BIG DATA, HEALTH LAW, AND BIOETHICS

When data from all aspects of our lives can be relevant to our health – from our habits at the grocery store and our Google searches to our FitBit data and our medical records – can we really differentiate between big data and health big data? Will health big data be used for good, such as to improve drug safety, or ill, as in insurance discrimination? Will it disrupt healthcare (and the healthcare system) as we know it? Will it be possible to protect our health privacy? What barriers will there be to collecting and using health big data? What role should law play, and what ethical concerns may arise? This timely, groundbreaking volume explores these questions and more from a variety of perspectives, examining how law promotes or discourages the use of big data in the healthcare sphere, as well as what we can learn from other sectors.

I. GLENN COHEN is Professor of Law and Faculty Director of the Petrie-Flom Center for Health Law Policy, Biotechnology, and Bioethics at Harvard Law School.

HOLLY FERNANDEZ LYNCH is Assistant Professor and Assistant Faculty Director of Online Education in the Department of Medical Ethics and Health Policy at Perelman School of Medicine of the University of Pennsylvania.

EFFY VAYENA is Professor of Bioethics at the Swiss Federal Institute of Technology (ETH Zurich).

URS GASSER is Executive Director of the Berkman Klein Center for Internet & Society at Harvard University and Professor of Practice at Harvard Law School.

Big Data, Health Law, and Bioethics

Edited by

I. GLENN COHEN
Harvard Law School

HOLLY FERNANDEZ LYNCH
Perelman School of Medicine, University of Pennsylvania

EFFY VAYENA
Swiss Federal Institute of Technology (ETH Zurich)

URS GASSER
Berkman Klein Center for Internet & Society, Harvard University

CAMBRIDGE
UNIVERSITY PRESS

CAMBRIDGE
UNIVERSITY PRESS

University Printing House, Cambridge CB2 8BS, United Kingdom

One Liberty Plaza, 20th Floor, New York, NY 10006, USA

477 Williamstown Road, Port Melbourne, VIC 3207, Australia

314–321, 3rd Floor, Plot 3, Splendor Forum, Jasola District Centre, New Delhi – 110025, India

79 Anson Road, #06–04/06, Singapore 079906

Cambridge University Press is part of the University of Cambridge.

It furthers the University's mission by disseminating knowledge in the pursuit of education, learning, and research at the highest international levels of excellence.

www.cambridge.org
Information on this title: www.cambridge.org/9781107193659
DOI: 10.1017/9781108147972

© Cambridge University Press 2018

This publication is in copyright. Subject to statutory exception and to the provisions of relevant collective licensing agreements, no reproduction of any part may take place without the written permission of Cambridge University Press.

First published 2018

Printed in the United States of America by Sheridan Books, Inc.

A catalogue record for this publication is available from the British Library.

Library of Congress Cataloging-in-Publication Data
NAMES: Cohen, I. Glenn, editor. | Lynch, Holly Fernandez, editor. | Vayena, Effy, 1972– editor. | Gasser, Urs, editor.
TITLE: Big data, health law, and bioethics / edited by I. Glenn Cohen, Holly Fernandez Lynch, Effy Vayena, Urs Gasser.
DESCRIPTION: Cambridge, United Kingdom : New York, NY : Cambridge University Press, 2018.
IDENTIFIERS: LCCN 2017041362 | ISBN 9781107193659 (Hardback)
SUBJECTS: | MESH: Data Mining | Health Policy | Legislation, Medical | Bioethical Issues | Privacy | United States
CLASSIFICATION: LCC RA425 | NLM W 26.55.I4 | DDC 362.1–dc23
LC record available at https://lccn.loc.gov/2017041362

ISBN 978-1-107-19365-9 Hardback
ISBN 978-1-108-44967-0 Paperback

Cambridge University Press has no responsibility for the persistence or accuracy of URLs for external or third-party internet websites referred to in this publication and does not guarantee that any content on such websites is, or will remain, accurate or appropriate.

For Will Zhang – I. Glenn Cohen
For Barbara Bierer – Holly Fernandez Lynch
For Martha Minow – Urs Gasser
For Bishop Nikolaos Chatzinikolaou – Effy Vayena

Contents

List of Editors and Contributors	*page* xi
Acknowledgments	xvii
Introduction	1
I. Glenn Cohen, Holly Fernandez Lynch, Effy Vayena, and Urs Gasser	
PART I SHIFTING PARADIGMS: BIG DATA'S IMPACT ON HEALTH LAW AND BIOETHICS	15
Introduction	15
Urs Gasser	
1 **Big Data and Individual Autonomy in a Crowd**	19
Barbara J. Evans	
2 **Big Data's Epistemology and Its Implications for Precision Medicine and Privacy**	30
Jeffrey M. Skopek	
3 **Correlation versus Causation in Health-Related Big Data Analysis: The Role of Reason and Regulation**	42
Tal Z. Zarsky	
4 **Big Data and Regulatory Arbitrage in Healthcare**	56
Nicolas P. Terry	
PART II OVERCOMING THE DOWNSIDES OF BIG DATA	69
Introduction	69
I. Glenn Cohen	

5	The Future of Pharmacovigilance: Big Data and the False Claims Act Efthimios Parasidis	73
6	Big Data's New Discrimination Threats: Amending the Americans with Disabilities Act to Cover Discrimination Based on Data-Driven Predictions of Future Disease Sharona Hoffman	85
7	Who's Left Out of Big Data? How Big Data Collection, Analysis, and Use Neglect Populations Most in Need of Medical and Public Health Research and Interventions Sarah E. Malanga, Jonathan D. Loe, Christopher T. Robertson, and Kenneth S. Ramos	98
8	Potential Roadblocks in Healthcare Big Data Collection: *Gobeille v. Liberty Mutual*, ERISA, and All-Payer Claims Databases Carmel Shachar, Aaron S. Kesselheim, Gregory Curfman, and Ameet Sarpatwari	112
	PART III THE INTERNET OF THINGS (IOT) AND HEALTH BIG DATA Introduction Nathan Cortez	125 125
9	Avoiding Overregulation in the Medical Internet of Things Dov Greenbaum	129
10	Data Policy for Internet of Things Healthcare Devices: Aligning Patient, Industry, and Privacy Goals in the Age of Big Data Marcus Comiter	142
	PART IV PROTECTING HEALTH PRIVACY IN THE WORLD OF BIG DATA Introduction Effy Vayena	157 157
11	Thought-Leader Perspectives on Risks in Precision Medicine Research Laura M. Beskow, Catherine M. Hammack, Kathleen M. Brelsford, and Kevin C. McKenna	161

12	From Individual to Group Privacy in Biomedical Big Data Brent Mittelstadt	175
13	Big Data and Informed Consent: The Case of Estimated Data Donna M. Gitter	193

PART V OVERSIGHT OF BIG DATA HEALTH RESEARCH:
PROPOSALS FOR IMPROVEMENT   205
Introduction   205
Holly Fernandez Lynch

14	Is There a Duty to Share Healthcare Data? I. Glenn Cohen	209
15	Societal Lapses in Protecting Individual Privacy, the Common Rule, and Big Data Health Research Laura Odwazny	223
16	The Common Rule and Research with Data, Big and Small Liza Dawson	237
17	Big Data, HIPAA, and the Common Rule: Time for Big Change? Margaret Foster Riley	251

PART VI BIG DATA, FDA, AND LIABILITY CONSIDERATIONS   265
Introduction   265
Jerry Avorn

18	Data Sharing that Enables Postapproval Drug and Device Research and Protects Patient Privacy: Best Practice Recommendations Ameet Sarpatwari, Bradley A. Malin, Aaron S. Kesselheim, Joshua J. Gagne, and Sebastian Schneeweiss	269
19	Big Data and Human Medical Judgment: Regulating Next-Generation Clinical Decision Support Jeffrey M. Senger and Patrick O'Leary	283
20	Medical Malpractice and Black-Box Medicine W. Nicholson Price II	295

PART VII INTELLECTUAL PROPERTY RIGHTS FOR HEALTH
BIG DATA   307
Introduction   307
Rachel E. Sachs

21	Big Data and Intellectual Property Rights in the Health and Life Sciences	311
	Timo Minssen and Justin Pierce	
22	The Pathologies of Data-Generating Patents	324
	Ted Sichelman and Brenda M. Simon	
	Epilogue: Professional Cooperation and Rivalry in the Future of Data-Driven Healthcare	337
	Frank Pasquale	
Index		341

Editors and Contributors

EDITORS

I. Glenn Cohen is Professor of Law and Faculty Director of the Petrie-Flom Center for Health Law Policy, Biotechnology, and Bioethics at Harvard Law School. He is one of the world's leading experts on the intersection of bioethics and the law, as well as health law. He also teaches civil procedure. He is the author of one hundred articles and book chapters in venues such as the *New England Journal of Medicine*, the *Journal of the American Medical Association*, *Nature*, and the *Harvard Law Review* and the author, editor, or coeditor of eight books. He has appeared on or been covered by PBS, NPR, ABC, CNN, MSNBC, *Mother Jones*, the *New York Times*, the *New Republic*, and the *Boston Globe*, among other media venues. He has been a fellow of the Radcliffe Institute and the Hastings Center.

Holly Fernandez Lynch is John Russell Dickson, MD Presidential Assistant Professor of Medical Ethics and Health Policy and Assistant Faculty Director of Online Education in the Department of Medical Ethics and Health Policy at the Perelman School of Medicine of the University of Pennsylvania. She is an expert on issues at the intersection of law, bioethics, and health policy, in particular, the regulation of research with human subjects and conflicts of conscience in healthcare. She published *Conflicts of Conscience in Health Care: An Institutional Compromise* in 2008 and has released several coedited volumes. In 2014, she was appointed as a member of the Secretary's Advisory Committee on Human Research Protections (SACHRP) at the US Department of Health and Human Services. She previously practiced Food and Drug Administration law, served as a bioethicist working with the National Institutes of Health's Division of AIDS, and staffed President Obama's Commission for the Study of Bioethical Issues.

Effy Vayena is Professor of Bioethics in the Department of Health Sciences and Technology at the Swiss Federal Institute of Technology (ETH Zurich). She is an international expert on issues of ethics and policy in digital health technologies. Her work has appeared in highly ranked journals such as the *Lancet*, *PLoS Medicine*, and the *Proceedings of National Academies of Science*. She has worked extensively in policy areas, consulting for the World Health Organization and the Organization of Economic Co-operation and Development, among others. She was elected a member of the Swiss Academy of Medical Sciences, and she chairs the Ethical, Legal and Societal Issues Advisory Group of the Swiss Personalised Health Network, a large-scale, federally funded national initiative advancing health data uses.

Urs Gasser is Executive Director of the Berkman Klein Center for Internet & Society at Harvard University and Professor of Practice at Harvard Law School. His research and teaching activities focus on information law, policy, and society issues and the changing role of academia in the digitally networked age. In addition to his appointments at Harvard, he is a guest professor at KEIO University (Japan), was a visiting professor at the University of St. Gallen (Switzerland), and taught at Fudan University School of Management (China). He has written and edited several books and published over a hundred journal articles and frequently acts as a commentator on digital technology, policy, and society issues for US and European media.

CONTRIBUTORS

Jerry Avorn, M.D. Chief of the Division of Pharmacoepidemiology and Pharmacoeconomics, Department of Medicine, Brigham and Women's Hospital and Professor of Medicine, Harvard Medical School, Boston, MA, USA

Laura M. Beskow, Ph.D., M.P.H. Professor in Health Policy and Director of Research Ethics in the Center for Biomedical Ethics and Society, Vanderbilt University Medical Center, Nashville, TN, USA

Kathleen M. Brelsford, Ph.D., M.P.H. Research Assistant Professor in Health Policy, Center for Biomedical Ethics and Society, Vanderbilt University Medical Center, Nashville, TN, USA

Marcus Comiter Ph.D. candidate in Computer Science, Harvard University, Cambridge, MA, USA

Nathan Cortez, J.D. Associate Dean for Research, Gerald J. Ford Research Fellow, and Adelfa Botello Callejo Endowed Professor of Law in Leadership and Latino Studies, Southern Methodist University Dedman School of Law, Dallas, TX, USA

Gregory Curfman, M.D. Editor-in-Chief, Harvard Health Publications, Harvard Medical School, Boston, MA, USA

Liza Dawson, Ph.D. Research Ethics Team Leader, Basic Sciences Program, Division of AIDS, National Institute of Allergy and Infectious Diseases, National Institutes of Health, US Department of Health and Human Services, Bethesda, MD, USA

Barbara J. Evans, M.S., Ph.D., J.D., LL.M. Alumnae College Professor of Law and Director of the Center on Biotechnology and Law, University of Houston Law Center, Houston, TX, USA

Joshua J. Gagne, Pharm.D., Sc.D. Associate Epidemiologist, Division of Pharmacoepidemiology and Pharmacoeconomics, Department of Medicine, Brigham and Women's Hospital and Associate Professor of Medicine, Harvard Medical School, Boston, MA, USA

Donna M. Gitter, J.D. Professor of Law, Zicklin School of Business, Baruch College, New York, NY, USA

Dov Greenbaum, J.D., Ph.D. Director of the Zvi Meitar Institute for Legal Implications of Emerging Technologies, Hertsliya, Israel
Assistant Professor, Department of Molecular Biophysics and Biochemistry, Yale University School of Medicine, New Haven, CT, USA

Catherine M. Hammack, J.D., M.A. Associate in Health Policy, Center for Biomedical Ethics and Society, Vanderbilt University Medical Center, Nashville, TN, USA

Sharona Hoffman, J.D., LL.M., S.J.D. Edgar A. Hahn Professor of Law, Professor of Bioethics, and Co-Director of the Law-Medicine Center, Case Western Reserve University School of Law, Cleveland, OH, USA

Aaron S. Kesselheim, M.D., J.D., M.P.H. Director of the Program on Regulation, Therapeutics, and Law (PORTAL), Division of Pharmacoepidemiology and Pharmacoeconomics, Department of Medicine, Brigham and Women's Hospital and Harvard Medical School and Associate Professor at Harvard Medical School, Boston, MA, USA

Jonathan D. Loe, J.D., LL.M. Associate, Business and Corporate Practice Group, Sherman & Howard, LLC, Scottsdale, AZ, USA

Sarah E. Malanga, J.D., M.P.H. Fellow of the Regulatory Science Program, University of Arizona James E. Rogers College of Law, Tucson, AZ, USA

Bradley A. Malin, Ph.D. Vice Chair for Research, Professor of Biomedical Informatics, Professor of Biostatistics, and Affiliated Faculty in the Center for Biomedical Ethics and Society, Vanderbilt University School of Medicine and Professor of Computer Science, Vanderbilt University School of Engineering, Nashville, TN, USA

Kevin C. McKenna, M.P.H. Research Program Leader, Department of Population Health Sciences, Duke University School of Medicine, Durham, NC, USA

Brent Mittelstadt, Ph.D. Postdoctoral Research Fellow in Data Ethics, Oxford Internet Institute, University of Oxford, Oxford, United Kingdom

Timo Minssen, M.I.C.L., LL.M., LL.D. Professor of Law, Mng. Director, Centre For Advanced Studies in Biomedical Innovation Law (CeBIL), University of Copenhagen Faculty of Law, Copenhagen, Denmark

Laura Odwazny, M.A., J.D. Senior Attorney, Public Health Division, Office of the General Counsel, US Department of Health and Human Services, Rockville, MD, USA

Patrick O'Leary, J.D. Deployment Strategist, Palantir Technologies, Washington, DC, USA

Efthimios Parasidis, J.D., M.Bioethics Associate Professor of Law and Public Health, Moritz College of Law and College of Public Health, and Faculty Affiliate, College of Medicine, The Ohio State University, Columbus, OH, USA

Frank Pasquale, M.Phil., J.D. Professor of Law, University of Maryland Francis King Carey School of Law, Baltimore, MD, USA

Justin Pierce, J.D. Postdoctoral Fellow, Department of Law, Lund University, Lund, Sweden

W. Nicholson Price II, J.D., Ph.D. Assistant Professor of Law, University of Michigan Law School, Ann Arbor, MI, USA

Kenneth S. Ramos, M.D., Ph.D., Pharma.D. Associate Vice President for Precision Health Sciences, University of Arizona Health Sciences, Interim Dean of the University of Arizona College of Medicine – Phoenix, Professor of Medicine in the Division of Pulmonary, Allergy, Critical Care, and Sleep Medicine, and Director of the Center for Applied Genetics and Genomic Medicine and the M.D.-Ph.D. Program, University of Arizona College of Medicine, Tucson, AZ, USA

Margaret Foster Riley, J.D. Professor of Law, General Faculty, Professor of Public Health Sciences, School of Medicine, Professor of Public Policy, Batten School of Leadership and Public Policy and Director of the Animal Law Program, School of Law, University of Virginia, Charlottesville, VA, USA

Christopher T. Robertson, J.D., Ph.D. Associate Dean for Research and Innovation and Professor of Law, University of Arizona James E. Rogers College of Law, Tucson, AZ, USA

Rachel E. Sachs, J.D., M.P.H. Associate Professor of Law, Washington University in St. Louis School of Law, St. Louis, MO, USA

Ameet Sarpatwari, J.D., Ph.D. Assistant Director of the Program on Regulation, Therapeutics, and Law (PORTAL), Division of Pharmacoepidemiology and Pharmacoeconomics, Department of Medicine, Brigham and Women's Hospital and Harvard Medical School, Boston, MA, USA

Sebastian Schneeweiss, M.D., Sc.D. Vice Chief of the Division of Pharmacoepidemiology and Pharmacoeconomics, Department of Medicine, Brigham and Women's Hospital, and Professor of Medicine, Harvard Medical School, Boston, MA, USA

Jeffrey M. Senger, J.D. Partner in the Food, Drug, and Medical Device Regulatory and Enforcement Group, Sidley Austin, LLP, Washington, DC, USA

Carmel Shachar, J.D., M.P.H. Executive Director of the Petrie-Flom Center for Health Law Policy, Biotechnology, and Bioethics, Harvard Law School, Cambridge, MA, USA

Ted Sichelman, J.D., M.S. Professor of Law, Director of the Center for Intellectual Property Law and Markets, Founder and Director of the Center for Computation, Mathematics, and the Law, and Founder and Director of the Technology Entrepreneurship and Intellectual Property Clinic, University of San Diego Law School, San Diego, CA, USA

Brenda M. Simon, J.D. Associate Professor of Law and Director of the Center for Law and Intellectual Property, Thomas Jefferson School of Law, San Diego, CA, USA

Jeffrey M. Skopek, Ph.D., J.D. Lecturer in Medical Law, Ethics, and Policy and Deputy Director of the Centre for Law, Medicine and Life Sciences, University of Cambridge Faculty of Law, Cambridge, United Kingdom

Nicolas P. Terry, LL.M. Hall Render Professor of Law and Executive Director of the William S. and Christine S. Hall Center for Law and Health, Indiana University Robert H. McKinney School of Law, Indianapolis, IN, USA

Tal Z. Zarsky, LL.M., J.S.D. Professor of Law and Vice Dean, University of Haifa Faculty of Law, Haifa, Israel

Acknowledgments

A book like this is the result of the hard work of many. We thank our student line editors Ethan Stevenson (lead line editor), Brian Yost, Colin Herd, and Wilfred Beaye for their meticulous work. We are also grateful to Cristine Hutchison-Jones and Justin Leahey for their administrative support in putting on the conference that gave rise to this book and Cristine in particular for her hard work shepherding all the many pieces of this manuscript. We also thankfully acknowledge the Petrie-Flom Center for Health Law Policy, Biotechnology, and Bioethics at Harvard Law School, with support from the Oswald DeN. Cammann Fund, for conference sponsorship and the Berkman Klein Center for Internet & Society at Harvard University and the Health Ethics and Policy Laboratory at the University of Zurich for their collaboration. Finally, of course, we thank the contributors for their thoughtful and important scholarly contributions.

Introduction

*I. Glenn Cohen, Holly Fernandez Lynch, Effy Vayena,
and Urs Gasser*

When data from all aspects of our lives can be relevant to our health – from our habits at the grocery store, to our Google searches, to our FitBit data, to our medical records – can we really differentiate between Big Data and *health* Big Data? Will health Big Data be used for good, for example, to improve drug safety, or ill, for example, for insurance discrimination? Will it disrupt healthcare (and the healthcare system) as we know it? Will it be possible to protect our health privacy? What barriers will there be to collecting and using health Big Data? What role will the law play, and what ethical concerns may arise? These questions, and many others, are at the heart of this book.

"Big data" is a term that has been used pervasively by the media and the lay public in the last several years. While many definitions are possible, the common denominator seems to include the "three V's" – volume (vast amounts of data), variety (significant heterogeneity in the type of data available), and velocity (the speed at which a data scientist or user can access and analyze the data). Some would add a fourth "V" of value, the idea that Big Data would allow us to improve healthcare. Defined as such, healthcare has become one of the key emerging-use cases for Big Data. For example, Fitbit and Apple's ResearchKit can provide researchers with access to vast stores of biometric data on users from which to test hypotheses on nutrition, fitness, disease progression, treatment success, and the like. The Centers for Medicare and Medicaid Services (CMS) have vast stores of billing data that can be mined to promote high-value care and prevent fraud; the same is true of private health insurers. And hospitals have attempted to reduce readmission rates by targeting patients who predictive algorithms indicate are at highest risk based on analysis of available data collected from existing patient records. Underlying these and many other potential uses, however, are a series of legal and ethical challenges relating to, among other things, privacy, discrimination, intellectual property, tort, and informed consent, as well as research and clinical ethics.

The contributions in this book examine the promise and perils of Big Data and related technological advancements in the health context from a number of analytically distinct but interrelated perspectives. In so doing, they follow a familiar pattern in assessing novel technologies and their impact on society by addressing three core themes.

The first theme involves development of a rich phenomenological understanding of the new technologies – here Big Data and to some extent the Internet of Things – and their implications for health and society at large: what changes, and what remains the same? What emerges from the nuanced accounts compiled in this volume is a picture of a world in which human lives, from media and communications to education and finance, are increasingly entangled in the data about them. Health and biomedicine are particularly affected by the rise of Big Data, with prominent examples found in clinical care, laboratories, genomic sequencing, and the wider range of genomics research.[1] Most notably, researchers predict a coming genomic data flood.[2] Due to the falling costs of genomic sequencing and an emphasis on genomic data for clinical and research applications, it is estimated that by 2025, between 100 million and 1 billion human genomes will be sequenced,[3] pushing data generation into the exabyte (one billion gigabyte) scale. Advances in bioinformatics and analytics are leveraging personal data to further health and biomedical knowledge and applications. New machine learning techniques, for instance, are now being used to analyze Big Data and help doctors provide diagnosis and treatment to patients.[4]

Health-related data are increasingly being derived from nonbiomedical sources as well. Data from online purchases reveal preferences, opinions, and health statuses, and Facebook "likes" can, with surprising accuracy, predict one's sexual orientation, ethnicity, religious and political views, personality traits, intelligence, happiness, use of addictive substances, parental separation, age, and gender.[5] Retail purchases have been used to predict whether particular customers are pregnant and therefore likely to use coupons for items related to pregnancy.[6] Users of social networks such as Facebook, Twitter, and PatientsLikeMe (a website where patients can "share their health data to track their progress, help others, and change medicine for

---

[1] Nuffield Council on Bioethics, The Collection, Linking and Use of Data in Biomedical Research and Health Care: Ethical Issues 4–18 (London, 2015).
[2] Zachary D. Stephens et al., Big Data: Astronomical or Genomical?, 13(7) *PLoS Biol.* e1002195 (2015).
[3] Erika Check Hayden, Genome Researchers Raise Alarm over Big Data, *Nature* 312, 312–14 (2015).
[4] See, e.g., Ariana Eunjung Cha, Watson's Next Feat? Taking on Cancer: IBM's Computer Brain Is Training alongside Doctors To Do What They Can't, *Washington Post*, June 27, 2015.
[5] Michal Kosinski et al., Private Traits and Attributes Are Predictable from Digital Records of Human Behavior, 110(15) *Proc. Natl. Acad. Sci. USA* 5802, 5802–5 (2013).
[6] Charles Duhigg, How Companies Know Your Secrets, *New York Times*, February 16, 2012.

good")[7] often reveal health-related information directly,[8] making it possible for their postings to be mined for research purposes.[9] These data can convey sensitive information such as whether an individual is experiencing symptoms associated with a medical condition. Recent pharmacovigilance studies have shown that Twitter posts containing a reference to a medical product can be used to identify adverse events related to a large number of conditions.[10] Other studies have shown that smartphones equipped with sensors allowing the capture of fine-grained geolocation and usage data can be used to detect depression symptoms and potentially with more accuracy than is possible using standard questionnaires. In addition, mobile phone data have been used for contact tracing and other public health surveillance activities, detecting human mobility in affected regions during the Ebola crisis, thus illustrating the value of such data in an infectious disease pandemic or other public health emergency.

At this point, a second core theme of this book emerges, addressing the many normative implications of these new technologies – how to evaluate the various shifts triggered by technological advancements and form new societal consensus around it? In this respect, this book's chapters demonstrate that while the highly penetrative power of Big Data analysis is revealing sought-after patterns in health and biomedicine, it is also challenging traditional approaches, prevailing social norms, and existing regulatory schemes with respect to autonomy, privacy, identity, and other values. Ethical codes and regulations dictate how biomedical research should be conducted when it involves human subjects, their samples, and their data. However, the systems currently in place, as several authors in this volume argue, do not necessarily address many new Big Data activities. For example, data generated on social media platforms are open to a broad range of uses authorized by the terms of service, but it is not clear that users are aware that their postings are often used for research purposes or that they are in agreement with the platform providers and the researchers regarding these uses of their data. There is a fundamental "impossibility of certainty concerning future uses of data" inherent to Big Data because its value largely stems from uses and insights unanticipated at the time of data generation. Hence subjects cannot be "informed" (in the sense contemplated by traditional informed-consent regimes) regarding future and often-unrelated

---

[7] About Us, PatientsLikeMe, available at www.patientslikeme.com/about [https://perma.cc/8D9L-DJKV] (last visited May 19, 2017).
[8] Susanne Fox, Pew Research Center, The Social Life of Health Information (2011), available at www.pewinternet.org/2011/05/12/the-social-life-of-health-information-2011 [https://perma.cc/VXU7-NM3E] (last visited May 19, 2017).
[9] Kate L. Mandeville et al., Using Social Networking Sites for Communicable Disease Control: Innovative Contact Tracing or Breach of Confidentiality?, 7(1) *Public Health Ethics* 47, 47–50 (2014); Effy Vayena et al., Ethical Challenges of Big Data in Public Health, 11(2) *PLoS Comp. Biol.* e1003904 (2015).
[10] Clark C. Freifeld et al., Digital Drug Safety Surveillance: Monitoring Pharmaceutical Products on Twitter, 37(5) *Drug Safety* 343, 343–50 (2014).

investigations based on shared, aggregated, and reused data from these services. Users often blithely agree to various terms of service or privacy policies without even reading them and cannot predict how the content of their future tweets, for example, will be used and by whom. Information asymmetries between researchers or institutions and subjects are amplified by the ambiguity of legal obligations and ethical practices for researchers using commercial Big Data sources for health-related purposes. Moreover, regulation and ethical guidelines may set requirements that are impossible to meet in the new paradigm of Big Data. An illustrative example discussed in several chapters is that of black-box medicine. These and related examples explored in greater depth in this volume demonstrate the difficult normative questions, including value conflicts, at the intersection of technology, law and ethics, social norms, and market forces that need to be addressed as Big Data is embraced in the health context.

Against this normative backdrop, a third cross-cutting theme emerges: what are the best available approaches and instruments to address the challenges and also embrace the opportunities afforded by new technological capabilities such as Big Data and the Internet of Things? The chapters that follow make clear that a series of approaches and "tools" is available as society responds to and otherwise interacts with the promises and challenges of emerging technologies in health. The set of available instruments ranges from technical to ethical approaches, mirroring the various modes of regulation that have become the standard repertoire when governing emerging technologies in the digitally connected environment.

Solutions to the Big Data challenges just highlighted are explored in detail across this volume's chapters. The solutions can themselves be divided into a few categories. They include market-based approaches, where different ethical and privacy standards compete for consumers in a marketplace. The idea of third-party auditing mechanisms available to users to audit the collection and use of their health data is an example of an approach discussed in this book that combines market-based mechanisms with technical solutions. Similarly, the proposal of implementing a middleware solution that serves as a gateway and point of control between patients and the end points of the data analysis is an illustration of an innovative solution space vis-à-vis Big Data, the Internet of Things, and related technologies. Many chapters in this book identify such novel approaches at both the conceptual and practical levels, not with the goal to replace traditional safeguards aimed at protecting the rights of individuals but to complement and bolster them in light of the phenomenological and normative challenges mentioned earlier. Reading this book as a whole suggests that no single approach or instrument is likely to be a "silver bullet" that solves the myriad challenges or is sufficient to harness the full benefits of the rapidly evolving digital technologies in the health sector. Rather, blended approaches that combine different instruments available in the "toolbox" seem most promising when dealing with both the challenges and opportunities of Big Data and related technologies, as many of the chapters suggest. At least in this respect, the solution space that emerges from the contributions in this book with its specific focus on health is consistent with an increasingly robust body of knowledge about the promise (and limits) of multimodal and multistakeholder governance of digital technologies more broadly.

Unsurprisingly, legal and regulatory responses to the challenges presented by Big Data and related technologies feature prominently among the chapters in this volume. From a cross-sectional perspective and at a conceptual level, two observations seem particularly noteworthy: (1) the different role law and regulation can (and should) play vis-à-vis the phenomenological changes described earlier in this Introduction and (2) the observation of a familiar set of patterns in how the interaction between law/regulation and technology unfolds in the health and Big Data discourse. With respect to the different functions that law and regulation can play, several chapters highlight the familiar (and often dominant) role of legal norms as a constraint on behavior. For instance, the requirement of informed consent – and what it means under the new technological conditions that set the context of this book – in order to protect the privacy and autonomy of individuals is a much-debated instance in which law clearly has a constraining function. Other chapters indicate a second way in which legal and regulatory approaches might contribute to problem solving by leveling the playing field among actors, for instance, by establishing more comprehensive accountability and oversight schemes that overcome traditional distinctions between regulated and nonregulated actors in a world of blurring lines of what constitutes health data and what does not. Some contributions make visible, or at least allude to, a third role that law and regulation can play: the role of an enabler of technological advancements that benefit the health of individuals and society at large. This enabling function of law finds its clearest expression in the context of the discussion of intellectual property rights and health Big Data and the question of appropriate incentive structures in order to promote the creation and access of beneficial big data frameworks. It also becomes visible where contractual mechanisms are used to enable new types of choice architectures for individuals through the creation of marketplaces for standards or trusted third-party services.

In terms of response modes, finally, the contributions in this volume reveal a pattern that is familiar from other fields where the legal system has to deal with technological developments that have disruptive effects. The default mode is what is known as *subsumption*, that is, the application of old rules to new phenomena. For instance, the discussion of whether new types of actors that are functionally in the health data business should fall under existing regulatory frameworks is such a question of subsumption. The debate about (existing) informed-consent requirements and how they can be applied in a Big Data environment with its new complexities is a good example of an attempt to use existing approaches to deal with a new phenomenon. As many chapters herein demonstrate, such a subsumption approach quickly reaches its limits when confronted with the deeper-layered structural changes in the health technology ecosystem diagnosed in this volume.

In such cases, the legal and regulatory system is itself forced to innovate, either by making gradual adjustments in the sense of evolution or engaging in more radical, paradigm-shifting innovations. An example of gradual adjustment is the updating of existing legislation (including by court interpretation) – such as the False Claims Act – or regulatory processes – such as the Sentinel System used by the Food and Drug Administration (FDA) – to address the unique challenges posed by Big Data and related technologies in the health context. The idea to extend privacy rights to groups that are otherwise inadequately shielded from harms that might result from biomedical Big Data might be seen as an illustration of an innovation within the legal system that goes beyond a gradual adjustment or "update" of existing norms and procedures.

Taken together, this volume provides a sense of the magnitude of the changes at the phenomenological and normative levels and outlines some of the instruments and strategies available when dealing with the rapidly evolving landscape of cutting-edge technologies such as Big Data, the Internet of Things, and artificial intelligence (AI), among others. To make things even more complex, the three challenges addressed in this book and outlined in this Introduction – phenomenological, normative, and designing solutions – cannot be addressed sequentially. In the case of Big Data in health, one needs to simultaneously gain a deeper understanding of the depth of change that has come about in the way we practice medicine and biomedical research, to explore and evaluate the normative pressure points and conflicts, and to develop, test, and revise the necessary legal, technological, incentive-based, and other tools that can help us deal with the challenges. This volume seeks to inform this debate but also demonstrates significant knowledge gaps and reveals remaining degrees of normative uncertainty in terms of the net outcome of the brave new world of health and digital technology. In this sense, it should be read as an open invitation for further research, collaboration, and discourse across a broad range of stakeholders to work toward a use of technology that benefits individual and public health.

This book is divided into seven parts. Part I, introduced by Urs Gasser, describes the ways in which Big Data is shifting existing paradigms of health law and bioethics. The contributions identify and discuss a series of seismic shifts in health-related data collection, aggregation, and use and engage in a thick analysis of their implications, including challenges related to traditional legal definitions and concepts, novel threats to privacy and autonomy, new power asymmetries, and potential ramifications from an epistemological perspective.

Barbara J. Evans in Chapter 1, "Big Data and Individual Autonomy in a Crowd," identifies privacy barriers, such as the risk of reidentification, and related normative challenges that prevent access to large and inclusive data resources, which would be required in order to harness the full benefits of Big Data. Evans' chapter also explores the question of how a new common purpose can emerge in bioethical and regulatory environments that currently emphasize individual autonomy. As a partial solution, she proposes the concept of consumer-driven commons as a way to empower individuals to protect themselves against research-related risks and to engage, collectively, in civic solidarity.

Privacy also plays a key role in Chapter 2, "Big Data's Epistemology and Its Implications for Precision Medicine and Privacy," in which Jeffrey M. Skopek examines from a broader epistemological perspective the extent to which the nature of scientific knowledge and inquiry is likely to change in the age of Big Data. After a critical examination of the often-discussed shifts from theory to data and from causation to correlation, Skopek explores how a separate shift from explanation to prediction may play out in the field of precision medicines and predicts a series of broad legal and ethical challenges in areas such as intellectual property, torts, and privacy as a result of this shift. Against this backdrop, he focuses on the privacy implications of predictive analytics, arguing that the threat to privacy posed by Big Data is more limited than has been widely thought.

Along similar thematic lines but with partially different results, in Chapter 3, "Correlation versus Causation in Health-Related Big Data Analysis: The Role of Reason and Regulation," Tal Z. Zarsky examines the epistemological implications of the new ways in which data are collected, aggregated, analyzed, and used in today's data-rich contexts that affect health. After analyzing the various forces at play, Zarsky engages in a review of the correlation versus causation debate and cautions, with some important exceptions, against practices in the medical and health context that rely increasingly and at times exclusively on mere correlation and ignore important questions of causation and mechanisms. He also examines the role law and regulation can and, under qualified circumstances, should play in setting requirements as to the appropriate way in which data must be analyzed prior to their use.

Finally, in Chapter 4, "Big Data and Regulatory Arbitrage in Healthcare," Nicolas P. Terry focuses on a series of scenarios concerning the misuse of healthcare data by the Big Data industry. With new commercial actors such as data brokers entering the arena, Terry diagnoses the problem that the current structure of healthcare data protection is insufficient and leaves individuals vulnerable to a series of serious risks, including discriminatory practices and privacy invasions. Terry calls for comprehensive federal legislation to create a level playing field in terms of protection from data-processing actors within and outside the traditional context of healthcare and to fix the current problem of regulatory arbitrage.

Next, in Part II, introduced by I. Glenn Cohen, the focus shifts to overcoming the potential downsides of health Big Data. The contributions in this part lie on a continuum, Cohen argues, between assimilation and disruption. Placement on the continuum depends on how easily the authors see Big Data in healthcare as fitting into existing legal paradigms versus breaking them open and requiring something new in their place.

In Chapter 5, "The Future of Pharmacovigilance: Big Data and the False Claims Act," Efthimios Parasidis looks at the role for Big Data in enforcement of the False

Claims Act, the federal government's main tool for combating healthcare fraud. He argues that the act should apply to fraud relating to Big Data manipulation – structuring data analysis to obscure information that might cause the submission of fewer claims. Among the intriguing questions Parasidis examines are "If Big Data analysis reveals questions about safety or efficacy, does a pharmaceutical company have an obligation to report the information or conduct further research?" and "What is the outcome if a learning algorithm is the sole entity to examine the new information?" Along the way, he also examines a role for Big Data in FDA pharmacovigilance.

In Chapter 6, "Big Data's New Discrimination Threats: Amending the Americans with Disabilities Act to Cover Discrimination Based on Data-Driven Predictions of Future Disease," Sharona Hoffman examines the threat posed by healthcare Big Data to protections from employment (and other forms) of discrimination. She focuses on one of the United States' primary antidiscrimination statutes, the Americans with Disabilities Act (ADA), and shows that it offers no protection to a group imperiled by improved Big Data analysis: "people who are currently healthy but are perceived as being at high risk of becoming sick in the future." Hoffman develops a proposal to expand the ADA to "prohibit discrimination based on predictions of future physical or mental impairment" and "require covered entities to disclose in writing their use of Big Data or other nontraditional means to obtain health-related information."

Chapter 7, "Who's Left Out of Big Data? How Big Data Collection, Analysis, and Use Neglect Populations Most in Need of Medical and Public Health Research and Interventions," by Sarah E. Malanga, Jonathan D. Loe, Christopher T. Robertson, and Kenneth S. Ramos, is a meditation on a major drawback of current healthcare Big Data sets: their failure to include marginalized populations such as racial minorities, people with low socioeconomic status, and immigrants. The authors examine the way these populations are also the ones that face the most acute health disparities and the way in which these gaps imperil moves toward precision medicine. Finally, they consider several ways to remedy these gaps. For example, the FDA, as part of the pharmaceutical and other product approval process, could require data to come from a diverse, inclusive pool of patients; regulation across several agencies could be "implemented, or strengthened, to push users of Big Data to acknowledge and reconcile the possibility for skewed data due to under- and overrepresentation, biases within algorithms, and overreliance on the findings of Big Data." While the authors are candid that these steps will not completely eradicate health disparities, they defend them as important steps for progress.

Finally, in Chapter 8, "Potential Roadblocks in Healthcare Big Data Collection: *Gobeille v. Liberty Mutual*, ERISA, and All-Payer Claims Databases," Carmel Shachar, Aaron S. Kesselheim, Gregory Curfman, and Ameet Sarpatwari focus on the Supreme Court's *Gobeille* decision, which held that the Employee Retirement Income Security Act (ERISA) preempted Vermont's attempt to gather healthcare data from plans governed by that act, prohibiting states from requiring self-insured employer-sponsored health plans to report data to their All-Payer Claims Database (APCD). The authors critique the decision and lament its effects on attempts to curb healthcare spending and to perform important health services research. At the end of this chapter, the authors explore several potential workarounds that would help to reduce the negative effects of the decision.

Part III, introduced by Nathan Cortez, addresses the Internet of Things and health Big Data. The chapters in this part identify a long list of concerns associated with these emerging technologies and corresponding practices, including interoperability, privacy, safety, transparency, and accountability challenges, among others. Both chapters also propose novel ways in which some of these concerns can be addressed using technological means and market mechanisms that supplement the work (and limited effectiveness) of the familiar regulatory bodies.

After analyzing the broad range of risks associated with mobile health technology such as wearables, smartphones, and other sensing devices that intend to track and assess the health of patients, Dov Greenbaum in Chapter 9, "Avoiding Overregulation in the Medical Internet of Things," proposes the introduction of a third-party clearinghouse, which would act as a transparent and accountable intermediary between Internet of Things devices and end users. The technological role of a third-party clearinghouse would include standardizing health data across multiple platforms and devices, ensuring both interoperability and usability. The regulatory role would be to embed more robust privacy and data security standards into spaces that fall outside the purview of federal privacy and security rules deriving from the Health Insurance Portability and Accountability Act (HIPAA), among others.

Similar in spirit, Marcus Comiter, in Chapter 10, "Data Policy for Internet of Things Healthcare Devices: Aligning Patient, Industry, and Privacy Goals in the Age of Big Data," introduces the idea of nongovernmental *third-party data auditors* (TPDAs) that could be hired or otherwise engaged by individuals to audit the use of their data by corporations, providers, data brokers, and others. Like Greenbaum's clearinghouses, Comiter's TPDAs would serve both a technological and a regulatory (or governance) function, specified in greater detail in the chapter. Comiter sees the primary benefit of independent TPDAs in an increased level of transparency and accountability in health Big Data, which, in turn, would deter misuses and promote consumer trust.

In Part IV, introduced by Effy Vayena, the contributors turn to focus on protecting health privacy in a world of Big Data. The chapters taken together provide a good illustration of the mixed approaches needed to address the privacy challenge. Some involve expanding the scope of existing regulation, such as informed consent; others entail the development of entirely new ethical and legal mechanisms.

In Chapter 11, "Thought Leader Perspectives on Risks in Precision Medicine Research," Laura M. Beskow, Catherine M. Hammack, Kathleen M. Brelsford, and Kevin C. McKenna report on empirical data that revealed shifts in the perception of harm with uses of biomedical Big Data, specifically an increased acknowledgment of group harm, which is little understood and even less addressed in current protection mechanisms. In the Big Data environment, risks are exacerbated by at least two factors: (1) the never-ending uses of multiple data sets and (2) the difficulty in predicting how data will be used and what they will yield. The uncertainty about what will emerge makes it virtually impossible to anticipate all potential risks a priori.

In his effort to address the issue of group harms, Brent Mittelstadt has formulated a particular right to privacy for algorithmically ad hoc groups: the right to "inviolate personality." In Chapter 12, "From Individual to Group Privacy in Biomedical Big Data," Mittelstadt proposes group privacy as a third interest to balance alongside individual privacy and social, commercial, and epistemic benefits when assessing the ethical acceptability of Big Data analytics. He examines two implementation models for group privacy, wherein group privacy can ground both anticipatory restrictions on processing and reactive redress for groups whose privacy has been violated.

Next, in Chapter 13, "Big Data and Informed Consent: The Case of Estimated Data," Donna M. Gitter addresses regulatory change and the increasing use in biomedical research of estimated data. To protect the privacy and autonomy of these individuals, Gitter argues that they also deserve the protection of the law of informed consent. She also explores the importance of the right not to know of the genetic incidental findings discovered by researchers as another component of the privacy right.

Part V, introduced by Holly Fernandez Lynch, addresses key questions regarding the regulatory and ethical requirements for research use of Big Data, either health research or health data. Contributors to this part agree that consent to such use is often unnecessary as long as appropriate protections of data sources are in place. What those protections ought to look like and how they ought to be implemented and enforced are where the real action is.

In Chapter 14, "Is There a Duty to Share Healthcare Data?," I. Glenn Cohen sketches an argument that there is, rooted in two distinct rationales. His first argument is that healthcare data should not be viewed as a patient's property, given that the patient has not added his or her labor or "sweat equity" to make the data valuable, and therefore, the patient has little claim to profit from or control them. Cohen's second argument, which may be viewed as either buttressing or alternative to the first, is that there is a duty based in reciprocity to contribute healthcare data to systems that generate benefits – health or otherwise – for all of us. Given these rationales, Cohen argues that consent is not required for the collection and use of healthcare data, although public education about these activities would be appropriate.

In Chapter 15, "Societal Lapses in Protecting Individual Privacy, the Common Rule, and Big Data Health Research," Laura Odwazny addresses application of the regulations governing research with human subjects to Big Data health research.

She notes that in many scenarios, such research will not fall within the existing regulatory structure because the data may not be either private (think of data collected via social media sites, for example) or individually identifiable. Nonetheless, given privacy concerns often raised around Big Data and health data, Odwazny recognizes that institutional review boards (IRBs) are often called on to review Big Data health research, sometimes under the regulations and sometimes because there may be no other good mechanism for checking that data sources are adequately protected. She explores the risks posed by Big Data health research, offering two rationales by which they can be deemed to satisfy the regulatory standard of "minimal risk" needed to support waiver of consent requirements: (1) privacy risks are ubiquitous in modern life, and (2) additional privacy protections may be implemented in the research context.

Next, in Chapter 16, "The Common Rule and Research with Data, Big and Small," Liza Dawson argues that Big Data research has exposed flaws in the existing regulatory structure governing research with data more generally and the lack of regulation of other data uses. She notes that current protections are avoidable, by removing identifiers from data, and based on a flawed foundation of seeking consent that is both ethically unnecessary and does nothing at all to address the key concern around data research, namely, privacy and informational risks. Accordingly, Dawson argues that regulation of data use – for research or other purposes – "ought to be systematically organized according to rational criteria that address (1) reducing the likelihood of a breach, (2) ensuring that responsible practitioners are the only ones with access, (3) ensuring that projects are designed with sound methodology addressing socially valuable goals, and (4) ensuring a level of transparency and communication appropriate to the activity."

The last chapter in this part, Chapter 17, "Big Data, HIPAA, and the Common Rule: Time for Big Change?," by Margaret Foster Riley, addresses data privacy protections more directly, assessing the suitability of the Health Insurance Portability and Accountability Act (better known as HIPAA) for health Big Data. Just as Dawson argued that the Common Rule is a poor fit, Riley concludes that HIPAA as applied to health Big Data is "both overregulatory because it makes it very difficult to use data that may have little informational risk and underregulatory because it does not apply to a great deal of data that falls out of the definition of [protected health information, or PHI]." In order to simultaneously protect individuals from risk of improper use of healthcare data and make those data more freely available for research, Riley argues that we need to abandon our currently fragmented approach with different privacy laws applicable to each sector and develop a national regulatory system that imposes "similar rules for similar contexts."

In Part VI, introduced by Jerry Avorn, the focus is on legal questions related to FDA oversight of health Big Data and liability concerns. In Chapter 18, "Data Sharing that Enables Postapproval Drug and Device Research and Protects Patient Privacy: Best Practice Recommendations," Ameet Sarpatwari, Bradley A. Malin,

Aaron S. Kesselheim, Joshua J. Gagne, and Sebastian Schneeweiss highlight legal and ethical tensions between federal privacy law and postapproval drug and device research. They detail how these laws limit data sharing and evaluate the ethical justifications for and against these restrictions. Of the ways to legally share data, they focus on the expert determination pathway and propose best practice recommendations for data protection (e.g., data censoring, generalization, perturbation, and access), linking, and risk assessment on the basis of an ethically proposed definition of very low risk, commonly implemented methods to determine reidentification risks, and the strengths and limitations of various data protection techniques.

Next, in Chapter 19, "Big Data and Human Medical Judgment: Regulating Next-Generation Clinical Decision Support," Jeffrey M. Senger and Patrick O'Leary focus specifically on the challenge of evaluating and regulating next-generation clinical decision support (CDS) systems that draw on massive data to make recommendations about clinical care decisions. The challenge for the FDA and other policymakers is that CDS will not be "low risk" in the traditional sense. They will have life-supporting and life-sustaining intended uses. Some will necessarily involve black-box analysis that may be too complicated for physicians to meaningfully second guess or even understand. The authors argue that the current FDA tools to manage this kind of risk are poorly calibrated to *any* software, let alone software that is designed to adapt to and learn from an ever-expanding universe of data and experiences.

Chapter 20, "Medical Malpractice and Black-Box Medicine," by W. Nicholson Price II, the last chapter in this section, addresses the question of medical malpractice liability in black-box medicine when the latter is used to direct care. Price posits that the question of medical malpractice arises both in the case of harms caused by the use of such algorithms and also when harms could have been avoided if algorithmic methods had been used. These novel medical malpractice risks arise for medical providers and healthcare enterprises and can have a significant impact on the adoption of black-box medicine. Price therefore argues that is important to develop correct liability rules for providers and enterprises, avoiding the extremes of lax liability and stringent liability.

Finally, Part VII, introduced by Rachel E. Sachs, examines ways that existing intellectual property regimes are conducive or in need of adjustment to deal with the problems posed by biomedical Big Data. How do we encourage incentives to produce Big Data frameworks in the first instance? And once we have them, how do we promote access to these frameworks and their products? The chapters in this part take up these questions, investigating both the strengths and weaknesses of intellectual property as a mechanism for promoting innovation in Big Data technologies and the potential difficulties this intellectual property may create from a social welfare perspective.

In Chapter 21, "Big Data and Intellectual Property Rights in the Health and Life Sciences," Timo Minssen and Justin Pierce examine five types of intellectual property rights relevant to big data: (1) patents, (2) copyrights, (3) the European database protection, and the important *sui generis* areas of (4) trade secret protection and (5) regulatory exclusivities. The authors compare these rights in EU and US law. They then turn to a set of emerging issues relevant for the future of law's intersection with Big Data, including the interface of competition law (i.e., antitrust) with the intellectual property rights of data owners, Big Data use for synthetic biology and biobank scientific enterprise, and private-sector use of public-sector Big Data.

Last but not least, in Chapter 22, "The Pathologies of Data-Generating Patents," Ted Sichelman and Brenda M. Simon focus on the implications of data-generating patents discussed elsewhere in the volume, such as patents covering genetic diagnostic tests, implantable and other medical devices, and consumer devices that track, store, and analyze information about patients and users. The authors propose and defend a two-factor test for determining which data-generating patents are likely to be problematic: whether the data-generating patent strongly preempts others from generating the same types of data and whether the patented invention generates data that can be used in secondary markets that are too distinct from that of the patented invention. To deal with problematic data-generating biomedical patents, the authors evaluate a series of legal solutions that include limiting patentability, mandating narrow disclosure or sharing of data, expanding defenses to infringement, and restricting available remedies.

Finally, an Epilogue by Frank Pasquale closes the book. Pasquale isolates some themes in the book and examines how rivalries among diverse professional groups could influence the future development and application of Big Data in healthcare.

As sports sage Yogi Berra once quipped, "It's tough to make predictions, especially about the future." The relationship between Big Data, health law, and bioethics is no exception. We are still at the dawn of the healthcare system's encounter with Big Data and the Internet of Things. We are even earlier in the development stage of the encounters of law and ethics with these topics. This is a daunting challenge for a volume such as this, but more important, it is an amazing opportunity. This is the moment when one can close one's eyes, point to a place on the intellectual globe, and find oneself in an undiscovered country. Some of the lands imagined by our authors will turn out to be mythical; others, quotidian. But at present they remain largely undiscovered, so we invite you to join us in exploring the possible worlds to come.

PART I

Shifting Paradigms

Big Data's Impact on Health Law and Bioethics

INTRODUCTION

Urs Gasser

The chapters in this part examine the wide-ranging impact of Big Data on individual and public health from different vantage points and offer a complementary set of epistemological, legal, and ethical perspectives and insights. The chapters cover a lot of ground and engage in a nuanced analysis of different facets of the Big Data phenomenon. At the outset, each chapter acknowledges a larger shift from "small" to "big" data that also embraces medical, health, and health-related data, confirming the notion of a paradigm shift that inspired this part of the book and the volume at large. Several chapters situate these structural changes in the specific context of information-based research trends, such as precision medicine, as well as specific projects, such as the Precision Medicine Initiative, the Cancer Moonshot, the NIH's Big Data to Knowledge Initiative, the BRAIN Initiative, and the like. Based on a discussion of the technological, economic, and regulatory undercurrents, each of the contributions in this part highlights a different aspect of the Big Data phenomenon that is likely to have significant ramifications for health law and bioethics. On a foundational level, several chapters discuss how the actors involved in data collection, aggregation, and analysis in the age of Big Data and the Internet of Things have expanded from traditional health institutions, such as hospitals, to a broad range of commercial enterprises that collect a wide array of sensitive health or health-relevant information. These developments, according to the authors, create a number of massive pressure points that need to be explored and addressed, including challenges regarding traditional legal definitions and concepts, amplified and new types of privacy risks, and the problem of an uneven legal and regulatory landscape.

The emerging asymmetry and unevenness of the legal and regulatory landscape are explored in depth in Nicolas P. Terry's contribution, "Big Data and Regulatory Arbitrage in Healthcare" (Chapter 4). Focusing on the creation, aggregation, and use of health-related data outside the regulated healthcare space, Terry identifies a series of pressing policy questions, including problems related to discriminatory practices by health insurance companies resulting from extensive data mining. At the core of the chapter is a detailed analysis of the elevated privacy and data-protection risks that emerge from data brokers who have entered the healthcare arena. Terry examines different dimensions of the healthcare data-protection challenge, which together lead to a problem of regulatory arbitrage. As a remedy to this problem, Terry proposes comprehensive federal legislation to ensure that personal health information, whether created inside or outside the healthcare system, enjoys the highest level of data protection.

While agreeing that Big Data will fundamentally transform health law and bioethics, Barbara J. Evans – in her chapter, "Big Data and Individual Autonomy in a Crowd" (Chapter 1) – looks at the inverse (privacy) problem by discussing the barriers to data resources "that are highly inclusive, with a large, diverse group of participating individuals, and with detailed health information about each" and that are required to unleash the full potential of Big Data research. In this context, Evans emphasizes that traditional legal pathways that have allowed unconsented access to data are under stress, particularly given the reidentification risks that characterize Big Data environments. She also points out that individual consent – as the most promising access pathway for researchers to obtain data resources in the future – might be an insufficient mechanism absent a new moral framework and sense of "common purpose" vis-à-vis the currently dominant "bioethical and regulatory landscape that celebrates individual autonomy." Moving to solutions, Evans introduces the idea of a "marketplace of ethics and privacy standards" in the form of a "[c]onsumer-driven data commons [that] would, in effect, be self-governing commonwealths, formed by consent of the members." Such a model rooted in civic solidarity seeks both to address new power imbalances and to reimagine the interplay between individual and society's rights.

The two other chapters in this part also start with a detailed account of the various forces at play that push toward a highly interconnected Big Data (and Internet of Things) health environment. The chapters touch on privacy risks but concentrate on a different dimension of the paradigm shift: to what extent Big Data will transform the nature of scientific knowledge and inquiry and the role law and policy should play in such a context. After critically evaluating popular claims that we are witnessing a trend from theory to data and from causation to correlation, Jeffrey M. Skopek argues in his chapter, "Big Data's Epistemology and Its Implications for Precision Medicine and Privacy" (Chapter 2), that the epistemological shifts are more limited than has been suggested. Nonetheless, using precision medicine as an example, Skopek demonstrates that the transformative potential of Big Data is significant, for instance, as a basis for predictive analytics that might provide novel insights about patients and their traits. These developments, Skopek argues, lead to a broad set of legal and ethical challenges for areas such as intellectual property, tort, and especially privacy. In examining the privacy issues more closely, Skopek argues that the "threat to privacy posed by Big Data is more limited than has been widely thought, because its predictions about us will often not cause privacy losses and its inferences about us will not constitute privacy violations." Acknowledging that these uses of Big Data might nevertheless be harmful, Skopek concludes that advances in Big Data may "require that we rethink the legal and ethical status of our bodies as bodies of data."

Using a similar analytical starting point as the other authors, Tal Z. Zarsky, in his chapter, "Correlation versus Causation in Health-Related Big Data Analysis: The Role of Reason and Regulation" (Chapter 3), examines the economic and related conditions of health data flows in the age of Big Data and diagnoses strong economic incentives for leading firms – and, as a result, a growing trend – to heavily rely on mere correlations to inform health-relevant predictions, decisions, and practices. Based on a critical review of the correlation versus causation debate, Zarsky concludes that there are strong arguments to opt for practices that rely not only on correlation but also on causation as far as health and medical data are concerned – with some notable exceptions where strong statistical evidence suggests causation even in the absence of a mechanism. With respect to the question of whether law should intervene, Zarsky provides a nuanced answer and examines a number of specific junctures at which the law should play a role by setting requirements as to the proper way the data must be analyzed prior to use in order to strengthen scientific knowledge and to avoid unnecessary harm resulting from wrongful generalization or neglected side effects.

Taken together, the contributions in this part provide a robust analysis of the seismic shifts and power implications that occur with respect to the creation, collection, storage, aggregation, and usage of medical, health, and health-related information within and outside the traditional sectors and set of actors. Combined, the chapters also provide a thorough mapping of the various risks associated with these new information-based practices and identify areas of particular normative concern such as privacy and autonomy but also equality and societal progress that benefit all. In their careful analyses of these multifaceted challenges, the authors not only identify problems but also suggest possible approaches and solutions ranging from legal and regulatory reform to a rethinking of ethical and other relevant norms. While a comprehensive roadmap still needs to be developed, the chapters in this part offer thought-provoking insights and provide conceptual building blocks that will contribute to future debates about the best ways to harness the full potential of Big Data for individual and societal health while also managing its risks and minimizing potential harms.

1

Big Data and Individual Autonomy in a Crowd

*Barbara J. Evans**

1.1 INTRODUCTION

Informational research studies people's preexisting data or biospecimens[1] and is an important tool for biomedical discovery in the twenty-first century. Examples of major informational research projects launched in recent years include the Precision Medicine Initiative,[2] the Cancer Moonshot,[3] and the BRAIN Initiative.[4] Such projects require access to data resources that are highly inclusive, with a large, diverse group of participating individuals and with detailed health information about each. The required level of detail includes data that raise important privacy concerns: genetic information, clinical information tracing a person's health history, data from research projects in which the person previously participated, and data bearing on behavior and lifestyle, such as data from the person's fitness tracker or at-home health monitoring devices.[5]

Faden et al. note that the moral framework to support informational studies "will depart in significant respects from contemporary conceptions of clinical and research

---

* This chapter was first developed for the 2016 Petrie-Flom Annual Conference and subsequently was published in a longer form in Power to the People: Data Citizens in the Age of Precision Medicine, 19 *Vand. J. Ent. Tech. L.* 243 (2017), parts of which are republished here with permission of the *Vand. J. Ent. Tech. L.* This research received financial support from the Robert Wood Johnson Foundation's Health Data Exploration Project (Kevin Patrick, M.D., M.S., PI).

[1] Federal Policy for the Protection of Human Subjects, 80 *Fed. Reg.* 53,933, 53,938 (September 8, 2015).
[2] See White House, The Precision Medicine Initiative, available at https://obamawhitehouse.archives.gov/node/333101 [https://perma.cc/GBS3-FYY8] (last visited May 21, 2017).
[3] See White House, Fact Sheet: Investing in the National Cancer Moonshot (February 1, 2016), available at https://obamawhitehouse.archives.gov/the-press-office/2016/02/01/fact-sheet-investing-national-cancer-moonshot [https://perma.cc/APJ2-AT78] (last visited May 21, 2017).
[4] See White House, Brain Initiative (September 30, 2014), https://obamawhitehouse.archives.gov/node/226036 [https://perma.cc/8R6L-PV94] (last visited May 21, 2017).
[5] Barbara J. Evans, Barbarians at the Gate: Consumer-Driven Data Commons and the Transformation of Citizen Science, 42 *Am. J. L. Med.* 651–85 (2016).

ethics" and may require a new "norm of common purpose ... a principle presiding over matters that affect the interests of everyone ... a shared social purpose that we cannot as individuals achieve."[6] This chapter explores an unresolved question: how can common purpose emerge on the present bioethical and regulatory landscape that celebrates individual autonomy? It is difficult to imagine why self-serving individuals, endowed with the right to make autonomous decisions to serve their own best interests, would willingly cede that right to embrace a new norm of common purpose. This chapter argues that common purpose may emerge, but only if bioethicists and members of the public embrace a richer conception of individual autonomy than the rugged go-it-alone individualism enshrined in twentieth-century bioethics.

1.2 EVOLVING CONCEPTIONS OF INDIVIDUAL AUTONOMY

The field of bioethics, as it emerged in the mid-twentieth century, embraced a Kantian atomistic concept of individual autonomy that conceives individuals as self-governing, self-reliant, individualistic, and fundamentally alone.[7] The concept resembles Richard Fallon's ascriptive autonomy,[8] which recognizes individuals' sovereignty over their own moral choices. At its inception, the field of bioethics sought to protect individuals facing binary us-versus-them challenges: the patient against the physician in a paternalistic healthcare system or the scientifically naive human research subject against the sophisticated investigator in research settings. The Kantian notion of autonomy was a "powerful antidote to the threats to personhood that result"[9] in these David-versus-Goliath settings characterized by disparities of expertise and bargaining power.

Twentieth-century bioethics emphasized the right of individuals to make their own decisions, but a criticism is that it empowered them to make decisions *only* as individuals and failed to lay out a roadmap for collective action.[10] Twentieth-century bioethics, for whatever reason, conceived patients and research subjects as weak, vulnerable, alone, disorganized, and in need of paternalistic protectors – for example, ethicists and institutional review boards (IRBs). This presumption of human disempowerment pervades federal ethical and privacy regulations such as the Common Rule[11] and the Health Insurance Portability and Accountability Act of 1996 (HIPAA) Privacy Rule.[12] Both regulations reject the approach of organizing

---

[6] Ruth R. Faden et al., An Ethics Framework for a Learning Health Care System: A Departure from Traditional Research Ethics and Clinical Ethics, 43 *Hastings Ctr. Rep.* S16 (2013).
[7] Alfred I. Tauber, *Patient Autonomy and the Ethics of Responsibility* (Basic Bioethics 17), 13, 117 (2005).
[8] Richard H. Fallon, Jr., Two Senses of Autonomy, 46 *Stan. L. Rev.* 875, 890–93 (1994).
[9] Tauber, Patient Autonomy, at 14.
[10] Evans, Barbarians at the Gate.
[11] 45 C.F.R. § 46 (2016).
[12] Health Insurance Portability and Accountability Act of 1996, Pub. L. No. 104–191, 110 Stat. 1936 (codified as amended in scattered sections of 18, 26, 29, and 42 U.S.C.); see 45 C.F.R. §§ 160, 164 (2010) (Privacy Rule).

and empowering individuals to protect themselves, for example, by allowing research subjects to elect IRB members and hold them accountable, or using referenda to establish ethical and privacy standards, or unionizing research subjects to defend their own interests through collective bargaining. This last approach – collective bargaining – has worked well in certain other contexts, such as labor relations, where the law seeks to protect vulnerable individuals who face disparities of bargaining power. The Common Rule and HIPAA Privacy Rule, despite their many merits, treat ethical and privacy standards as gifts to be handed down from above to vulnerable, cowering "subjects" too disempowered to negotiate the protections they desire.

In the years after 1980, some bioethicists explored alternative visions of what individual autonomy means, such as an interactive or relational[13] view where autonomy is "not merely an internal, psychological characteristic but also an external, or social [one]."[14] By this view, individuals enhance their autonomy by working together rather than by acting alone.[15] The "self is understood as a confluence of relationships and social obligations that are constitutive of identity," and autonomy may, at times, "legitimately be subordinated to other moral principles that determine how the self is governed within a social context."[16] The individual is autonomous yet simultaneously embedded in social relationships and shared institutions that are instrumental to the realization of individuals' autonomy. Individuals acting alone are weak; individuals acting together are stronger. Social institutions are the soil in which common purpose can emerge. But such views were side currents in twentieth-century bioethics.

In connection with data access, insistence on atomistic autonomy has had the unintended consequence of keeping individuals disorganized and, therefore, weak. Those who assert a right of individuals to block access to their data in all circumstances – even when other people's health depends on data access – may be blurring the line between individual autonomy and narcissism, "a pattern of traits and behaviors which signify infatuation and obsession with one's self *to the exclusion of all others.*"[17] One sometimes hears that even if research has high social value and consent is difficult or impossible to obtain, and even if requiring consent may undercut the scientific validity of results, these problems "do not in themselves constitute valid ethical reasons for waiving a requirement of informed consent."[18] This vision of "go-it-alone" autonomy risks consigning individuals to the condition

---

[13] See, e.g., Tauber, Patient Autonomy, at 121.
[14] Ibid., at 120 (citing Grace Clement, *Care, Autonomy, and Justice: Feminism and the Ethic of Care* 22 [1996]).
[15] Ibid., at 122.
[16] Ibid., at 85.
[17] See Definition of Narcissistic Personality Disorder, HealthyPlace, available at www.healthyplace.com/personality-disorders/malignant-self-love/narcissistic-personality-disorder-npd-definition [https://perma.cc/VB7G-FMUQ] (last visited May 22, 2017) (emphasis added).
[18] Franklin G. Miller, Research on Medical Records without Informed Consent, 36 *J.L. Med. Ethics* 560 (2008) (discussing but not necessarily endorsing this view).

Thomas Hobbes referred to as "the confusion of a disunited multitude,"[19] unable to act together for the common purpose of promoting wellness and public health.

In Hobbes' scheme, these confused, disunited people are empowered when they come together to form "commonwealths," institutions they form to advance common purposes. When forming a commonwealth, people agree "every one with every one" to create mechanisms for deliberating and making collective decisions that bind all of them: "every one, as well he that voted for it as he that voted against it," shall embrace decisions made by the "consent of the people assembled ... in the same manner as if they were his own."[20]

Twentieth-century bioethics downplayed the capacity of individuals to work together to form commonwealths to solve their own problems. It instead empowered IRBs and ethicists to decide what is best for them. Governance "in the sense of binding collective decisions about public affairs" is one of a basic set of universal concepts that anthropologists observe in both primitive and advanced cultures; other such concepts include giving, lending, reciprocating, and forming coalitions.[21] This core concept was poorly developed in twentieth-century bioethics. This gap is an important failing in the era of twenty-first-century informational research.

1.3 GIVING DATA PARTICIPANTS A MEANINGFUL VOICE

Creating data "commonwealths" or finding common purpose requires civic solidarity. Richard Rorty has reflected on the long struggle, dating back at least as far as the Greek philosophers, to reconcile individual autonomy with membership in a community.[22] There is an obvious potential for autonomy to undermine solidarity. People are deeply divided about the privacy, ethical, and moral issues in bioethics,[23] making solidarity difficult, if not impossible, to achieve. Some people desire near-absolute control over their health data, whereas others would like to see everybody's data openly accessible for research and other projects perceived to advance the public good. These differences are deep and intractable and cannot be resolved through persuasion because the disputants lack a shared set of principles – and sometimes even a common set of perceived facts – by which to judge whose view is correct. Members of the public are "moral strangers" to one another, to use Engelhardt's phrase about the perils of bioethical discourse.[24]

---

[19] Thomas Hobbes, *Leviathan* 101 (1651).
[20] Ibid.
[21] Stuart P. Green, The Universal Grammar of Criminal Law: Basic Concepts of Criminal Law, 98 *Mich. L. Rev.* 2104, 2112 (2000) (citing Donald E. Brown, *Human Universals* [1991]); see also Robin Bradley Kar, The Deep Structure of Law and Morality, 84 *Tex. L. Rev.* 877, 885 (2006) (same).
[22] Richard Rorty, *Contingency, Irony, and Solidarity* xiii (1989).
[23] See H. Tristram Engelhardt, *The Foundations of Bioethics* 3–7 (2nd edn, 1996).
[24] Ibid., at 7.

A troubling aspect of twentieth-century bioethics was its presumption that ethical and privacy standards governing research data access should be developed "top down" – by national commissions, a privacy protection study commission, expert advisory bodies, or federal agency officials – rather than "bottom up" through collective decisions of the people whose data researchers wish to use. The top-down approach to setting ethical standards for data access may have reflected a pragmatic assessment that the people, if asked, would never be able to agree what the standards should be. Policymakers may simply have deemed civic solidarity to be impossible.

Top-down ethical and privacy standards, such as those reflected in the Common Rule and the HIPAA Privacy Rule, unfortunately have failed to persuade enough people to contribute their data to ensure that twenty-first-century scientists will have the vast data resources they need. There is a striking disconnect between empirical surveys that show that most people feel favorably about letting researchers use their data[25] and the very low rates at which people actually consent for their data to be used in research. Existing ethical and privacy standards, designed with little direct, organized collective public engagement, may not be what people want. Those standards were, after all, minimal regulatory standards, not designed for the purpose of pleasing the public, and apparently they have not done so. Why not engage the public in the challenge of designing a better set of standards that can satisfy concerns of data contributors while still making data available for socially valuable research uses?

A mistake we may all be making is to assume that public engagement is fruitful only if there is a prospect that a broad public consensus will emerge. Too often we assume that the public will never agree on appropriate ethics and privacy standards to govern data access, and the perceived intractability of their disagreement becomes an excuse to cut them out of the debate. The real mistake here lies in presuming that everyone *needs* to agree on a single set of uniform access and privacy standards, applicable to all, in order for data access to work. The reality may be that a vibrant framework of research data access can exist in the presence of multiple competing visions of what ethical data access requires. If Big Data is as big as it purports to be, perhaps it is big enough to accommodate a marketplace of ethics and privacy standards.

Elsewhere I proposed the formation of consumer-driven data commons, which would be institutions that enable groups of consenting individuals to collaborate to assemble powerful, large-scale health data resources for use in scientific research, on terms the group members themselves would set.[26] Consumer-driven data commons

---

[25] See, e.g., Leonard J. Kish & Eric J. Topol, Unpatients: Why Patients Should Own Their Medical Data, 11 *Nat. Biotech.* 921–24 (2015) (discussing individuals' willingness to participate in research); Eric Topol, The Big Medical Data Miss: Challenges in Establishing an Open Medical Resource, 16 *Nat. Rev. Genet.* 253–54 (2015) (same).

[26] Evans, Barbarians at the Gate.

would, in effect, be self-governing data commonwealths formed by consent of the members – people self-selected because they share at least some degree of common purpose. These commons could be organized and operated by the members themselves, by disease advocacy groups, or by commercial data-management companies acting as trustees to manage members' collective data resources according to rules the members themselves would set.

Each commons-forming group would establish its own rules of access to – and use of – their shared data resources, privacy practices, duties and rights of membership in the group, policies on entry and exit from the group, and collective decision-making processes. This would not necessarily lead to adoption of ethical and privacy norms that differ starkly from today's Common Rule and the HIPAA Privacy Rule. A commons-forming group might decide, after considering alternatives, to embrace norms similar to those reflected in current regulations. They might choose to modify them slightly, for example, by electing members of the IRB that can grant consent waivers on behalf of their group and making these members fireable at the group's discretion. Presumably, however, if people had been happy with the norms reflected in current regulations, they already would have contributed their data for scientific use, which most people have not done. Groups would be free to enunciate ethical and privacy standards significantly different from the regulations that currently govern access to their data.

The real value of consumer-driven data commons is that they offer a laboratory for modernizing ethical and privacy norms to function in Big Data environments. Commons-forming groups would enunciate their privacy and ethical standards bottom up – that is, for themselves – rather than having standards imposed top down by regulators, external ethics advisory bodies, and IRBs. Some commons-forming groups might reject traditional regulatory norms altogether, replacing them with collectively agreed norms that are more (or less) favorable to research uses of data. Groups would enunciate their own visions of what constitutes an ethical use of their members' data. Some groups, to enhance the value of their collective data resources, might agree to abolish individual consent and instead make collective decisions about how their entire data resource – including the data of all group members – can be used. The more inclusive a data resource is, the greater is its value to science.

No individual would be required to join a commons-forming group. Individuals wishing to participate would first obtain their own health data by exercising their HIPAA Section 164.524 access rights (for traditional healthcare data) or as allowed under the policies of non-HIPAA-covered data sources such as wearable device manufacturers. Thereafter, individuals could choose to deposit their data in one or more consumer-driven data commons. Once in, individuals would give up their right of traditional, granular informed consent to specific data uses and would instead agree to be governed by whatever norms to which the group had agreed. The individual right of consent thus would be conceived as a right to enter or not enter a specific commons group, to remain in or exit it in accordance with its rules, and to participate in the group's collective decision-making processes.

An advantage of consumer-driven data commons is that they offer the prospect of a workable revenue model to fund the costs of making data interoperable and hiring skilled technical and legal advisors to manage privacy and data access. The Common Rule and the HIPAA Privacy Rule do not restrict individuals' ability to sell their own data. In contrast, institutional data holders such as hospitals face limits, such as the HITECH Act's restrictions on the sale of data, which make it hard to finance the development of large-scale data resources and to sustain them for long-term use. Consumer-driven data commons could make collective decisions about the revenue model they wish to adopt, using proceeds to retain legal and other consultants to help manage their data assets and to convert their data resources into consistent formats that enhance their value and scientific utility. However, consumer-driven data commons would be free to decide that commodification of their data is ethically objectionable and instead donate their data resources for scientific uses chosen through the group's collective decision making processes.

As different commons-forming groups enunciate their respective visions of ethical data access, there would arise a marketplace of ethical and privacy policies. Individuals could compare these as they make decisions about which consumer-driven data commons best satisfy their own vision and goals for ethical use of their data. A successful consumer-driven commons would be one that attracts members (by enunciating ethical and privacy standards that satisfy concerns of data contributors) yet is able to supply data for useful lines of research on terms that are satisfactory to those members (by threading the needle of ethically acceptable research data access). As successful consumer-driven data commons expand, their expansion would supply empirical data on what works and what does not work. Commons-forming groups could learn from one another, perhaps converging on people-driven ethical and privacy standards that outperform those handed down by ethics experts.

In setting ethical standards for data sharing, there is every reason to trust the wisdom of the people. In normative ethics (the study of what constitutes an ethical course of action), experts "disagree so much and so radically that we hesitate to say that they are experts."[27] Courts consider normative ethics so standardless and nonreproduceable that there is ongoing controversy whether normative ethics testimony even meets the threshold for admissibility as legal evidence.[28] Government-appointed expert advisory bodies add value in fields – such as setting consumer product safety standards or water-quality standards – where recognizable

---

[27] Bethany Spielman, The Future of Bioethics Testimony: Guidelines for Determining Qualifications, Reliability, and Helpfulness, 36 *San Diego L. Rev.* 1044, 1056 (1999) (citing J. R. Bambrough, Plato's Political Analogies, in *Plato, Popper and Politics* 152, 158 [Renford Bambrough ed., 1967]).

[28] Edward J. Imwinkelried, Expert Testimony by Ethicists, 76 *Temp. L. Rev.* 91, 105–6, 96–99 (2003).

bodies of expert knowledge exist. But when answering the question, "What is an ethical use of an individual's personal health data?," meaningful public engagement offers expertise as credible as that of self-declared ethics experts.

1.4 WHY THE TIME MAY BE RIGHT FOR SOLIDARITY TO EMERGE

Self-serving people may be willing to eschew rugged individualism if it ceases to promote their personal aims. In Big Data environments, traditional norms of individual informed consent may no longer serve the principal aim for which they were designed: that is, empowering individuals to protect themselves against research-related risks.

The traditional informed consent norms in regulations such as the Common Rule and the HIPAA Privacy Rule were designed several decades ago with clinical research and relatively small informational studies in mind. In those contexts, individual informed consent is a rather effective instrument for protecting people from research-related risks: a person can effectively avoid the physical risks of clinical research by refusing to consent to the research. Refusals to volunteer for clinical research are strongly respected in our legal system, which treats unconsented touching of a person's body as a battery. Only in rare circumstances, such as emergency clinical research where participants are not able to consent, can their right of consent be waived and then only under oversight of an IRB.

In informational research that uses a person's data, the principal risks individuals face are privacy and dignitary risks related to data disclosure. In past small-data contexts, a right of informed consent gave individuals considerable power to manage those risks. The degree of privacy risk individuals faced, it was thought, was proportional to how widely they shared their data. The Common Rule and the HIPAA Privacy Rule do allow some unconsented uses of data in research, but only subject to constraints: for example, requiring data to be deidentified (which was believed to neutralize privacy risks) or requiring a consent waiver (which requires an IRB or privacy board to assess the privacy risks and judge them to be minimal). In twentieth-century data environments, the consent norms reflected in current regulations plausibly advanced the individual's wish to be shielded from privacy risks.

Is this still true in the twenty-first-century Big Data environment? Can individual informed consent still protect people's privacy? As noted previously, the most valuable data resources for twenty-first-century informational research are deeply descriptive in the sense of linking, for each included individual, multiple streams of personal genomic, health, and lifestyle data. Deeply descriptive data resources defy attempts to deidentify them. Access to identifiers is often necessary, in certain phases of database development, to link these multiple streams of data to assemble a comprehensive description of each individual.[29] Even if overt identifiers such as

---

[29] Barbara J. Evans, Much Ado about Data Ownership, 25 *Harv. J. L. Tech.* 69, 93–94 (2012), available at http://jolt.law.harvard.edu/articles/pdf/v25/25HarvJLTech69.pdf [https://perma.cc/A4JU-CV79].

names are subsequently discarded, the resulting data resources can potentially be reidentified by cross-correlating data elements with external data sets that link those same elements back to the person's name.[30] Reidentification risk is not the only threat to individual privacy, however.

Modern, interconnected Big Data environments may exhibit privacy interdependence: individuals' privacy is "affected by the decisions of others, and could be out of their own control."[31] Such interdependence exists, for example, in online social networks: person A chooses to share a group photo that displays an embarrassing image of person B, which the latter would prefer to suppress.[32] Particularly with genomic data, which display similarities among related individuals, one family member's willingness to share data in identifiable form may reveal information about others who did not consent to data sharing. When people's privacy preferences are misaligned and some of the people reveal even a limited set of attributes, "it is almost impossible for a specific user to hide in the crowd."[33] Moving past petty traditional conceptions of clan and kinship, we are all one large human family, sharing genomic data that are 99.9 percent alike and sharing weight gain within our social networks.[34] Even when familial interrelationships are not an issue, data scientists have demonstrated reidentification attacks that can infer (sometimes with surprising accuracy) to whom a given genome belongs by applying algorithms that rule out identifiable individuals to whom the data could not possibly belong.[35]

In twenty-first-century data environments, the individual's traditional right of informed consent may cease to protect individual privacy. To protect one person's privacy, it might be necessary to constrain other people's rights to consent to sharing their own data. In effect, respecting one person's autonomy would require crushing

---

[30] See Khaled El Emam et al., A Systematic Review of Re-Identification Attacks on Health Data, 10(4) *PLoS One* e0126772 (2011); Federal Trade Commission, *Protecting Consumer Privacy in an Era of Rapid Change: A Proposed Framework for Businesses and Policymakers* 35–38 (2010) (warning that the distinction between personally identifiable information and nonidentifiable information is increasingly irrelevant in light of the potential for data to be reidentified); Paul Ohm, Broken Promises of Privacy: Responding to the Surprising Failure of Anonymization, 57 *UCLA L. Rev.* 1701, 1706 (2010) (discussing the risks to individual privacy if deidentified data were to be reidentified); Mark A. Rothstein, Is De-identification Sufficient to Protect Health Privacy in Research?, 10 *Am. J. Bioethics* 3, 5 (2010) ("Despite using various measures to de-identify health records, it is possible to reidentify them in a surprisingly large number of cases").

[31] Gergely Biczók & Pern Hui Chia, Interdependent Privacy: Let Me Share Your Data, in *Financial Cryptography and Data Security* 338 (Ahmad-Reza Sadeghi ed., 2013).

[32] Mathias Humbert, When Others Impinge upon Your Privacy: Interdependent Risks and Protection in a Connected World (March 13, 2015) (unpublished doctoral thesis), available at https://infoscience.epfl.ch/record/205089/files/EPFL_TH6515.pdf [https://perma.cc/HU3P-GXJN].

[33] Ibid., at v.

[34] Nicholas A. Christakis & James H. Fowler, The Spread of Obesity in a Large Social Network over 32 Years, *N. Engl. J. Med.*, July 26, 2007, at 370–79.

[35] Arvind Narayanan, New Genetic Re-identification Methods and Implications for Privacy at the University of Wisconsin Big Data, presented at Policy Meets Data Science Symposium (October 15, 2015).

the autonomy of others. When this is true, then atomistic, autonomous decision making breaks down as a mechanism for advancing the individual's interest.

This critique differs starkly from the oft-heard criticism that individual decisions fail to advance the *public's* interests (e.g., by making it impossible to assemble data resources that could be used to advance public health and the well-being of other patients). This critique – that atomistic autonomy undermines public interests – has never proved persuasive among strong proponents of data privacy, who may view autonomy as encompassing a right to disregard the interests of others. In contrast, the critique grounded in privacy interdependence highlights a different problem: individuals cannot, through their own autonomous decision making, protect *their own* interests anymore. No man is an island in the age of Big Data, and protecting individual privacy requires collective decision making.

The Big Data environment thus offers two incentives for people to band together to pursue common purposes. The first incentive is the one that Faden et al. highlight: sharing individual health data offers a prospect of public health benefits, and it may improve the health of other people such that the balance of individual and public interests justifies a moral obligation to share one's own data. The second incentive is more self-serving: individuals, acting alone, may no longer be able to protect the privacy of their own health data. Collective action of many individuals will be required, even to serve one's own selfish aims. This latter point may prove to be the more compelling rationale for collective action in the age of Big Data. It is possible that some people value their individual autonomy so greatly that they would be willing to let other people die to protect their own data privacy. Such people, though unwilling to work with other people to protect the public, may nevertheless be willing to cooperate with other people if that is the only way to protect individual privacy. In the age of Big Data, public health and privacy *both* are collective enterprises.

1.5 CONCLUSION

Traditional legal pathways for accessing data under the Common Rule and the HIPAA Privacy Rule are under stress and may not be able to meet the needs of twenty-first-century science. Deidentification of data, a major pathway for accessing data under current regulations, has ceased to provide the comfort it once did: reidentification risks are real. Even if deidentification worked, deidentified data have limited scientific utility because it is hard to link them together to form the deeply descriptive longitudinal health records most useful to science. Waivers of consent and privacy authorization, another important way to free data for research under HIPAA and the Common Rule, are also increasingly problematic: how can IRB members, in good conscience, deem the privacy risks of big, deeply descriptive general-purpose data resources to be minimal, as waiver criteria require? Individual consent may soon be the only remaining regulatory pathway for researchers to obtain data resources. Yet even today individuals do not consent to share their data in the numbers that would be required to assemble the very large-scale, inclusive data resources that modern science needs. They may grow even more reluctant to consent in coming years amid growing public awareness of reidentification risks and privacy interdependencies.

The consumer-driven commons discussed here are not proposed as a panacea but as one possible approach for organizing people and engaging them in helping to enunciate a new bioethics for twenty-first-century informational research. The transition from twentieth-century small-data bioethics to twenty-first-century Big Data bioethics in many respects resembles a shift from self-consciousness to social consciousness. In the Big Data environment, all of us are interdependent, and collective action is necessary both to overcome the scientific challenges that lie ahead and to protect our privacy as we do so. Regulatory frameworks of the past have served well and will continue to deliver good service in the contexts for which they were designed: clinical research and small-data studies. They are not adequate, however, for the challenges of Big Data science. In developing new frameworks, top-down approaches of the past must be treated with skepticism. The people whose data are used in research possess an expertise of what is ethical that is as valid as what regulators and ethics experts can offer. Consumer-driven data commons offer a laboratory in which groups of consenting individuals can discover the common purposes that they share and enunciate ethical and privacy standards that, after six decades of bioethical debate, will at last be of the people, by the people, and for the people.

2

Big Data's Epistemology and Its Implications for Precision Medicine and Privacy

Jeffrey M. Skopek

2.1 INTRODUCTION

It is generally thought that Big Data poses a substantial threat to privacy and that this threat is especially pressing in the health context. This chapter critically evaluates this view, revealing that the data revolution and its implications for privacy are often both misunderstood. This analysis has three parts. The first part explores the epistemological claims that are frequently made about how new data-mining techniques will transform scientific knowledge and inquiry, rejecting or identifying limits to some of the core claims. The second part looks at how the rise of prediction-oriented science will play out in the biomedical context, identifying a substantial transformation in field of precision medicine. The third part evaluates the implications of these developments for privacy, concluding that data mining will not generate many of the privacy losses and violations that have been envisioned.

2.2 THE BIG DATA REVOLUTION

Three core claims are often made about how Big Data will transform the nature of scientific inquiry and knowledge. The first is that new data-mining techniques and opportunities will free science of the constraints of theory, allowing data to speak for themselves. The second is that the search for causation will no longer be paramount, as correlation takes center stage. The third is that science will no longer focus solely on understanding, with prediction trumping explanation in some domains. The following analysis will demonstrate that the first claim should be rejected, that the second must be significantly amended, and that only the third is generally correct.

2.2.1 *From Theory to Data?*

The claim that new data-mining techniques and opportunities will free science of the constraints of theory and the hypotheticodeductive method, allowing the data to "speak for themselves," appears frequently in the literature. It is a claim made by the scientists who are using new data-mining techniques,[1] as well as by social scientists who are describing these uses.[2] Yet, on critical analysis, the claim does not hold up and should be rejected for both philosophical and empirical reasons.

The philosophical reasons can be found in a centuries-old debate in epistemology, given that the claim that pure induction can free science of the constraints of theory is not new but rather dates to Francis Bacon in the 1600s. This view, sometimes called "naive inductivism," has generally been rejected on several grounds. First, with respect to data collection, the critique is that data are not merely found but rather are generated in ways that presuppose theoretical commitments (e.g., the collection of genetic data may rely on theories about genetic expression, models of the biological processes involved, etc.). Second, with respect to data aggregation, the critique is that there are infinite ways in which the same set of facts can be classified, so the choice between them must presuppose some sort of theory of relevance or point of view. Third, regarding the final act of inference, the critique is that data cannot speak for themselves – that to elicit an answer, one must ask a question, which again presupposes at least a minimal hypothesis.

There are also empirical reasons to reject the "end-of-theory" claim, which are revealed by an analysis of the techniques actually employed in data mining. For example, as Wolfgang Pietsch demonstrates in an analysis of two widely used algorithms in data mining (classificatory trees and nonparametric regression), these algorithms will only identify the causal connections needed to reliably predict and manipulate a phenomenon if (1) the data in the training set include the parameters that are causally relevant, (2) the data do not contain too many parameters that are causally irrelevant, and (3) the parameters reflect adequate causal categories.[3] In these ways, the creation of the training set requires theory. Further, while machine learning may free humans of the need to generate hypotheses and thus create an illusion of discovering insights without asking questions, the algorithms generated through machine learning are themselves hypotheses that are tested against the training sets.

This does not mean, however, that there is nothing epistemologically novel about machine learning and science grounded in data mining. The fact that data-intensive science is theory laden externally (in its framing of an inquiry) does not mean that it must be theory laden internally (in its assumptions about the causal structure of the phenomenon under investigation).[4] Rather, machine learning may be able to

---

[1] See, e.g., Eric S. Lander, The Heroes of CRISPR, 164 *Cell* 18 (2016).
[2] See, e.g., Viktor Mayer-Schönberger & Kenneth Cukier, *Big Data: A Revolution That Will Transform How We Live, Work, and Think* 14, 61 (2013) ("hypotheses are no longer crucial for correlational analysis"); Rob Kitchin, Big Data, New Epistemologies and Paradigm Shifts, 1 *Big Data Soc'y*. 1, 2 (2014).
[3] Wolfgang Pietsch, Aspects of Theory-Ladenness in Data-Intensive Science, 82 *Phil. Sci.* 905, 913 (2015).
[4] Ibid. There may also be interesting epistemic differences between theory-directed and theory-informed science. See, generally, C. Kenneth Waters, The Nature and Context of Exploratory

generate powerful predictions on the basis of correlations without relying on any hypothesis about the underlying cause of the correlations. So when people talk about the end of theory, perhaps what they really mean is science free of a certain type of theory, such as causal theory – which is the second promise of the data revolution.

2.2.2 *From Causation to Correlation?*

The second way in which Big Data is said to revolutionize scientific inquiry is by bringing about a shift "from causation to correlation."[5] This claim can be found throughout the legal and social sciences literature, and there is certainly some truth to it. However, it must be qualified in ways that have not been recognized. To identify these limits, some clarification of the concept of "causation" is necessary. While this is a complex topic in philosophy that cannot be discussed fully here, it is helpful to recognize three basic points.

First, causation can be defined in either "mechanistic" or "difference-making" terms.[6] Mechanistic accounts of causation suggest that there is a causal connection between two variables if they are connected by an appropriate sort of physical mechanism (e.g., a chemical reaction). Difference-making accounts, by contrast, suggest that there is a causal connection between two variables if the occurrence of one variable makes the "right type of difference" in the occurrence of the other: for example, if the occurrence of one increases the probability of the other, if one would not occur but for the occurrence of the other, or if manipulating one allows for a manipulation of the other.

Second, to capture the full range of relationships that we ordinarily deem to be causal, both of these accounts of the nature of causation are needed. For example, to capture causation by omissions or absences (e.g., a missed flight that causes one to be late), a difference-making account is needed, whereas to capture cases of causation that are preempted or overdetermined (e.g., two fires that would have independently burned a single house but end up doing so together), a mechanistic account is needed.

Third, difference-making causation plays a central role in prediction, whereas mechanistic causation plays a central role in explanation – especially in the life sciences.[7] For example, to explain why smoking causes cancer, it is not sufficient to identify the series of difference-making relationships between smoking, the number of cilia in the lungs, and the occurrence of cancer. Rather, what is needed is an

---

Experimentation: An Introduction to Three Case Studies of Exploratory Research, 29 *Hist. Phil. Life Sci.* 275 (2007).

[5] See, e.g., Mayer-Schönberger & Cukier, *Big Data*, at 14, 15, 18.
[6] Jon Williamson, How Can Causal Explanations Explain? 78 *Erkenntnis* 257, 260–63 (2013).
[7] Federica Russo & Jon Williamson, Interpreting Causality in the Health Sciences, 21 *Int'l Stud. Phil. Sci.* 157, 158–59 (2007).

account of the underlying mechanisms: the fact that smoke destroys cilia, which allows carcinogenic particles to become trapped in the mucus that lines the respiratory tract, which allows them to mutate the DNA of the lung cells.

Recognizing these three features of causation reveals a problem with the way in which the shift from "causation to correlation" is often equated with a shift from "asking why to asking what." Take, for example, Mayer-Schönberger and Cukier's statement that "non-causal analyses ... aid our understanding of the world by primarily asking *what* rather than *why*."[8] The assumption underlying this claim is that causal analyses are different – that they do ask why. However, as the preceding discussion reveals, this is not always the case. While mechanistic causes may explain, difference-making causes may not (as in the case of cancer discussed earlier). Further, this error matters because it can lead to the mistaken conclusion that data-mining tools that tell us "what rather than why" are not capturing causal relationships or, more radically, to the conclusion by Mayer-Schönberger and Cukier that "Big Data does not tell us anything about causality."[9]

By failing to recognize that data mining can reveal difference-making causes that are nonexplanatory, this account obscures a transformative power of large-scale data mining: the power to identify multivariable causal relationships that are too complex to be identified through experimental science. Note that identifying causation is different from understanding or even proving it. Black-box medicine, discussed by Nicholson Price in this volume,[10] is just one example of how science might be transformed in this way, which is arguably more significant than our increased power to discover predictive correlations.

Further, looking beyond prediction to the goal of intervention, it is relevant that many of the interventions that we may want to make on the basis of data mining will only work if difference-making causes have been identified. Imagine, for example, that data mining reveals that a combination of variables is associated with a negative outcome. This could support two types of preventative interventions: (1) we might try to prevent the combination of variables from materializing or (2) if they do materialize, we might use this knowledge to adopt other preventative measures. The second type of intervention can work if the association is noncausal, but the first cannot.

For these reasons, we should reject the claim that the data revolution is about a general shift from causation to correlation. While our increased ability to uncover predictively useful correlations is transformative, so is our ability to uncover complex difference-making causes that might otherwise be undiscoverable; both are central to the power of data mining.

---

[8] Mayer-Schönberger & Cukier, *Big Data*, at 63. See also ibid., at 60 ("The system does not rely on causality but on correlations. It tells us what, not why.").
[9] Ibid., at 163.
[10] See Chapter 20.

2.2.3 *From Explanation to Prediction?*

The third way in which Big Data is said to transform scientific inquiry is by shifting its focus from explanation to prediction. Unlike the first two claims, this is not a methodological claim but rather a claim about the way in which data is being used which seems to be correct. What is worth highlighting, however, is that this shift in ambition implicitly entails a methodological shift in focus: either from causation to correlation (as the literature has recognized) or from mechanistic causation to difference-making causation (which has gone unrecognized). The reason this matters is that mechanistic knowledge allows not only for explanation but also for the generalization of causal claims based on probabilistic evidence. Without an understanding of the mechanism, we do not know what is behind a causal relationship (e.g., whether it is particular to specific populations or circumstances or is otherwise "fragile") and thus do not know what might cause that relationship and the prediction it generates to break down. For this reason, among others, it is unlikely that prediction will generally come to replace explanation as a goal of science – especially in areas such as the life sciences, which have historically placed great importance on both mechanistic and difference-making causation.[11] This does not mean, however, that these areas of science will not be significantly transformed.

2.3 BIG DATA AND PRECISION MEDICINE

The transformative potential of our new data-mining techniques and opportunities is clearly visible in the field of precision medicine, where predictive analytics will bring about a fundamental change in how patients and their medical traits are known, departing from the trajectory along which the personalization of medicine has progressed over the past century.

2.3.1 *Precision Medicine Prior to Big Data*

To see the potential impact on precision medicine, one must recognize that while the term "precision medicine" is new, there is significant continuity between past and present attempts to increase the precision of diagnosis and treatment. Modern attempts to increase the granularity of disease categories, for example, build on hundreds of years of history, dating back at least as far as Carolus Linnaeus' 1763 *Genera Morborum*. The core difference between the past and present is the nature of the classification criteria being used. Whereas classification was once based largely on measurable symptoms together with descriptions of tissues or cells,

---

[11] Russo & Williamson, Interpreting Causality in the Health Sciences, at 158–59.

precision medicine today is looking beyond the clinical manifestation of diseases to their genetic and molecular characteristics or their pathogenic pathways.

The same can be said of precision treatments. Take, for example, a *HER2* biomarker test (which is used to determine whether to treat cancer with the paradigmatic precision medicine drug Herceptin) and a blood type test (which has been used to determine which type of blood to use in a transfusion for more than 100 years). In both cases, a diagnostic is used to support a treatment decision that is based on a mechanistic understanding of how the treatment will work on the individual at issue. Thus, although modern precision drugs are designed to target specific pathogenic pathways (including those that might only be present in a minority of patients with a given disease), rather than developed on the basis of clinical manifestations (and for the average patient with a given disease), there is a fundamental epistemological continuity.

2.3.2 *Precision Medicine in the Era of Big Data*

Advances in machine learning, however, promise to give us an entirely new form of precision medicine – a form that Nicholson Price has described as "black-box medicine."[12] There are two defining features of this shift.

The first way in which machine learning will transform precision medicine is by allowing us to identify causal relationships and correlations that are inaccessible to the methodologies at the core of modern medicine: bench science (used to develop knowledge of mechanisms) and randomized controlled trials (used to develop knowledge of difference making). Both of these experimental techniques are only capable of identifying or testing a relatively small number of causal relationships because they both need to hold constant as many variables as possible. In the drug trial, this is needed to achieve statistically significant results, and in laboratory science, this is needed to isolate the causal mechanisms at issue. Machine learning techniques, by contrast, do not face the same constraints when the data set is large enough. As discussed earlier, these tools allow us to identify complex difference-making causes and correlations that have too many variables to study in randomized controlled trials (e.g., a complex set of genetic and environmental factors that increase the risk of a disease) and that arise from mechanistic causes that are too complex to identify through laboratory science (e.g., the biological pathways that link genetic and environmental factors). In these ways, we are able to discover previously unidentifiable relationships hidden within the vast information that is being generated in medical research and practice.

The second way in which advances in machine learning will transform precision medicine is by providing us with predictive algorithms that work on the basis of causal relationships and correlations that we are unable to understand.

[12] See Chapter 20.

This nontransparency may take one of two forms, as Price has identified. One possibility is that machine learning will generate algorithms that we can state as a formal matter but that we cannot comprehend as a practical matter due to the complexity of the relationships they identify: for example, an algorithm that can predict how a tumor will respond to a drug based on allelic patterns among thousands of genes. Another possibility is that machine learning will generate an algorithm that is inherently nontransparent: for example, an artificial neural network that has been trained to determine whether an image likely shows a tumor or not, but its process remains opaque to everyone, including the initial programmer.

Thus, in the future, precision medicine will not need to rely solely on a predictive model based on biomarkers and biological mechanisms that we understand. Rather, we will be able to make even more powerful predictions on the basis of data sets that include not only nonmedical data but also data whose relevance is not known and might never be known. The development of this form of precision medicine will give rise to a broad set of legal and ethical challenges for areas including intellectual property[13], torts (discussed in Chapter 20), and privacy, to which I now turn.

2.4 PRIVACY AND BIG DATA

It is often suggested that Big Data poses a novel threat to our privacy through its ability to reveal personal information about us. A frequently cited example of this is the story of how Target correctly inferred that one of its female teenage customers was pregnant on the basis of her purchasing patterns of items that were not obviously linked to pregnancy. It is a mistake, however, to think that privacy rights are implicated in cases such as this.

To recognize the limits of the threat to privacy, it necessary to differentiate between two issues that are often conflated in the privacy literature. The first is the purely factual question of whether someone has suffered a privacy loss. The second is the legal and normative question of whether someone has suffered a privacy violation. Differentiating these issues helps to reveal that large-scale data mining (1) will not cause privacy losses when it generates personal predictions based on various types of probabilistic information and (2) will not cause privacy violations when it reveals private information through mere inference.

This does not mean, however, that data mining cannot implicate privacy in other ways. For example, the aggregation of the underlying data sets might itself violate privacy, as may the use of these data to deanonymize personal information. Such issues are outside the scope of my argument, though it is worth noting that the way in which aggregation is often said to violate privacy is by revealing new information about us – a claim that is undermined if inferences cannot violate privacy.

---

[13] W. Nicholson Price II, Big Data, Patents, and the Future of Medicine, 37 Cardozo L. Rev. 1401 (2016).

Either way, the threat to privacy is more limited than has been widely thought and for reasons that have not been recognized.

2.4.1 Privacy Losses

In evaluating the extent to which data aggregation and mining might cause privacy losses, I will assume that a privacy loss can be best defined – as a factual rather than a normative matter—as occurring when a piece of personal information about someone is accessed by someone else.[14] If this is right, the central question here is whether these processes will reveal personal information about individual people. While it is generally assumed that they will, one of the core types of information about people that is revealed by data mining (specifically, probabilistic information) often will not.[15]

To illustrate why, it is helpful to begin with an example. Imagine that a computer analyzed data on the distribution of Huntington's disease and found that 1/20,000 people with my personal characteristics develop the disease. If, on this basis, it predicted that I have a 1/20,000 chance of developing the disease, it would be incorrect. The reason for this is that the disease is caused by a gene, which I either have or do not have. Thus my chance of developing the disease must be 1 or 0.

What this example highlights is the danger of conflating two different types of probability: objective and epistemic. Objective probabilities are features of reality that exist independently of human knowledge, whereas epistemic probabilities are a feature of our knowledge about the world.[16] Unfortunately, we often fail to differentiate between them in ordinary language. For example, we would say that the probability of rolling a five on a normal unweighted die is 1/6, and we would say the same for a die that we know is weighted in a way that we cannot discover. In the former case, though, the probability would be objective, whereas in the latter it would be epistemic. The objective probability in the latter case would be either 1 or 0, assuming that the weighting was strong enough.

The reason that this distinction is important here is that reveals that the predictive analytics generated by machine learning will often not identify facts about

---

[14] I take this to be the most compelling nonnormative account of what constitutes a privacy loss. While privacy scholars have also defined privacy losses as losses of control over one's personal information, closer analysis reveals that informational control is neither necessary nor sufficient for privacy. See Jeffrey M. Skopek, Reasonable Expectations of Anonymity, 101 Va. L. Rev. 691, 702 (2015).

[15] The assumption that data mining will cause privacy losses might also be partly challenged by arguing (a) that an individual's privacy can only be lost if someone gains a justified true belief (i.e., knowledge) about that person and (b) that black-box algorithms do not provide us with justified true beliefs about individuals due to the nontransparency issues identified earlier. But this is an argument that must be set aside for another day.

[16] See, generally, Michael Strevens, Probability and Chance, in 8 *Encyclopedia of Philosophy* 24, 27–37 (Donald M. Borchert ed., 2nd edn, 2006).

individual persons – at least not if the underlying probabilities are partly epistemic (which may often be given the shift away from mechanistic causation in data-intensive science). As applied to populations, predictions based on these probabilities will be meaningful, but as applied to individuals, they will not.

However, there will no doubt also be cases in which predictive analytics do reveal objective probabilities, and it might seem that in these cases privacy will be implicated. For example, if it is discovered that a person has a gene that has a 1/3 tendency to generate cancerous cells, then this probabilistic knowledge would seem to be individual knowledge about the person, giving rise to a privacy loss. But even this might not be right.

Whether objective probabilities can reveal information about individuals – and thereby cause privacy losses – depends on whether single-case objective probabilities exist. This is a much-debated question in philosophy that cannot be fully addressed here, but it is worth briefly identifying the two core competing accounts. According to "propensity accounts," objective probabilities refer to a kind of causal tendency or disposition of the entity being described (e.g., a gene's propensity to result in cancer), which would mean that single-case probabilities do exist.[17] According to "frequentist accounts," by contrast, an event's objective probability is the limit of its relative frequency in a large number of cases, which would mean there are no single-case probabilities.[18] It is, of course, beyond the scope of this chapter to take a position in this debate. The distinction is relevant, however, because it helps to clarify the limited extent to which probabilistic information may cause privacy losses.

To cause a privacy loss, probabilistic information about an individual must capture not only an objective probability (rather than epistemic one) but also a propensity (rather than a frequency). For these reasons, privacy may not be implicated by much of the probabilistic information that will be generated by predictive analytics.

2.4.2 *Privacy Violations*

Having explored data mining's relationship with privacy losses, I will now turn to the distinct issue of its relationship with privacy violations. The key difference between privacy losses and privacy violations, which is often overlooked in the literature, can be stated simply: whereas privacy is lost when knowledge of a person is accessed, privacy is violated when such knowledge is accessed through an impermissible means. Or, in other words, privacy losses turn on epistemic states, whereas privacy violations turn on epistemic pathways. Failure to recognize this difference can lead to the mistaken conclusion that all unwanted privacy losses constitute privacy violations.

---

[17] Ibid., at 34–35.
[18] Ibid., at 32–33.

The idea that privacy violations turn on epistemic pathways is implicitly recognized in both legal scholarship and case law on privacy.[19] For example, Hellen Nissenbaum's theory of privacy as "contextual integrity" defines privacy violations as the breach of context-specific norms governing the transfer of personal information,[20] and Dan Solove's "family resemblance" theory of privacy identifies specific forms of information collection, processing, and dissemination as being at the core of privacy violations.[21] Likewise, under the "reasonable expectation of privacy test" that is applied across various areas of privacy law, privacy violations depend not on whether personal information has been discovered but rather on how. Thus, while there might be disagreement among scholars and courts about which specific means of generating and transferring personal information are capable of violating privacy, there is widespread agreement that privacy violations depend on the permissibility of the pathways through which knowledge about a person is generated or accessed.

Recognizing the centrality of epistemic pathways in privacy violations reveals a potential problem for the common view that data mining can violate privacy. The problem is that data mining often generates knowledge about people through the process of inference rather than direct observation or access, and there are both legal and normative grounds for rejecting the notion that inferences can violate privacy.

While the question of whether inferences can violate privacy has received little attention in the law, the Supreme Court case of *Kyllo v. United States* (which may be the only case that has explicitly addressed this issue) held that it is not possible for an inference to violate a reasonable expectation of privacy in the Fourth Amendment context.[22] The case addressed the constitutionality of using thermal imaging to draw conclusions about what was happening inside a house. And while the case was decided in a five-four split – with disagreement centering on whether the technology should be understood as measuring something occurring inside the house (the majority's view) or merely drawing inferences from the outside of the house (the dissent's view) – what is significant for present purposes is that both sides agreed that inferences were not capable of violating a reasonable expectation of privacy. This point was stated most concisely by the majority, which simply stated: "an inference is not a search."[23] The dissent elaborated in more detail:

> There is ... a distinction of constitutional magnitude between "through-the-wall surveillance" that gives the observer or listener *direct access to information* in a private area, on the one hand, and the thought processes used to *draw inferences*

---

[19] This view can also be found in the very limited work on the epistemology of privacy. See Klemens Kappel, Epistemological Dimensions of Informational Privacy, 10 *Episteme* 179, 190 (2013).
[20] Helen Nissenbaum, *Privacy in Context: Technology, Policy, and the Integrity of Social Life* 127 (2009).
[21] Daniel J. Solove, A Taxonomy of Privacy, 154 *U. Penn. L. Rev.* 477, 488 (2006).
[22] *Kyllo v. United States*, 533 U.S. 27, 37 n. 4 (2001).
[23] Ibid.

from information in the public domain, on the other hand ... The process of drawing inferences from data in the public domain should not be characterized as a search.[24]

The *Kyllo* case not only directly addresses the legal status of inferences but also provides a useful analogy for thinking about privacy in the medical context, as it held – in line with cases from across various fields of privacy law – that privacy is violated by looking inside closed spaces. Applied in the medical context, this approach suggests that the shift from traditional medicine to black-box medicine (discussed earlier) might be privacy enhancing. Take, for example, privacy in the context of biobank research. Under conventional approaches to research on biobanks, the human body is translated into a body of data that is disaggregated and studied: the researcher gains direct access to facts about the individual and their medical relevance, "looking inside" the body in a way that implicates privacy. With new machine-learning techniques, by contrast, the human body will not be translated into data that are disaggregated and studied but rather turned into black box: the researcher will not look inside the body and discover facts about the person but rather draw inferences and predictions from the outside. For this reason, under traditional principles of privacy law, the shift to black-box medicine might be seen as a shift toward greater privacy.

Of course, one might argue that what this reveals is that the law should be modified. However, on further reflection, it should become quickly apparent that it would be deeply problematic to treat inferences as capable of violating privacy. The core problem with this is that it would, without a limiting principle, impose restrictions on a purely mental activity. And although a limit could be imposed by drawing a line between mental inferences and technology-assisted inferences, it is not clear that anything of normative relevance turns on this distinction. While technological assistance might be normatively relevant with respect to other issues that arise with data mining (e.g., the question of whether the aggregation and collection of data on which inferences are based violate privacy), it appears to be irrelevant to the act of inference itself. Thus, while large scale data analysis may allow us to infer facts about people that they would rather keep secret, and thereby cause them privacy losses, such inferences should not be treated as privacy violations.

2.5 CONCLUSION

The threat to our privacy posed by the analysis of Big Data is more limited than has been widely thought, as predictions about us will often not cause privacy losses and inferences about us can not constitute privacy violations. This is not to say, however,

---

[24] Ibid., at 41 (Stevens, J., dissenting).

that we should not regulate how these predictions and inferences are used (e.g., in the setting of insurance premiums). Yet, if these uses do not actually implicate privacy, the normative justification for their regulation is weakened, and an alternative basis must be found. One might argue that what this means is that we should develop a conception of privacy that captures these potential harms. But the mere fact that a harm arises from the use of personal information does not mean that it should be considered a privacy harm. Nor does it mean that the tools we have developed in a privacy framework will be well suited to the problem. Further, it may not just be privacy that is a poor fit for the challenges of the data revolution but also other principles that govern medicine and medical research, such as informed consent. It may be that across these areas, scientific and technological advances will require that we rethink the legal and ethical status of our bodies as bodies of data.

3

Correlation versus Causation in Health-Related Big Data Analysis

The Role of Reason and Regulation

Tal Z. Zarsky

3.1 INTRODUCTION

Technological developments, as well as the rise of new business environments and practices, have brought Big Data to the forefront.[1] In many data-rich contexts, entities are seeking new ways to gather data and aggregate them with sources already obtained in order to use this information in novel ways. At the core of many of these initiatives is the aspiration to reveal data relationships previously unknown.[2] In some instances, the data-driven results of the analysis are applied without any further examination of the underlying facts and reasons. In other words, entities rely on mere *correlations*.[3]

Relying on mere correlations as the basis for actions, recommendations, or even distinctions generates a variety of concerns. Correlation is often the first step in scientific inquiry and is followed by steps and measures seeking causation between the relevant parameters. Recently, commentators began arguing that correlation should constitute not only the first step of an inquiry but also the last one as well.[4] The speed and power of Big Data analysis render the search for causation

---

[1] Jonathan Shaw, Why "Big Data" Is a Big Deal: Information Science Promises to Change the World, *Harvard Magazine*, March 2014, available at http://harvardmagazine.com/2014/03/why-big-data-is-a-big-deal [https://perma.cc/7UF7-GM3Y]; Steve Lohr, The Age of Big Data, *New York Times*, February 11, 2012, available at www.nytimes.com/2012/02/12/sunday-review/big-datas-impact-in-the-world.html.

[2] Viktor Mayer-Schönberger & Kenneth Cukier, *Big Data: A Revolution That Will Transform How We Live, Work, and Think* 51.

[3] Ibid., at 56–57. See also Ryan Calo, Digital Market Manipulation, 82 Geo. Wash. L. Rev. 995, 1009 (2014).

[4] Chris Anderson, The End of Theory: The Data Deluge Makes the Scientific Method Obsolete, *Wired*, June 23, 2008, available at www.wired.com/2008/06/pb-theory/ [https://perma.cc/PD7A-BHCX]. See also the debate regarding this issue in Gil Press, Big Data News Roundup: Correlation vs. Causation, *Forbes*, April 19, 2013, available at www.forbes.com/sites/gilpress/2013/04/19/big-data-news-roundup-correlation-vs-causation/#3b9c4cb64936 [https://perma.cc/32Z6-S69H].

and mechanisms a thing of the past, making correlation a sufficient attribute in this new age.[5] Indeed, a number of business practices have begun to unfold along these lines.[6]

Must causation have a substantial role in the use of Big Data? If this is the case, what would a call for causation even entail; perhaps law and legislation must move in and provide a response. How can law and regulation promote this objective? And what are the possible shortcomings of such proactive steps? In the context of both health-related data and health-related recommendations, these questions are both intuitively alarming and intriguing. They are alarming given the centrality of causation and scientific reasoning to health and medical issues. However, they are intriguing because they challenge us to consider whether a paradigmatic shift in the manner health- and medical-related information is handled is afoot or whether setting causation aside is merely a troubling yet temporary turn.

This chapter maps out the discussion on the role correlation, statistical causation, and mechanisms should play in the age of health Big Data, as well as the proper role of law and policy – a discussion almost absent in the legal literature.[7] It first addresses changes in the health data environment while accounting for new technologies and business models that enhance data collection and analysis. It explains that entities controlling health data, as well as the processes they are motivated to now apply, have changed, thus requiring the analysis to follow. It then elaborates on the pros and cons of relying on correlation alone or, in some cases, on statistical analyses suggesting causation without incorporating a hypothesis, study, experiment, or manipulation in the field into the decision-making process. It also maps a variety of scenarios and errors such practices might include. Finally, it explores the crucial nexuses between legal and policy hooks and the correlation/causation debate in the health and medical realm. The chapter claims that policymakers and legislators must clearly establish when and whether law and policy should ignore, encourage, accept, or reject reliance on mere correlations while distinguishing between the interests and rights of data subjects, affected individuals, investors, and society in general.

Even though a discussion addressing the role of correlation and causation in Big Data analysis pertains to a very broad array of contexts, this chapter focuses on that of health data. This focus is with good reason because policies pertaining to health Big Data call for a unique balance. On the one hand, the data are considered highly sensitive. Individuals will feel that their rights and autonomy were substantially

---

[5] See notes 37–46.
[6] See Daniel Bjorkegren & Darrell Grissen, Behavior Revealed in Mobile Phone Usage Predicts Loan Repayment, July 13, 2015 (unpublished manuscript), available at http://papers.ssrn.com/sol3/papers.cfm?abstract_id=2611775 [https://perma.cc/T6QX-QC2U] (showing, for instance, the use of Big Data in the context of credit).
[7] As an exception, see, generally, Skopek, Reasonable Expectations of Anonymity; Bart H. M. Custers, *The Power of Knowledge* (2004).

violated if health data end up in the wrong hands or if they are treated wrongfully on the basis of such personal information. Indeed, the European Union has provided greater protection to such data,[8] as well as US law as defined by the Health Insurance Portability and Accountability Act (HIPAA) and related regulations.[9] On the other hand, the benefits of the analysis of "health data" are substantial. It could promote medical research as well as the discovery of ailments and possibly hints as to their cures.[10] The unique balance that the regulation of "health law" requires will therefore guide the discussion to follow.

3.2 BIG DATA, HEALTH DATA, HEALTH BIG DATA

Big Data is a big deal. The attributes, benefits, and perils of analyzing and using vast data sets, which often include personal information, have been widely acknowledged and discussed in academic journals,[11] policy papers,[12] and the popular press.[13] However, within this broader issue, the use of Big Data in the health data context deserves its own discussion.

The association of the Big Data–related concerns with the health-related context comes at a crucial time. This is a time in which the definition of "health data," as well as the identities of the entities controlling it, is in flux. The fact that such changes are afoot renders the current discussion – that is, the reliance on correlation (or causation) – of even greater importance. Indeed, until recently, the flow of health-related information was substantially different from the flow of advertising, marketing, financial, and credit data – the context policy debates on associated harms of Big Data often unfolded.[14] Health-related data were a relatively confined and somewhat limited corpus of knowledge. The data sources were mostly trusted entities, such as health practitioners or other actors in highly regulated industries (e.g., hospitals, insurance firms, and pharmacies). Therefore, exercising the regulation of health Big Data analysis and use did not likely cause substantial challenges and problems because the entities controlling the data were few, of a conservative nature, heavily regulated, and bound by ethical codes. Furthermore, the state,

---

[8] Regulation 2016/679 of the European Parliament and of the Council of 27 April 2016 on the protection of natural persons with regard to the processing of personal data and on the free movement of such data, and repealing Directive 95/46/EC, Article 9, 2016 O.J. (L 119).

[9] See, e.g., Chapter 17.

[10] See, e.g., Wayne Parslow, How Big Data Could be Used to Predict a Patient's Future, *The Guardian*, January 17, 2014, available at www.theguardian.com/healthcare-network/2014/jan/17/big-data-nhs-predict-illness [https://perma.cc/R5LW-ENHG]. See also Skopek, Reasonable Expectations of Anonymity (discussing precision medicine in the age of Big Data).

[11] See, e.g., Omer Tene & Jules Polontesky, Big Data for All: Privacy and User Control in the Age of Analytics, 11 *Nw. J. Tech. Intell. Prop.* 239 (2013).

[12] See, e.g., Executive Office of the President, White House, Big Data: Seizing Opportunities, Preserving Values (2014).

[13] See Lohr, The Age of Big Data.

[14] Danielle K. Citron & Frank Pasquale, The Scored Society, 89 *Wash. L. Rev.* 1 (2014) (generally addressing the risks Big Data generates in the context of finance and credit).

government-funded entities, and academic researchers were often key entities engaged in analyzing health data – again, entities that are relatively simple to regulate and hold accountable.[15]

Yet, the age of Big Data has revolutionized the meaning of "health data," substantially expanding it and placing data in the hands of additional entities, which will not hesitate to apply the novel practices detailed below while setting causation aside. Big Data allows researchers to draw conclusions and inferences on individual health conditions from a much broader set of factors and variables, especially those regarding lifestyle choices and individual preferences. Therefore, health data are now obtained by numerous entities that have general knowledge on an individual's activities and can make health predictions (with arguable strength and accuracy) – predictions that may be driven by mere correlations. Entities collecting, obtaining, analyzing, and using health data are to some extent all the usual suspects – large vendors, communication firms that can also track users' location, and employers.

The growth of the "health data" category has already generated legal implications. The recently-passed EU General Data Protection Regulation (GDPR) includes a specific subcategory of "data concerning health" that demands a higher level of protection.[16] Article 4(15) of the GDPR defines "data concerning health" as "personal data related to the physical or mental health of a natural person ... which reveal information about his or her health status," while Recital 35 explains that health data should also include information on "disease risk."[17] In a variety of contexts, Big Data analysis of various databases related to human conduct exposes information on an individual's health status or risk of disease, and therefore, the processes' outputs are considered health-related personal data, worthy of special legal status. This was indeed the opinion of the Article 29 EU Working Party addressing this matter.[18]

Yet another technological development – the rising popularity of the Internet of Things (IoT) and especially the growing use of wearables – has rendered these service providers key health data aggregators because they can now collect an abundance of health-related data. "IoT" is a broadly-used term that describes a growing market of sensor gadgets that are connected to computer networks.[19] Many of these sensors provide information from which health data could be derived – thus enabling enhanced collection capabilities of health-related data.[20] "Wearables" are

---

[15] Kristen Madison, Regulators as Data Stewards, 92 N.C. L. Rev. 1605, 1611–21 (2014).
[16] See Regulation 2016/679, at Article 9.
[17] Ibid., at Recital 35.
[18] Article 29 Working Party, Letter, Annex: Health Data in Apps and Devices (February 5, 2015), available at http://ec.europa.eu/justice/data-protection/article-29/documentation/other-document/files/2015/20150205_letter_art29wp_ec_health_data_after_plenary_annex_en.pdf [https://perma.cc/RWW9-5PPN].
[19] See Mckinsey Global Institute, Unlocking the Potential of the Internet of Things (July 2015), available at http://healthcare.mckinsey.com/unlocking-potential-internet-things [https://perma.cc/6C6L-JKY5].
[20] Scott R. Peppet, Regulating the Internet of Things: First Steps Toward Managing Discrimination, Privacy, Security & Consent, 93 Tex. L. Rev. 85, 99 (2014).

IoT gadgets affixed to the users' body that collect biometric (heartbeat or temperature) and behavioral (number of steps taken during a set time) information and at times allow for such data's aggregation.[21] Health data could even be collected, at times, directly from one's smartphone. For instance, correlations were found between specific phone uses and sleeping patterns, overall well-being, and the progression of Parkinson's disease.[22]

Interestingly, the entities providing these IoT services might be startups with no assets beyond their noted data sets and powerful ambition to formulate a sustainable business model to capitalize on these valuable data. Furthermore, these tools also provide existing large data aggregators with the means to collect, analyze, and use health data with far greater precision, thus exacerbating existing privacy concerns. Indeed, recent news reports indicate that employers[23] and even insurance companies[24] are showing great interest in data derived from these sources. Again, this point regarding the expansion of the category of health data aggregators has not escaped policymakers. The previously noted Article 29 Working Party found that when these gadgets gather medical information (e.g., body temperature and heart rate) over time, they might be considered to be collecting health data (with all the legal implications that follow) even though they are not marketed as medical devices.[25]

To conclude, a broad array of entities is collecting and thereafter engaging in various analyses of "health data" (now broadly defined) and applying novel practices with questionable legitimacy. The law has already responded (at least in the European Union) by bringing these practices under its wings in the context of enhanced forms of data protection. The following discussion is an early step in figuring out whether the law must intervene with regard to other aspects of this matter and how. One such aspect that this chapter now explores in depth is these firms' tendency to merely rely on findings of correlation between factors.

3.3 BIG HEALTH DATA AND (MERE) CORRELATION: AN ACCEPTABLE PRACTICE OR AN ABOMINATION?

3.3.1 Background, Hypotheticals, and Possible Failures

The noted technological and economic developments have brought health research and ethics to a brave new world. In this reality, entities controlling vast data sets of

---

[21] Ibid., at 100–2.
[22] Ibid., at 114–17.
[23] Parmy Olson & Aaron Tilley, The Quantified Other: Nest and Fitbit Chase a Lucrative Side Business, Forbes, April 17, 2014, available at www.forbes.com/sites/parmyolson/2014/04/17/the-quantified-other-nest-and-fitbit-chase-a-lucrative-side-business/#551fdfb15403 [https://perma.cc/F5Y5-AHHT].
[24] Ibid.
[25] See Article 29 Working Party, Letter, Annex, at 2.

health data have various incentives to seek correlations between personal factors/ medical symptoms/attributes. Importantly, they can act on the basis of found correlations without engaging in any further inquiry. As these business dynamics unfold, let us pause and examine whether such practices are acceptable. To do so, we must first establish the various options firms engaging in the analysis of health-related data face at this juncture while offering a menu of hypotheticals.

The starting point for all the following hypotheticals is the existence of an entity with Big Data at its disposal. The entity uses Big Data to analyze and correlate health-related phenomenon with other factors as well as to predict the occurrence of health-related events and outcomes with some accuracy. Yet, note that there are at least five variations to this story. Consider that the relevant firm decides to move forward while deciding

1. To only rely on correlation when statistical analysis indicates a significant relationship between the factors. This option is the basic prerequisite for the following discussion. Let us therefore assume that competitive forces, as well as other standards of responsibility, will ensure, at least over time, that the firm's managers refrain from relying on weak correlations.
2. To rely on correlation when statistical analysis indicates that a causal relationship exists between the factors and the health-related data.
3. To only rely on correlation when experimental evidence indicates the cause-and-effect linkage between the two factors. Note that many of the entities now collecting health data are not in a position to initiate such manipulations and experimental studies given their unique limited interaction with their data subjects.
4. To only rely on correlation when a reasonable explanation as to the existence of a mechanism (more on this concept later) has been set forth.
5. To only rely on correlation when a solid mechanism has been proven using scientific methods and tools. Note that even this option has its limits because the "true" cause of an effect is actually impossible to reveal and most likely does not exist.[26]

While some of these options might seem redundant, they are all in fact quite distinct. One key difference pertains to the notion of a *mechanism*,[27] a term of art referring to an explanation of a phenomenon.[28] Mechanisms serve a dual role. First,

---

[26] Mayer-Schönberger and Cukier, Big Data, at 63. Given space constraints, this chapter will set aside the debate regarding Karl Popper's work concerning this issue. See also Karl Popper, *The Logic of Scientific Discovery* 249–52 (2005) (discussing the challenge of verification of hypotheses)

[27] See Skopek, Reasonable Expectations of Anonymity.

[28] Phyllis McKay-Illari et al., Why Look at Causality in the Sciences?, in *Causality in the Sciences*, 3, 16 (Phyllis Illari et al. eds., 2011).

they provide additional proof of the existence of a causal relationship that has been hypothesized. Second, they satisfy scientific curiosity.[29] The role mechanisms ought to serve in the setting described earlier (in which a firm strives to use a causal finding it encounters in its data) is debatable. Some argue that without offering a remotely plausible mechanism (option 4), any causation found is at best tentative.[30] A more radical stance calls for establishing a confirmed mechanism prior to acting on a correlation (option 5).[31] Another, more lenient option relies on other methods to establish causation, such as experimental design (option 3) or "mere" statistical proof of causation often established via computer modeling (option 2), thus forgoing the need to establish a mechanism.[32]

Selecting one of these five options is a complicated task. In the interest of further simplifying the discussion, let us consider and list possible failures (outcomes that are both inefficient and unfair) in the prediction/induction process noted to assist in indicating which processes should be avoided and which should be selected. To demonstrate, consider a simplified case of hypothetical option 1. Here, a firm discovers a correlation between measured factor A and health factor B and assumes that factor A should be tracked and measured. When factor A meets a specific threshold, it would predict health factor B (which might constitute a negative outcome). Note that the previous statement regarding the firm's practices was carefully worded because it does not necessarily rely on, or refer to, causality. The firm is merely interested in predicting B with a reasonable level of accuracy. To assess this firm's conduct, let us consider a few possible simplified alternative descriptions of the firm's actions, their outcomes, and the implications for the prediction's accuracy:

i. A causes B (either on its own or with other confounding factors having a joint effect) – this would be the ideal, yet not only, result.
ii. A does *not* cause B. This correlation is unreliable because the data used were faulty. This outcome could indeed unfold within the Big Data context because data sets are collected in various commercial contexts with lax quality control and are later used in the highly sensitive health context. Note that various methods could be applied

---

[29] Alex Broadbent, Inferring Causation in Epidemiology: Mechanisms, Black Boxes, and Contrasts, in *Causality in the Sciences*, 45, 51.
[30] Ibid., at 52.
[31] Donald Gillies, The Russo-Williamson Thesis and the Question of Whether Smoking Causes Heart Disease, in *Causality in the Sciences*, 110, 114.
[32] In other words, these researchers rely on a "black-box stance." Here there are several methods for doing so, such as "scored-based" and "constraint-based" algorithms, using "screening-off" methods. See McKay-Illari et al., Why Look at Causality in the Sciences?, at 13. See also Jan Lemeire et al., When Are Graphical Models Not Good Models, in *Causality in the Sciences*, 562, 569; Ricardo Silva, Measuring Latent Causal Structure, in *Causality in the Sciences*, 673, 678.

to "cleanse" the data and limit this concern, yet this problem might, nonetheless, persist.[33]

iii. A does not cause B, and although the data themselves are accurate, the relationship between these factors is spurious.[34] In other words, the correlation found is merely coincidental and will prove false as time goes by. This outcome is often noted in the financial context, where correlations are sought between many thousands of economic factors and a very limited number of events.[35]

iv. A does not cause B. Rather, it is B that causes A. In such a case, factor A would have only limited success in predicting B, and learning of this correlation will not contribute substantially to preventing this health condition (insofar as such a condition is preventable). However, this correlation would still prove helpful in providing an early warning that condition B is afoot.[36]

v. A does not cause B. Rather, it is C that causes both A and B (a fact unknown to the analysts). C is, in other words, a confounding factor.[37] Here, and as with alternative option iv, revealing this correlation provides some predictive yet very limited preventive abilities. Furthermore, note that the existence of the confounding factor also indicates that there are more accurate correlations and predictive practices to be found and applied (i.e., between C and B). Relying on the correlation linking A to B could even undermine incentives to further seek out and reveal more accurate indicators of condition B.

This brief analysis was meant to highlight the implications of relying on mere correlations (option 1) and therefore possibly encountering the noted four pitfalls (alternative options ii–v). If this is the case and mere correlations are unacceptable given the high risk of error, which of the other four options (2–5) should a firm choose? And is indeed the practice of mere reliance on correlations always unacceptable? To provide a partial response to these questions while balancing the relevant factors and accounting for the specific intricacies health data entail, let us briefly turn to a debate currently unfolding regarding this matter.

---

[33] Danah Boyd & Kate Crawford, Critical Questions for Big Data, 15 *Info. Comm. Soc.* 662, 668 (2012).

[34] Note that this term is used in various forms in this unfolding discussion and thus must be approached with care.

[35] Larry Swedroe, What Butter Production Means for Your Portfolio, *CBS News*, April 29, 2013, available at www.cbsnews.com/news/what-butter-production-means-for-your-portfolio/ [https://perma.cc/B3QD-DFYB]; Nate Silver, *The Signal and the Noise: Why So Many Predictions Fail – But Some Don't*, 185–86 (2012). See also Tyler Vigen, Spurious Correlations, tylervigen.com, available at http://tylervigen.com/spurious-correlations [https://perma.cc/Y369-CXRV].

[36] See Custers, The Power of Knowledge, at 57.

[37] Bert Leuridan & Erik Weber, The IARC and Mechanistic Evidence, in *Causality in the Sciences*, 91, 99.

3.3.2 *The Correlation/Causation Debate*

The shift toward reliance on mere correlations has not gone unnoticed in both the popular and academic contexts. Chris Anderson (of *Wired*) recently declared that the "End of Theory" has arrived.[38] Mayer-Schönberger and Cukier argue that we must rid ourselves of our obsession with causality. As these authors note, merely relying on correlations provides several clear benefits that perhaps supersede the failures and detriments noted earlier. The first benefit is speed. Practice options 2–5 are time-consuming. Practice option 1 can be carried out quickly, automatically, and on a grand scale.[39] A closely related factor to speed is cost. Engaging in mere correlation finding is relatively inexpensive, as opposed to the other, costly practices listed earlier, especially in the health context.[40] These factors are very important when considering how startups operate, particularly when contemplating the use health data at their disposal to reveal interesting correlations. To some extent, both arguments also justify relying on mere statistical causation as well (as opposed to requiring that a mechanism be found).

In addition, seeking causality and adding mechanisms could compromise the process's precision; a fully automated and algorithm-driven process might generate highly elaborate, noninterpretable models. This means that they are not easily explainable to humans and therefore not conveniently tested for causality. While these models lack transparency, they could be precise and efficient, but the simplification required to interpret and thereafter seek causal proof and explanations could undermine the efficiency of the models.[41]

Furthermore, exclusively relying on causation – especially by requiring evidence of mechanisms (as in hypotheticals 4 and 5) – steers science and thus society in a problematic direction. Rather than approaching data-based findings with an open mind, the mechanism requirement generates a bias toward findings that could be explained by existing scientific literature and models.[42] Insisting on the development of mechanisms brings the risk of rejecting correlations that current science cannot prove or even explain and yet nonetheless have predictive value. Such a policy choice thus will tilt the balance of expected outcomes in favor of existing knowledge.[43]

---

[38] Anderson, The End of Theory. See also discussion in Skopek, Reasonable Expectations of Anonymity, regarding the "Death of Theory" argument (explaining that the claim should be understood in a narrower form. It is not that "theory" in general is rejected but merely a causal theory).

[39] Mayer-Schönberger and Cukier, *Big Data*, at 54, 66.

[40] Ibid.

[41] Tal Z. Zarsky, Transparent Predictions, 2013 U. Ill. L. Rev. 1503, 1519–20 (2013); See also Antoinette Rouvroy, "Of Data and Men": Fundamental Rights and Freedoms in a World of Big Data, Council of Europe, Directorate General of Human Rights and Rule of Law, T-PD-BUR (2015) 09REV, 11 (2016), available at https://works.bepress.com/antoinette_rouvroy/64/ [https://perma.cc/435V-F9QZ].

[42] Mayer-Schönberger and Cukier, *Big Data*, at 71.

[43] Broadbent, Inferring Causation in Epidemiology, at 56.

These statements have not gone uncontested in academic writing, the popular press, and the blogosphere. For example, consider Nate Silver's (a famous blogger on statistical matters) response.[44] His recent book, *The Signal and the Noise*, warns of confusing mere noise with meaningful data signals. Silver also worries about "overfitting" – a situation in which correlations are "forced" on the data.[45] This concern is akin to that of "apopehnia" – the phenomenon of seeing patterns where they do not exist, which too could lead to problematic results if causation is not sought.[46] Therefore, finding causation is crucial to promote the quality of the entire process and to ensure that in the end individuals are treated fairly.

It is again unclear whether statistical analyses aimed at verifying causal connections (as noted in option 2 earlier) sufficiently overcome these concerns. Silver, in fact, goes on to argue that data must be explained through the telling of a "story" (which seems to be another word for mechanism) to prevent the analyst from mistaking noise for a signal, an error that would delude others as well.[47] He further notes that "statistical inferences are much stronger when backed up by theory or at least some deeper thinking about their root causes."[48] In other words, greater concerns for errors of the various forms noted earlier mandate a substantial inquiry into the nature of causal connections. Beyond popular science, the debate whether option 2 or options 4 and 5 noted earlier are required to ensure reliable results unfolds in a variety of scientific disciplines with no clear outcome at this time.[49]

Yet the justifications for revealing causation backed by a mechanism go beyond the notions of quality assurance. Without a theory to understand the prediction, the lesson learned via correlation cannot be *generalized*[50] and thus can only be used in the specific context and population found. Relying on a theory prior to making data-driven predictions allows us to understand when such generalizations are acceptable and when they go too far.[51]

In addition, relying on correlations without investigating causal effects that are backed by mechanisms could ignore the impact of side effects. For instance, allowing for merely (even correctly) predicting that A indicates health factor/problematic outcome B could ignore the fact that reducing behavior A could lead to negative outcomes – the damage of which could even surpass the benefits of reducing health outcome B.[52] Understanding the mechanism (options 4 and 5)

---

[44] See, e.g., FiveThirtyEight, available at http://fivethirtyeight.com [https://perma.cc/Y8P3-CJ9J] (last visited March 14, 2017). See also Skopek, Reasonable Expectations of Anonymity, for an additional discussion of the perils of mere reliance on correlations rather than a mechanism.
[45] Silver, The Signal and the Noise, at 162.
[46] Boyd & Crawford, Critical Questions for Big Data, at 668.
[47] Silver, *The Signal and the Noise*, at 196.
[48] Ibid., at 197.
[49] See notes 27–32.
[50] Broadbent, Inferring Causation in Epidemiology, at 45; Leuridan & Weber, The IARC and Mechanistic Evidence, at 100.
[51] Leuridan & Weber, The IARC and Mechanistic Evidence, at 100.
[52] Julian Reiss, Third Time's a Charm: Causation, Science, and Wittgensteinian Pluralism, in *Casuality in the Sciences*, 907, 918–19.

would limit this concern. While this argument is true in a variety of settings, given the substantial risk of bodily harm, it is of greatest relevance in the context of health data.

Finally, relying on mere correlations fails to generate some of the positive externalities and effects derived from a process premised on causation, especially when seeking a mechanism. In the latter case, the practices generate substantial knowledge about nature and human conditions – knowledge that very often will become public. In addition, and even without mechanisms, publishing causal rules allows individuals to engage in self-improvement, at least when relevant factors are mutable. This is as opposed to situations in which mere proxies are applied or when an unknown confounding factor exists – all instances in which the prediction scheme does not provide individuals with the necessary measures to avoid the final outcome the model strives to predict.

In conclusion, while there are some arguments for relying on mere correlations, the case for causation is strong. Balancing these options calls, however, for a context-specific approach and requires a tradeoff, at times pitting efficiency against fairness. With mere correlations, more patterns will emerge, but additional errors will be introduced. With a causation requirement, relevant patterns could be missed, thus generating detriments and costs of a different kind.

3.4 THE LAW OF CAUSATION/THE LAW OF REASON

As previous chapters demonstrate, reliance on mere correlations to carry out predictions and other actions based on the results of such analyses has become a growing trend in health data analysis. While correlations hold intrinsic value, solely relying on them can prove inaccurate and limit other social benefits; thus the outcome of such reliance is problematic. Should the law strive to directly intervene (most notably by restricting practices merely relying on correlation or lacking sufficient mechanisms) and influence one form of analysis over the other?

At face value, specific legal intervention at this juncture is unwarranted. Indeed, data analyses relying on mere correlations might be severely flawed. Yet so are many other business practices that are destined to fail. In addition, intervening with these practices could impinge on the speech rights of data holders to analyze data at their disposal and use them as they deem fit. In addition, society may want to encourage (or at least enable) startups to challenge existing scientific paradigms and introduce new ways of thought. Therefore, enabling reliance on mere correlation seems to be a step in the right direction.

Finally, it might prove unwise to allow law to meddle unnecessarily in scientific criteria. To promote both science and innovation, governments and courts should refrain from steering scientific methods in specific directions. Legal, and thus government, intervention might be generated by self-interest or be just outdated and wrong.

Nonetheless, law should play a role in this debate at specific junctures, intervening and setting requirements regarding acceptable data analysis and use. Establishing the point of entry and the proper time to do so is challenging because intervening in the actions of private actors to merely enhance efficiency (when a substantial market failure is absent) is often not a recommended strategy. Rather, law must intervene when other hooks are available. For instance, when striving to protect investor interests in firms using data (i.e., situations in which relying on correlations would be considered a reckless business practice). In addition, regulatory intervention might follow from steps taken to protect the interests of those whose data are collected and analyzed – the data subjects. Here intervention could be justified by arguing that data analysis that relies on mere correlation cannot be assumed to be in line with data subjects' preferences and the uses they find permissible. With that, intervention premised on these legal hooks is limited and remains to be explored elsewhere. The most promising hook for legal intervention in this context is the social interest in protecting those affected by the analysis of health data. Such an impact might be the denial or degrading of medical services, the charging of higher prices, or other detrimental outcomes.[53]

To further articulate the harm caused to the affected individual, consider the concept of "fairness," which at this juncture is somewhat aligned with the interest of enhancing efficiency.[54] Clearly, a comprehensive analysis of this issue calls for a discussion that goes beyond fairness and will explore notions of autonomy, desert, and virtue, as well as a deeper analysis of the process's efficiency. Such a detailed discussion is beyond the confines of this chapter. Fairness, however, is a good place to launch an analysis of this conundrum. When a firm relies on a faulty correlation, its conduct could, intuitively, be considered unfair. Fairness here is being derived from the notion of equality – all individuals should be treated similarly, unless there is a relevant difference between them. Yet, when a faulty correlation

---

[53] For a discussion of instances in which the regulator directly addresses this issue, see James Grimmelmann & Daniel Westreich, Incomprehensible Discrimination, *Cal. L. Rev. Online* (forthcoming 2017) (manuscript at 12–13) (on file with author). The authors provide two important examples: one in which the regulator implemented a causation requirement (with a basic mechanism needed as well); see Office of the Comptroller of the Currency, OCC Bull. No. 97-24, Credit Scoring Models, at 11 (1997), available at www.occ.treas.gov/news-issuances/bulletins/1997/bulletin-1997-24.html [https://perma.cc/TF55-C337]. It also includes an additional example in which such a requirement was not introduced, and reliance on mere correlation was found sufficient; see The Uniform Guidelines on Employment Selection Procedures, 29 C.F.R. § 1607.14(B)(5) (1978).

[54] For an extensive discussion of the notion of "fairness" in this context and its relation with efficiency, see Tal Z. Zarsky, The Trouble with Algorithmic Decisions: An Analytic Road Map to Examine Efficiency and Fairness in Automated and Opaque Decision Making, 41 *Sci. Tech. Human Values* 118, 123 (2015). For a general discussion regarding the distinction and overlap between these concepts, see, generally, Barak Medina & Eyal Zamir, Law, Morality, and Economics: Integrating Moral Constraints with Economic Analysis of Law, 96 *Calif. L. Rev.* 323 (2008).

(revealed in a process which did not seek out causation) is used to distinguish between individuals that are in fact equal, the outcome that follows is unfair – those that are equal will receive unequal treatment from the relevant firm. Furthermore, damages inflicted when relying on such a faulty correlation could exceed this limited and specific instance of unequal mistreatment. Being (wrongfully) considered to be at a higher risk of suffering from a health condition could also cause secondary reactions such as a negative stigma. Of course, such unfair outcomes might follow when a firm seeks out causation as well. After the fact, the causal reasoning used could be found to be false. Thus individuals who were virtually the same were wrongfully treated differently. Still, in the latter case, the firm could perhaps be shielded from liability attached to unfair conduct because it acted diligently (yet, erred nonetheless).

Note, however, that private entities are not necessarily required to meet fairness standards. While discriminating against protected groups (such as racial minorities or on the basis of gender), even by private parties, is very often considered illegal and normatively unacceptable, arbitrary actions are more difficult to prohibit.[55] Therefore, a fairness-based justification to intervene and prohibit reliance on mere correlations will have limited bite when generally applied to private firms that gather and use health-related data. However, general fairness-related requirements indeed apply to government processes, in government's capacity as a public custodian of health data, or when providing a public good. These requirements can also be applied to firms providing health-related services while operating under public licenses or as monopolies. This broad fairness-based argument may also justify intervention in the somewhat arbitrary actions of heavily regulated industries – such as the insurance industry, which presumably undertakes the crucial social role of spreading and sharing risk. In all these instances, law often steps in and broadly promotes fairness, even at the cost of undermining private entities' prerogatives. Therefore, in the name of fairness and in these cases, mere correlation could be considered as normatively insufficient.

Finally, it is important to note that the regulatory steps addressed thus far focus on process errors and how causation could mitigate them. Yet opting to rely on mere correlation could have broader societal effects. While such practices can provide inexpensive, quick responses, they deprive society of additional knowledge and scientific inquiry. However, this justification may only have limited regulatory reach. Nonetheless, it certainly should be considered when government facilitates scientific studies, such as when it provides funding or data. In such cases, and in exchange, government could mandate reliance on a causal element (with or without a mechanism).

---

[55] For a discussion of the possible legal remedies applicable in this context, see Tal Z. Zarsky, Understanding Discrimination in the Scored Society, 89 Wash. L. Rev. 1375, 1405 (2014).

3.5 CONCLUSION

This chapter confronts a novel flow of health information in the age of Big Data. It addresses economic pressures leading firms to consider relying on mere correlation to guide their predictions, decisions, and practices. It further notes the benefits and detriments of these steps, as well as the legal hooks that enable regulatory intervention regarding this issue.

In the context of health and medical data, stronger arguments opt for adopting and even mandating practices that rely on causation (and mechanisms) – and not just correlation. The benefits of the rich array of information mere correlations bring about are great; still, the harms of wrongful generalization or missed side effects are substantial. With that, for some industries, exceptions should be made to the mechanism requirement in situations where strong statistical evidence suggests causation, given the benefits of reliance on such limited inquiries and their findings to health-related research and practices. In any event, the full breadth of options addressed in this chapter must be considered by regulators prior to deciding on these matters.

4

Big Data and Regulatory Arbitrage in Healthcare

*Nicolas P. Terry**

4.1 INTRODUCTION

This chapter highlights the misuse of healthcare data by the Big Data industry. This is occurring notwithstanding our rich history of healthcare data protection and existing legal protections such as the Health Insurance Portability and Accountability Act (HIPAA) federal privacy and security rules. Euphemistically stated, the reason for this misuse is that healthcare data exist in an "uneven policy environment."[1] Translated, this means that the current structure of healthcare data protection allows for sensitive healthcare data to exist in a lightly regulated space outside the reach of traditional healthcare data-protection regimes. This leads to regulatory disruption as patients, providers, and healthcare policymakers struggle not only with underregulation but also with costly indeterminacy as to the when and how such data may or may not be protected. Meanwhile, data brokers practice successful regulatory arbitrage, doing in lightly protected space what they are prohibited from doing in HIPAA-regulated space.

4.2 THE HEALTHCARE BIG DATA DEBATE

When used by healthcare stakeholders for clinical practice or research, Big Data should improve "personalization of care, assessment of quality and value for many more conditions" as well as helping "providers better manage population health and risk-based reimbursement approaches."[2] Other touted uses include disease

---

* I have examined some of these issues in greater depth in Big Data Proxies and Health Privacy Exceptionalism, 24 *Health Matrix* 65 (2014), and Regulatory Disruption and Arbitrage in Healthcare Data Protection, 17 *Yale J. Health Pol'y L. Ethics* 143 (2017).
[1] Privacy and Security Workgroup, Health IT Policy Committee, *Recommendations on Health Big Data* 17 (2015).
[2] Robert Kocher & Bryan Roberts, Meaningful Use of Health IT Stage 2: The Broader Meaning, Health Affairs (March 15, 2012), available at http://healthaffairs.org/blog/2012/03/15/meaningful-use-of-health-it-stage-2-the-broader-meaning/ [https://perma.cc/36J9-UEEB].

modeling,[3] epidemic prediction,[4] public health surveillance,[5] pharmacovigilance,[6] decreasing antimicrobial resistance,[7] reducing readmissions while improving outcomes,[8] identifying high-risk patients,[9] and combating fraud.[10] Even the Federal Trade Commission (FTC), no friend of Big Data brokers, has noted Big Data's potential role in improving healthcare and ushering in precision medicine.[11]

Some of the positive claims for health Big Data may be premature. Critics argue that healthcare is still working with "small data"[12] or that analytics do not yet successfully "capture and weigh ... psychosocial data elements."[13] Notwithstanding, the substantial investment in Big Data–led projects such as the Precision Medicine Initiative[14] and the National Institutes of Health's (NIH's) BD2K project[15] likely are accurate predictors of the transformational potential of data analytics on healthcare.

The *commercial use* of sensitive data *exported from or created outside the healthcare space* impacts quite different policy questions. For example, the Affordable Care Act (ACA) prohibits preexisting condition exclusions and discriminatory premium rates and generally requires guaranteed issue.[16] However, some health

---

[3] Steve Lohr, Sizing Up Big Data, Broadening Beyond the Internet, *New York Times*, June 19, 2013.
[4] Jeremey Ginsberg et al., Detecting Influenza Epidemics Using Search Engine Query Data, 457 *Nature* 1012, 1012–14 (2009).
[5] Amy B. Bernstein & Marie Haring Sweeney, Public Health Surveillance Data: Legal, Policy, Ethical, Regulatory, and Practical Issues, 61 *MMWR* 30, 30–34 (2012).
[6] Ryen W. White et al., Web-Scale Pharmacovigilance: Listening to Signals from the Crowd, 20 *J. Am. Med. Inform. Assoc.* 404, 404–8 (2013).
[7] David N. Schwartz et al., Deriving Measures of Intensive Care Unit Antimicrobial Use from Computerized Pharmacy Data: Methods, Validation and Overcoming Barriers, 32 *Infect. Control Hosp. Epidemiol.* 472, 472–80 (2011).
[8] Anna Wilde Mathews, Hospitals Prescribe Big Data to Track Doctors at Work, *Wall St. J.*, July 11, 2013, at A1; Sarah E. Neddleman, Rx to Avoid Health-Law Fines, *Wall St. J.*, August 7, 2013.
[9] L. R. Haas et al., Risk-Stratification Methods for Identifying Patients for Care Coordination, 19 *Am. J. Manag. Care* 725, 725–32 (2013).
[10] Roger Foster, Top 9 Fraud and Abuse Areas Big Data Tools Can Target, *Healthcare IT News* (May 14, 2012), available at www.healthcareitnews.com/news/part-3-9-fraud-and-abuse-areas-big-data-can-target [https://perma.cc/4CSD-25MU].
[11] Federal Trade Commission, Big Data: A Tool for Inclusion or Exclusion?, in *Understanding the Issues* 7 (2016) (hereinafter FTC, Inclusion).
[12] Tom Sullivan, Big Data: Hardest Part of Population Health and Precision Medicine?, *Healthcare IT News*, March 28, 2016, available at www.healthcareitnews.com/news/big-data-hardest-part-population-health-and-precision-medicine [https://perma.cc/TG37-MYLK].
[13] James Colbert & Ishani Ganguli, To Identify Patients for Care Management Interventions, Look Beyond Big Data, Health Affairs Blog (April 19, 2016), available at http://healthaffairs.org/blog/2016/04/19/to-identify-patients-for-care-management-interventions-look-beyond-big-data/ [https://perma.cc/Y6NC-2XXS].
[14] The Precision Medicine Initiative, White House, available at https://obamawhitehouse.archives.gov/precision-medicine [https://perma.cc/7MHS-SLM6].
[15] Big Data to Knowledge (BD2K), National Institutes of Health, available at https://datascience.nih.gov/bd2k [https://perma.cc/HKN2-NGS3].
[16] Patient Protection and Affordable Care Act of 2010, 42 U.S.C. § 1201 (2010).

insurers continue their discrimination against high-cost patients and frustrate the guaranteed issue by misusing prescription drug data.[17] For example, there is evidence that health insurers use data-mined prescription drug data to continue their discrimination against high-cost patients by moving drugs associated with patients with expensive chronic conditions to high cost-sharing tiers in the hope of discouraging those patients from applying for coverage.[18] As a result, lightly regulated Big Data has the potential to frustrate some of the mainstay policies of our healthcare system.

Concentrating more narrowly on data-protection policies, a number of objections can be raised. One of the most frequent is the lack of transparency associated with the data brokers industry, "retaining the information in dossiers that we know nothing about, much less consent to."[19] Next, discrimination; some "discriminatory uses of health information are either not prohibited or are expressly permitted (for example, use of health information in life and disability insurance decisions)."[20] As a result, data brokers are harnessing health or medically inflected data to create "body scores [that] may someday be even more important than your credit score."[21] These scores not only sort us into health-related categories such as pregnant or diabetic[22] but by reference to our adherence to medication or likelihood to face medically complex procedures.[23] Beyond concerns about discriminatory electronic "redlining" based on health status, this "data-determinism" argument is that persons will become judged by "inferences or correlations drawn by algorithms suggest[ing] they may behave in ways that make them poor credit or insurance risks, unsuitable candidates for employment or admission to schools or other institutions, or unlikely to carry out certain functions."[24]

---

[17] See, e.g., Jordan Robertson, The Pitfalls of Health-Care Companies' Addiction to Big Data, Bloomberg (September 23, 2015), available at www.bloomberg.com/news/articles/2015-09-23/the-pitfalls-of-health-care-companies-addiction-to-big-data [https://perma.cc/4RJD-3V5D].

[18] Douglas B. Jacobs & Benjamin D. Sommers, Using Drugs to Discriminate: Adverse Selection in the Insurance Marketplace, 372 N. Eng. J. Med. 399, 399–402 (2015); see also Julie Appleby, Got Insurance? You Still May Pay a Steep Price for Prescriptions, Kaiser Health News (October 13, 2014), available at http://khn.org/news/got-insurance-you-still-may-pay-a-steep-price-for-prescriptions/ [https://perma.cc/7SE2-Q3CG].

[19] Julie Brill, Commissioner, Federal Trade Commission, Keynote Address at the 23rd Computers, Freedom, and Privacy Conference: Reclaim Your Name 11–12 (June 26, 2013).

[20] Privacy and Security Workgroup, Recommendations on Health Big Data, at 12.

[21] Frank Pasquale, The Black Box Society: The Secret Algorithms That Control Money and Information 26 (2015).

[22] Federal Trade Commission, Data Brokers: A Call for Transparency and Accountability 47 (2014) (hereinafter FTC, Data Brokers).

[23] Jane Sarasohn-Kahn, Here's Looking at You: How Personal Health Information Is Being Tracked and Used, California HealthCare Foundation (July 2014), at 8, available at www.chcf.org/~/media/MEDIA%20LIBRARY%20Files/PDF/PDF%20H/PDF%20HeresLookingPersonalHealthInfo.pdf [https://perma.cc/E934-8HAY].

[24] Edith Ramirez, Chairwoman, Federal Trade Commission, Keynote Address at the Tech. Pol'y Inst. Aspen Forum, The Privacy Challenges of Big Data: A View from the Lifeguard's Chair 7 (August 19, 2013).

4.3 THE DEPRECATION OF HEALTHCARE DATA PROTECTION

With the decades spent framing healthcare protection as disclosure-centric, fiduciary duties inherent in the physician-patient relationship have taken their toll. Specifically, healthcare has expressed little interest in broader data-protection principles such as those embraced by the fair information practice principles (FIPPs).[25] For example, healthcare has embraced the collection of *all* patient data, probably seeing only negatives in data minimization. Similarly, healthcare's pre–electronic health record (her) data storage "technology" (manila folders in a doctor's siloed file room) unintentionally minimized concerns that data could be used for any purpose other than for which they were collected. As a result, healthcare presents as an ingénue to the modern environment of threats to data protection.

There are several reasons for the limitations of contemporary healthcare data protection. First, US privacy law uses a sectoral approach. This dates back to the Privacy Act of 1974,[26] which, contrary to the original expectations of its architects, adopted a comprehensive approach to data protection *only* with regard to federal agencies. Absent an overarching protective model, the sector-based patchwork of resulting protections led to "Congress ... sporadically creating individual pieces of ad hoc legislation."[27] As a result, "most Federal data privacy statutes apply only to specific sectors, such as healthcare, education, communications, and financial services or, in the case of online data collection, to children."[28]

Second, policymakers have taken a notably conservative approach to data protection, using only a few of data-protection levers available to them. Worse, of those levers, policymakers have preferred "downstream" models. Typical downstream models only place limitations on data disclosure[29] or require notification of breaches[30] rather than in any way placing "upstream" constraints on the collection of data.[31]

Third, data protection always seems to be playing catch-up with threatening technologies. Apologists might protest that no data-protection regime could predict the technology challenges – the rise of mobile computing, the growth of cloud services, the power of data analytics, and the increase in cyber attacks, to name but a few. Assuredly, data protection cannot be future-proofed. However, new business practices or technologies would be less likely to outflank a comprehensive

---

[25] Ibid., at xx–xxi, xxiii.
[26] 5 U.S.C. § 552a (2014).
[27] Department of Commerce, *Commercial Data Privacy and Innovation in the Internet Economy: Dynamic Policy Framework* 60 (2010).
[28] White House, *Consumer Data Privacy in a Networked World: A Framework for Protecting Privacy and Promoting Innovation in the Global Digital Economy* 6 (2012).
[29] See, e.g., 45 C.F.R. § 164.508 (HIPAA requirement for authorization for some disclosures).
[30] See, e.g., 45 C.F.R. § 164.408 (HIPAA breach notification).
[31] Cf. Genetic Information Nondiscrimination Act of 2008 (GINA) § 202(b), 42 U.S.C. 2000ff-1(b) (2008) (prohibiting most collection of genetic information by employers).

data-protection system built on broad (and broadly accepted) principles and making use of an array of data-protection models.

4.4 REGULATORY ARBITRAGE

As emphasized by the FTC, "Big Data is big business [and] [d]ata brokers – companies that collect consumers' personal information and resell or share that information with others – are important participants in this Big Data economy."[32] Concerns about the underregulation of data brokers are not new. It has been recognized that the US sectoral or vertical approach to data protection allowed data brokers "to have frequently slipped through the cracks of US privacy law" and "found ways to avoid"[33] the Fair Credit Reporting Act (FCRA). Other have observed, "Not only does Big Data's use have the potential to circumvent existing antidiscrimination regulations, but it may also lead to privacy breaches in healthcare."[34]

Big Data raises two healthcare data-protection questions. First, to what extent are sources of data used to create health Big Data subject to regulation? Second, should there be any regulatory limits on how the products built from the data may be used? The answers to both these questions raise issues of regulatory arbitrage. The opportunity for arbitrage occurs when there is a regulatory differential between two vertical domains or markets. In this case, the regulatory differential is stark, between the HIPAA-regulated conventional healthcare domain and the general data-collecting domain that is untouched by HIPAA and only lightly regulated by laws such as the FCRA. There is reason to believe that arbitrage is occurring from the way data brokers have built a surrogate or proxy business in the less regulated vertical market.

In some cases, data analytics companies will enter into business associate agreements with healthcare entities to provide, for example, analysis of readmissions data. Presumably, in such a case, the covered entity will assert that such outcomes research is a permitted use under healthcare operations.[35] That business associate agreement presumably would prohibit shared clinical data from migrating out of the healthcare system. Indeed, data brokers should not find dealing directly with HIPAA-covered entities to be a good source of clinical data. Generally, covered entities would be unable to supply clinical data without data subject (patient) authorization,[36] a heightened form of consent. Or, if the brokers request for a "limited data set" were agreed to, the disclosure would be restricted to "research" processing and subject to a reidentification-limiting data-use agreement.[37]

[32] FTC, *Data Brokers*, at i.
[33] Daniel J. Solove & Chris Jay Hoofnagle, A Model Regime of Privacy Protection, 2006 *U. Ill. L. Rev.* 357, 359 (2006).
[34] Kate Crawford & Jason Schultz, Big Data and Due Process: Toward a Framework to Redress Predictive Privacy Harms, 55 *B.C. L. Rev.* 93, 99 (2014).
[35] 45 C.F.R. § 164.506(c)(4) (2013).
[36] 45 C.F.R. § 164.508 (2013).
[37] 45 C.F.R. § 164.514 (2013).

Data brokers do not completely ignore data that have been subject to HIPAA protection. For example, they acquire deidentified data – HIPAA data that, once deidentified, are no longer subject to HIPAA.[38] Also, they acquire HIPAA data that have been legally shared with public health authorities,[39] who then make deidentified data sets available[40] without prohibitions on reidentification.

In the main, however, the brokers source their data (particularly their identified or identifiable data) outside the HIPAA-protected zone. They purchase personal, including health-related, information from a variety of commercial sources.[41] These sources provide troves of medical-inflected data harvested from social media interactions, retail stores, web trackers, online transactions, mobile phone location trackers, fitness wearables, and so on. The opportunities for such wide-scale harvesting are only mounting. Increasingly, our everyday interactions will trigger unrealized or unconsented collection of data about us from Internet of Things (IoT) devices, specifically our location and physical (even medical) condition or even from the unwitting "nonconsensual collection and use of genetic material."[42]

One major data broker has claimed, "Our scaled and growing data set, containing over 10 petabytes of unique data, includes over 85% of the world's prescriptions by sales revenue and approximately 400 million comprehensive, longitudinal, anonymous patient records."[43] In many cases, data brokers leverage their computing power and the breadth of their triangulation databases to reidentify the data.[44] Subsequently, they apply their sophisticated algorithms "to help [their] clients run their organizations more efficiently and make better decisions to improve their operational and financial performance."[45]

Regulatory disruption is clear and arbitrage highly likely. Data brokers, generally shut out of protected healthcare data, are able to create proxies for those data in a lightly regulated HIPAA-free zone. Crawford and Schultz go further, noting that the "predictive privacy harms" caused by Big Data are such that traditional upstream and downstream data-protection models ("collection, processing and disclosure")

---

[38] See, generally, US Department of Health and Human Services, *Guidance Regarding Methods for De-identification of Protected Health Information in Accordance with the Health Insurance Portability and Accountability Act (HIPAA) Privacy Rule* (2012).
[39] 45 C.F.R. § 164.512(b) (2013).
[40] See, e.g., Sean Hooley & Latanya Sweeney, Harvard Survey of Publicly Available State Health Databases, University Data Private Lab 3 (2013), available at https://dataprivacylab.org/projects/50states/1075-1.pdf [https://perma.cc/PJH6-VF4T].
[41] See also FTC, Big Data, at 3–4; FTC, *Data Brokers*, at 13.
[42] Elizabeth R. Pike, Securing Sequences: Ensuring Adequate Protections for Genetic Samples in the Age of Big Data, 37 *Cardozo L. Rev.* 1977, 2013 (2015).
[43] IMS Health Holdings, Inc., Form S-1, Registration Statement under the Securities Act of 1933, available at www.sec.gov/Archives/edgar/data/1595262/000119312514000659/d628679ds1.htm [https://perma.cc/85FD-CX66].
[44] See, generally, Nicolas Terry, Developments in Genetic and Epigenetic Data Protection in Behavioral and Mental Health Spaces, 33 *Behav. Sci. L.* 653 (2015).
[45] IMS Health Holdings, Form S-1.

can be circumvented.[46] With only few exceptions (such as FCRA prohibitions), the products they sell are essentially unregulated.

4.5 REFORM PROPOSALS

There appears to be broad agreement that Big Data poses significant data-protection issues that need to be addressed lest the historically high levels of protection given to healthcare data are nullified.[47] Legislation providing for data minimization and context-based limitations is urgently required. Such protections have been part of European law for decades.[48] Data minimization and a purpose limitation are now being preserved, even strengthened, by new EU data-protection regulation.[49] Along with data minimization, the EU "purpose" limitation creates major limitations on Big Data collection and analytics.[50]

However, in the United States, there is little agreement as to the specifics of any reform and almost no indication of imminent congressional action.[51] With silence on Capitol Hill, the major sources of proposals for reform have been the White House and the FTC. In 2012, the former recommended a "Consumer Privacy Bill of Rights," strongly rooted in FIPPS and promotive of both upstream and downstream protections.[52] As to Big Data, it noted that as "third parties become further removed from direct interactions with consumers, it may be more difficult for them to provide consumers with meaningful control over data collection."[53] As a result, the report argued, data brokers "may need to go to extra lengths to implement other principles such as Transparency ... as well as providing appropriate use controls once information is collected under the Access and Accuracy and Accountability principles to compensate for the lack of a direct consumer relationship."[54]

---

[46] Kate Crawford & Jason Schultz, Big Data and Due Process: Toward a Framework to Redress Predictive Privacy Harms, 55 B.C. L. Rev. 93, 106 (2014).
[47] Cf. Skopek, Reasonable Expectations of Anonymity (pushing back on a model of medical exceptionalism).
[48] Council Directive 95/46 1995 O.J. (L 281) 31–50.
[49] Regulation (EU) 2016/679 of the European Parliament and of the Council of 27 April 2016 on the Protection of Natural Persons with Regard to the Processing of Personal Data and on the Free Movement of Such Data, and Repealing Directive 95/46/EC, 2016 O.J. (L 119) 1–88.
[50] Compare Article 29 Data Protection Working Party, Opinion 03/2013 on Purpose Limitation, 2013 O.J (WP 203) 45–47, Example 9, with President's Council of Advisors on Science and Technology, Report to the President on Big Data and Privacy: A Technological Perspective 41 (2014) ("[A] focus on the collection, storage, and retention of electronic personal data will not provide a technologically robust foundation on which to base future policy").
[51] See, generally, Nicolas Terry, Navigating the Incoherence of Big Data Reform Proposals, 43 J. L. Med. Ethics 44 (2015).
[52] White House, Consumer Data Privacy in a Networked World: A Framework for Protecting Privacy and Promoting Innovation in the Global Digital Economy, 95 J. Priv. Confidentiality 139–42 (2012).
[53] Ibid., at 107.
[54] Ibid.

In 2014, in a more focused report, the administration directly addressed data mining and Big Data processing,[55] noting "the wide variety of potential uses for big data analytics raises crucial questions about whether our legal, ethical, and social norms are sufficient to protect privacy and other values in a big data world" and cautioned how Big Data capabilities, "most of which are not visible or available to the average consumer, also create an asymmetry of power between those who hold the data and those who intentionally or inadvertently supply it."[56] A key finding was, "[t]he powerful connection between lifestyle and health outcomes means the distinction between personal data and health care data has begun to blur. These types of data are subjected to different and sometimes conflicting federal and state regulation."[57]

Additionally, the report recognized that "big data technologies can cause societal harms beyond damages to privacy, such as discrimination against individuals and groups" – including the "intent to prey on vulnerable classes" – and recommended that federal "civil rights and consumer protection agencies should expand their technical expertise to be able to identify practices and outcomes facilitated by big data analytics that have a discriminatory impact on protected classes, and develop a plan for investigating and resolving violations of law."[58] A companion report issued by the President's Council of Advisors on Science and Technology (PCAST) took issue with notice and consent privacy models, viewing them as "increasingly unworkable and ineffective."[59]

Notwithstanding these major and broadly circulated reports, there has been no congressional action. Perhaps frustrated by the inaction, in 2015, the White House published its own "Draft Consumer Privacy Bill of Rights Act."[60] This was based on the 2012 proposed legislation but exhibited regrettable enthusiasm for enforceable codes of conduct. Even so, there was no legislative uptake.

In its 2012 report, "Protecting Consumer Privacy in an Era of Rapid Change,"[61] the FTC also called for the general adoption of FIPPS. However, its sole detailed legislative recommendation was for "targeted legislation to provide greater transparency for, and control over, the practices of information brokers" to "provide consumers with access to information about them held by a data broker."[62] The FTC

---

[55] See, generally, White House, *Big Data: Seizing Opportunities and Preserving Values* (2014).
[56] Ibid., at 3.
[57] Ibid., at 23.
[58] Ibid., at 48, 51, 60.
[59] President's Council of Advisors on Science and Technology, A Technological Perspective, at 40–50.
[60] White House, Administration Discussion Draft: Consumer Privacy Bill of Rights Act of 2015 (2015) (hereinafter White House, Draft Bill).
[61] Federal Trade Commission, *Protecting Consumer Privacy in an Era of Rapid Change: Recommendations for Businesses and Policymakers* (2012) (hereinafter FTC, *Protecting Consumer Privacy*).
[62] Ibid., at iv–v, 73.

also argued that access and correction rights should be calibrated such that "[c]ompanies should provide reasonable access to the consumer data they maintain; the extent of access should be proportionate to the sensitivity of the data and the nature of its use."[63] For example, with regard to credit data, differing levels of access would "reflect different levels of data sensitivity: (1) entities that maintain data for marketing purposes; (2) entities subject to the FCRA; and (3) entities that may maintain data for other, non-marketing purposes that fall outside of the FCRA."[64]

The FTC's 2014 "Data Brokers" report analyzed the markets and practices of nine major data brokers.[65] It noted, "[i]n the nearly two decades since the Commission first began to examine data brokers, little progress has been made to improve transparency and choice."[66] The report makes frequent reference to mobile data being collected by data brokers.[67] It also noted the amount of sensitive information, including health information, being collected and how "[d]ata brokers infer consumer interests from the data that they collect" and "place consumers in categories," including "potentially sensitive categories [that] highlight certain health-related topics or conditions, such as 'Expectant Parent,' 'Diabetes Interest,' and 'Cholesterol Focus.'"[68] Finally, the agency made a specific proposal for legislation to require opt-in consent for Big Data collection of healthcare data, "requiring that consumer-facing sources obtain consumers' affirmative express[ed] consent before collecting and sharing such information with data brokers."[69]

The FTC issued yet another report in 2016, "Big Data: A Tool for Inclusion or Exclusion?" The report expressed concerns that some uses of big data would

- Result in more individuals mistakenly being denied opportunities based on the actions of others
- Create or reinforce existing disparities
- Expose sensitive information
- Assist in the targeting of vulnerable consumers for fraud
- Create new justifications for exclusion
- Result in higher-priced goods and services for lower-income communities
- Weaken the effectiveness of consumer choice[70]

Comprehensive federal legislation remains the preferable option for dealing with these risks, particularly when faced with an industry that is adept at regulatory

---

[63] Ibid., at 64.
[64] FTC, *Protecting Consumer Privacy*, at 65.
[65] See, generally, FTC, *Data Brokers*.
[66] Ibid., at 1.
[67] See, e.g., ibid., at 57.
[68] See, e.g., ibid., at iv–v.
[69] Ibid., at 52.
[70] FTC, Big Data, at 9–12.

arbitrage and does not take self-regulation seriously.[71] This is the consistent recommendation of the FTC, and the agency continues to press for "federal legislation that would (1) strengthen its existing data security authority and (2) require companies, in appropriate circumstances, to provide notification to consumers when there is a security breach."[72] Given Congress's apparent disinterest in such a comprehensive solution, we will see, at most, more patchwork sectoral legislation aimed at narrow privacy or security threats. Although unlikely, it is not impossible that we may see some additional "point-of-use" nondiscrimination legislation aimed at Big Data brokers. Yet even narrow, targeted legislation such as the FTC's 2014 proposal for data custodians to be required to obtain opt-in consent from data subjects before releasing personal information to data brokers seems to lack legislative traction.

4.6 EXISTING FTC POWERS

Given the absence of expanded regulation or the passage of comprehensive federal privacy legislation, the practical legal limitations placed on Big Data collection, processing, and use are thin. Compared with HIPAA's regulation of healthcare privacy, security, and breach notification, the HIPAA-free zone in which the data brokers operate is sparsely regulated – hence the regulatory arbitrage that the brokers have enjoyed in constructing their health information products. However, while the HIPAA-free zone is sparsely regulated, it is not unregulated. Most of the regulation that does exist is enforced by the FTC.[73]

For example, the FTC uses the FCRA to regulate consumer reporting agencies (CRAs) to maintain accurate, fair, and private files and provide notices of adverse actions.[74] A CRA is a person who "regularly engages in whole or in part in the practice of assembling or evaluating consumer credit information or other information on consumers for the purpose of furnishing consumer reports to third parties."[75] The FCRA's scope is somewhat broader than its title would suggest, extending "beyond traditional credit bureaus"[76] and applying to CRAs "that compile and sell consumer reports, which contain consumer information that is used or

---

[71] See, e.g., Direct Marketing Association, *DMA Guidelines on Ethical Business Practice* (2014). See also Individual Reference Services Group, *Industry Principles: Commentary* (1997).
[72] Opportunities and Challenges in Advancing Health Information Technology before the House Oversight and Government Reform Commission, 114th Congress (2016) (statement of Jessica L. Rich, Director, Bureau of Consumer Protection) (reference omitted). See also Federal Trade Commission, *Internet of Things, Privacy & Security in a Connected World* (2015).
[73] See, generally, Daniel J. Solove & Woodrow Hartzog, The FTC and the New Common Law of Privacy, 114 *Colum. L. Rev.* 583 (2014).
[74] 15 U.S.C §§ 1681a–1681i (2012).
[75] Ibid., at § 1681(a)(f).
[76] FTC, Big Data, at 14.

expected to be used for credit, employment, insurance, housing, or other similar decisions about consumers' eligibility for certain benefits and transactions."[77]

During congressional testimony in 2013, the FTC reported that it had collected more than $30 million in civil penalties in more than 100 FCRA cases. Several of these cases were brought against data brokers, with the agency arguing that brokers who compiled personal profiles and marketed them to human resources (HR) departments were CRAs subject to FCRA requirements of accuracy and transparency or had otherwise failed to follow FCRA dispute procedures.[78] Two recent FCRA settlements were also with data brokers who sold public record information about consumers to employers or landlords performing background checks. Specific complaints included that some information was inaccurate or that it was supplied to persons who lacked the requisite FCRA-defined permissible purpose.[79]

The FTC has argued that several data uses can fall afoul of "federal equal opportunity laws [that] prohibit discrimination based on protected characteristics such as race, color, sex or gender, religion, age, disability status, national origin, marital status, and genetic information."[80] The FTC has brought several cases against lenders alleging disparate treatment or disparate impact under the Equal Credit Opportunity Act.[81]

The agency also has broader powers under Section 5(a) of the Federal Trade Commission Act, which prohibits "deceptive" and "unfair" acts.[82] The "deceptive" cases will generally be premised on some misrepresentation or broken promise. The "unfair" cases are far more broadly based.

For example, in *ChoicePoint*, the FTC settled security data breach complaints against the data broker after alleging that it had supplied credit histories to subscribers who did not have a permissible purpose to obtain them (FCRA) and made misleading statements about its privacy policies such as only selling to customers who had been vetted (Section 5[a]).[83]

---

[77] Ibid., at 13.
[78] See What Information Do Data Brokers Have on Consumers, and How Do They Use It? Before the Senate Committee on Commerce, Science, & Transportation, 113th Congress 4–6 (2013) (statement of Jessica L. Rich, Director, Bureau of Consumer Protection).
[79] Federal Trade Commission, Press Release, Two Data Brokers Settle FTC Charges That They Sold Consumer Data without Complying with Protections Required under the Fair Credit Reporting Act (April 9, 2014), available at www.ftc.gov/news-events/press-releases/2014/04/two-data-brokers-settle-ftc-charges-they-sold-consumer-data [https://perma.cc/UCB7-966H].
[80] FTC, Big Data, at 18.
[81] Ibid., at 17–21.
[82] 15 U.S.C. § 45 (2012).
[83] Federal Trade Commission, Press Release, ChoicePoint Settles Data Security Breach Charges; to Pay $10 Million in Civil Penalties, $5 Million for Consumer Redress (January 26, 2006), available at www.ftc.gov/news-events/press-releases/2006/01/choicepoint-settles-data-security-breach-charges-pay-10-million [https://perma.cc/LQ87-2BKT].

The recent developments in the FTC's "unfairness" jurisprudence suggest that this may develop into a potent weapon to use against data brokers who sell poor-quality or otherwise harmful data.[84] For example, in *FTC v. Wyndham Worldwide Corp.*,[85] the agency successfully argued that some privacy or security failures are intrinsically "unfair," suggesting an avenue of attack in cases involving data breaches at data brokers.[86]

The FTC has refuted any notion that its jurisdiction in privacy and security matters is in any way limited by the existence of domain-specific regulatory models such as HIPAA.[87] This somewhat reduces the likelihood of a health information case "falling between the cracks" if it is unclear whether or not HIPAA applies, and "so long as the requirements of those statutes do not conflict with one another, a party cannot plausibly assert that because it complies with one of these laws, it is free to violate the other."[88]

Although the FTC's clear intent to closely scrutinize the data broker industry and these victories aside, the FTC's powers must still be recognized as severely limited. Even interpreted broadly, the FCRA applies to only a small range of data broker practices. And, although broadly based, Section 5(a) is a fact intensive, "thin" law that only applies ex post facto. As such, its development will depend on the FTC being successful in a very large number of cases, an eventuality that is unlikely given the agency's limited enforcement resources.

4.7 CONCLUSION

Healthcare data analytics may well offer our healthcare system something that its homegrown small data, beset by lack of interoperability and limited nonclinical insights into patients, currently lacks. However, health-related Big Data *outside* the healthcare system raises orthogonal issues. The concern addressed here is the commercial use of sensitive personal health information data exported from or created outside the regulated healthcare space. Data brokers no doubt will seek to collapse the issues, arguing for a light regulatory hand that allows for reidentification and does not clearly distinguish between use cases (e.g., healthcare systems research and marketing) or whether best practices are developed inside or outside the data broker industry.[89] This chapter argues that whether created inside or outside the

---

[84] See, e.g., *POM Wonderful, LLC v. FTC*, 777 F.3d 478 (D.C. Cir. 2015).
[85] *FTC v. Wyndham Worldwide Corp.*, 799 F.3d 236 (3d Cir. 2015).
[86] See FTC, Big Data, at 22–23 (citations omitted).
[87] *LabMD, Inc., In the Matter of*, Federal Trade Commission, available at www.ftc.gov/enforcement/cases-proceedings/102-3099/labmd-inc-matter [https://perma.cc/S8V4-VMLX].
[88] Ibid.
[89] See Quintiles IMS Institute, *Closing the Healthcare Gap: The Critical Role of Non-Identified Information*, 32–33 (2015).

healthcare system, personal health information is our most sensitive data and deserves the highest level of data protection. Regulatory arbitrage has been enabled by a sectoral approach to data protection and "creates complexity and costs for businesses and confuses consumers."[90] The culture of healthcare and the expectations of patients demand uniform protection for healthcare data that can only be guaranteed by comprehensive federal legislation.

[90] Department of Commerce, Commercial Data Privacy, at 59.

PART II

Overcoming the Downsides of Big Data

INTRODUCTION

I. Glenn Cohen

The chapters in this part cover a myriad of distinctive legal topics – Food and Drug Administration (FDA) pharmacovigilance, the False Claims Act, discrimination under the Americans with Disabilities Act (ADA), the inclusion of minorities (and their data) in research design and healthcare deployment, and the interplay of state all-payer claims databases (APCDs) and the Employment Retirement Income Security Act of 1974 (ERISA). At a deeper level, the chapters represent two distinct reactions to the way in which Big Data and health law intersect – assimilation and disruption.

Assimilation, as the word suggests, is a view that new technologies require bending but not breaking existing legal categories. A threat emerges to the kingdom from a neighboring kingdom. The attackers seek to storm the castle, and their initial barrage is quite threatening to the kingdom's existing citizens. But, before long, the kingdom realizes that it shares much with the interlopers and that their cultural and other forms of distinctiveness can be accommodated by making just a few changes to the kingdom's laws and culture; indeed, in many cases the kingdom finds that the new recruits make it stronger. To borrow from a different body of law, consider the way in which family law has approached same-sex marriage. Many initially (and perhaps some still) considered this form of marriage to be very disruptive of the law of marriage. How would, for example, family law react to the inclusion of a third reproductive partner (a sperm donor, a surrogate) in determining the parentage of children born to same-sex married couples? Now that the dust has settled, though, we see that same-sex marriage has been relatively well assimilated into the canon of American family law, and such questions as "who goes on the birth certificate" have been answered without too much fuss.

Disruption is a quite different model.[1] A new technology causes movement of tectonic plates, and the result more deeply reconfigures existing kingdoms. Sometimes the kingdom is torn apart into two or more pieces with oceans between them, each of which can now develop on its own according to its own organizing principles. On other occasions, separate kingdoms get pushed together with volcanoes peppering their seams and clashes of organizing principles until there is some accommodation. Sometimes both happen at once. Whether the new configuration is better or worse depends very much on where one sits – those who built homes where volcanoes now erupt will surely be unhappy. To borrow again from a very different body of law, consider the way in which the development of the automobile and increased flow of goods and persons across state lines radically changed the law of personal jurisdiction. The centrality of territoriality as the basis for personal jurisdiction was sufficient in the old world of *Pennoyer v. Neff*[2] but wholly insufficient for the world of *International Shoe Co. v. Washington*.[3] At that point, the law switched from a focus on "is it there" to a focus on "is it fair," producing winners and losers and completely changing the way courts, corporations, and others thought about who has the power to adjudicate disputes.

The chapters in this part fall – if not neatly then at least recognizably – into these two paradigms and indeed can be seen as points on a continuum from assimilation to disruption roughly in the following order: in Chapter 5, "The Future of Pharmacovigilance: Big Data and the False Claims Act," Efthimios Parasidis is squarely in the assimilation camp. He seeks to accord a "transformative role" to Big Data in FDA processes, one that uses it to expand and improve approaches that the FDA is already using – most notably the Sentinel System for monitoring adverse events. He sees a role for Big Data monitoring to "highlight anomalies (for example, people over the age of sixty who are prescribed drug X have an unusually high rate of heart attacks) that can trigger a need for further research." He also sees a second potential assimilative role for Big Data, the possibility that government "can leverage algorithmic analysis of Big Data to prosecute and disincentivize fraud and thus gain valuable ground in addressing the massive exploitation of the public fisc," primarily through the False Claims Act (FCA). He also argues that "courts should find that the reverse false claims provision of the FCA applies if a defendant used Big Data tools to conceal an obligation owed to the government," in addition to any direct FCA liability.

In Chapter 7, "Who's Left Out of Big Data? How Big Data Collection, Analysis, and Use Neglects Populations Most in Need of Medical and Public Health Research and Interventions," Sarah E. Malanga, Jonathan D. Loe, Christopher T. Robertson, and Kenneth S. Ramos focus on the problem that Big Data is not

---

[1] The locus classicus, such that it is, is probably the idea of "disruptive innovation" from Clayton M. Christensen, *The Innovator's Dilemma* (1997). However, the term has been used in an increasingly broad and amorphous sense since that seminal work.
[2] 95 U.S. 714 (1877).
[3] 326 U.S. 310 (1945).

big enough, in that the existing collection in the health area has "not captured certain marginalized demographics," especially "racial minorities, people with low socioeconomic status, and immigrants." But it gets worse, for these "are the very people most in need of increased health research, intervention, and care." But all is not lost. The authors consider a series of possible solutions. All are partial; some are technological – such as "standard post-hoc statistical adjustments that yield unbiased estimates notwithstanding known disparities in the way the data are collected"; some are regulatory – for example, requiring the FDA to "follow NIH's lead to require that drug and device applications exhibit the use of diverse data sets in order to inform the safety and efficacy of these drugs and devices."

In Chapter 8, "Potential Roadblocks in Healthcare Big Data Collection: *Gobeille v. Liberty Mutual*, ERISA, and All-Payer Claims Databases," Carmel Shachar, Aaron S. Kesselheim, Gregory Curfman, and Ameet Sarpatwari look for a way to harness Big Data to improve evaluation of prescription drug and medical device safety and effectiveness through APCDs. In *Gobeille v. Liberty Mutual*,[4] the Supreme Court decided that ERISA preempted Vermont's attempt to gather healthcare data from plans governed by ERISA, thus prohibiting Vermont and others states from requiring that self-insured employer-sponsored health plans report data to their APCDs. At first, this does not seem like much of a story of assimilation, but instead only conflict – for as the authors put it, *Gobeille* 's permitting "self-funded insurance plans to use ERISA as a shield against reporting their health care claims data may undermine the ability of health care and services researchers to improve the quality of care and to address health care costs and other trends by reducing APCDs from a complete data set to a fragmented one." But the last part of the chapter reviews ways in which existing ERISA law could accommodate APCDs in the wake of *Gobeille*, for example, by having the Department of Labor collect data for APCDs, by explicitly granting permission for APCDs to require data reporting from self-insured plans, or by having states offer incentives to those who share the data in the correct format. Therefore, there is at least some hope that peace might reign in the kingdom and the value of Big Data would be harnessed, notwithstanding the apparent conflict with ERISA.

All three of these chapters view the Big Data revolution in relatively benign terms. The legal system will face challenges but also great opportunities if it can only accommodate Big Data – the hallmarks of the assimilationist approach. They differ primarily on how easy or hard that assimilation will be.

Chapter 6, "Big Data's New Discrimination Threats: Amending the Americans with Disabilities Act to Cover Discrimination Based on Data-Driven Predictions of Future Disease," by Sharona Hoffman, by contrast, falls squarely in the disruption camp. This is evident from the chapter's very first line: "While Big Data holds great promise to improve the human condition, it also creates new and previously unimaginable opportunities for discrimination." That is, "[w]hile the ADA protects

---

[4] 136 S. Ct. 936 (2016).

individuals who have existing disabilities, records of past disabilities, or are regarded as having mental or physical impairments, it does not reach people who are currently healthy but are perceived as being at high risk of becoming sick in the future," which is precisely the group that harnessing Big Data will allow employers, financial institutions, marketers, universities, and others to identify and treat adversely. Hoffman offers several fixes that might be thought of as assimilationist – primarily expanding the "regarded as" prong of protection under the ADA to cover "individuals who are perceived as likely to develop physical or mental impairments in the future" and amending the ADA to require disclosure of data-mining practices – but I think this understates that which is radical about this chapter and portrays it as more assimilationist than it actually is.

Hoffman is actually taking an existing legal kingdom governing discrimination against those with disabilities or who are wrongfully regarded as disabledand suggesting an extension of the ADA's protection to a wholly new kingdom: discrimination against those who are *predicted* (using Big Data mechanisms) to become disabled in the future, even though they are neither disabled nor regarded as disabled at present. At one point she hints at the radicalism of this proposal – that instead of protecting a "discrete and insular minority" of the disabled, this approach would "expand the ADA to reach all Americans." But Hoffman does not dwell on just how disruptive a move this is. Among other things, especially as to cases where prediction is *accurate*, it may be transformative of our conception of disability discrimination and raise deep questions as to what makes such discrimination wrongful. To hum only the first few bars of this claim, one might argue that the wrongfulness of disability discrimination, akin to sex or race discrimination, stems from its reliance on stereotype and overbreadth. "Able-ist" society (i.e., the society of those without disability that may be intolerant of those with disability) wrongfully views people with disabilities as unable to perform the essential function of a job when, in fact, those people could perform those functions with a reasonable accommodation. But at least as to some subsets of those who are "algorithmically regarded as disabled" (my term, not hers), the prediction is accurate and not the result of stereotype. If systems could be put in place to limit the use of Big Data discrimination to those groups, would it be wrongful?

Among the intriguing questions raised by these chapters viewed through this lens is whether the assimilation-disruption continuum is best understood as a reflection of subject matter or timing. To put the point differently, do technological innovations such as Big Data's encounter with law cluster around a predictable chronologic path – first attempts at assimilation until that which can bend no more breaks and disruption ensues – or is the path chronologically unpredictable? Is zigzagging between assimilation to disruption and back to assimilation possible, or once disruption sets in to some magnitude, is the old paradigm unrecoverable?

5

The Future of Pharmacovigilance

Big Data and the False Claims Act

Efthimios Parasidis*

5.1 INTRODUCTION

Big Data's virtues are touted far more than its vices. Just as Big Data can be leveraged to incentivize innovation, assess healthcare quality, and improve health outcomes, Big Data also can be used to conceal wasteful spending, suppress negative findings, or seek reimbursement for care that is not medically necessary. The healthcare industry is not unique in this sense – twenty-first-century technologies permit twenty-first-century fraud across all market sectors. While the False Claims Act (FCA) is the US government's primary tool for combating healthcare fraud, in recent years it has recovered no more than 5 percent of the estimated fraudulent claims paid by the US Centers for Medicare and Medicaid Services (CMS).[1] This is significant because healthcare fraud is estimated to cost taxpayers close to $100 billion per year, which equates to about 10 percent of annual CMS expenditures.[2] While healthcare fraud comes in many forms, I focus this chapter on the role of the FCA as a means of prosecuting companies that use Big Data to manipulate safety or efficacy information for marketed medical products.

As other chapters in this book detail, the healthcare industry is in the midst of a Big Data revolution. Government and industry investments in health information

---

* For illuminating comments on this chapter, I thank Glenn Cohen and participants at the Petrie-Flom Center conference, Big Data, Health Law, and Bioethics, which was held at Harvard Law School in May 2016. I thank the Greenwall Foundation Faculty Scholars Program in Bioethics for providing financial support for this project. COI Disclosure: I provide counsel to relator in *United States ex rel. Petratos v. Genentech, Inc.*, which is discussed in this chapter; the views expressed herein are my own and may not reflect those of relator or co-counsel.

[1] Shantanu Agrawal, Testimony on the Use of Data to Stop Medicare Fraud, Committee on Ways and Means, Subcommittee on Oversight, US House of Representatives (March 24, 2015); T. R. Goldman, Eliminating Fraud and Abuse, *Health Affairs* (July 31, 2012); Health-Care Fraud: The $272 Billion Swindle, *Economist* (May 31, 2014).

[2] Ibid.

technology (IT) have led to a proliferation of electronic health records (EHRs), patient registries, adverse-event databases, and data-mining tools. Data from social media and health apps are aggregated, shared, and sold. Researchers can access de-identified health data to conduct studies on quality management, health outcomes, and comparative effectiveness, while states have established health information exchanges whereby patients and providers can access and learn from health data.

Notwithstanding the explosion of health Big Data, health policy experts underscore the fact that how Big Data is analyzed is more important than the amassing of Big Data. As Ziad Obermeyer and Ezekiel Emmanuel succinctly explain, "[I]t is algorithms – not data sets – that will prove transformative."[3] This maxim also holds true in the world of healthcare fraud. While healthcare fraud existed before Big Data, Big Data has altered the dynamics of healthcare fraud, creating new options for fraudsters and new challenges for regulators and prosecutors.

A significant component of FCA prosecutions addresses healthcare overbilling, which includes billing for care that was not provided or not medically necessary. Although the FCA "is not an all-purpose anti-fraud statute,"[4] Congress drafted the act "expansively ... to reach all types of fraud, without qualification, that might result in financial loss to the Government."[5] Yet, the extent to which the FCA applies to Big Data manipulation of risk-benefit information that affects physician prescribing is unclear.[6] For example, if Big Data analysis reveals questions about safety or efficacy, does a pharmaceutical company have an obligation to report that information or conduct further research? What if material information is revealed only if a query is structured in a certain way, or if data sources are combined in a certain way? What is the outcome if a learning algorithm is the sole entity to examine the new information? Is it truthful for a company to say that no new risks exist if the data suggest, but do not demonstrate, new risks?

Insofar as companies are increasingly outsourcing clinical development and Big Data analytics,[7] these issues become more complex. For instance, the law is unclear on the extent to which third parties have an obligation to disclose negative information on safety and efficacy to regulators, the public, and the company that requested assistance with Big Data analysis. Equally unclear is the extent to which the FCA applies to these scenarios.

This chapter explores the role of Big Data in pharmacovigilance, fraud detection, and fraud prosecution. I examine whether the FCA encompasses false claims where the alleged fraud relates to Big Data manipulation, which I define as structuring data

---

[3] Ziad Obermeyer & Ezekiel Emanuel, Predicting the Future: Big Data, Machine Learning, and Clinical Medicine, 375 N. Engl. J. Med. 1216 (2016).
[4] Universal Health Services, Inc. v. United States ex rel. Escobar, 136 S. Ct. 1989, 2003 (2016).
[5] Cook County v. United States ex rel. Chandler, 538 U.S. 119, 129 (2009).
[6] See, e.g., Joan H. Krause, Reflections on Certification, Interpretation, and the Quest for Fraud that "Counts" Under the False Claims Act, 2017 Ill. L. Rev. 1811 (2017).
[7] See, e.g., Jane E. Winter & Jane Baguley, eds., Outsourcing Clinical Development (2016).

analysis to obscure information that might cause the submission of fewer claims. I conclude by arguing that the FCA should apply to such claims, and set forth the legal, public health, and normative rationales for this conclusion.

5.2 THE ROLE OF BIG DATA IN PHARMACOVIGILANCE AND HEALTHCARE FRAUD

While the FDA's premarket review process is robust, it also is limited – premarket studies may not capture rare adverse events, latent adverse events, or adverse events that occur because of comorbidities.[8] As such, postmarket research plays an integral role in providing evidence regarding the safety and efficacy of marketed medical products. As the FDA has noted, "[P]ostmarketing safety data collection and risk assessment based on observational data are critical for evaluating and characterizing a product's risk profile and for making informed decisions on risk minimization."[9]

The need for comprehensive postmarket analysis is magnified by the FDA's premarket reliance on surrogate endpoints. Via surrogate endpoints, manufacturers can satisfy efficacy requirements by relying on biomarkers, rather than demonstrating that a product provides a clinical benefit such as relieving disease symptoms, extending life, or improving the quality of life.[10] Although studies have called into question the causal relationship between positive outcomes on surrogate endpoints and positive outcomes on clinical endpoints,[11] reliance on surrogate endpoints is expanding. For example, between 2005 and 2011, nearly half of FDA approvals for new molecular entities were granted solely on the basis of surrogate endpoints.[12] In addition, the Twenty-First-Century Cures Act broadens accelerated approval and the FDA's reliance on surrogate endpoints during premarket review.[13] Increased reliance on surrogate endpoints (particularly for new molecular entities, which are drugs that have never been approved for human use) calls for increased emphasis on postmarket review for safety and efficacy.

In this context, Big Data can play a transformative role – by helping to create, manage, and analyze health-related information. The FDA maintains an arsenal of Big Data tools, including adverse-event databases and the Sentinel System, which

---

[8] Keith B. Hoffman et al., A Pharmacovigilance Signaling System Based on FDA Regulatory Action and Post-Marketing Adverse Event Reports, 39 *Drug Safety* 561 (2016).
[9] *Guidance for Industry: Good Pharmacovigilance Practices and Pharmacoepidemiologic Assessment*, Food and Drug Administration, US Department of Health and Human Services, at 3 (March 2005) (hereinafter, FDA, *Guidance: Pharmacovigilance*).
[10] Thomas R. Fleming, Surrogate Endpoints and FDA's Accelerated Approval Process, 24 *Health Affairs* 67, 68 (2005).
[11] Ibid.
[12] N. S. Downing et al., Clinical Trial Evidence Supporting FDA Approval of Novel Therapeutic Agents, 2005–2012, 311 *JAMA* 368 (2014).
[13] Pub. L. 114-225 (2016).

is a distributed data network in which participating organizations own and share their health data. As studies have detailed, however, these tools are limited in their ability to capture relevant information in a timely manner or to prove a causal relationship between an adverse event and a product.[14] Nonetheless, the resources can serve as signal-generating mechanisms that put companies, the FDA, and physicians on notice for the need for further inquiry into a product's risks and benefits. For example, data monitoring can highlight anomalies (e.g., people over the age of sixty who are prescribed drug X have an unusually high rate of heart attacks) that can trigger a need for further research.

5.2.1 Regulatory Requirements

While postmarket data are valuable, the general rule governing postmarket research is that manufacturers must report known adverse events to the FDA. FDA regulations do not mandate that manufacturers actively monitor their products, nor do the regulations contain a general requirement that manufacturers seek out and analyze safety and efficacy data.[15] Under existing regulations, the FDA has the legal authority to require postmarket analysis only in two circumstances: as a condition of approval and when a new safety signal arises.[16]

At the same time, however, the law states that manufacturers cannot introduce or maintain "misbranded" drugs in interstate commerce.[17] A drug is misbranded when the manufacturer's labeling (which is defined to include not only the drug's physical packaging, but also all written, audio, or visual communications about the drug) is "false, lacking in fair balance or otherwise misleading."[18] The omission of information relevant to approved and known intended uses is a form of misbranding.[19] Moreover, once a drug earns FDA approval, the manufacturer must

> promptly review all adverse drug experience information obtained or otherwise received by the applicant from any source, foreign or domestic, including information derived from commercial marketing experience, postmarketing clinical investigations, postmarketing epidemiological/surveillance studies, reports in the scientific literature, and unpublished scientific papers.[20]

---

[14] R. Harpaz et al., Big Data and Adverse Drug Reaction Detection, 99 *Clin. Pharmacol. Ther.* 268 (2016); Thomas Moore & Curt Furberg, Electronic Health Data for Postmarket Surveillance: A Vision Not Realized, 38 *Drug Safety* 601 (2015).

[15] See, generally, *Guidance for Industry: Postmarketing Studies and Clinical Trials*, Food and Drug Administration, US Department of Health and Human Services (April 2011) (hereinafter FDA, *Guidance: Postmarketing Studies*).

[16] Ibid., at 4.

[17] 42 U.S.C. § 331(a) (2016).

[18] 21 U.S.C. § 352 (2016).

[19] 21 U.S.C. § 321(n) (2016).

[20] 21 C.F.R. § 314.80(b) (2016).

A manufacturer also has a duty to update a drug's label in light of new information related to safety and efficacy.[21] To reflect newly acquired information in a drug's label, a manufacturer may, without first gaining FDA approval, "add or strengthen a contraindication, warning, precaution, or adverse reaction" or "add or strengthen an instruction about dosage and administration that is intended to increase the safe use of the drug."[22] According to the FDA, "[N]ewly acquired information is not limited to new data, but also encompasses new analyses of previously submitted data. The rule accounts for the fact that risk information accumulates over time and that the same data may take on a different meaning in light of subsequent developments."[23]

As the US Supreme Court has indicated, "[I]t has remained a central premise of federal drug regulation that the manufacturer bears responsibility for the content of its label at all times. It is charged both with crafting an adequate label and with ensuring that its warnings remain adequate as long as the drug is on the market."[24] For example, a sponsor must include "the most clinically significant information" related to a drug's indications and use.[25] This includes "information that would affect decisions about whether to prescribe a drug, recommendations for patient monitoring that are critical to safe use of the drug, and measures that can be taken to prevent or mitigate harm."[26] As such, pharmacovigilance can create obligations to update product labels.

5.2.2 Big Data and Pharmacovigilance

Pharmacovigilance involves "the science and activities relating to the detection, assessment, understanding and prevention of adverse effects or any other drug-related problem."[27] The fundamental goal of pharmacovigilance is "identifying adverse events and understanding, to the extent possible, their nature, frequency, and potential risk factors."[28] Notwithstanding the importance of pharmacovigilance, the FDA faces several challenges in adverse-event reporting, which include missing information, underreporting of information, and the timeliness of reporting.[29] Indeed, studies estimate that only 10 percent of serious adverse events are reported to the FDA.[30] The agency is working to address these challenges – for example, by

---

[21] 21 C.F.R. § 201.57 (2016).
[22] *Wyeth v. Levine*, 555 U.S. 555, 568 (2009).
[23] Ibid., at 569.
[24] Ibid., at 570–71.
[25] 21 C.F.R. § 201.57(a)(10).
[26] Ibid.
[27] World Health Organization, *Medicines and Health Products, Pharmacovigilance* (2016).
[28] FDA, *Guidance: Pharmacovigilance*, at 4.
[29] Hesha J. Duggirala et al., Use of Data Mining at the Food and Drug Administration, 23 *J. Am. Med. Inform. Assoc.* 428, 432 (2016).
[30] R. Harpaz et al., Combing Signals from Spontaneous Reports and Electronic Health Records for Detection of Adverse Drug Reactions, 20 *J. Am. Med. Inform. Assoc.* 413, 414 (2013).

including more data (e.g., from EHRs, mobile devices, and social media) and by examining how best to evaluate the utility of data sources.[31] Incorporation of relevant data into the postmarket surveillance regime can facilitate earlier detection of material information related to safety and efficacy of marketed products.[32]

Data mining of patient registries, EHRs, or adverse-event databases also can facilitate the identification of rare or latent adverse events, and can be "especially useful for assessing patterns, time trends, and events associated with drug-drug interactions."[33] One of the primary tools for pharmacovigilance involves use of signal-detection algorithms (SDAs), which monitor statistical associations between medical products and adverse events.[34]

The consensus view is that SDAs are valuable, yet "their performance characteristics are not well understood."[35] Although there are some guidelines for evaluating SDAs, there is variation in the quality of SDAs and the ability of an SDA to produce clinically meaningful information.[36] SDA queries must balance sensitivity and specificity – that is, queries must be structured to be sensitive enough to pick up relevant information but also specific enough to have predictive value (e.g., trying to minimize false positives or false negatives).[37]

The FDA employs several SDAs and data-mining techniques. These include (1) disproportionality methods, which compare observed information with expected information, (2) change-point analysis, which examines the slope or variability of adverse events in large databases, (3) text mining, which evaluates unstructured data (such as narratives and descriptions), and (4) disproportionality analysis of published literature, whereby adverse-event evaluation in publications is compared with data in new drug applications or supplemental applications.[38] Each SDA can help provide signals for further evaluation. In this respect, the FDA's data-mining techniques are hypothesis generating – data mining of adverse-event databases rarely, if ever, can determine whether a causal relationship exists between a product and an adverse event.[39]

To examine whether a causal relationship exists, the signals generated from data mining can be used to create pharmacoepidemiologic studies. Pharmacoepidemiologic studies can take many forms, but each typically is designed to assess risk by including a protocol and control group.[40] As the FDA explains,

---

[31] Duggirala et al., Use of Data Mining, at 432.
[32] Harpaz et al., Combing Signals, at 414.
[33] FDA, *Guidance: Pharmacovigilance*, at 8.
[34] R. Harpaz et al., Performance of Pharmacovigilance Signal-Detection Algorithms for the FDA Adverse Event Reporting System, 93 *Clin. Pharmacol. Ther.* 539 (2013).
[35] Ibid., at 540.
[36] Ibid.
[37] Ibid., at 542.
[38] Duggirala et al., Use of Data Mining, at 428–30.
[39] Ibid.; FDA, *Guidance: Pharmacovigilance*, at 8–9.
[40] Ibid., at 12–13.

"Pharmacoepidemiologic studies can allow for the estimation of the relative risks of an outcome associated with a product and some (for example, cohort studies) can also provide estimates of risk (incidence rate) for an adverse event."[41]

While sponsors may initiate pharmacoepidemiologic studies at any time, they are not obligated to do so absent an FDA requirement or other regulatory obligation. In guidance documents, the FDA indicates that sponsors should conduct pharmacoepidemiologic studies when a new safety signal arises,[42] but the FDA also notes that the guidance constitutes nonbinding recommendations and does not create a legal obligation to conduct the studies.[43] Yet, for rare adverse events (e.g., adverse events that occur 1/2000), pharmacoepidemiologic studies often are the only practical means for assessing risk.[44] Additionally, premarket studies are limited in their ability to identify safety concerns that arise from chronic use of a product, or to identify risk factors for adverse events.[45] Consequently, the signal-generation phase of postmarket research is significant because pharmacoepidemiologic studies typically will not be initiated unless a new safety signal arises.

5.3 DATA MANIPULATION AND THE FALSE CLAIMS ACT

Patients, providers, and payers rely on accurate risk-benefit disclosures to determine whether a medical product constitutes medically necessary treatment. As the World Health Organization (WHO) notes, "Pharmacovigilance and all drug safety issues are relevant for everyone whose life is touched in any way by medical interventions."[46] Insofar as pharmacovigilance facilitates improvements in patient care, public health, and the effective use of health care resources,[47] diligent Big Data analysis is essential. Yet, Big Data analysis also can facilitate nefarious ends, such as the manipulation of data to cause the administration of medically unnecessary treatment. At the same time, Big Data analysis enables the detection of claims that are based on such data manipulation. Here is where the FCA enters the equation.

Historically, the government has invoked a "pay and chase" model for combating healthcare fraud, but this model has failed to capture the overwhelming majority of fraudulent claims.[48] Recently, the government also has employed Big Data analysis (e.g., SDAs and other data-mining techniques) to catch fraudulent claims prior

---

[41] Ibid.
[42] Ibid., at 13; FDA, *Guidance: Postmarketing Studies*, at 6–12.
[43] Ibid., at 1; FDA, *Guidance: Pharmacovigilance*, at 1.
[44] Ibid., at 12–13.
[45] Ibid.
[46] World Health Organization, *The Importance of Pharmacovigilance: Safety Monitoring of Medicinal Products*, 8 (2002).
[47] Ibid., at 4.
[48] See notes 1 and 2 and accompanying text.

to payment.[49] Looking ahead, an integral question is whether the government can leverage algorithmic analysis of Big Data to prosecute and disincentivize fraud, and thus gain valuable ground in addressing the massive exploitation of the public fisc.

5.3.1 *False Claims Act Primer*

The FCA was enacted during the American Civil War, at a time when public coffers were pillaged by opportunistic companies that overbilled the US government or provided the government with worthless products. Examples include "suppliers who sold blind and deaf mules to the military, substituted sand for gunpowder, and packed crates with sawdust in lieu of muskets."[50] Although healthcare fraud was not a key concern in the 1860s, the creation of Medicare and Medicaid in 1965, and the subsequent increase in government spending on healthcare, set the stage for an increase in the use of the FCA as a means of combating healthcare fraud.

Amendments to the FCA in 1986 expanded the government's ability to prosecute false claims – these amendments were enacted, in part, to provide the government with additional tools to prosecute healthcare fraud.[51] While healthcare fraud accounted for 12 percent of FCA suits in 1987, by 1998 the rate had risen to 61 percent.[52] In 2009, further amendments to the FCA broadened the reach of the law, including expanded liability for conspiracies and "reverse" false claims.

FCA liability may attach when any person

1. Knowingly presents, or causes to be presented, a false or fraudulent claim for payment or approval[53];
2. Knowingly makes, uses, or causes to be made or used a false record or statement material to a false or fraudulent claim[54]; or
3. Knowingly makes, uses, or causes to be made or used a false record or statement material to an obligation to pay or transmit money or property to the government or knowingly conceals or knowingly and improperly avoids or decreases an obligation to pay or transmit money or property to the government.[55]

The first two instances are commonly referred to as *direct false claims*[56] and the third as *reverse false claims*.[57] Direct false claims are subdivided into factually false and

---

[49] Agrawal, Testimony on the Use of Data to Stop Medicare Fraud.
[50] Joan H. Krause Twenty-Five Years of Health Law through the Lens of the Civil False Claims Act, 19 *Ann. Health L.* 13 (2010).
[51] Ibid., at 14–16.
[52] Ibid.
[53] 31 U.S.C. § 3729(a)(1)(A) (2009).
[54] 31 U.S.C. § 3729(a)(1)(B) (2009).
[55] 31 U.S.C. § 3729(a)(1)(G) (2009).
[56] See, e.g., *United States ex rel. Wilkins v. United Health Group, Inc.*, 659 F.3d 295, 303–7 (3d Cir. 2011).
[57] See, e.g., *United States v. Caremark, Inc.*, 634 F.3d 808, 814–17 (5th Cir. 2011).

legally false claims, and legally false claims are further subdivided into express false certifications and implied false certifications.[58]

Liability under the FCA is independent of liability for violations of the Food, Drug and Cosmetic Act (FDCA). Furthermore, under the Racketeer Influenced and Corrupt Organizations Act (RICO), third-party payers (e.g., pension funds or health insurance companies) have brought suits against companies that engage in fraudulent conduct that conceals risks material to the payment for, or cost of, medical care.[59] The laws are not mutually exclusive – a fraud can give rise to liability under the FCA, FDCA, RICO, and/or other state or federal laws. While each is a meaningful and necessary legal tool in the fight against healthcare fraud, I focus this chapter on the overlap between data manipulation and the FCA.

5.3.2 Data Manipulation as a Direct False Claim

A handful of courts have considered whether data manipulation can give rise to a direct false claim, and some FCA settlements have included allegations that a defendant manipulated material information related to safety or efficacy. For example, in the government's $3 billion settlement with GlaxoSmithKline (involving Paxil, Avandia, and other drugs) and $2.2 billion settlement with Johnson & Johnson (involving Risperdal and other drugs), defendants were accused of data manipulation and other violations, such as improper off-label marketing.

Of the courts that have directly addressed the issue of data manipulation, inconsistent rulings have resulted. In *United States ex rel. Krahling v. Merck & Co., Inc.*, relator alleged that defendant "omitted, concealed, and adulterated material information" related to the effectiveness of the mumps vaccine.[60] Relator further alleged that defendant knew that the data manipulation "would likely overstate the vaccine's effectiveness" and that defendant "falsified, abandoned, and manipulated" data in order to fraudulently mislead the government into purchasing the vaccine.[61] In ruling on a motion to dismiss, the court held that such data manipulation could constitute a factually false claim (because it was material to the government's purchase of the vaccine) or a legally false claim (because it violated express and implied legal duties to report material information on safety and efficacy).[62] As of this writing, the case was pending, and a ruling on the merits has yet to be reached.

Compare *Krahling* with *United States ex rel. Petratos v. Genentech, Inc.*, in which defendants were alleged to have engaged in a broad scheme to suppress the risks of the cancer drug Avastin.[63] Relator alleged that defendants intentionally used

---

[58] See, e.g., *Universal Health Services*, 136 S. Ct. at 1995–96; *Wilkins*, 659 F.3d at 303–7.
[59] See, e.g., *In re Avandia Mktg., Sales Practices, & Prods. Liab. Litig.*, 804 F.3d 633 (3d Cir. 2015).
[60] 44 F. Supp. 3d 581, 587 (E.D. Pa. 2014).
[61] Ibid., at 587–88.
[62] Ibid., at 592–97.
[63] 141 F. Supp. 3d 311 (D.N.J. 2015).

databases that understated Avastin's risks in order to minimize the financial "business risk" to the company. The district court held that the FCA does not reach fraud that affects physician prescribing because CMS has sole authority to determine whether a drug is medically necessary, and physicians play no role in making this determination.[64] On appeal, the Third Circuit disagreed, arguing that since physicians play a "critical role" in CMS's reimbursement regime, "the claims at issue here are false if Avastin was not 'reasonable and necessary'" for individual patients.[65] However, the court affirmed the dismissal of the case on other grounds, finding that the relator did not adequately plead that the suppressed information was material to the government's decision to pay for the drug.[66] Nonetheless, the Third Circuit made clear that FCA liability may attach when data manipulation leads to overprescribing.

5.3.3 Data Manipulation as a Reverse False Claim

As with data manipulation as a direct false claim, few courts have examined whether data manipulation can give rise to a reverse false claim. In *United States ex rel. Booker v. Pfizer, Inc.*, relator alleged that defendant suppressed safety information and intentionally misled physicians into prescribing various drugs.[67] The court held that the reverse false claim provision of the FCA does not apply in cases where a defendant's obligation to repay money to the government is conditioned on the government's decision to ask for the money. As the court noted, the "mere fact that Pfizer's failure to report *might* result in a fine or penalty is insufficient to establish an 'obligation' to pay the government."[68]

However, in *United States v. Lakeshore Medical Clinic, Ltd.*, the court determined that relator had stated a plausible claim for relief under the FCA, finding that "[i]f the government overpaid ... and defendant intentionally refused to investigate the possibility that it was overpaid, it may have unlawfully avoided an obligation to pay money to the government."[69] Indeed, a reverse false claim may exist where the initial data error was unintentional. In *United States ex rel. Kane v. HealthFirst, Inc.*, the court held that the reverse false claim provision was implicated where a software

---

[64] Ibid., at 320. But see *United States ex rel. Strom v. Scios, Inc.*, 676 F. Supp. 2d 884, 890–91 (N.D. Cal. 2009) (ruling that FCA applies where "[d]efendants' reckless misrepresentation of scientific evidence caused doctors to submit claims for treatment that were not reasonable and necessary, and hence were not eligible for reimbursement under Medicare").
[65] 855 F.3d 481, 487–88 (3d Cir. 2017).
[66] Ibid., at 489–93.
[67] 9 F. Supp. 3d 34, 40 (D. Mass. 2014).
[68] Ibid., at 49 (emphasis in original).
[69] No. 11-CV-00892, 2013 WL 1307013, at *4 (E.D. Wisc. March 28, 2013). See also *United States ex rel. Matheny v. Medco Health Solutions, Inc.*, 671 F.3d 1217, 1229 (11th Cir. 2012) (finding that data manipulation implicates the reverse false claims provision of the FCA when, due to defendants' misrepresentations, "the government was unable to identify and recover excess government payments").

glitch caused hospitals to submit false claims for payment from the government.[70] Once the glitch was discovered, relator provided his superiors with an analysis that revealed that the extent of overbilling was more than that previously disclosed to the government.[71] HealthFirst did not disclose relator's analysis to the government, nor did the company conduct further analysis to examine the extent of overbilling.[72] On these facts, the court held that by "intentionally or recklessly" failing to take the necessary steps to identify the claims affected by the software glitch, HealthFirst violated the reverse false claim provision of the FCA.[73]

5.4 CONCLUSION

Every business day CMS processes, on average, over 4.5 million claims from 1.5 million providers.[74] Although CMS is "applying advanced analytics to claims" and is developing tools that permit evaluation of "claims for episodes of care that span multiple legacy claims processing systems as well as those that span multiple visits over a period of time,"[75] it is difficult for CMS to capture fraudulent claims involving data manipulation where the data might have affected physician prescribing. This is problematic, according to Shantanu Agrawal, deputy administrator and director of the Center for Program Integrity at CMS, because such practices pose grave risks to patients and the public fisc. In testimony before the US House of Representatives, Agrawal indicated that "[b]eneficiaries are at risk when fraudulent providers perform medically unnecessary tests, treatments, procedures, or surgeries, or prescribe dangerous drugs without thorough examinations of medical necessity."[76] Agrawal further testified that preventing fraud helps to ensure that patients obtain "improved access to quality health care."[77]

The statutory language makes clear that liability under the FCA attaches when a party's conduct causes the submission of a false claim.[78] As such, in cases where Big Data tools were used to manipulate material information that caused physicians to prescribe more than they otherwise would have, courts should find that the FCA applies. A similar analysis should apply to manipulation of Big Data and reverse false claims: namely, courts should find that the reverse false claims provision of the FCA applies if a defendant used Big Data tools to conceal an obligation owed to the government.

---

[70] 120 F. Supp. 3d 370, 375–76 (S.D.N.Y. 2015).
[71] Ibid., at 377.
[72] Ibid., at 377–78.
[73] Ibid., at 378.
[74] Goldman, Eliminating Fraud and Abuse.
[75] Agrawal, Testimony on the Use of Data to Stop Medicare Fraud.
[76] Ibid.
[77] Ibid.
[78] 31 U.S.C. § 3729(a)(1).

These conclusions not only are squarely in line with the language and purpose of the FCA, but they also help to ensure that patients do not suffer unnecessarily. Adverse drug reactions are a significant "public health problem accounting for up to 5% of hospital admissions, 28% of emergency department visits, and 5% of hospital deaths."[79] Studies estimate that adverse drug reactions "occur in 30% of hospital stays, causing 2 million injuries, hospitalizations, and deaths each year in the United States at a cost of $75 billion."[80] Data manipulation that conceals risks will harm patients and unnecessarily increase healthcare expenditures.

Insofar as entities engage in black-box decision making that is outside the reach of regulators and the public,[81] whistleblowers can play a unique role in the healthcare industry by bringing fraudulent practices into the public eye and helping to build transparency and accountability into the healthcare system. Applying the FCA to data manipulation will further the public policy goals of improving health outcomes and lowering the cost of healthcare.

---

[79] Mei Liu et al., Comparative Analysis of Pharmacovigilance Methods in the Detection of Adverse Drug Reactions Using Electronic Medical Records, 20 *J. Am. Med. Inform. Assoc.* 420, (2013).

[80] Guan Wang et al., A Method for Systematic Discovery of Adverse Drug Events from Clinical Notes, 22 *J. Am. Med. Inform. Assoc.* 1196 (2015).

[81] Donald Light, *The Risks of Prescription Drugs* 15–17 (2010).

6

Big Data's New Discrimination Threats

Amending the Americans with Disabilities Act to Cover Discrimination Based on Data-Driven Predictions of Future Disease

Sharona Hoffman*

6.1 INTRODUCTION

While Big Data holds great promise to improve the human condition, it also creates new and previously unimaginable opportunities for discrimination. Employers, financial institutions, marketers, educational institutions, and others can now easily obtain a wealth of Big Data about individuals' health status and use it to make adverse decisions relating to data subjects.[1]

The Americans with Disabilities Act (ADA) is a federal law that prohibits employers and other public and private entities from discriminating against individuals because of their disabilities.[2] This chapter argues that in the era of Big Data, the ADA does not go far enough. While the ADA protects individuals who have existing disabilities or records of past disabilities or are regarded as having mental or physical impairments, it does not reach people who are currently healthy but are perceived as being at high risk of becoming sick in the future. This is a gap that should not be ignored at a time when decision makers have many newly available data tools that enable them to make predictions about medical problems that individuals will face in later years.

This chapter recommends that the ADA be amended to expand its antidiscrimination mandate. Specifically, the statute should (1) prohibit discrimination based on predictions of future physical or mental impairments and (2) require covered entities to disclose in writing their use of Big Data or other nontraditional means to obtain health-related information.[3]

---

* This chapter is based in part on Big Data and the Americans with Disabilities Act, 68 *Hastings L. J.* 777 (2017).
[1] Sharona Hoffman, Citizen Science: The Law and Ethics of Public Access to Medical Big Data, 30 *Berkeley Tech. L. J.* 1741, 1773–80 (2015); Executive Office of the President, Big Data: Seizing Opportunities, Preserving Values 51–53 (2014).
[2] Americans with Disabilities Act of 1990. Pub. L. No. 101-336 (codified primarily in 42 U.S.C. §§ 12101–12213).
[3] Nontraditional means are means other than medical examinations or inquiries.

6.2 WHO MIGHT BE INTERESTED IN MEDICAL BIG DATA?

A number of parties are likely to have an interest in individuals' predictive health data. Among them are employers, financial institutions, marketers, and educational institutions.

First and foremost, employers are highly motivated to hire the healthiest possible employees. Employers hope to avoid absenteeism problems, productivity problems, and most important, high healthcare and health insurance costs. Some employers already reject candidates who are obese or smoke because of anticipated health problems.[4] Consequently, employers will likely be keen to obtain further information that will allow them to determine which applicants and employees will develop serious illnesses in the future for purposes of employment decisions.

Likewise, financial institutions are eager to collect information about individuals who seek their services. Banks routinely maintain databases with data about customers who previously overdrew their accounts or bounced checks.[5] In the future, if it is easily available, financial institutions may well add health information to their databases to improve their ability to screen out applicants with a high risk of defaulting on loans because of medical difficulties.

Marketers and advertisers have a similar interest in individuals' health data. The more they know about potential customers, the more accurately they can tailor their materials to appeal to particular consumers or determine who should and who should not receive various offers.[6] A 2014 Presidential Report explained marketers' pricing practices as follows:

> [S]ome ... retailers were found to be using an algorithm that generated different discounts for the same product to people based on where they believed the customer was located. While it may be that the price differences were driven by the lack of competition in certain neighborhoods, in practice, people in higher-income areas received higher discounts than people in lower-income areas.[7]

Similarly, individuals who are perceived as being at high risk of imminent illness may not receive generous promotional offers because marketers will assume that they will not be devoted customers and big spenders in the long term. Retailers have developed considerable skill in collecting and analyzing health-related data, as

---

[4] Jessica L. Roberts, Healthism and the Law of Employment Discrimination, 99 *Iowa L. Rev.* 571, 577–79 (2014).
[5] Jessica Silver-Greenberg & Michael Corkery, Bank Account Screening Tool Is Scrutinized as Excessive, *New York Times*, June 15, 2014, available at http://dealbook.nytimes.com/2014/06/15/bank-account-screening-tool-is-scrutinized-as-excessive [https://perma.cc/ZP7K-AA9Y].
[6] Lori Andrews, Facebook Is Using You, *New York Times*, February 4, 2012, available at www.nytimes.com/2012/02/05/opinion/sunday/facebook-is-using-you.html [https://perma.cc/4C8Q-XPGS].
[7] Executive Office of the President, Big Data, at 46–47.

demonstrated by a 2012 *Forbes* magazine article entitled, "How Target Figured Out a Teen Girl Was Pregnant Before Her Father Did."[8]

It is even possible that financially focused educational institutions would be interested in Big Data medical information about applicants. Universities hope to enroll students who will become successful professionals, bring honor to the school, and donate generously for many years. Therefore, applicants who are likely to have abbreviated careers and limited earnings because of medical challenges may be unappealing prospects to some institutions of higher learning.

6.3 THE MANY SOURCES OF HEALTH-RELATED BIG DATA

Employers, financial institutions, marketers, universities, and others may obtain health-related Big Data from myriad sources. By "health-related Big Data," I mean both specifically medical data and other types of data from which analysts may infer information about individuals' health. Several data sources are discussed next.

6.3.1 *Social Media*

Facebook, Twitter, Instagram, and other social media platforms provide a treasure trove of information, including medical data, for interested parties. Many users post personal and sensitive details about themselves and are not scrupulous about their privacy settings.

An online article entitled, "How Social Media Strengthens Your Loan Application," informs borrowers that a "growing number of lenders – mostly online lenders – are using social media as part of their loan underwriting process."[9] A different article entitled, "Lots More College Admissions Officers Are Checking Your Instagram and Facebook," cautions the public that "fully 40 percent of admissions officers say they visit applicants' social media pages to learn about them."[10]

Employers are particularly notorious in this regard. According to CareerBuilder's annual social media recruitment survey of more than 2,000 hiring managers, 60 percent of employers acknowledged that they read job candidates' social

---

[8] Kashmir Hill, How Target Figured Out a Teen Girl Was Pregnant before Her Father Did, *Forbes*, February 16, 2012, available at www.forbes.com/sites/kashmirhill/2012/02/16/how-target-figured-out-a-teen-girl-was-pregnant-before-her-father-did/#29525f3e6668 [https://perma.cc/D6TG-PKWT] (discussing Target's practice of data mining its customers' purchasing records in order "to figure out what you like, what you need, and which coupons are most likely to make you happy").

[9] Rieva Lesonsky, How Social Media Strengthens Your Loan Application, Funderaledger, July 13, 2015, available at www.fundera.com/blog/2015/07/13/how-social-media-strengthens-your-loan-application.

[10] Kaitlin Mulhere, Lots More College Admissions Officers Are Checking Your Instagram and Facebook, *Time*, January 13, 2016, available at http://time.com/money/4179392/college-applications-social-media/ [https://perma.cc/KV38-MYE9].

networking sites in the process of assessing them.[11] Moreover, employers do in fact base adverse decisions on information they discover on social media.[12] For example, one employer terminated an employee for abusing his leave time after finding photos that the worker posted from vacations he took while on medical leave following shoulder surgery.[13]

6.3.2 Wellness Programs

Wellness programs are increasingly popular among employers who hope to improve employees' health and thereby save healthcare costs.[14] According to the Kaiser Family Foundation, in 2016, 83 percent of firms with 200 or more workers that offered health benefits had some type of wellness program.[15] These programs routinely require participants to disclose details about their health either directly to employers or to wellness vendors, who may share certain information with employers and enable them to make adverse decisions about applicants and employees.[16]

6.3.3 Data Brokers

A growing industry of data brokers is operating in the United States, collecting personal information from a variety of public and private sources and selling them to interested parties.[17] Data brokers mine sources such as social media, personal

---

[11] CareerBuilder, Number of Employers Using Social Media to Screen Candidates Has Increased 500 Percent over the Last Decade, April 28, 2016, available at www.careerbuilder.com/share/aboutus/pressreleasesdetail.aspx?sd=4/28/2016&siteid=cbpr&sc_cmp1=cb_pr945_&id=pr945&ed=12/31/2016 [https://perma.cc/DLH8-Z7V7].

[12] Steven L. Thomas et al., Social Networking, Management Responsibilities, and Employee Rights: The Evolving Role of Social Networking in Employment Decisions, 27 *Emp. Resps. Rts. J.* 307 (2015).

[13] *Jones v. Gulf Coast Health Care of Del., LLC*, No. 8:15-CV-T-24EAJ, 2016 WL 659308 (M.D. Fla. Feb. 18, 2016).

[14] Reed Abelson, Employee Wellness Programs Use Carrots, and Increasingly, Sticks, *New York Times*, January 24, 2016, available at www.nytimes.com/2016/01/25/business/employee-wellness-programs-use-carrots-and-increasingly-sticks.html?_r=0 [https://perma.cc/K7Z9-F9QJ].

[15] Kaiser Family Foundation, *2016 Employer Health Benefits Survey*, September 14, 2016, available at http://kff.org/report-section/ehbs-2016-summary-of-findings/ [https://perma.cc/6HAL-7A6J].

[16] Jay Hancock, Workplace Wellness Programs Put Employee Privacy at Risk, CNN, October 2, 2015, available at www.cnn.com/2015/09/28/health/workplace-wellness-privacy-risk-exclusive/ [https://perma.cc/X3RC-CRST]; Rachel Emma Silverman, Bosses Tap Outside Firms to Predict Which Workers Might Get Sick, *Wall Street Journal*, February 17, 2016, available at www.wsj.com/articles/bosses-harness-big-data-to-predict-which-workers-might-get-sick-1455664940 [https://perma.cc/Q7SA-ZZRP]; How to Set Up a Wellness Plan, *Wall Street Journal*, September 12, 2008, available at http://guides.wsj.com/small-business/hiring-and-managing-employees/how-to-set-up-a-wellness-plan/tab/print/ [https://perma.cc/SK22-NAKJ].

[17] Brian Naylor, Firms Are Buying, Sharing Your Online Info. What Can You Do About It?, NPR, July 11, 2016, available at www.npr.org/sections/alltechconsidered/2016/07/11/485571291/firms-are-buying-sharing-your-online-info-what-can-you-do-about-it [https://perma.cc/C5SX-4YSE].

websites, US Census records, state hospital records, retailers' purchasing records, real property records, insurance claims, and more.[18] They are known to sell lists of people with sexually transmitted diseases, Alzheimer's disease, dementia, AIDS, depression, and other ailments.[19] By some estimates, several thousand data brokers already exist, including well-known companies such as Spokeo and Axciom.[20]

Lenders turn to data brokers to purchase information that identifies financially distressed consumers.[21] Likewise, marketers commonly use the services of data brokers. For example, according to one source, each year, "Pfizer spends $12 million to buy health data from a variety of sources."[22]

Employers too have not shied away from the offerings of data brokers. Walmart reportedly hired a company called Castlight to identify workers with back problems and those who are likely to become pregnant, purportedly in order to give them advice about good healthcare.[23] It takes little imagination, however, to conclude that employers could also use such information for discriminatory purposes.

6.3.4 Open Data Sources

The federal government, state governments, and private-sector entities have established numerous large databases that offer the public access to patient-related health information.[24] For instance, the Centers for Disease Control and Prevention's CDC WONDER allows users to search for a broad range of health information. Thus one

---

[18] Gary Anthes, Data Brokers Are Watching You, 58 *Communications of the ACM* 28, 28–30 (2015), available at http://cacm.acm.org/magazines/2015/1/181629-data-brokers-are-watching-you/fulltext [https://perma.cc/QFJ9–3VZ9].

[19] Frank Pasquale, The Dark Market for Personal Data, *New York Times*, October 16, 2014, available at www.nytimes.com/2014/10/17/opinion/the-dark-market-for-personal-data.html?_r=0 [https://perma.cc/PYS3-TRSZ].

[20] Ibid.; Paul Boutin, The Secretive World of Data Brokers, *Newsweek*, May 30, 2016, available at www.newsweek.com/secretive-world-selling-data-about-you-464789 [https://perma.cc/9CGH-PV3F]; Spokeo, available at www.spokeo.com/?g=name_gs_C000213&gclid=CK6I70WG-MoCFYsAaQod2moCkQ [https://perma.cc/H96Z-6EU4] (last visited July 4, 2016); Acxiom, available at www.acxiom.com/ [https://perma.cc/NST7-ZB6Y] (last visited July 4, 2016).

[21] Stephanie Armour, Data Brokers Come under Fresh Scrutiny: Consumer Profiles Marketed to Lenders, *Wall Street Journal*, February 12, 2014, available at www.wsj.com/articles/SB10001424052702303874504579377164099831516 [https://perma.cc/HS5X-M7HQ].

[22] Adam Tanner, How Data Brokers Make Money Off Your Medical Records, *Sci. Am.*, February 1, 2016, available at www.scientificamerican.com/article/how-data-brokers-make-money-off-your-medical-records/ [https://perma.cc/95QK-2RBL].

[23] Rachel Emma Silverman, Bosses Tap Outside Firms to Predict Which Workers Might Get Sick, *Wall Street Journal*, February 17, 2016, available at www.wsj.com/articles/bosses-harness-big-data-to-predict-which-workers-might-get-sick-1455664940 [https://perma.cc/P2CZ-Q8G3]; Aimee Picchi, The "Big Data" App That Predicts Employees' Health, CBS News, February 18, 2016, available at www.cbsnews.com/news/the-big-data-app-that-predicts-employees-health/ [https://perma.cc/3NVM-TZZK].

[24] Hoffman, Citizen Science, at 1748–54.

can search for cancer incidence by "year, state, metropolitan area, age group, race, ethnicity, gender, childhood cancers and cancer site classifications."[25]

Similar data can be garnered from the Healthcare Cost and Utilization Project (HCUP) databases. These offer "a core set of clinical and nonclinical information found in a typical [hospital] discharge abstract, including all listed diagnoses and procedures, discharge status, patient demographics, and charges for all patients."[26]

Employers, lenders, and others may use these demographic and other data to create profiles of individuals who are particularly vulnerable to certain diseases such as cancer. They then may make adverse decisions concerning people that fit those profiles.

6.3.5 What about Privacy Protections?

One might wonder why so much health information is widely available despite the existence of the Health Insurance Portability and Accountability Act (HIPAA) Privacy Rule. The answer is that the HIPAA Privacy Rule is limited in its reach. It covers only healthcare providers, insurers, healthcare clearinghouses, and their business associates.[27] Therefore, many of those who produce and handle medical Big Data, including social media operators, wellness vendors, data miners, and government entities, are not governed by HIPAA.

In addition, the HIPAA Privacy Rule protects only "individually identifiable health information."[28] The rule therefore does not govern deidentified data,[29] and many Big Data sources are deidentified at least to some extent.[30] Finally, it covers only "protected health information," and thus nonmedical data that are used to make health predictions or determinations are exempted from the regulations.[31] Consequently, the HIPAA Privacy Rule does not significantly infringe on the Big Data market.

---

[25] Centers for Disease Control and Prevention, United States Cancer Statistics Public Information Data, available at https://wonder.cdc.gov/cancer.html [https://perma.cc/M3WB-8JPX] (last visited August 15, 2016).

[26] Agency for Healthcare Research and Quality, Databases and Related Tools from HCUP: Fact Sheet, available at http://archive.ahrq.gov/research/findings/factsheets/tools/hcupdata/datahcup.html [https://perma.cc/8L4M-W7RY] (last visited February 2, 2017).

[27] 45 C.F.R. §§ 160.102–160.103 (2016); 42 U.S.C. § 17934 (2010).

[28] 45 C.F.R. § 160.103 (2016).

[29] See 45 C.F.R. § 164.514(b) (2016) for details regarding deidentification.

[30] Tanner, How Data Brokers Make Money (stating that "data brokers are not restricted by medical privacy rules in the US, because their records are designed to be anonymous – containing only year of birth, gender, partial zip code and doctor's name"); Jay Hancock, Workplace Wellness Programs Put Employee Privacy at Risk, CNN, October 2, 2015, available at www.cnn.com/2015/09/28/health/workplace-wellness-privacy-risk-exclusive/ [https://perma.cc/DX5P-8X8W] (explaining that "HIPAA [does not] protect the de-identified health information that wellness providers routinely share with employers and other, unidentified outside parties ... includ[ing] blood pressure, cholesterol, drug use and disease history").

[31] 45 C.F.R. § 160.103 (2016) (defining protected health information).

6.4 HEALTH-RELATED BIG DATA AND DISEASE PREDICTION

Big Data is useful to employers, lenders, educators, marketers, and others because it can enable them to make predictions about individuals' future health status. Increasingly, scientists are recognizing that particular behaviors or traits render individuals vulnerable to future ailments.[32] The most obvious example is smoking, which is associated with risks of various cancers, heart disease, stroke, and other serious conditions.[33] Alcoholism is associated with impairments of the heart, liver, pancreas, and other systems.[34] Women who never bore children or have their first child when they are older than age thirty are at increased risk of breast and ovarian cancers.[35]

Medical researchers are also pursuing biomarkers that can help them identify disease risks. A "biomarker" is a "biological molecule found in blood, other body fluids, or tissues that is a sign of a normal or abnormal process, or of a condition or disease."[36] For example, in a study published in 2014, researchers determined that people with lower levels of ten phospholipids in their blood were more likely than others to be suffering from cognitive impairments either at the time of the blood draw or within a few years.[37]

Emerging science further enables researchers to use data algorithms to predict certain diseases before the patient becomes symptomatic.[38] Researchers have

---

[32] Francie Diep, How to Predict a Lifetime of Diseases, *Popular Science*, June 24, 2014, available at www.popsci.com/article/science/how-predict-lifetime-diseases. [https://perma.cc/TN9Q-3GZ4]

[33] National Heart, Lung, and Blood Institute, What Are the Risks of Smoking?, available at www.nhlbi.nih.gov/health/health-topics/topics/smo/risks [https://perma.cc/GKE7-9VSL] (last visited July 4, 2016); National Cancer Institute, Harms of Cigarette Smoking and Health Benefits of Quitting, available at www.cancer.gov/about-cancer/causes-prevention/risk/tobacco/cessation-fact-sheet [https://perma.cc/24KW-6H9E] (last visited July 4, 2016).

[34] National Institute on Alcohol Abuse and Alcoholism, Alcohol's Effects on the Body, available at www.niaaa.nih.gov/alcohol-health/alcohols-effects-body [https://perma.cc/HQF4-SP6Y] (last visited July 4, 2016).

[35] National Cancer Institute, Reproductive History and Breast Cancer Risk, available at www.cancer.gov/about-cancer/causes-prevention/risk/hormones/reproductive-history-fact-sheet [https://perma.cc/2FM5-BW2A] (last visited July 4, 2016); American Cancer Society, What Are the Risk Factors for Ovarian Cancer? (2016), available at www.cancer.org/cancer/ovariancancer/detailedguide/ovarian-cancer-risk-factors [https://perma.cc/QU7C-58TA]; American Cancer Society, What Are the Risk Factors for Breast Cancer? (2016), available at www.cancer.org/cancer/breastcancer/detailedguide/breast-cancer-risk-factors [https://perma.cc/2JBP-NHPW].

[36] National Cancer Institute, NCI *Dictionary of Cancer Terms*, available at www.cancer.gov/publications/dictionaries/cancer-terms?cdrid=45618 [https://perma.cc/GG4K-HMW8] (last visited July 4, 2016).

[37] Alison Abbott, Biomarkers Could Predict Alzheimer's before It Starts, *Nature*, March 9, 2014, available at www.nature.com/news/biomarkers-could-predict-alzheimer-s-before-it-starts-1.14834 [https://perma.cc/53TH-AVMV].

[38] Mohana Ravindranath, IBM Used Predictive Analytics to Find Patients at Risk of Heart Failure, *Washington Post*, February 20, 2014, available at www.washingtonpost.com/business/on-it/ibm-used-predictive-analytics-to-find-patients-at-risk-of-heart-failure/2014/02/20/9b0ddb3c-9a47-11e3-b88d-f36c07223d88_story.html [https://perma.cc/DH2M-8WVJ].

published algorithms used to predict clinical depression, diabetes, and heart failure based on patients' medical record data, insurance claims, and other sources.[39]

Researchers are becoming ever more creative in excavating data sources in order to discover health predictors. The *Wall Street Journal* reported findings that bicycle shop customers are generally in good health and midterm election voters are healthier than their nonvoting counterparts.[40] By contrast, individuals with low credit scores are in poorer health than others because they are less likely to fill prescriptions and get follow-up care.[41]

If employers, lenders, marketers, educators, or others obtain predictive health information about individuals, they will likely be sorely tempted to use the data for decision-making purposes. It is known that some employers already reject candidates who are obese or smoke because of anticipated health problems.[42] In the future, entities might disqualify applicants because of a variety of traits or behaviors (e.g., sleeping, exercise, and purchasing habits) that are believed to forecast future medical ailments.

6.5 THE AMERICANS WITH DISABILITIES ACT (ADA)

The ADA prohibits disability-based discrimination. Title I of the statute applies to employers, Title II relates to public services, and Title III governs "public accommodations and services provided by private entities."[43] The antidiscrimination mandate is straightforward. For example, Title III provides that "[n]o individual shall be discriminated against on the basis of disability in the full and equal enjoyment of the goods, services, facilities, privileges, advantages, or accommodations of any place of public accommodation by any person who owns, leases (or leases to), or operates a place of public accommodation."[44] Such discrimination

---

[39] Arthur Allen, Big Brother Is Watching Your Waist, *Politico*, July 21, 2014, available at www.politico.com/story/2014/07/data-mining-health-care-109153 [https://perma.cc/LN7Z-KT33]; IBM, IBM Predictive Analytics to Detect Patients at Risk for Heart Failure, IBM News Release, February, 19, 2014, available at http://www-03.ibm.com/press/us/en/pressrelease/43231.wss [https://perma.cc/C9ZC-5KFP]; Susan H. Babey et al., Prediabetes in California: Nearly Half of California Adults on Path to Diabetes, UCLA Center for Health Policy Research Health Policy Brief (March 2016), available at http://healthpolicy.ucla.edu/publications/Documents/PDF/2016/prediabetes-brief-mar2016.pdf [https://perma.cc/G3YL-FNBR] (using data from the National Health and Nutrition Examination Survey).

[40] Rachel Emma Silverman, Bosses Tap Outside Firms to Predict Which Workers Might Get Sick, *Wall Street Journal*, February 17, 2016, available at www.wsj.com/articles/bosses-harness-big-data-to-predict-which-workers-might-get-sick-1455664940 [https://perma.cc/2H9Z-5CTW].

[41] Ibid.

[42] Jessica L. Roberts, Healthism and the Law of Employment Discrimination, 99 *Iowa L. Rev.* 571, 577–79 (2014).

[43] 42 U.S.C. §§ 12111–89 (2010).

[44] 42 U.S.C. § 12182 (2010). Title III "public accommodations" include banks, insurance offices, private educational institutions, sales establishments, service establishments, and many other private entities. 42 U.S.C. § 12181(7). Note that public colleges and universities are covered

includes "the imposition or application of eligibility criteria that screen out or tend to screen out" individuals with disabilities.[45]

The question of what does and does not constitute a disability is a more complicated matter. The term "disability" is defined as "(A) a physical or mental impairment that substantially limits one or more major life activities of such individual; (B) a record of such an impairment; or (C) being regarded as having such an impairment."[46]

This definition is quite broad in scope. Individuals can be covered by the ADA even if they do not have existing disabling conditions. They are covered so long as they have records of past disabilities or are wrongly perceived as having disabilities. Moreover, individuals are covered under the statute's "regarded as" provision as long as they have any mental or physical impairment that is not "transitory and minor."[47] For purposes of the "regarded as" provision, impairments do not need to substantially limit a major life activity, and thus they need not be severe enough to be considered disabilities.[48]

Nevertheless, in the era of Big Data, the definition of disability is not broad enough. This is because the ADA does not reach predictions of future disabilities. It does not forbid discrimination against individuals who have never had disabilities and are not perceived as having existing impairments but are deemed to be at risk of being unhealthy later in life.[49] Consequently, the ADA does not stop decision makers from basing determinations on concern that individuals will become ill in the future because of their health habits, stress levels, exposure to environmental pollutants, or a multitude of other hazards.

Note that the Genetic Information Nondiscrimination Act (GINA) prohibits employers and health insurers (but not others) from discriminating based on genetic information.[50] Thus employers and health insurers cannot legally seek genetic data about individuals, including family health histories.[51] They also cannot lawfully make adverse decisions based on findings of genetic abnormalities or family

---

under Title II, which applies to public services. 42 U.S.C. § 12131 (defining a "public entity" as including any instrumentality of a state or local government).

[45] 42 U.S.C. § 12182(b)(2)(A)(i) (2010). Such eligibility criteria are not unlawfully discriminatory if they "can be shown to be necessary for the provision of the goods, services, facilities, privileges, advantages, or accommodations being offered."

[46] 42 U.S.C. § 12102 (2010).

[47] 42 U.S.C. § 12102(3)(B) (2010). "Transitory impairments" are defined as those "with an actual or expected duration of 6 months or less," such as a broken leg or influenza.

[48] 42 U.S.C. § 12102(3)(A) (2010).

[49] Ibid.

[50] Genetic Information Non-Discrimination Act, Pub. L. No. 110–233, 122 Stat. 881 §§ 201(4) & 202(a) (2008); 29 U.S.C. § 1182 (2010); 42 U.S.C. § 2000ff-1(a) (2010). "Genetic information" is defined as including (i) an individual's genetic tests, (ii) the genetic tests of an individual's family members, and (iii) the manifestation of a disease or disorder in an individual's family members. 42 U.S.C. §§ 2000ff(4)(A) (2010).

[51] 29 U.S.C. § 1182 (c) & (d) (2010); 42 U.S.C. § 2000ff-1(b) (2010).

histories that indicate susceptibility to diseases that could manifest later in life.[52] However, GINA's sole focus is genetic information, and it does not reach any other predictive data.

Other laws also forbid disability-based discrimination. For example, the Rehabilitation Act of 1973 prohibits federal-sector employers and "any program receiving federal financial assistance" from discriminating against individuals because of their disabilities.[53] Such programs include colleges and universities that receive direct federal financial assistance or even indirect assistance in the form of federal financial aid for their students.[54] Almost all states have also adopted statutory antidiscrimination in employment mandates that include disability as a protected classification.[55]

The definition of "individual with a disability" in these laws, however, is generally similar to the ADA's definition of the term. No law covers individuals who are currently healthy but are regarded as being vulnerable to illness in the future.[56]

6.6 RECOMMENDATIONS

The ADA and other disability rights laws should be amended to respond to emerging discrimination threats in the era of Big Data. Specifically, the laws should account for the likelihood that third parties will obtain information that will enable them to make predictions about data subjects' future health status and to discriminate based on these data. For the sake of brevity, I will focus on the ADA in this section, but all antidiscrimination laws could follow the model I propose.

6.6.1 Expanding the "Regarded As" Provision

The easiest fix would be to amend the ADA's "regarded as" provision.[57] The provision should be broadened to cover individuals who are perceived as likely to

---

[52] 29 U.S.C. § 1182 (a) & (b) (2010); 42 U.S.C. § 2000ff-1(a) (2010).
[53] 29 U.S.C. §§ 791 and 794(a) (2010).
[54] Disability Rights California, Rights of Students with Disabilities in Higher Education, July 2013, available at www.disabilityrightsca.org/pubs/530901.pdf [https://perma.cc/ZBT8-8LNL].
[55] National Conference of State Legislatures, State Laws on Employment-Related Discrimination, July 2015, available at www.ncsl.org/documents/employ/Discrimination-Chart-2015.pdf [https://perma.cc/G4ES-XMAV].
[56] 29 U.S.C. § 705(20)(B) (2010) (referring to the ADA's definition); Georgetown Law, Chart Comparing State Definitions of Disability, available at www.law.georgetown.edu/archiveada/documents/statebystatechart–updated.pdf [https://perma.cc/5YYV-FMJX]; see. e.g., *Ohio Rev. Code Ann.* § 4112.01 (West) (defining "disability" as "a physical or mental impairment that substantially limits one or more major life activities, including the functions of caring for one's self, performing manual tasks, walking, seeing, hearing, speaking, breathing, learning, and working; a record of a physical or mental impairment; or being regarded as having a physical or mental impairment").
[57] 42 U.S.C. §§ 12102(1)(C) and (3) (2010).

develop physical or mental impairments in the future. Thus the law would reach not only people who are considered to be currently impaired but also those who are thought to be at risk of impairment in later years based on information about their habits, purchases, biomarkers, or other indicators. As is generally true in "regarded as" cases, a plaintiff should not have to establish that the decision maker believed that he or she would develop a condition that rises to the level of a disability. Instead, plaintiffs should have to prove only that decision makers were worried about future nontransitory physical or mental impairments.[58]

Opponents might object that the proposed change would expand the ADA to reach all Americans rather than to protect a "discrete and insular minority."[59] One of the traditional justifications for antidiscrimination laws is that they cover only specific, well-defined vulnerable populations, and extending coverage to any worker who might be subject to data mining would be a departure from this approach. In truth, however, the ADA's existing "regarded as" provision is already expansive and covers anyone and everyone who is incorrectly perceived as disabled, including those who are perfectly healthy.[60] Thus Congress did not intend the ADA's target population to be narrow in scope.

Moreover, the ADA's broad coverage would be consistent with that of many other federal antidiscrimination laws.[61] Title VII of the Civil Rights Act of 1964 covers anyone who suffers discrimination based on race, color, religion, sex, or national origin, including males and whites.[62] The Equal Pay Act prohibits sex-based wage discrimination against both men and women.[63] Likewise, GINA protects all individuals against discrimination based on genetic information.[64] This includes individuals who are perfectly healthy but who are believed to be at risk of future ailments because of genetic abnormalities. Thus GINA already embraces the approach that I propose in this chapter, and the suggested ADA modification would bring the two statutes into better alignment.

Expanding the "regarded as" prong of the ADA's definition of "disability" is also consistent with the statute's central mission. The ADA declares that its purpose is "to provide a clear and comprehensive national mandate for the elimination of discrimination against individuals with disabilities."[65] Moreover, the "regarded as" provision

---

[58] See note 56 and accompanying text.
[59] See Sharona Hoffman, The Importance of Immutability, 52 Wm. Mary L. Rev. 1483, 1500–4 (2011) (critiquing the theory that employment discrimination laws are designed to protect discrete and insular minorities).
[60] See notes 56 and 57 and accompanying text.
[61] The only federal antidiscrimination in employment law that explicitly limits its protected class is the Age Discrimination in Employment Act, which covers only individuals who are age forty or older. 29 U.S.C. § 631(a) (2010).
[62] 42 U.S.C. § 2000e-2 (2010).
[63] 29 U.S.C. § 206(d)(1) (2010).
[64] 42 U.S.C. § 2000ff-4(a) (2010).
[65] 42 U.S.C. § 12101(b)(1) (2010).

intends to combat "myths, fears, and stereotypes associated with disabilities."[66] The law was enacted in 1990, long before the emergence of the Big Data phenomenon. Today, individuals' health vulnerabilities can increasingly be detected before their disabilities become apparent, and discrimination based on predictive data is just as pernicious as discrimination based on existing symptoms. Data analysis practices that enable health status projections can fuel and exacerbate "myths, fears, and stereotypes" about disabilities. Consequently, extending the ADA's reach is both logical and necessary.

6.6.2 *Disclosing Data-Mining Practices*

Standing alone, language prohibiting discrimination based on predictions of future impairments may not provide adequate protection. This is so because data subjects may never discover that employers, lenders, educators, or anyone else used data mining or data broker services to collect predictive information about them and therefore will have no evidence with which to establish discrimination cases.

In order to provide meaningful protection, the ADA will need to include disclosure requirements for Big Data use. Title I of the ADA has a section that governs how and when employers can obtain medical information about workers.[67] The provision should be revised to instruct employers that they must inform applicants and employees in writing if they intend to obtain health-related data about them by any means other than traditional medical examinations and inquiries. In Title III, a similar disclosure requirement could be added after the statement that discrimination includes "the imposition or application of eligibility criteria that screen out or tend to screen out an individual with a disability."[68] Title II of the ADA would require the addition of a separate provision to address the use of predictive data or should reference the provision in another title.

6.7 CONCLUSION

In today's data-driven world, employers, lenders, marketers, educators, and many others are able to obtain a bounty of health-related information about individuals. These parties may then use data to identify those with future health risks and make adverse decisions concerning them. This chapter has argued that legislators must respond to the availability of new data tools. It does not suggest that the use of Big Data be banned altogether. Instead, legislators should amend the ADA (and other

---

[66] Risa M. Mish, "Regarded as Disabled" Claims under the ADA: Safety Net or Catch-All?, 1 U. Pa. J. Lab. Emp. L. 159, 160 (1998) [quoting *School Board of Nassau County v. Arline*, 480 U.S. 273, 279 (1987) (discussing the Rehabilitation Act's "regarded as" provision)].
[67] 42 U.S.C. § 12112(d) (2010).
[68] 42 U.S.C. § 12182(b)(2)(A)(i) (2010).

antidiscrimination laws) to prohibit discrimination based on predictive health information and to require disclosure of Big Data use to data subjects.

These requirements should not open the floodgates of litigation. In order to prevail, plaintiffs would need to show that (1) decision makers engaged in data mining or sought information from data brokers, (2) they discovered health-predictive information, and (3) they based an adverse decision on those data. Doing so may prove extremely difficult, if not impossible, for many plaintiffs. Therefore, attorneys are not likely to pursue weak cases.

The great hope of the antidiscrimination statutes is that the vast majority of covered entities are law abiding and will voluntarily comply with regulatory mandates. The proposed approach aligns the law with new technology and provides the public with much-needed protection.

7

Who's Left Out of Big Data?

How Big Data Collection, Analysis, and Use Neglect Populations Most in Need of Medical and Public Health Research and Interventions

Sarah E. Malanga, Jonathan D. Loe, Christopher T. Robertson, and Kenneth S. Ramos

7.1 INTRODUCTION

Scholars and commentators, including many of those found in this book, have expressed concern that Big Data may be getting too big because too much of our lives is being tracked, captured, and analyzed, sometimes without our knowledge or permission. Here we express a different concern: in one important way, Big Data is not big enough.

Big Data refers to a set of emerging technologies designed to "extract value from large volumes of a wide variety of data by enabling high-velocity capture, discovery, and analysis."[1] These technologies include pattern recognition, data repositories, and natural-language recognition.[2] The information gleaned from Big Data can be extremely useful to those in the medical and public health fields engaged in research, intervention, program implementation, and behavioral analysis.[3] Furthermore, Big Data can be helpful in recruiting study participants and designing specific interventions.

The problem is that Big Data is largely homogeneous, failing to reflect the growing diversity of the US population. To date, Big Data has not captured certain marginalized demographics. Particularly concerning are racial minorities, people with low socioeconomic status, and immigrants.[4] Many of the people missing from the data that come from sources such as Internet history, social media presence, and

---

[1] Richard L. Villars et al., *Big Data: What It Is and Why You Should Care*, Independent Directors Council (June 2011).
[2] Fabricio F. Costa, Big Data in Biomedicine, 19(4) *Drug Disc. Today* 433, 435 (April 2014).
[3] Ronald Margolis et al., The National Institutes of Health's Big Data to Knowledge (BD2K) Initiative: Capitalizing on Biomedical Big Data, 21 *J. Am. Med. Inform. Assoc.* 957 (July 2014).
[4] Cecilia Esther Rabess, Can Big Data Be Racist?, The Bold Italic (March 30, 2014), available at www.thebolditalic.com/articles/4502-can-big-data-be-racist [https://perma.cc/D3B6-A62B]; Jonas Lerman, Big Data and Its Exclusions, 66 *Stan. L. Rev. Online* 55 (2013).

credit-card use are also missing from other sources of Big Data, such as electronic health records (EHRs) and genomic databases. The factors responsible for these gaps are diverse and include lack of insurance and the inability to access healthcare, to name just two, which leaves those missing from the data at an even greater disadvantage and more susceptible to missing out on the healthcare advantages and benefits that Big Data can provide.

Further exacerbating the problem is the fact that many of the people who are unable to integrate into the Big Data trail are the very people most in need of increased health research, intervention, and care. Compelling evidence increasingly supports the association between social determinants of health and health disparities among certain populations.[5] Minority populations, for instance, can suffer a higher burden of disease, which can be disproportionately concentrated in certain conditions.[6] Moreover, drug effectiveness varies among groups based on specific variations in their genomes.[7] Thus, using precision medicine to target populations disproportionately affected by health disparities is of utmost importance. However, in order to effectively use Big Data in conjunction with individualized medicine to tailor medical and public health research, programming, and interventions to specific populations, the necessary information must be available in the databases used to advance Big Data platforms. If Big Data can be made representative of the diversity of the US population, we will be better able to realize the benefits of precision medicine, as evidenced by improvements in early diagnosis, development of targeted therapies with increased effectiveness and reduced toxicities, prevention of disease, and improved health outcomes.

This chapter posits that the scope of Big Data and the subsequent studies and interventions designed around the information gathered need to be broadened to increase the diversity of the data by capturing the heterogeneity of the population not only in conventional demographic terms but also, importantly, in terms of those most vulnerable to diminished health outcomes. The first section of this chapter discusses Big Data and its value for medicine and public health, including behavioral policy, healthcare, and precision medicine. The second section discusses the failure of Big Data to adequately represent certain populations, which also suffer from the most severe health disparities – a problem that stymies the utility of Big Data. Finally, the third section provides recommendations on how best to increase the amount of Big Data being collected on specific populations.

[5] Ana Penman-Aguilar et al., Measurement of Health Disparities, Health Inequities, and Social Determinants of Health to Support the Advancement of Health Equity, 22(Suppl. 1) *J. Pub. Health Mgmt. Pract.* S33 (2016).
[6] Tom Bodenheimer et al., Confronting the Growing Burden of Chronic Disease: Can the U.S. Health Care Workforce Do the Job?, 28(1) *Health Aff.* 64 (2009); Leonard E. Egede & Samuel Dagogo-Jack, Epidemiology of Type 2 Diabetes: Focus on Ethnic Minorities, 89 *Med. Clin. North Am.* 949 (2005).
[7] Micheline Piquette-Miller & Denis M. Grant, The Art and Science of Personalized Medicine, 81(3) *Clin. Pharmacol. Ther.* 311 (2007).

7.2 BIG DATA AND THE PROMISE FOR HEALTH

Traditionally defined by the three V's – volume, velocity, and variety – Big Data is the compilation, sorting, and organization of vast amounts of data.[8] Essentially, new and emerging technologies ease the processing of large amounts of data and make searching and categorizing the data to address specific needs much more feasible.[9] With such ease comes the potential to use Big Data in a number of sectors, including medicine, where the data collected can provide information about genomics, proteomics, metabolomics, and the physiologic features of a given individual, among other information.[10]

Big Data is collected from many diverse sources, such as credit-card use information, social media profiles, and webpage visits. Information is also mined from health insurance claims, EHRs, and data on pharmaceutical drug prescription and usage trends,[11] as well as health applications and wearables, and everyday consumer products equipped with data-tracking sensors and microchips.[12] The data produced are being applied to the healthcare industry in a number of ways.[13] One approach uses the data to spot trends that might otherwise go unnoticed, and the analysis of search terms has allowed health officials and clinicians to respond to influenza, breast cancer, and bariatric surgery.[14] As Efthimios Parasidis notes in his chapter on pharmacovigilance (Chapter 5), the Food and Drug Administration (FDA) employs a number of programs to monitor the safety of FDA-regulated medical products, including drugs, vaccines, and medical devices. One such program is the Sentinel Initiative, which combines surveillance, assessment, and simple, efficient probing of diverse automated healthcare data holders – such as EHR systems, administrative and insurances claims databases, and registries.[15]

Many industries use Big Data to tailor their products to better serve the populations to which they cater. Manufacturers, for instance, use Big Data to adapt their product designs and features to meet specific needs. In this vein, Big Data can help

---

[8] Javier Andreu-Perez et al., Big Data for Health, 19(4) *IEEE J. Biomed. Health Inform.* 1193, 1194 (July 2015).
[9] Steve G. Peters & James D. Buntrock, Big Data and the Electronic Health Record, 3(3) *J. Ambulatory Care Mgmt.* 206 (2014).
[10] Andreu-Perez, Big Data for Health.
[11] Eberechukwu Onukwugha, Big Data and Its Role in Health Economics and Outcomes Research: A Collection of Perspectives on Data Sources, Measurement, and Analysis, 34 *Pharmacoeconomics* 91 (2016).
[12] Charles F. Hofacker et al., Big Data and Consumer Behavior: Imminent Opportunities, 33(2) *J. Consumer Marketing* 89 (2016).
[13] Costa, Big Data in Biomedicine.
[14] Ramone F. Williams & Gideon P. Smith, Using "Big Data" to Optimize Public Health Outreach, 151(4) *JAMA Dermatol.* 367 (2015).
[15] See Chapter 5; FDA's Sentinel Initiative, US Food and Drug Administration (2016), available at www.fda.gov/Safety/FDAsSentinelInitiative/ucm2007250.htm [https://perma.cc/V9LE-2AFQ].

to create and adapt medical interventions to meet the needs identified.[16] One of the main elements of public health, for example, is the design and implementation of health interventions, such as smoking-cessation counseling via "quitlines" and workplace programs aimed at decreasing obesity.[17] Big Data can be used to make such interventions more specific and relevant to the communities and populations being served.

Big Data is also valuable when applied to precision medicine because it allows more "targeted diagnostics and treatment based on each patient's history, ancestry and genetic profile."[18] The field of precision medicine uses Big Data to improve clinical trials, repurpose pharmaceuticals, optimize therapies, define the heterogeneity of chronic disease, and redefine the taxonomy of disease, among others.[19] Genome sequencing and genetic testing, for example, enable clinicians to identify whether or not an individual may be at risk for specific cancers or conditions, such as hyperparathyroidism, and can screen patients accordingly while avoiding unnecessary screening in those who do not present a higher risk.[20]

7.3 BIG DATA EXCLUSIONS AND HEALTH DISPARITIES

Unfortunately, if Big Data is not sufficiently inclusive, these benefits may not extend to populations who are already underserved and marginalized by society, such as racial and ethnic minorities, people with low socioeconomic status, and immigrants – the very same groups who are at risk for increased health disparities.[21]

Consumer data are the first major source of Big Data that may be exploited for health purposes. Such data come from smartphone applications, wearable devices, and general Internet use (e.g., patterns of health-related searching). Approximately 20 percent of Americans do not use the Internet in any form – at home, at work, at school, or by mobile phone.[22] Moreover, home Internet access reflects and reproduces deeper social and economic disparities. Only 57 percent of African-American households and 58 percent of Hispanic households use the Internet compared with

---

[16] Alex Pentland et al., Revolutionizing Medicine and Public Health, World Innovation Summit for Health Big Data and Health Working Group (2013).
[17] Educational and Community-Based Programs: Evidence-Based Resources, Healthy People (2016), available at www.healthypeople.gov/2020/topics-objectives/topic/educational-and-community-based-programs/ebrs [https://perma.cc/76H9-72J2].
[18] Costa, supra note 2, at 433.
[19] J. Larry Jameson & Dan L. Longo, Precision Medicine: Personalized, Problematic, and Promising, 327(23) N. Engl. J. Med. 2229 (June 4, 2015).
[20] Ibid.
[21] Rabess, Can Big Data Be Racist?
[22] Edward Wyatt, Most of U.S. Is Wired, but Millions Aren't Plugged In, New York Times, August 18, 2013, available at www.nytimes.com/2013/08/19/technology/a-push-to-connect-millions-who-live-offline-to-the-internet.html?_r=0 [https://perma.cc/PW2J-PJPW].

76 percent of white households.[23] Education is important too – only 37 percent of households without a high school diploma have Internet access at home, versus 90 percent of households with a college degree.[24] Older Americans have less access – just over half of Americans aged over sixty-five, compared with over three-fourths for those under.[25] And the overall rate of Internet adoption has not improved since roughly 2009.[26]

Similarly, smartphone ownership reflects some disparities. Only 30 percent of Americans over age sixty-five own smartphones, compared with 86 percent of those between the ages of eighteen and twenty-nine and 83 percent of thirty- to forty-nine-year-olds.[27] Educational disparities continue too: 41 percent of those without a high school diploma own such a phone, whereas 81 percent of those with a college degree do.[28] Low-income populations do not have access to smartphones at the same rate as richer Americans: 52 percent of those making less than $30,000 as opposed to 87 percent for those making more than $75,000. Finally, rural populations own phones at a 52 percent rate compared with 72 percent of those in urban areas.[29] Nonetheless, African-American, white, and Hispanic adults own smartphones at similar rates.[30]

Statistics for wearables are not as clear. Overall, the ownership rate for wearables is lower than that for smartphones (only 10 percent of American adults own a fitness tracker).[31] It does seem likely that we can expect their uptake to continue to reflect this trend. For example, 48 percent of fitness tracker owners have an income above $100,000, a far higher number than the general population.

The second major source of Big Data is derived from EHRs and health insurance claims. As technology has improved, the ability to store health-related information electronically has become increasingly easier. This information includes health history, doctor and emergency room visits, prescription and treatment history, and insurance claims. In 2009, as part of the American Recovery and Reinvestment Act,

---

[23] Department of Commerce, Exploring the Digital Nation: America's Emerging Online Experience, 26 (2013), available at www.ntia.doc.gov/files/ntia/publications/exploring_the_digital_nation_-_americas_emerging_online_experience.pdf [https://perma.cc/43R7-YTZM].
[24] Ibid.
[25] Ibid.
[26] Wyatt, Most of U.S. Is Wired.
[27] Monica Anderson, Technology Device Ownership: 2015, Pew Research Center, 7 (October 29, 2015), available at www.pewinternet.org/files/2015/10/PI_2015-10-29_device-ownership_FINAL.pdf [https://perma.cc/5GLP-3CFN].
[28] Ibid.
[29] Ibid.
[30] Ibid.
[31] NPD Group, The Demographic Divide: Fitness Trackers and Smartwatches Attracting Very Different Segments of the Market (January 6, 2015), available at www.npd.com/wps/portal/npd/us/news/press-releases/2015/the-demographic-divide-fitness-trackers-and-smartwatches-attracting-very-different-segments-of-the-market-according-to-the-npd-group/ [https://perma.cc/4Q8A-STZA].

the Health Information Technology for Economic and Clinical Health (HITECH) Act was passed to "advance the implementation of a nationwide health IT [information technology] infrastructure that improves health care quality, reduces health disparities, and advances delivery of patient-centered medical care, among other goals."[32] Included in the HITECH Act are the Medicare and Medicaid Electronic Health Record Incentive Programs, which provide funding to professionals and hospitals that meaningfully use EHR technology.[33] The act also emphasizes the use of health technology to treat underserved populations, providing technical assistance and EHR implementation at federally qualified health centers and favorable incentives to Medicaid providers.[34]

As of 2014, 97 percent of all reported nonfederal acute-care hospitals had certified EHR technology, and 74.1 percent of all office-based physicians had a certified EHR system.[35] The data suggest disparities between medical specialties, but use of EHRs is not shown to be associated with patient demographics.[36] Moreover, even if the use of EHRs is widespread among physicians, 53 percent of patients say that they are unable to access their health records, either because they do not have Internet access or do not know how to do so and therefore will not receive the potential benefits of EHRs, such as improved communication between patients and physicians.[37] Minorities are also significantly less likely to enroll in online patient portals, which are useful for both accessing EHRs and providing additional patient interactions and data.[38]

Although the use of EHRs continues to expand, they, of course, only cover persons who have sought healthcare, a predicate which itself suffers from disparities due to lack of health insurance coverage. Minorities continue to have higher

---

[32] NORC, Understanding the Impact of Health IT in Underserved Communities and Those with Health Disparities, University of Chicago, 3 (October 29, 2010) (hereinafter NORC), available at www.healthit.gov/sites/default/files/pdf/hit-underserved-communities-health-disparities.pdf [https://perma.cc/Q4C3-WF4B].

[33] Ibid.

[34] Ibid.

[35] Dustin Charles et al., Adoption of Electronic Health Record Systems among U.S. Non-Federal Acute Care Hospitals: 2008–2014, Office of the National Coordinator for Health Information Technology, 1 (April. 2015), available at www.healthit.gov/sites/default/files/data-brief/2014HospitalAdoptionDataBrief.pdf [https://perma.cc/WW9P-UQJ6]; Eric W. Jamoom, Adoption of Certified Electronic Health Record Systems and Electronic Information Sharing in Physician Offices: United States, 2013 and 2014, US Department of Health and Human Services, 1 (January 2016), available at www.cdc.gov/nchs/data/databriefs/db236.pdf [https://perma.cc/K7HH-K7HU].

[36] Erik W. J. Kokkonen et al., Use of Electronic Medical Records Differs by Specialty and Office Settings, 20(1) *J. Am. Med. Inform. Assoc.* e33 (June 1, 2013).

[37] Sara Heath, 53% of Consumers Can't Access Electronic Health Record Info, EHR Intelligence (December 31, 2015), available at https://ehrintelligence.com/news/53-of-consumers-cant-access-electronic-health-record-info [https://perma.cc/XCX8-682G].

[38] Mita Sanghavi Goel et al., Disparities in Enrollment and Use of an Electronic Patient Portal, 26(10) *J. Gen. Intern. Med.* 1112 (May 3, 2011).

uninsured rates. In 2014, 11.8 percent of African Americans, 9.3 percent of Asians, and 19.9 percent of Hispanics were uninsured compared with 7.6 percent of non-Hispanic whites.[39] People living in poverty also experienced much higher uninsured rates. Those living below 100 percent poverty had the highest uninsured rate (19.3 percent), whereas those living at 400 percent or above poverty had the lowest rate (4.8 percent).[40] Uninsured individuals are less likely to access healthcare,[41] and even if they do so, they will not appear in health insurance claims databases, which means that these specific populations will be absent from data analysis based on insurance claims and the subsequent uses of that analysis.

Another problem that arises when collecting data from these specific populations is the distrust that many members have toward the medical community. This distrust, especially among minority populations, stems from instances of exploitation and unethical treatment at the hands of medical professionals as well as the ingrained discrimination found throughout history within the medical community.[42] Instances of exploitation and discrimination include the Havasupai diabetes project, the Tuskegee experiment on African-American men, and lower survival rates among African-American cancer patients due to discriminatory access to cancer care.[43] These incidents have led to a wariness among minorities and a lack of participation in research studies, organ donation, and other healthcare initiatives that are beneficial to their health.[44] This history not only may deter people from participating in research but also may deter them from seeking medical care altogether.

As mentioned earlier, these exclusions reflect preexisting health disparities and may amplify them. The medical, public health, and scientific literature emphasize the many factors that can influence an individual's health outcomes. The unequal dissemination of socioeconomic status, race, ethnicity, and education leads to unequal health outcomes among certain sectors of the population.[45] Racial and ethnic minorities in the United States are at greater risk for a number of diseases and

[39] Jessica C. Smith & Carla Medalla, Health Insurance Coverage in the United States: 2014, US Census Bureau, 4 (September 2015).
[40] Ibid., at 13.
[41] Dominic Coey, The Effect of Medicaid on Health Care Consumption of Young Adults, 24(5) Health Econ. 558 (February 27, 2014).
[42] Dayna Bowen Matthew, Legal Battles against Discrimination in Healthcare, in I. Glenn Cohen et al., eds., The Oxford Handbook of US Healthcare Law (2016).
[43] Christina M. Pacheco et al., Moving Forward: Breaking the Cycle of Mistrust between American Indians and Researchers, 103(12) Am. J. Pub. Health 2152 (December 2013); Bernice Roberts Kennedy et al., African Americans and Their Distrust of the Healthcare System: Healthcare for Diverse Populations, 14(2) J. Cult. Diversity 56 (2007); Matthew, Legal Battles against Discrimination in Healthcare.
[44] Pacheco, Moving Forward; Emily Russell et al., Distrust in the Healthcare System and Organ Donation Intentions among African Americans, 37(1) J. Commun. Health 40, (May 2011).
[45] Elizabeth Brondolo et al., Race, Racism, and Health: Disparities, Mechanisms, and Interventions, 31 J. Behav. Med. 1 (December 17, 2008).

health issues, including heart disease and hypertension, diabetes, and poor birth outcomes.[46] Health disparities include not only heightened levels of morbidity and mortality but also an unequal degree of access to healthcare, health insurance, and other factors that have an impact on health outcomes.[47]

It is apparent that these disadvantaged categories are the same as those groups with less representation in the sources of Big Data. Given their poorer outlook as it stands, it is troubling that the promise of Big Data for health improvement discussed earlier in this chapter may not fully be shared and the gap in health outcomes potentially increased. In particular, the absence of applicable data makes it nearly impossible to apply precision medicine to these populations.

To decrease the disproportionate effect these factors have on select populations, policy change, interventions, and research are needed. The health issues themselves must be addressed as well as the underlying causes, including poor nutrition, inadequate healthcare, lack of infrastructure, unsuitable programming, and outright neglect, to list a few. Unfortunately, when available data on a given population are skewed, interventions and research studies aimed at addressing the needs of those specific populations will not be successful. For instance, using Facebook check-ins to determine popular locations to set up roving vaccination clinics will likely include fewer Americans who do not use social media or smartphones or who do not have continuous access to the Internet, such as racial minorities and older Americans. This could lead to biased estimates as to the likely effects of interventions, distortions of the research agenda, or less effective recruitment of study participants.

These problems may be most trenchant in the domain of precision medicine, which promises to individualize care using research and clinical practice.[48] This field is harnessing diagnostic, prognostic, and therapeutic strategies precisely tailored to each patient's requirements[49] but depends on a robust data set that allows easier classification of diseases, sequencing of genomes, and the making of diagnoses based on imaging.[50] The proliferation of Big Data influences precision medicine in that it can provide information on everything from prescription drug use and popular dietary trends to the prevalence of smoking within a certain community. However, this precision cannot occur without the necessary data to inform diagnosis and treatment.

[46] Ibid.
[47] Health Disparities and Inequalities Report: United States, 2011, Centers for Disease Control and Prevention (2011), available at www.cdc.gov/mmwr/pdf/other/su6001.pdf [https://perma.cc/XH2K-64X5].
[48] Reza Mirnezami et al., Preparing for Precision Medicine, 366(6) N. Engl. J. Med. 489 (February 9, 2012).
[49] Jane Mohler et al., Precision Medicine: A Wider Definition, 63)9) J. Am. Geriatr. Soc. 1971 (September 21, 2015).
[50] Jameson & Longo, Precision Medicine.

Although much of the discussion on Big Data tends to focus on issues of privacy and civil liberties, it is important to note that Big Data's underinclusivity is troublesome because of its potential ramifications in terms of national health. Neglecting to gather information about minority populations, those who live below the poverty line, and other marginalized sectors of society does not simply mean there is a dearth of information about these populations; it also means that these populations will not benefit from the tailored attention, care, and benefits that Big Data can yield.

7.4 RECOMMENDATIONS

Given the documented absence of vulnerable populations from sources of Big Data and the profoundly positive effect on the individuals and populations who are recipients of the benefits of Big Data, there is a strong incentive to develop solutions to this absence – to make Big Data inclusive enough. Although addressing and correcting deficits within the world of Big Data constitute an effort that will require collaborations among the federal government, medical professionals, and industry, here we document some efforts to do so and propose others.

We should acknowledge that for some purposes these problems can be solved through standard post hoc statistical adjustments that yield unbiased estimates notwithstanding known disparities in the way the data are collected. For example, statisticians using EHRs to track population health have acknowledged that the data are likely to suffer from a selection bias on an income gradient.[51] However, patient-level income is not likely to appear in the EHR data, making simple stratification techniques unavailable.

During his 2015 State of the Union Address, President Obama announced the Precision Medicine Initiative.[52] Enabled with $215 million in funding, the initiative aims to encourage investment and research into precision medicine and to provide medical professionals with the appropriate tools and knowledge to integrate precision medicine into clinical practice.[53] The main objectives of the initiative include increasing and improving cancer treatment, the creation of a

---

[51] NYC Department of Health and Mental Hygiene, Developing an Electronic Health Record-Based Population Health Surveillance System (2013), available at www1.nyc.gov/assets/doh/downloads/pdf/data/nyc-macro-report.pdf.

[52] Office of the Press Secretary, FACT SHEET: President Obama's Precision Medicine Initiative (2015) (hereinafter Press Secretary, FACT SHEET), available at www.whitehouse.gov/the-press-office/2015/01/30/fact-sheet-president-obama-s-precision-medicine-initiative [https://perma.cc/AC7T-NE5D].

[53] Brady Dennis, Obama Touts 'Lifesaving' Potential of Personalized Medicine, *Washington Post*, January 20, 2015, available at www.washingtonpost.com/national/health-science/obama-seeks-215-million-for-personalized-medicine-initiative-using-genetic-data/2015/01/29/75789342-a7f4-11e4-a7c2-03d37af98440_story.html [https://perma.cc/8RJ6-87PB].

national research cohort that will include the voluntarily contributed data of 1 million Americans, modernizing the current regulatory scheme, and collaboration between public and private sectors.[54] We applaud the goal expressed by the Precision Medicine Initiative that the proposed research cohort will "broadly reflect the diversity of the U.S. population" and will include participants from different social and ethnic groups.[55] While the new funds made available through the initiative in February 2016 are currently focused on building the cohort, additional resources could be leveraged to increase the number of grants focused on diverse populations in the future.

The increased attention on precision medicine by the National Institutes of Health (NIH) grew out of a number of factors. These factors not only include the initiative but also the growing ability to sequence the human genome, improvements in analytical technologies, and new tools that enable the use of large data sets as well as enthusiasm from the medical community. The NIH has rapidly responded to the call of the initiative. In March 2015, for example, a team of experts in precision medicine and clinical research was formed to seek public input, define a vision for cohort participation, and outline what can be gained from the study as well as what obstacles might arise.[56] Funding was also provided to Vanderbilt University to begin a pilot project focused on the cohort.[57] These steps are important advances, but it is critical that they are not limited to specific groups and in fact reach across the diverse segments of the population.

The FDA may be a powerful ally in helping to alleviate these unintended downfalls of the incomplete use of Big Data. The FDA has broad discretion on how and what it enforces. In its approval of certain pharmaceuticals and other health-related products, the FDA could require that the data used to inform the efficacy and safety of these items come from a diverse, inclusive pool. Currently, the NIH's Policy on Inclusion of Women and Minorities in Clinical Research only applies to research funded by the NIH.[58] The goal of the policy, which was

---

[54] Press Secretary, FACT SHEET.
[55] National Institutes of Health, About the Precision Medicine Initiative Cohort Program, available at www.nih.gov/precision-medicine-initiative-cohort-program [https://perma.cc/8MP6-CCU2].
[56] National Institutes of Health, NIH Taking First Steps to Huge Precision Medicine Project, NIH news release (March 30, 2015), available at www.nih.gov/news-events/news-releases/nih-forms-team-experts-chart-course-presidents-precision-medicine-initiative-research-network [https://perma.cc/G7CS-J8KK].
[57] Lauren Neergaard, NIH Taking First Steps to Huge Precision Medicine Project, Associated Press (February 25, 2016), available at www.pbs.org/newshour/rundown/nih-taking-first-steps-to-huge-precision-medicine-project/ [https://perma.cc/CP6A-YRGJ].
[58] National Institutes of Health, NIH Policy and Guidelines on the Inclusion of Women and Minorities as Subjects in Clinical Research – Amended, October, 2011 (October 1, 2001), available at https://grants.nih.gov/grants/funding/women_min/guidelines_amended_10_2001.htm [https://perma.cc/K9E9-WP5A].

mandated by Congress in 1993 following a number of iterations that grew out of the women's health movement, is to guarantee that women and minorities are included in human subject research and requires inclusion "in numbers adequate for valid analysis."[59]

The FDA's own recommendations, however, do not require the inclusion of minorities in industry-sponsored trials but rather suggest the use of "a standardized approach for collecting and reporting race and ethnicity information in clinical trials conducted in the United States and abroad for certain FDA-regulated products."[60] In 1997, the Clinton administration enacted its Modernization Act, which, among other issues, addressed the inclusion of women and minorities in clinical trials.[61] The agency's "Dialogues on Diversifying Clinical Trials" expanded on this theme, providing a number of strategies that could increase the involvement of minorities in clinical trials, including community outreach, trial redesign, and more efficient regulation.[62] While these guidelines provide information on how to uniformly collect the racial and ethnic data of study participants, they do not "address the level of participation of racial and ethnic groups in clinical trials."[63] The FDA should follow the NIH's lead in requiring that drug and device applications exhibit the use of diverse data sets in order to inform the safety and efficacy of these drugs and devices.

Additionally, the FDA is increasingly relying on "omics" data to carry out its regulatory mandate.[64] These efforts have now been framed within the context of guidelines that have been open for public comment. The report outlines the initiatives and efforts undertaken by the agency to ensure that its scientific base is robust, effective, and targeted to its regulatory responsibility to protect and promote health through ensuring the safety and effectiveness of human and veterinary drugs, biologics, and devices and the safety of foods and cosmetics. The scientific strategy builds on five principles designed to specify implementation plans, deliverables and timelines, development of a preemptive approach, enhancement of

---

[59] US Food and Drug Administration Office of Women's Health, Dialogues on Diversifying Clinical Trials: Successful Strategies for Engaging Women and Minorities in Clinical Trials, 4 (2011) (hereinafter FDA, Dialogues), available at www.fda.gov/downloads/ScienceResearch/SpecialTopics/WomensHealthResearch/UCM334959.pdf [https://perma.cc/Q66R-5FQK].

[60] US Food and Drug Administration, Guidance for Industry: Collection of Race and Ethnicity Data in Clinical Trials, 1 (October 26, 2016) (hereinafter FDA, Guidance), available at www.fda.gov/ucm/groups/fdagov-public/@fdagov-afda-gen/documents/document/ucm126396.pdf [https://perma.cc/M9JZ-YJAJ].

[61] US Food and Drug Administration, FDAMA Women and Minorities Working Group Project (July 20, 1998), available at www.fda.gov/downloads/Drugs/GuidanceComplianceRegulatoryInformation/Guidances/ucm080616.pdf [https://perma.cc/677R-WE4K].

[62] FDA, Dialogues.

[63] FDA, Guidance, at 3.

[64] Frank M. Torti, Report on Status of Regulatory Science at FDA: Progress, Plans and Challenges, Food and Drug Administration (2013), available at https://perma.cc/9VZG-9BPX.

infrastructure and core expertise in modern technologies, and effective communication. Several reports have been published to address these priorities.[65] In parallel, other federal agencies such as the National Cancer Institute have developed a checklist for determining the readiness of omics-based tests for guiding patient care in clinical trials.[66] The criteria cover issues related to specimens, assays, modeling, design, and ethical, legal, and regulatory aspects. As such, more effort should be made to increase participation of stakeholders in vetting and updating these recommendations.

The FDA could also leverage its enforcement discretion over a number of mobile apps, such as those that provide assistance with smoking cessation or help track medication usage.[67] Similar to the pharmacoepidemiologic studies mentioned by Parasidis in Chapter 5, the FDA recognizes that many of these apps may meet the definition of a medical device and may be intended for use in diagnosis, treatment, or prevention, but the administration has decided, for now, not to subject such apps to regulatory requirements.[68] In the mobile apps space, the FDA could require compliance with some of the suggestions made in "Dialogues on Diversifying Clinical Trials," in an effort to diversify the pool from which data are mined. Beyond the safety and efficacy mandate that applies to drugs and devices, however, it is not clear that the FDA has such authority to require diversification of data collection for other purposes.

Another remedy may be for the federal government to issue new regulations aimed at this particular issue. Currently, much of the legal discussion around Big Data has centered on privacy and other issues of autonomy. For instance, any personal data collected are usually preceded by collection of informed consent from the individual to use his or her data.[69] In addition, data often are anonymized to protect privacy when both collecting and disseminating the information gathered from individuals, especially if the information may be considered to be sensitive.[70] Much of the dialogue is also concentrated on an individual's control over the information he or she produces and how the information should be managed by the individuals creating it.[71]

---

[65] US Food and Drug Administration, FDA Science and Mission at Risk: Report of the Subcommittee on Science and Technology (2007); The Future of Drug Safety: Promoting and Protecting the Health of the Public, Institute of Medicine, National Academy (2006); Challenges for the FDA: The Future of Drug Safety, Institute of Medicine (2007).

[66] Lisa McShane et al., Criteria for the Use of Omics-Based Predictors in Clinical Trials, 502 Nature 317 (2013).

[67] US Food and Drug Administration, Examples of Mobile Apps for Which the FDA Will Exercise Enforcement Discretion (September 22, 2015) (hereinafter FDA, Mobile Apps), available at www.fda.gov/MedicalDevices/DigitalHealth/MobileMedicalApplications/ucm 368744.htm [https://perma.cc/M7P9-N8PX].

[68] See Chapter 5; FDA, Mobile Apps.

[69] Charith Perera et al., Big Data Privacy in the Internet of Things Era, 17(3) IT Pro. 32 (2015).

[70] Ibid.

[71] Ibid.

Perhaps what is needed to address this specific issue and curb what Lerman identifies as the "reinforcement of the status of already disadvantaged groups" is a regulatory scheme that guarantees that, at the very least, any data being used to inform healthcare initiatives, development, and delivery are inclusive.[72] Because Big Data comes from so many unique sources, it may not be realistic or even possible to regulate *how* Big Data is collected, but it may be possible to regulate the ways in which data are searched, analyzed, and ultimately used.[73] The Federal Trade Commission (FTC), for example, released a report that mentions a number of existing acts and regulations that may be applicable to Big Data, including the Fair Credit Reporting Act, the Federal Trade Commission Act, and equal opportunity laws.[74] Further, regulations could be implemented, or strengthened, to push users of Big Data to acknowledge and reconcile the possibility for skewed data due to under- and overrepresentation, biases within algorithms, and overreliance on the findings of Big Data.[75]

Regulating the way in which Big Data is mined and used could face a number of barriers, including difficulty in defining Big Data, privacy concerns, and conflicting interests regarding the sharing and use of Big Data. It is also not a remedy that could be put in place immediately. Nevertheless, regulation has the potential to provide safeguards in terms of who is benefiting from the collection of data. Increased regulation targeting the mining of data may force those using the data to include information from more diverse populations, sources, and geographic locations – helping to guarantee that those who leave a smaller data trail are still included in the overall analysis and application of the data.

One model for solving the problem of collecting Big Data on certain populations is the federal Lifeline program. Introduced in 1985 as part of the Federal Communications Commission (FCC), it provides discounted, affordable phone services to low-income consumers.[76] The program aims to give consumers the "opportunities and security" that come with telephone access.[77] Lifeline was expanded in 1996 when it was made available to consumers across the country and again in 2005 when wireless services were included in the program.[78] Additionally, in 2016, the

---

[72] Lerman, Big Data and Its Exclusions.
[73] Alessandro Mantelero & Giuseppe Vaciago, Data Protection in a Big Data Society: Ideas for a Future Regulation, 15 *Digital Invest.* 104 (December 2015).
[74] US Federal Trade Commission, Big Data: A Tool for Inclusion or Exclusion?, Understanding the Issues (2016), available at www.ftc.gov/system/files/documents/reports/big-data-tool-inclusion-or-exclusion-understanding-issues/160106big-data-rpt.pdf [https://perma.cc/VTK6-JNL8].
[75] Ibid.
[76] US Federal Communications Commission, Lifeline Support for Affordable Communications, available at www.fcc.gov/consumers/guides/lifeline-support-affordable-communications [https://perma.cc/ZH57-3ALS] (last visited June 9, 2017).
[77] Ibid.
[78] Ibid.; David Honig, The Truth about Lifeline, *Huffington Post*, July 13, 2013, available at www.huffingtonpost.com/david-honig/the-truth-about-lifeline_b_3266143.html [https://perma.cc/6ZY3-G3NS].

FCC announced that broadband services would be added to the program, giving low-income Americans the opportunity for "full and meaningful participation in society."[79] The adoption of cell phones into the program, as well as the proposal to expand services to include broadband, has the potential to increase the data produced by populations that may not otherwise have access to or engage with technology on a regular basis. The expansion of the program also suggests that this specific problem with regard to Big Data demographics may be remedied over time as more and more people own cell phones and have greater Internet access.[80] It is important to note, however, that the services provided by Lifeline are limited, which, in turn, may limit the scope of data derived from these specific sources.

7.5 CONCLUSION

Big Data is proving to be extremely useful in the medical and public health fields. It can provide degrees of information on practices, attitudes, beliefs, and medical needs at both the individual and group levels that have not been previously available. As such, the benefits of Big Data and its application to research, pharmaceutical innovation, intervention design, and treatment plans are significant. Regrettably, not everyone is able to receive the benefits that Big Data provides because information is not currently being gathered in ways that ensure adequate representation of all segments of society. This is particularly significant in the United States given the diversity of the population.

In order to address and remedy this oversight, Big Data collection must be augmented to include diverse populations. While this will not eradicate the health disparities that plague disadvantaged populations, the use of Big Data to design and implement more tailored medicine will be better poised to benefit the populations most at risk for health disparities. These precise studies, interventions, and treatments have the potential to have a positive impact on the health outcomes of these populations both over the life course of the individuals and among future generations.

---

[79] US Federal Communications Commission, FCC Modernizes Lifeline Program for the Digital Age: New Rules Will Help Make Broadband More Affordable for Low-Income Americans, 1, available at https://apps.fcc.gov/edocs_public/attachmatch/DOC-338676A1.pdf [https://perma.cc/8CEU-W2J5].

[80] Anderson, Technology Device Ownership.

8

Potential Roadblocks in Healthcare Big Data Collection

Gobeille v. Liberty Mutual, *ERISA*, and All-Payer Claims Databases

Carmel Shachar, Aaron S. Kesselheim, Gregory Curfman, and Ameet Sarpatwari

8.1 INTRODUCTION

In an era of heightened demand for healthcare cost control, transparency, and quality, state all-payer claims databases (APCDs) are well positioned to unlock an array of value. APCDs systematically collect medical and pharmacy claims from public and private payers within a state, offering a comprehensive view of patients' interactions with the healthcare system. State APCDs have accordingly become a popular means through which to generate critical data on the cost, use, and impact of healthcare services. As discussed in other chapters of this book, there is an important need for healthcare Big Data sets, including those generated by APCDs. Indeed, APCDs are perhaps one of the better methods of developing Big Data for healthcare services and payments within a state, encompassing both the private and public payer systems. APCDs could also be harnessed to evaluate prescription drug and medical device safety and effectiveness. Currently, more than thirty states have or are in the process of developing an APCD.[1]

The advantage of APCDs over other healthcare databases is that they contain a complete set of data for a well-defined population. Research that draws only on data from government payer programs, such as Medicare and Medicaid or from individual insurance companies, although valuable, is often not generalizable to the entire population. Important healthcare research using the Big Data generated by APCDs includes pinpointing healthcare spending trends to control costs, identifying rare but important adverse events, and building predictive models. Spending data are based on the prices negotiated between the payer and provider. APCDs are therefore a critical tool for the development and implementation of health policies and to tracking the impact of policy changes on health and healthcare.

---

[1] APCD Council, The Basics of All-Payer Claims Databases, Robert Wood Johnson Foundation (2014).

The growth of state APCDs, however, has raised important legal questions about the government's ability to demand participation in them. In *Gobeille v. Liberty Mutual Insurance Co.*,[2] the Supreme Court concluded that due to the Employment Retirement Income Security Act of 1974 (ERISA),[3] state governments did not have the ability to mandate participation of so-called self-insured employer-sponsored health insurance plans. This surprising decision will undermine the utility of state APCDs in promoting evidence-based prescribing and healthcare policymaking. We review the context of the *Gobeille* decision and the potential ways forward to help protect the vital role these databases can play.

In order to mitigate the effects of *Gobeille*, policymakers, regulators, and employers should work together to maximize employer participation in APCDs. Although the US Department of Labor is attempting to promulgate mitigating regulations under the authority granted to it by ERISA, the more fruitful approach may be to encourage voluntary participation in healthcare data reporting through state-based incentives such as tax benefits and regulations to shield reporting employers from liability.

The second section of this chapter places *Gobeille* in the context of ERISA and discusses the pivot in healthcare data collection caused by this case. The third section unpacks the impact that *Gobeille* and ERISA will have on healthcare research that typically depends on Big Data generated by APCDs. The final section evaluates several solutions, from federal, state, and private actors, to the problems posed by *Gobeille*.

8.2 GOBEILLE V. LIBERTY MUTUAL: AN EXPANSIVE PREEMPTIVE DECISION

The central issue in *Gobeille* was whether a federal employee benefit statute, ERISA, preempts state laws, in particular, the Vermont law[4] requiring all in-state healthcare payers, including self-funded insurance plans, to report claims and healthcare services data to the state. In 2008, the Vermont Department of Banking, Insurance, Securities, and Health Care Administration promulgated regulations to implement a healthcare claims reporting system and establish an APCD. Health insurers were required to regularly submit medical claims data, pharmacy claims data, member eligibility data, provider data, and other information regarding healthcare provided to Vermont residents and healthcare provided by Vermont healthcare providers to Vermont residents and nonresidents in a specified electronic format. This information is compiled into a publically accessible resource.

---

[2] 136 S. Ct. 936 (2016).
[3] 29 U.S.C. § 1001 (2015).
[4] Vt. Stat. Ann. Tit. 18 § 9410(a)–(d) (2012).

ERISA is a federal statute setting minimum standards for most voluntarily established pensions and other employee benefit plans, including self-funded healthcare plans or plans in which an employer assumes the direct risk for payments of the employees' claims for benefits. In creating ERISA, Congress intended to establish the regulation of such plans "as exclusively a federal concern."[5] ERISA was intended to protect the interests of beneficiaries of employee benefit plans by standardizing certain financial disclosure and reporting requirements, as well as establishing standards of conduct, responsibility, and obligation for fiduciaries of these plans.

In service of this aim, ERISA is notable in that it includes one of the broadest preemption clauses of any federal statute in its Section 514(a). As the Supreme Court noted in *New York State Conference of Blue Cross & Blue Shield Plans v. Travelers Insurance Co.*, "[t]he governing text of ERISA is clearly expansive ... Section 514(a) marks for pre-emption 'all state laws insofar as they ... relate to any employee benefit plan' covered by ERISA, and one might be excused for wondering, at first blush, whether the words of limitation ('insofar as they ... relate') do much limiting."[6] Prior to *Gobeille*, the Supreme Court concluded that state law is preempted if "it has a connection with or reference to such a[n employee benefit] plan."[7]

Nevertheless, leading up to *Gobeille*, it was unclear that ERISA would bar states from mandating the collection of healthcare data from self-insured employer-sponsored plans. The Supreme Court repeatedly cautioned that even in cases "where federal law is said to bar state action in fields of traditional state regulation ... [the Court has] worked on the 'assumption that the historic policy powers of the States were not to be superseded by the Federal Act unless that was the clear and manifest purpose of Congress.'"[8] Therefore, this Court limited ERISA preemption to only "state statutes that mandate[d] employee benefit structures or their administration."[9] Under these limitations to ERISA's preemption provision, courts prior to *Gobeille* preserved a role for state regulations that did not overlap with or burden compliance with ERISA's requirements or core purposes.

Writing for the majority, Justice Anthony Kennedy[10] nevertheless concluded in *Gobeille* that ERISA preempted Vermont's attempt to gather healthcare data from plans governed by ERISA.[11] The Court interpreted ERISA's broad preemption clause[12]

---

[5] *Alessi v. Raybestos-Manhattan, Inc.*, 451 U.S. 504, 523 (1981).
[6] 514 U.S. 64 (1995).
[7] *Shaw v. Delta Airlines, Inc.*, 463 U.S. 85, 97 (1983).
[8] *Travelers*, 514 U.S. at 655 (quoting *Rice v. Santa Fe Elevator Corp.*, 331 U.S. 218, 229 [1947]).
[9] *California Div. of Labor Standards Enforcement v. Dillingham Constr.*, N.A., 519 U.S. 316, 328 (1997) (quoting *Travelers*, 514 U.S. at 658).
[10] Justice Kennedy was joined by Chief Justice Roberts and Justices Thomas, Breyer, Alito, and Kagan.
[11] *Gobeille*, 136 S.Ct. at 936 (2016).
[12] 29 U.S.C. § 1444(a) (stating that ERISA shall preempt "any and all State laws insofar as they may now or hereafter relate to any employee benefit plan").

to preclude laws with a "reference to"[13] or a "connection with"[14] ERISA plans. The latter prong focuses on two aspects of a state law – whether the law "governs ... a central matter of plan administration" and whether it "interferes with nationally uniform plan administration."[15] The Court held that the Vermont law was thus preempted because "reporting, disclosure, and recordkeeping are central to, and an essential part of" ERISA,[16] and the statute would interfere with a "nationally uniform plan administration."[17] Therefore, Vermont and other states are unable to require self-insured employer-sponsored health plans to report data to their APCDs.

In a separate concurrence, Justice Stephen Breyer highlighted the "serious administrative problems" that could emerge if self-insured health plans were subject to more than fifty information-reporting requirements.[18] However, he also noted the importance of APCDs and stated that rather than creating "unnecessary, duplicative, and conflicting" reporting requirements,[19] the states' interests would be better served by working with the Department of Labor or the Department of Health and Human Services to obtain that information.[20]

By contrast, Justice Ruth Bader Ginsburg argued in dissent that Vermont's law did "not impermissibly intrude on ERISA's dominion over employee benefit plans."[21] ERISA's reporting requirement is focused largely on demonstrating that applicable employee benefit plans, including self-funded insurance plans, are financially sound. The Vermont statute established a regulatory scheme to collect healthcare claims data intended to evaluate and improve the quality and cost of healthcare provided in Vermont and not to evaluate the financial soundness of the plans themselves. As the law and ERISA's reporting requirements "elicit[ed] different information and serve[d] distinct purposes,"[22] and because the law does not impose a "substantial burden" on ERISA,[23] Justice Ginsburg concluded that ERISA should not preempt the Vermont law.[24]

8.3 POST-*GOBEILLE* CONCERNS

Gobielle places ERISA on a collision course with healthcare data trends. Before *Gobeille*, states could take refuge in the Supreme Court's repeated emphasis that

---

[13] *Gobeille*, 136 S.Ct. at 943 (quoting *Dillingham Constr., N.A., Inc.*, 519 U.S. at 325 ["[w]here a State's law acts immediately and exclusively upon ERISA plans ... or where the existence of ERISA plans is essential to the law's operation ... that 'reference' will result in pre-emption"]).
[14] Ibid., at 942.
[15] Ibid. (quoting *Egelhoff v. Egelhoff*, 532 U.S. 141, 148 [2001]).
[16] Ibid., at 945.
[17] Ibid.
[18] Ibid., at 949 (Breyer, J., concurring).
[19] Ibid.
[20] Ibid., at 949–50.
[21] Ibid., at 950 (Ginsburg, J., dissenting).
[22] Ibid., at 954.
[23] Ibid., at 955.
[24] See ibid.

ERISA's "relate to" provision, which sets the scope of its preemption reach, must remain reasonable. Otherwise, there would be no reasonable limits on ERISA preemption because, "as many a curbstone philosopher has observed, everything is related to everything else."[25] *Gobeille* now extends the reach of ERISA into laws of general application, for example, state laws that allow employers to offer whatever benefits they see fit and do not dictate the products available to employees. The Vermont statute in question in *Gobeille* did not dictate the structure of health plans available to employees; it only asked for information. Because the law struck down in *Gobeille* was of a general nature, it is unclear now where the defining limits of ERISA's reach are now.

8.3.1 *Potential Impact on States' Programs and Initiatives*

The rate of growth of healthcare spending in the United States has moderated in recent years due in large part to the downturn in the economy. Still, healthcare spending growth continues to exceed the rate of growth of the economy as a whole (gross domestic product [GDP]), and healthcare spending now represents nearly 18 percent of GDP. Spending on healthcare and the rate of growth in spending, however, are not uniform across states, with wide variation in both spending and spending growth. For example, Kaiser Family Foundation data (1991–2009) indicate that average per capita spending varied nearly twofold from $5,434 in Arizona to $10,349 in the District of Columbia. Similarly, the average annual per capita rate of growth in spending varied from 4.5 percent in the District of Columbia to 7.3 percent in Alaska. Thus, spending on healthcare is straining all state budgets, but some states are affected substantially more than others.

It is understandable that states, with their budgets stretched, are making a concerted effort to control the growth of healthcare spending. To accomplish this objective, states need detailed data on healthcare spending from payers across their state to better understand variations in spending according to geographic area and by individual hospitals and hospital networks, physician groups, and individual providers. Such data, however, have been difficult to access from private insurance companies because they have been considered proprietary.

APCDs were developed to solve the problem of lack of access to healthcare spending data at the state level. At least eighteen states have established APCDs, whereas another dozen states have them under consideration. But *Gobeille* essentially guts the value of APCDs in this field. Over 60 percent of private healthcare plans are self-insured, so preemption of the reporting requirement greatly reduces the amount of healthcare data that state governments can obtain from private payers. States will need to seek other solutions to obtain essential data on healthcare spending to control spending growth.

---

[25] *Dillingham Construction, Inc.*, 519 U.S. at 335 (Scalia, J., concurring).

8.3.2 Potential Impact on Health Services Research

But *Gobeille* has an even more significant detrimental effect on trends in healthcare delivery and data collection. Prior to *Gobeille*, APCDs functioned as a potentially powerful source of comprehensive claims data within a state and thus as a key resource for identifying trends and variation in the cost, use, and quality of healthcare services. Colorado, for example, began using its APCD data to promote price transparency and competition for maternity services and hip and knee replacements in the state. Consumers can access a convenient-to-use website and obtain the median price of care at nearby hospitals as well as gain insight into the relative complexity of cases seen at these institutions.[26] In Massachusetts, the Health Policy Commission used the state's APCD to set targets for healthcare spending to contain spending growth.

APCD data have also helped to uncover important discrepancies in pediatric care. Using APCDs in New England, researchers found that psychotropic drug use among Medicaid-enrolled children was over fourfold higher than among commercially insured children between 2007 and 2010.[27] Overall, prescription drug use in the Medicaid population was 62 percent higher,[28] raising the question of how Medicaid policies fueled inappropriate off-label use of powerful medications with considerable side effects.

APCDs have additionally facilitated prediction modeling. An analysis of Maine's APCD revealed that men aged eighteen to thirty-four who either filled prescriptions for opioids – addictive pain relief medications such as morphine and oxycontin – at multiple pharmacies or refilled their opioid prescriptions early were significantly more likely to abuse prescription opioids.[29] Several state prescription drug monitoring programs have indicated an interest in using claims data to develop additional algorithms for screening patients receiving opioid prescriptions to help combat the nation's opioid abuse epidemic.

By prohibiting mandatory reporting by self-funded insurance plans, *Gobeille* will hinder these and other uses of ACPDs in two critical respects. First, the loss of data on the 61 percent of employees receiving insurance through self-funded plans[30] will dramatically reduce the number of claims in APCDs. This reduction will limit statistical power – the ability to detect nonrandom differences in outcomes between

---

[26] CO Medical Price Compare, Center for Improving Value in Health Care (March 2016), available at www.comedprice.org/#/home [https://perma.cc/NK59-VVPA].

[27] Shelsey J. Weinstein, Small Geographic Area Variations in Prescription Drug Use, 132 *Pediatrics* 3 (September 2014).

[28] Ibid.

[29] Alan G. White et al., Analytic Models to Identify Patients at Risk for Prescription Opioid Abuse, 15 *Am. J. Managed Care* 12 (December 2009).

[30] Kaiser Family Foundation and Health Research & Education Trust, *Employer Health Benefits: 2014 Annual Survey*, 6 (September 10, 2014), available at http://files.kff.org/attachment/2014-employer-health-benefits-survey-full-report [https://perma.cc/66SR-LRP8].

populations with a specified level of certainty under a frequentist paradigm[31] – rendering it more difficult to identify rare but important adverse events associated with prescriptions drugs or device use. The case of the multiple sclerosis drug natalizumab (Tysabri) is illustrative in this regard. A Swedish team was able to link natalizumab use with progressive multifocal leukoencephalopathy (PML), a serious, rare, and usually fatal viral infection resulting in inflammation of the brain,[32] but only by drawing on several sources, including manufacturer-conducted postapproval studies and a Swedish registry. Claims derived from only a limited number of payers in a state would not have generated a sufficiently large number of PML cases from which to establish an association.

Removal of self-funded insurance plans will also affect the external validity of post-*Gobeille* APCD data. Data lacking self-insured plans will disproportionately reflect Medicare and Medicaid enrollees, who differ considerably from their privately insured counterparts. Medicare enrollees are older and Medicaid enrollees are sicker than patients in self-funded insurance plans. Among Medicaid enrollees at or below 100 percent the federal poverty level, 38 percent were in fair or poor health, 26 percent reported physical or mental chronic conditions, and 36 percent were unable to work or could only pursue limited work due to their health; by contrast, among privately insured Americans at or below 100 percent of the federal poverty level, only 12 percent were in fair or poor health, 13 percent reported physical or mental chronic conditions, and 6 percent were unable to work or could only pursue limited work due to their health.[33] Important demographic differences likewise exist between employees in self-funded and non-self-funded insurance plans. As the American Hospital Association and Association of American Medical Colleges noted, "Whereas only around 20% of employers in the construction industry and agriculture industry offer a self-insured plan ... over 55% of retail employers do."[34]

---

[31] Frequentist statisticians define "probability" as the long-run frequency of a certain measurement or observation. The more data collected, the closer a frequentist statistician can come to the "truth" of the matter. See Maarten H. P. Ambaum, Frequentist vs Bayesian Statistics: A Non-Statisticians View, Department of Meteorology, University of Reading (July 2012), available at www.met.reading.ac.uk/~sws97mha/Publications/Bayesvsfreq.pdf [https://perma.cc/AZN5-UJHH]. By convention, a *p*-value of less than 0.05 is often required for researchers to conclude that the differences between the studied sample populations are statistically significant and hence worth reporting. A *p*-value depends on the size of the samples, the frequency of the outcome, and the magnitude of the difference in outcome between the samples; the larger the samples, the more frequent the outcome, and the greater the difference in outcome between the samples, the more likely a health services researcher can trust what was observed.

[32] Gary Bloomgren et al., Risk of Natalizumab-Associated Progressive Multifocal Leukoencephalopathy, 366 *N. Engl. J. Med.* 1870–80 (May 2012).

[33] Kaiser Family Foundation, Medicaid Enrollees Are Sicker and More Disabled than the Privately-Insured (March 14, 2013), available at http://kff.org/medicaid/slide/medicaid-enrollees-are-sicker-and-more-disabled-than-the-privately-insured/ [https://perma.cc/GQ4K-E777].

[34] Brief for American Hospital Association and Association of American Medical College as Amici Curiae.

The resulting loss of a key resource for gauging the health status and needs of a state will hamper efforts to allocate scarce and expensive public health resources efficiently. Moreover, as the following example of the antibiotic azithromycin illustrates, policymakers and researchers will face difficulty drawing actionable conclusions from post-*Gobeille* APCD analyses. In 2012, an American team used Tennessee Medicaid data to document a twofold greater risk of cardiovascular death among people taking azithromycin compared with people taking amoxicillin – another common antibiotic – or not using antibiotics.[35] In response to this study, a team from Denmark used their country's national registries[36] to evaluate the same question, finding no such risk.[37] Access to a comprehensive database, akin to the APCD data, was helpful; as the Danish team noted, "Given the large, nationally representative study population," their results were likely generalizable to young and middle-aged adults, who are common users of these antibiotics, whereas those of the Tennessee team were likely confined to high-risk populations receiving Medicaid coverage.

Thus *Gobeille* has the potential to undermine the comprehensiveness of APCDs across the country by applying ERISA to regulations intended to gather healthcare data. Allowing self-funded insurance plans to use ERISA as a shield against reporting their healthcare claims data may undermine the ability of healthcare and services researchers to improve the quality of care and to address healthcare costs and other trends by reducing APCDs from a complete data set to a fragmented one.

8.4 POTENTIAL SOLUTIONS

8.4.1 *Department of Labor Regulations*

The Court in *Gobeille* suggested that an appropriate response to its establishment of ERISA's broad preemption sweep would be for the Department of Labor to mitigate the impact that ERISA would have on healthcare data collection. In his concurrence, Justice Breyer specifically proposed having the Department of Labor collect data for APCDs or explicitly grant permission for APCDs to require data reporting from self-insured plans.

> I see no reason why the Secretary of Labor could not develop reporting requirements that satisfy the States' needs, including some State-specific requirements, as appropriate. Nor do I see why the Department could not delegate to a particular

---

[35] Wayne A. Ray et al, Azithromycin and the Risk of Cardiovascular Death, 366 N. *Engl. J. Med.* 1881–90 (May 17, 2012).
[36] The Danish registries are not strictly an APCD in that Denmark has only one payer – the Danish Government – but functions as one in that they collect all healthcare claims for the Danish population.
[37] Henrik Svanstrom et al., Use of Azithromycin and Death from Cardiovascular Causes, 368 N. *Engl. J. Med.* 1704–12 (May 2, 2013).

State the authority to obtain data related to that State, while also providing the data to the Federal Secretary for use by other States or at the federal level.[38]

His proposal is not without some merit. ERISA allows the Secretary of Labor to use any data disclosed by plans, including self-insured health insurance plans, "for statistical and research purposes, and [to] compile and publish such studies, analyses, reports, and surveys based thereon as he may deem appropriate."[39] Additionally, the Secretary may "in connection" with *any* research "collect, compile, analyze, and publish data, information, and statistics relating to" plans.[40] It is because of the broad reporting powers bestowed on the Secretary of Labor that the Court concluded that "reporting, disclosure, and recordkeeping are central to, and an essential part of, the uniform system of plan administration contemplated by ERISA."[41] As a result, the Court suggests that the Secretary of Labor "may be authorized to require ERISA plans to report data similar to that which Vermont seeks, though that question is not presented here."[42]

The Department of Labor took the Court's suggestion to heart and proposed to expand plan reporting to capture some of the data that would be otherwise lost as a result of *Gobeille*.[43] While these regulations will be better than allowing self-insured plans to forgo all data reporting, the regulations as proposed do not include enough information to maintain the value of APCDs' data sets. For example, the regulations require only summary statistics and not detailed information on payment and quality collected on a per-encounter, per-provider basis. Additionally, the Department of Labor proposed collecting data on an annual basis, as opposed to the monthly or quarterly basis that most APCDs, prior to *Gobeille*, collected data. Some of the flaws in the proposed regulations likely reflect the Department of Labor's limited experience with healthcare data reporting and the limited time it had to promulgate regulations due to the change in presidential administrations.

Several groups, including the National Academy for State Health Policy (NASHP), the National Association of Health Data Organizations (NAHDO), and the APCD Council are developing a "Common Data Layout" (CDL) in response to the insufficient regulations proposed by the Department of Labor. The purpose of the CDL is to create a single national standard for claims data submission and remove the burden of deciding which data reporting elements are important for healthcare reporting from the Department of Labor. Potentially, the CDL could help to mitigate the inexperience that the Department of Labor has with healthcare data

---

[38] *Gobeille*, 136 S. Ct. at 950 (Breyer, J., concurring).
[39] 29 U.S.C. § 1026(a).
[40] Ibid., at § 1143(a)(1).
[41] *Gobeille*, 136 S. Ct. at 945.
[42] Ibid.
[43] Department of Labor, Proposed Revision of Annual Information Return/Reports: Proposed Rules, 81 *Fed. Reg.* 47534 (July 21, 2016).

reporting and analysis. It would also have the added benefit of establishing a de facto standard for fully insured plans, which still are required to report into the APCDs directly and whose obligations were not modified by *Gobeille*.[44]

The success of Department of Labor regulations in preserving the APCDs remains an open question. The Trump administration already has a complicated and adversarial relationship with recent healthcare reforms. It is unclear as to whether the Trump Department of Labor will prioritize collecting healthcare data for APCDs, or if they will undo the proposed regulations. Even if the Trump Department of Labor agrees to collect a certain amount of healthcare data, it is unclear whether it will collect enough data elements to preserve the data integrity of APCDs or adopt the CDL as proposed by interested groups. As a result, it is important to also consider complementary strategies to promote healthcare data reporting outside of relying on Department of Labor regulations.

8.4.2 *Voluntary Data Contributions by Payers*

With the elimination of comprehensive APCDs and the uncertain guidance of the Department of Labor, is it realistic to believe that private payers would voluntarily contribute healthcare information, and specifically data on healthcare spending, to a centralized data repository? Although facially implausible, there is reason to believe that a voluntary system might work. Recently, three large health insurers – Aetna, Humana, and UnitedHealthcare – deposited economic data with the nonprofit, nonpartisan Health Care Cost Institute. The data from the three insurers are accessible to institute-approved academic research teams through a secure data enclave and represent nearly 28 percent of all persons insured by employer-sponsored health insurance in the United States, so although the data set is not complete, it is sufficiently large to yield robust conclusions. Thirty percent of overall US healthcare spending is in private health insurance, whereas a lesser amount, 20 percent of spending, is in Medicare.

Cooper et al.[45] used the Health Care Cost Institute data set to examine geographic variation in healthcare spending and in hospital prices based on hospital referral regions (HRRs) as defined by the Dartmouth Atlas of Health Care. Their analyses revealed significant findings about American healthcare spending, including (1) that private insurance spending varied by a factor of three across the United States, (2) variation in private spending was driven by providers' prices and not intensity of services provided, (3) the prices for specific procedures ranged greatly even within HRRs, and (4) hospital prices were significantly influenced by market

---

[44] John D. Freedman, et al., All-Payer Claims Databases: Uses and Expanded Prospects after *Gobeille*, 375 N. Engl. J. Med. 2215–17 (November 23, 2016).

[45] Zack Cooper et al., The Price Ain't Right? Hospital Prices and Health Spending on the Privately Insured, National Bureau of Economic Research Working Paper No. 21815 (2015).

power. These important findings extend results reported in the Dartmouth Atlas of Health Care on geographic variation in healthcare spending in Medicare.

Voluntary deposition of spending data by the three insurers provided novel insights into variation in healthcare spending in private insurance that were not previously possible to achieve because such data had been considered proprietary. Given that Aetna, Humana, and UnitedHealthcare provided their data for purposes of research, we believe that other payers may also find it beneficial to voluntarily deposit their data. Payers benefit from having the results of analyses such as these, which are possible only when large, pooled data sets are available. For example, payers may benefit from cost-containment studies performed using the pooled data. The development of the CDL will make it easier to compare data across voluntarily data deposits.

This example provides compelling evidence that voluntary data deposits into pooled repositories can yield important findings that may contribute to healthcare policymaking that can contribute to cost control. If all payers contributed their data to the Health Care Cost Institute or some other similar depository, more robust examinations of patterns in healthcare spending could result. Insights into how best to control the rate of growth of healthcare spending will clearly benefit payers as well as consumers.

8.4.3 Incentives for Data Sharing

To promote healthcare claims data sharing from employers who self-insure, perhaps beyond the skeleton to be required by the Department of Labor, states could consider offering incentives to those who share the data in the correct format. Employers, in contrast to private insurance companies, are not invested in the healthcare system beyond insuring their employees. Therefore, unlike private insurance companies, they may feel less motivated to contribute their data for the sake of improving the healthcare system. Other considerations may instead be paramount, such as avoiding the cost of compiling the data or protecting their privacy. Therefore, to have a voluntary database that would have the greatest reach, states may want to offer incentives to participate in a voluntary APCD.

The incentives could take a variety of forms. Most logically, they could be tax incentives relating to health insurance costs. APCDs also could offer incentives to the third-party administrators that generally run the self-insured employer plans. This would encourage third-party administrators, such as Blue Cross Blue Shield in the case of Liberty Mutual, to urge their clients to participate. For example, states could offer some reimbursement to be split between the third-party administrator that furnishes the data and the employers that consent to the sharing of their employees' data. Because virtually all self-insured employers use third-party administrators to implement their health plans, providing buy-in for the third-party administrators may reach a greater number of employers than offering the incentives to the employers themselves.

Lastly, states should consider nonfinancial incentives. For example, voluntary participation of employers may be jeopardized by nondisclosure agreements and privacy requirements in the post-*Gobeille* world. Because pre-*Gobeille* APCDs mandated data reporting, employers sidestepped liability under nondisclosure agreements and privacy laws such as the Health Insurance Portability and Accountability Act (HIPAA). Self-insuring employers may now not be able to use APCD requirements as a shield from privacy liabilities. States interested in encouraging voluntary participation in APCDs and other data-sharing initiatives should consider passing legislation explicitly protecting employers that disclose employee healthcare information.[46] Within the first month of the *Gobeille* decision, the New Hampshire legislature took up a bill to explicitly shield participating employers from disclosure liability. Such legal protections are especially important because APCDs often use nondeidentified information.

Incentives have an advantage over merely relying on employers to volunteer their healthcare claims data because they provide a measure of control over the scope and format of the data. Employers may not want to share as much data as the states would find helpful for healthcare services analysis. To resolve this difference, states could choose to offer the incentive only to employers and insurers who meet certain standards in scope. Likewise, tying the incentives to a particular format for the data would allow APCDs to avoid situations in which they have to reformat the data before they could be added to the database. Of course, the more onerous the requirements, the greater the incentives must be for employers to find contributing to the APCDs worthwhile.

8.5 CONCLUSION

Undoubtedly *Gobeille* changed the landscape for APCDs and healthcare claims data collection, as well as the potential for health services research that requires the sort of Big Data commonly generated by APCDs. Because the Supreme Court explicitly concluded that ERISA preempts state data collection from self-insured employer plans, even if the information states collect is of a different nature and a different purpose than the information collected under ERISA, states can no longer mandate that employers that self-insure report data to their APCDs. This presents serious concerns for the future of healthcare services research because APCDs will

---

[46] HIPAA is a federal statue, so states cannot normally waive its protections. HIPAA, however, includes a disclosure exception for public health activities. See 45 C.F.R. 164.512(b)(1)(i) (2016). In order to allow covered entities to disclose without authorization under this exception, the entity receiving the information must be responsible for public health as part of its official mandate or act under a grant of authority from a public health agency. APCDs should be explicitly authorized by state legislatures as public health authorities, and their purposes should be officially recognized as servicing public health interests to make explicit that this exception applies to these disclosures.

no longer present complete large data sets for researchers. Solutions to the problems imposed by *Gobeille* and ERISA must be found to avoid chilling some Big Data healthcare research.

There are some workarounds to these detrimental impacts of the *Gobeille* decision. The Department of Labor has taken Justice Breyer's suggestion to use its authority under ERISA to collect additional healthcare data to funnel into APCDs. It remains, however, an open question as to whether the Department of Labor will collect sufficient information to preserve the value of APCDs. Private insurers are increasingly starting to voluntarily contribute their data to databases. This trend should be commended, and states could further build on it by offering incentives to employers to participate. Incentives could greatly increase the rates of participation while also offering a further measure of control over the data reported.

PART III

The Internet of Things (IoT) and Health Big Data

INTRODUCTION

Nathan Cortez

The use of Big Data in healthcare is promising, in part, because of the remarkable volume and variety of data sources – ranging from electronic health records (EHRs) and insurance claims to diagnostic imaging, bedside monitoring, and laboratory testing. But these traditional sources are being augmented by a torrent of data generated by the Internet of Things (IoT) – connected devices such as wearables, ingestibles, implantables, and dozens of other permutations – that can collect data in more continuous and granular ways. IoT devices can capture not only transient health events that might be difficult to capture in traditional settings, such as hospitals, physician offices, and diagnostic laboratories, but also baselines in between. Thus one clear implication of the IoT is that neither data capture nor the point of care will be confined to traditional settings. In short, Big Data will not be nearly so "big" without the IoT. When coupled with the evolving tools of artificial intelligence and predictive analytics (e.g., machine learning, deep learning, neural networks, and data mining), Big Data can be deployed to make healthcare more efficient and effective. In this way, IoT devices could be the great extender in healthcare.

Of course, the very novelty of IoT devices has put a strain on existing legal, regulatory, and ethical frameworks that were crafted long ago with more traditional medicine in mind. As such, Big Data methods raise somewhat novel concerns centered on privacy, bias, and error. For example, will patients be able to maintain the privacy and security of their data? Will data be used to discriminate against patients based on their race, gender, sexuality, socioeconomic indicators, or predispositions to sickness? And how will we identify errors, not to mention resolve or prevent them? For the most part, our existing legal and regulatory frameworks do not offer satisfactory answers to these questions.

The two chapters in this part, by Dov Greenbaum and Marcus Comiter, both contemplate novel ways to address the various concerns raised by IoT technologies and health Big Data. Both authors are doubtful that traditional regulation by traditional regulators will suffice. Thus both look to nontraditional regulation by technological intermediaries or "layers" that can complement, rather than necessarily displace, the usual crop of regulators, such as the US Food and Drug Administration (FDA), the Federal Trade Commission (FTC), and the US Department of Health and Human Services Office of Civil Rights (HHS OCR).

Greenbaum, in Chapter 9, calls for "third-party clearinghouses" to act as a transparent, standardized conduit between IoT devices and end users. The clearinghouses could be created, funded, or associated in some way with the government, or perhaps a trusted nongovernmental organization, and could serve both technological and regulatory ends. For example, the technological role of a third-party clearinghouse would be to standardize health data across multiple platforms and devices, ensuring both interoperability and usability. The regulatory role would be to embed more robust privacy and data security standards in spaces that fall outside the purview of federal privacy and security rules deriving from the Health Insurance Portability and Accountability Act (HIPAA). Importantly, the clearinghouses could provide patients/consumers with centralized access to their own health data and perhaps ideally also some control over their access and use. Companies and organizations that wished to access, use, or transmit health data through the clearinghouses would have to agree to comply with the conditions of use – much like Medicare providers must agree to Medicare's long list of "conditions of participation." Companies and organizations that complied with clearinghouse standards could signal and thus market their compliance to users, who would have more reason to trust such transactions. Someday, perhaps, compliance with clearinghouse standards could form the basis for insurance reimbursement – almost a prerequisite for health innovations that wish to endure.

In similar spirit, Comiter, in Chapter 10, calls for "third-party data auditors" (TPDAs), nongovernmental entities that could be hired by patients/consumers to audit the use of their data by corporations, providers, data brokers, and others. Like Greenbaum's third-party clearinghouses, Comiter's third-party auditors would serve both technological and regulatory functions. Technology-wise, such auditing would require individual data to be tagged and tracked – features that are currently lacking in the new "data layer" in healthcare. Regulation-wise, auditors would help to promote more transparent data uses and disclosures, allow better enforcement of existing laws, provide important inputs to shifting societal norms regarding health data, and encourage further innovation with health data. Comiter envisions that the primary benefit of independent third-party auditors would be to increase transparency and accountability in health Big Data and thus to deter abuses and promote consumer trust in the long run.

In introducing their responses, both chapters catalog a range of looming concerns with health Big Data, including suboptimal interoperability, privacy, security, safety, accuracy, reliability, usability, transparency, and accountability. Compounding these problems is deep uncertainty regarding which regulators have jurisdiction to address which concerns. Thus the health Big Data space is marbled with tentative guidelines and enforcement actions by the usual suspects – the FDA, FTC, HHS OCR, and state medical boards and professional societies.

In many ways, then, health Big Data (amplified by the IoT) may represent a shifting paradigm for modern medicine. Historically an intuitive profession, medicine now grapples with how to process and make use of massive amounts of data. Like other scholars now grappling with the legal and policy implications of health Big Data, Greenbaum and Comiter acknowledge that the benefits of these technologies generally outweigh their risks and thus seek accommodations rather than solutions, relying appropriately on creative, nontraditional responses. We should expect the usual cycles of excess and correction that often accompany technological shifts in major sectors such as healthcare, and these two chapters offer compelling responses.

9

Avoiding Overregulation in the Medical Internet of Things

Dov Greenbaum

9.1 INTRODUCTION

Mobile health (mHealth) attempts to integrate varied technologies, including smartphones, wearables, and software applications (apps) to deliver health-related services. It is a rapidly growing industry with projected revenues of 20 billion US dollars by 2018.[1] The US Food and Drug Administration (FDA), Federal Trade Commission (FTC), Federal Communications Commission (FCC), Office of the National Coordinator for Health Information Technology (ONC), and the US Department of Health and Human Services Office for Civil Rights (OCR) have all provided unconvincing, vague, and expansive language to support their role in regulating this sector.[2] But, with advancements in mHealth far ahead of oversight and regulation, heavy-handed government regulation in this area is likely impracticable because it is too slow to adequately keep pace with innovation.

This chapter will review the status quo of smartphones, wearables, and apps in healthcare, including current regulatory oversight, and propose an alternative solution: succinctly, some form of industry-agreed-upon, government-sanctioned virtual clearinghouse that can scale as more people look to their smartphones for interaction with the health system. The system is intended to specifically overcome regulatory limitations, as well as even more pressing ethical and legal concerns.

---

[1] Things Are Looking App, *Economist*, March 12, 2016, at 55.
[2] Zachary Brennan, FDA Collaborates with FTC on Mobile Health App Regulatory Tool, Regulatory Affairs Professionals Society (April 5, 2016), available at http://raps.org/Regulatory-Focus/News/2016/04/05/24700/FDA-Collaborates-With-FTC-on-Mobile-Health-App-Regulatory-Tool/ [https://perma.cc/YLA6-WY75].

9.2 YOUR SMARTPHONE: LIKELY NOT THE SAME ONE THAT YOUR NEIGHBOR IS USING

The ubiquity of smartphones belies the exceedingly fractured nature of the market, particularly as that market continues to grow worldwide. Although the open-source Android operating system (OS) has a dominant market share of around 80 percent[3] (with remaining consumers split between Apple's iOS, Microsoft's Windows Phone, and others), there is not one monolithic Android OS. Available since 2008, there are numerous versions of the operating system and various iterations thereof.[4] The Android hardware market is similarly splintered, with at least half a dozen leading manufacturers, and an even greater number of smaller, lesser-known manufacturers,[5] each manufacturer with its own ever-expanding family of smartphone models. Apple, the distant second in world market share, similarly has its own varied versions of its operating system, iOS, and various versions of its hardware.

No matter the manufacture or the operating system, all smartphones have myriad sensors: proprioceptive (i.e., inward-looking) and exteroceptive (the opposite), analog and digital, integrated and external, passive and active, physical and virtual. This plethora of embedded sensors can measure, among other things, humidity, magnetism, mechanical movement, force, voltage, current, light, pressure, speed, temperature, moisture, proximity, motion, acceleration, direction, sound, and GPS coordinates.[6] New sensors continue to be developed and integrated.[7]

Each smartphone manufacturer incorporates its own subset of sensors. Even the same sensor type may be manufactured to different specifications by different manufactures. These differences can be inconsequential, or they can be substantial, differing in accuracy, range, calibration, resolution, signal-to-noise ratio, repeatability, and optimal operating conditions. For most applications, all of this inconsistency should not matter, but when app developers rely on the onboard sensors working in a particular fashion, subtle differences, especially in health, can make all the difference.

---

[3] Doug Olenick, Apple iOS and Google Android Smartphone Market Share Flattening: IDC, *Forbes*, May 27, 2015.

[4] Palak Khanna & Amandeep Singh, Google Android Operating System: A Review, 147 *Int'l J. Comput. App.* 26, 27 (2016). See also, e.g., Android Version History, Wikipedia, available at en.wikipedia.org/wiki/Android_version_history [https://perma.cc/X46V-3YZC] (last visited April 3, 2017).

[5] Margaret Butler, Android: Changing the Mobile Landscape, 10(1) *IEEE Pervasive Computing* 4–7 (2011).

[6] S. Ali et al., Sensors and Mobile Phones: Evolution and State-of-the-Art, 66 *Pakistan J. Sci.* 386–400 (2014).

[7] Javier Cañete & Sergey Y. Yurish, Sensors Systems for Smartphones, Tablets and IoT: New Advanced Design Approach, 187(4) *Sensors & Transducers* 1 (2015).

Finally, with over 1 million available apps for each of the leading operating systems, each and every one of the nearly 6 billion smartphones[8] is effectively a unique hardware and software ecosystem.[9]

9.3 HEALTH AND SMARTPHONES

This huge variety of sensors in everyone's pocket has helped spur the growth in the number of consumers who monitor, catalogue, and analyze various aspects of their daily lives: the "quantified-self movement." This movement has a relatively long history of association with healthcare.[10] Generally, "quantified-self" refers to the manual or automatic collection of physical, environmental, biological, or other forms of personal data such as vital signs or number of steps taken per day.[11] Often these data are collected automatically through the consumer's phone (with or without the consumer's knowledge) or through wearable sensor technology that automatically collect various types of data. The wearables sector is projected to have a compound annual growth rate of over 40 percent over the next five years,[12] representing a 1,000 percent increase in sales to just under 20 billion US dollars.[13]

In many instances, data collected by wearables can also be used for healthcare – including, for example, blood pressure monitors, pulse oximeters, glucose monitors, sleep apnea monitors, cardiac monitors, and others – and are passed onto local smartphone apps and eventually often to distant off-site third parties.

As with the smartphone market, the wearable market is equally fragmented, with major players ranging in diversity and nationality, including sporting goods manufacturers, computer and technology companies, and consumer electronics companies.[14] This diversity leads to the current lack of standardization within the

---

[8] Arjun Kharpal, Smartphone Market Worth $355 Billion, with 6 Billion Devices in Circulation by 2020: Report, CNBC (January 17, 2017), available at www.cnbc.com/2017/01/17/6-billion-smartphones-will-be-in-circulation-in-2020-ihs-report.html [https://perma.cc/6PYZ-CLEE].

[9] Matias Martinez & Sylvain Lecomte, Towards the Quality Improvement of Cross-Platform Mobile Applications, CNBC arXiv:1701.06767 (2017).

[10] Melanie Swan, Emerging Patient-Driven Health Care Models: An Examination of Health Social Networks, Consumer Personalized Medicine and Quantified Self-Tracking, 6(2) Int'l J. Envntl. Res. Pub. Health 492–525 (2009).

[11] Melanie Swan, The Quantified Self: Fundamental Disruption in Big Data Science and Biological Discovery, 1(2) Big Data 85, 85–99 (2013).

[12] IDC Forecasts Worldwide Shipments of Wearables to Surpass 200 Million in 2019, Driven by Strong Smartwatch Growth, IDC (December 17, 2015), available at https://perma.cc/6BV2-G2D2.

[13] Facts and Statistics on Wearable Technology, Statistia, available at www.statista.com/topics/1556/wearable-technology/ [https://perma.cc/523M-8ZET] (last visited April 4, 2017).

[14] Wearable Technology Market Worth 31.27 Billion USD by 2020, MarketsandMarkets (December 15, 2015), available at https://marketsandmarkets.com/PressReleases/wearable-electronics.asp [https://perma.cc/WKU8-W7Z9].

wearables field, potentially resulting in similar but different wearables returning similar but different data for the same individual.[15]

In addition to apps-associated wearables, mHealth apps all interact with the onboard sensors of the smartphone itself. These apps range in focus from simplistic and wildly inaccurate recreational-related software to disease-specific apps, often even developed by drug manufactures with an interest in a particular disease and its management.[16]

The less-recreational apps are part of the emerging mHealth app market, forecasted to reach nearly 60 billion US dollars by 2020.[17] It is estimated that there are at least half a billion smartphone users who currently have at least one mHealth app installed on their phone.[18] mHealth apps are especially useful for monitoring the vital signs of the elderly, diabetes management, cancer management, women's health, fertility, nutrition, management of chronic diseases such as asthma and chronic obstructive pulmonary disease (COPD), infectious disease, kidney disorders, and many other areas of health.[19] There are already more than 150,000 mHealth apps published by 45,000 different publishers; even with larger companies entering the market, a large percent of apps is still developed by stereotypical garage-based-type innovators.[20] It is likely that many of these companies do not appreciate the extent to which their apps could be regulated by the US government, particularly the FDA,[21] and possibly even the FCC[22] or the FTC.

---

[15] UL Introduces Comprehensive Compliance Services for the Wearable Technology Industry, UL Consumer Technology (January 14, 2015), available at http://ul.com/newsroom/press releases/ul-introduces-comprehensive-compliance-services-for-the-wearable-technology-industry/ [https://perma.cc/9JQS-MA9R]; P360: Standard for Wearable Consumer Electronic Devices. Overview and Architecture, IEEE Project (2017), available at standards.ieee.org/develop/project/360.html [https://perma.cc/UU8C-58NW].

[16] Things Are Looking App.

[17] Health Solutions Market Worth 59.15 Billion USD by 2020, MarketsandMarkets (November 17, 2015), available at marketsandmarkets.com/PressReleases/mhealth-apps-and-solutions.asp [https://perma.cc/7FGB-F3MG].

[18] Kevin Khachatryan, Medical Device Regulation in the Information Age: A Mobile Health Perspective, 55(4) Jurimetrics 477 (2015).

[19] Ibid.

[20] R2G, mHealth App Developer Economics 2015: 5th Annual Study on mHealth App Publishing Based on 5,000 Plus Respondents 8 (November 2015), available at https://research2guidance.com/r2g/r2g-mHealth-App-Developer-Economics-2015.pdf [https://perma.cc/ZXV8-JF5G].

[21] Keith Barritt, How to Avoid FDA Regulation Of Your Mobile Medical App, Med Device Online (July 7, 2015), available at meddeviceonline.com/doc/how-to-avoid-fda-regulation-of-your-mobile-medical-app-0001 [https://perma.cc/8HYN-968A].

[22] Sonali P. Gunawardhana & Scott Delacourt, An Introduction to FDA and FCC Regulations Impacting mHealth, Med Device Online (August 24, 2015), available at meddeviceonline.com/doc/an-introduction-to-fda-and-fcc-regulations-impacting-mhealth-0001 [https://perma.cc/N4KL-NE5H].

In addition to the apps, a number of large corporations have developed mHealth software platforms/environments. These software ecosystems include Microsoft's Health,[23] Google's Fit,[24] Apple's Healthkit,[25] Researchkit,[26] and CareKit.[27]

While some of these corporations have also attempted to regulate the health-related apps that run in these environments to protect consumer security and privacy,[28] at the same time, the same companies have concomitantly pushed to prevent their ecosystems from being heavily regulated by the FDA.[29] Perhaps reflecting an arrangement between Apple and the FDA, the FDA's list of mobile medical applications (MMAs) not requiring regulation[30] was recently updated to include something that sounds a lot like HealthKit.[31]

While these apps empower the lay public to become more involved in their healthcare[32] – people even tend to lie less to their phone than to their

---

[23] Microsoft Health, Microsoft, available at www.microsoft.com/microsoft-health/en-us [https://perma.cc/4VE3–8VVD] (last visited June 14, 2017).

[24] Thomas Claburn, Google Fit: Another Try At Health Data?, *Information Week*, June 14, 2014, available at www.informationweek.com/mobile/mobile-applications/google-fit-another-try-at-health-data—/d/d-id/1269680 fit.google.com/fit/u/0/ [https://perma.cc/LC8K-EX9H].

[25] Diane J. Skiba, The Connected Age: Digital Tools for Health, 35(6) *Nursing Educ. Perspect.*, 415 (2014).

[26] J. Ardine et al., Apple's ResearchKit: Smart Data Collection for the Smartphone Era?, 108(8) *J. Soc. Med.* 294–96 (2015).

[27] Matthias Mettler, #FocusOnTheEndUser: The Approach to Consumer-Centered Healthcare, in *Health 4.0: How Virtualization and Big Data Are Revolutionizing Healthcare* 109–23 (2017).

[28] Allison Grande, FTC's Brill Praises Apple HealthKit Data Privacy Policy, Law360 (May 20, 2015), available at www.law360.com/articles/658275/ftc-s-brill-praises-apple-healthkit-data-privacy-policy [https://perma.cc/Y492–5AWB].

[29] Jordan Kahn, FDA Details High-Level Meeting with Apple: "Moral Obligation to Do More" with Health, Innovative Sensors, 9To5Mac (June 9, 2014), available at 9to5mac.com/2014/06/09/fda-details-high-level-meeting-with-apple-moral-obligation-to-do-more-with-health-innovative-sensors/ [https://perma.cc/2RLY-A7G9]; Apple Works Hard to Avoid FDA Regulations, Klick Wire (June 18, 2014), available at klick.com/health/news/blog/mhealth/apple-works-hard-to-avoid-fda-regulations/ [https://perma.cc/3FZW-EU2G].

[30] US Food and Drug Administration, Guidance for Industry and Food and Drug Administration: Staff Document (February 9, 2015), available at www.fda.gov/downloads/MedicalDevices/.../UCM263366.pdf [https://perma.cc/DR92–85RY]; Mary Beth Hamel et al., FDA Regulation of Mobile Health Technologies, 371(4) *N. Engl. J. Med.* 372–79 (2014).

[31] Brian Dolan, FDA Makes Clear It Won't Regulate Apps like Apple's HealthKit, mobihealthnews (June 16, 2014), available at www.mobihealthnews.com/34173/fda-makes-clear-it-wont-regulate-apps-like-apples-healthkit [https://perma.cc/GVT7–5NGR]. See also added definitions as of June 11, 2014, US Food and Drug Administration, Mobile Medical Applications (August 1, 2016), available at www.fda.gov/MedicalDevices/DigitalHealth/MobileMedicalApplications/ucm368744.htm [https://perma.cc/VF8A-AXVE] ("Mobile apps that allows a user to collect, log, track and trend data such as blood glucose, blood pressure, heart rate, weight or other data from a device to eventually share with a heath care provider, or upload it to an online (cloud) database, personal or electronic health record [added June 11, 2014]").

[32] Gartner Survey Shows Wearable Devices Need to Be More Useful, Gartner (December 7, 2016), available at http://www.gartner.com/newsroom/id/3537117 [https://perma.cc/5N34-UT8S]; Teena Maddox, Wearables Have a Dirty Little Secret: 50% of Users Lose Interest, TechRepublic

doctor[33] – these mostly commercial and sometimes academic efforts – for example, the National Institutes of Health MD2K endeavor[34] – present substantial ethical and legal concerns.

9.4 REGULATORY CONCERNS WITH CURRENT MHEALTH APPS

By law, the FDA's jurisdiction could extend to many mHealth apps.[35] However, FDA guidance in this area is particularly problematic: its reviews are not designed with the typical app developer in mind and do not address some of the more relevant concerns in mHealth, including privacy, encryption, sensor calibration, consistency of data, transferability of data, and usefulness and efficacy of data, among others.

Any comprehensive FDA or other agency oversight in this area will be nearly impossible to implement given, for example, the huge number of apps.[36] Any concerted effort will likely only serve to inhibit growth and chill innovation through the uncertainty of regulatory intrusion, particularly for the large cohort of neophyte developers. "[I]t'll be quite a few years before we have a handle on this technology and how it's going to be regulated by the FDA, if at all ... The FDA doesn't have a depth of experience here that necessarily justifies them heavily regulating this area ... FDA involvement in the regulation of these products may kill off the innovation that we're looking for."[37]

Perhaps in recognition of this incapability of the FDA, Congress has attempted to preemptively take away the FDA's ability to regulate in this area. The Sensible Oversight for Technology which Advances Regulatory Efficiency Act (SOFTWARE Act) proposes to amend Section 201 of the US Food, Drug, and Cosmetic Act[38]: "Health software, as defined by the act, is exempted from regulation by the FDA except for software that provides patient-specific recommendations and poses a significant risk to patient safety."[39] Similarly, the Medical Electronic Data Technology Enhancement for Consumers Health (MEDTECH) Act seeks to amend the US

(February 13, 2014), available at www.techrepublic.com/article/wearables-have-a-dirty-little-secret-most-people-lose-interest/ [https://perma.cc/H2N4-ACCG].

[33] Jenna Worthman, On Technology: We're More Honest with Our Phones than with Our Doctor, *New York Times*, March 23, 2016.

[34] Santosh Kumar et al., Center of Excellence for Mobile Sensor Data-to-Knowledge (MD2K), 22(6) *J. Am. Med. Inform. Assoc.* 1137–42 (2015).

[35] Food and Drug Administration Safety and Innovation Act of 2012 Pub. L. No. 112–44 (2012).

[36] Karen Taylor, Connected Health: How Digital Technology Is Transforming Health and Social Care, *Deloitte* 11 (2015).

[37] Dana A. Elfin, FDA Struggles with Regulation of Mobile Health, Bloomberg (December 17, 2015), available at bna.com/fda-struggles-regulation-n57982065240/ [https://perma.cc/DSQ2-B5UR] (quoting Jeffrey K. Shapiro, a member of the Washington, DC, law firm of Hyman Phelps & McNamara P.C.).

[38] 21 U.S.C.S. § 321 (LEXIS through Pub. L. No. 115–22).

[39] H.R. 2396, 114th Cong. (2015).

Food, Drug, and Cosmetic Act to exclude many mHealth apps from regulation.[40] However, even this proposed legislation – which divides software into regulated medical software and mostly unregulated health software – remains too broad for useful and efficacious oversight.

In addition to congressional efforts to limit FDA oversight, the FDA itself may have already arguably effectively relinquished its authority over software-based medical devices, as recently indicated by efforts by a competing agency, the FTC, to police these devices,[41] with a focus more on cybersecurity than health.[42]

As this chapter was going to press, the FDA has signalled a renewed interest in this area with the recent introduction of a digital health unit at the FDA as part of its Digital Health Innovation Action Plan, and the even more recent selection of participants for its Digital Health Software Precertification Program (pre-cert).[43]

However it happens, less FDA oversight in this area is probably a good thing. Given (1) the sheer number of apps that could be regulated, (2) the number of iterations the software goes through before and after introduction to the market, (3) the lack of experience of both the FDA and most app publishers regarding the application of regulations in this sphere, and (4) the time it would take to regulate an app in comparison with the actual lifespan of that app – especially in consideration of the need to be first to market – any comprehensive Class II or III regulation in this area is effectively untenable.

9.5 PRACTICAL CONCERNS WITH MHEALTH APPS

In addition to the regulatory concerns raised earlier, there is the general realization that the nature of a global marketplace of app developers could prevent any individual jurisdiction from effectively enforcing preconditions or actual oversight on many mHealth apps. As such, there are vanishingly few options for any jurisdiction to control the apps that are available to smartphone owners. Moreover, even initial regulatory oversight of an app will not guarantee that (1) it works as intended

---

[40] S.1101, 114th Cong. (2015–16).
[41] US Food and Drug Administration, Regulatory Information: Food and Drug Administration Safety and Innovation Act (FDASIA) (October 6, 2015), available at www.fda.gov/RegulatoryInformation/LawsEnforcedbyFDA/SignificantAmendmentstotheFDCAct/FDASIA/ucm358951.htm [https://perma.cc/RV3Q-RGGQ]; Eric Wicklund, FTC Takes the Lead in mHealth App Regulation, mHealth Intelligence (March 24, 2016), available at http://mhealthintelligence.com/news/ftc-takes-the-lead-in-mhealth-app-regulation [https://perma.cc/ADB6-2FH8].
[42] But cf. 81 Fed. Reg. 71, 105 (October 14, 2016) (recent FDA guidance in the area of mHealth apps).
[43] US Food and Drug Administration Digital Health Innovation Action Plan (June 15, 2017) available at https://www.fda.gov/downloads/MedicalDevices/DigitalHealth/UCM568735.pdf; US Food and Drug Administration, FDA Selects Participants for New Digital Health Software Precertification Pilot Program (September 26, 2017), available at www.fda.gov/NewsEvents/Newsroom/PressAnnouncements/ucm577480.htm.

on every available platform, both hardware and software, and (2) that the inevitable consumer modifications, for example, through selective updates or the introduction of other apps to those platforms, will not alter the interaction of the app with the patient.

Further, there may be other, more pressing concerns relating to mHealth apps regardless of their regulatory status and that are not even dealt with by theFDA: privacy and security.[44] In fact, cybersecurity has been, until late in 2016,[45] conspicuously lacking from the FDA's mHealth app guidance.[46]

Whereas the FCC has suggested some arguably unrealistic solutions[47] to deal with these issues, and the FTC has even recently challenged "the public to create an innovative tool that will help protect consumers from security vulnerabilities in the software of home devices,"[48] it is generally assumed that wearables and consumer mobile platforms, and the software that runs on them, are insecure. For example, Google's recently disclosed that the vast majority of unencrypted traffic through Google's servers originates in mobile devices.[49]

Further, "[a] recent study cites the healthcare sector as the most immature industry in terms of personal mobile device security, endpoint compliance discovery and remediation."[50] As such, it is no surprise that "[c]linicians and patients are adopting mobile technologies faster than providers can protect security and privacy."[51] These security concerns are nearly insurmountable if mHealth relies on

---

[44] Kathryn C. Montgomery et al., Health Wearable Devices in the Big Data Era: Ensuring Privacy, Security, and Consumer Protection (2016), available at www.democraticmedia.org/sites/default/files/field/public/2016/aucdd_wearablesreport_final121516.pdf [https://perma.cc/2SHV-5A4P].

[45] US Food and Drug Administration, Postmarket Management of Cybersecurity in Medical Devices: Guidance for Industry and Food and Drug Administration Staff (December 28, 2016), available at www.fda.gov/downloads/MedicalDevices/DeviceRegulationandGuidance/GuidanceDocuments/ucm482022.pdf [https://perma.cc/66FR-QW8X].

[46] Katherine Booth Wellington, Cyberattacks on Medical Devices and Hospital Networks: Legal Gaps and Regulatory Solutions, 30 *Santa Clara Computer High Tech. L. J.* 139, 186 (2014).

[47] Karl Bode, The FCC Suggests Some Wishy Washy, Highly Unlikely Solutions to the Poorly-Secured Internet of Things, Techdirt (December 12, 2016), available at www.techdirt.com/articles/20161207/06540336216/fcc-suggests-some-wishy-washy-highly-unlikely-solutions-to-poorly-secured-internet-things.shtml [https://perma.cc/D3GF-SEY2].

[48] US Federal Trade Commission, FTC Announces Internet of Things Challenge to Combat Security Vulnerabilities in Home Devices (January 4, 2017), available at www.ftc.gov/news-events/press-releases/2017/01/ftc-announces-internet-things-challenge-combat-security [https://perma.cc/D6BM-R33C].

[49] Google, Transparency Report, available at www.google.com/transparencyreport/https/metrics/?hl=en [https://perma.cc/PE4B-F6SU] (last visited April 6, 2017).

[50] Judy Mottl, mHealth Success Hinges on Security, Workflow Adaptability, Fierce Mobile Healthcare (October 4, 2014), available at fiercemobilehealthcare.com/story/mhealth-success-hinges-security-workflow-adaptability/2014-10-04 [https://perma.cc/7WWK-LZ4D].

[51] Bari Faudree & Mark Ford, Security and Privacy in Mobile Health, *Wall Street Journal*, August 6, 2013, available at http://deloitte.wsj.com/cio/2013/08/06/security-and-privacy-in-mobile-health/ [https://perma.cc/XYQ9-LZX8].

the consumer's smartphone to collect and/or to mediate the analysis of health-related data. "Mobile phones are one of the most insecure devices that were ever available ... they're very easy to tap."[52]

This lack of security directly leads to privacy concerns; experts estimate, for example, that 60 percent of Android phones have been infected by malicious code.[53] Health data are at risk for privacy breaches while they are being collected by smartphones or via remote sensors, while they sit on the phone, and while they are in transit to other systems, such as to third-party devices or the cloud.[54] This inability to properly accommodate all the private data resulting from mHealth apps could be a huge liability for mHealth apps, and needs to be addressed.

Overall, any leaking, stealing, or sniffing of data could also expose risk-averse app developers to fines and lawsuits, chilling innovation. Guidelines and even regulations could attempt to enforce encryption protocols and other efforts to protect data, but in consumer-facing apps, this type of enforcement is often not feasible because it requires the unprecedented and unlikely cooperation of the multitudes of mHealth app developers and/or consumers to be implemented.[55] It is unlikely that even suggested guidelines will be heeded: app developers uninterested in cumbersome and user-unfriendly encryption are unlikely to impose encryption without consumer demand. And consumers are unlikely to demand encryption because both hardware- and software-level encryption can affect phone performance and battery life. Most consumers do not protect their mobile phones with any technological protections.[56] Even consumers who encrypt data on their own devices are unlikely to be sufficiently technologically savvy to encrypt communications between their

---

[52] Dov Greenbaum, Direct Digital Engagement of Patients and Democratizing Health Care, 32 *Santa Clara Computer High Tech. L. J.* 93 (2015).

[53] Breaking Down the mHealth Security Landscape, Smart Clinic Blog (September 25, 2014), available at http://smartclinicapp.com/breaking-mhealth-security-landscape/ [https://perma.cc/45DW-XDZY].

[54] Marc Goodman, *Future Crimes* 117 (2015); David Kotz, A Threat Taxonomy for mHealth Privacy, COMSNETS (2011); Your Secrets Aren't Safe: Data Thieves Are after Your Most Private Info – When You Use Wi-Fi and Shop Online, and Even When You Store Files in the Cloud, *Consumer Reports*, May 2014, available at www.consumerreports.org/cro/magazine/2014/07/your-secrets-aren-t-safe/index.htm [https://perma.cc/DVD9-XUHP].

[55] Bruno M. Silva et al., A Data Encryption Solution for Mobile Health Apps in Cooperation Environments, 15(4) *J. Med. Internet Res.* (2013).

[56] Sophos, Press Release, 67 Percent of Consumers Don't Have Password Protection on Their Mobile Phones (August 9, 2011), available at sophos.com/en-us/press-office/press-releases/2011/08/67-percent-of-consumers-do-not-have-password-protection-on-their-mobile-phones.aspx [https://perma.cc/UHH7-NDCL]; Herb Weisbaum, Most Americans Don't Secure Their Smartphones, CNBC (April 26, 2014), available at cnbc.com/2014/04/26/most-americans-dont-secure-their-smartphones.html [https://perma.cc/39H9-3AL8]; Smart Phone Thefts Rose to 3.1 million in 2013: Industry Solution Falls Short, While Legislative Efforts to Curb Theft Continue, *Consumer Reports*, May 28, 2014, available at www.consumerreports.org/cro/news/2014/04/smart-phone-thefts-rose-to-3-1-million-last-year/index.htm [https://perma.cc/8DKD-HZVF].

applications and third parties. Moreover, the government itself is against strong encryption for smartphone data.[57]

The standardization concerns just described are not only an issue vis-à-vis the hardware configurations of the mobile platforms, standardization will also be necessary to promote data consistency, for example, such that readings are all provided using the same formulas and the same units to allow for comparisons across wearable platforms. A lack of standardization makes it harder to collect, decrypt, and analyze the data and keep those private data safe and secure. Standardized data also help to make the data useful for large-scale analysis and comparison of data. It also helps to prevent mistakes that can result when more incompatible data accounting methods are employed.[58]

With thousands of apps available to consumers and an inherent grading and reporting system built into most app markets, it would seem unlikely that inefficacious apps would remain popular for long. However, this is not always the case.[59] There needs to be a better system to monitor and regulate the market while also making sure that the patient's data are actionable, safe, and secure. Weighty top-down regulation will likely be ineffective and not be agile enough to account for changes in these emerging industries.

9.6 CLEARINGHOUSES

According to FTC Chairwoman Edith Ramirez, "The only way for the Internet of Things to reach its full potential for innovation is with the trust of American consumers."[60] This trust is currently being eroded by the concerns of privacy and security, as well as the lack of consistency and efficacy in the apps and wearables.

To this end, and to specifically solve many of the technical issues reported herein, I suggest the implementation of a third-party clearinghouse. This would allow for the trusted exchange of information between the smartphone (and any wearables communicating through it) and the end point for the data, either corporate, medical, or academic. These one or more third-party clearinghouses would act as

---

[57] Maggie Ybarra, FBI Pushes to Weaken Cell Phone Security, Skirt Encryption, *Washington Times*, May 26, 2015; FBI Director Lashes Out at Apple, Google for Encrypting Smartphones, RT (September 26, 2014), available at http://rt.com/usa/190980-comey-fbi-encryption-phones/ [https://perma.cc/2ZV4-4HAG].

[58] Douglas Isbell et al., RELEASE 99–113: Mars Climate Orbiter Team Finds Likely Cause of Loss (September 30, 1999), available at http://mars.nasa.gov/msp98/news/mco990930.html [https://perma.cc/VDY3-3GPB].

[59] Timothy B. Plante et al., Validation of the Instant Blood Pressure Smartphone App, 176(5) JAMA Intern. Med. 700–2 (2016).

[60] US Federal Trade Commission, Report on Internet of Things Urges Companies to Adopt Best Practices to Address Consumer Privacy and Security Risks (January 27, 2015), available at ftc.gov/news-events/press-releases/2015/01/ftc-report-internet-things-urges-companies-adopt-best-practices [https://perma.cc/CQ2Z-LTVR].

transparent shared interfaces for mHealth data, collecting, tracking, aggregating, and transmitting data to the end user.

The proposed clearinghouses could be associated, funded, and/or run by a government, a nongovernmental organization (NGO), or a multinational organization that would have the necessary and sufficient levels of trust for this task. For example, the US government could develop regulations akin to the Fair Credit Reporting Act (FCRA),[61] which ostensibly promotes efficiency and protects privacy in the collecting and conveying of consumer credit data. As with credit reporting agencies (CRAs) under the FCRA that collect financial and personal information from data furnishers, the proposed clearinghouses would similarly collect data and have imposed duties. Similar to CRAs, the proposed clearinghouses would be regulated by one or more agencies, perhaps the FTC and the FDA, which would leave much of the practical details to the clearinghouses. And like CRAs, these clearinghouses – through directing all voluntarily provided patient data through a single or limited number of gateways – could help consumers to keep track of the overwhelming amount of data that they generate and export and warn consumers of any malicious hijacking of those data.

The mostly unobtrusive clearinghouses would receive and report data provided voluntarily from each smartphone and/or wearable. The clearinghouses would be configured to encourage data integration and device interoperation, for example, by requiring all data passing through to be in a standardized format. "As it is right now, all the wearable gear out there is marching to its own tune, doing its own thing, and grabbing data in its own way with marginal accuracy. By and large, these are closed ecosystems or proprietary applications within an open architecture that have limited scalability."[62] Nonstandardized data would be rejected.

The development of these standards is nontrivial because it also requires scientists, statisticians, medical doctors, and engineers to agree on universal standards. However, like the CRAs mentioned earlier, data, encryption, and other relevant standards could be developed through a trade organization such as the Consumer Data Industry Association (CDIA).

The clearinghouses would also query the reporting smartphones and wearables to confirm that, through regular firmware updates, the phone or associated wearable is calibrated, and that the outputs are normalized to account for known variability associated with the sensor environments. This might be more useful than outputting raw data because the clearinghouse lacks context to properly evaluate those data. Alternatively, the clearinghouses could bench test devices to determine the inherent variability of sensors depending on environment, sensor placement, and

[61] Fair Credit Reporting Act, 15 U.S.C.S. § 1681 (LEXIS through Pub. L. No. 115–18).
[62] R. Maxwell, Samsung's "Voice of the Body" Is an Open Hardware and Software Platform for Personal Health Monitoring, PhoneArena (May 28, 2014), available at phonearena.com/news/Samsungs-Voice-of-the-Body-is-an-open-hardware-and-software-platform-for-personal-health-monitoring_id56601 [https://perma.cc/HYD6-GW7R].

other factors.[63] Periodic user-independent recalibration of the sensors could also potentially be enforced. A clearinghouse could also require that all data that it receives be encrypted via standard encryption methods and refuse the data if any of these concerns have not been met.

Once the desired condition of transmitted data is established, unencrypted, unstandardized, or noninteroperable data would bounce back, frustrating the user and putting market pressure on the app developers to comply with the necessary encryption and data standards. Clearinghouses could change these conditions and provide sufficient notice to manufacturers to update their outputs. These manufacturers could also advertise, as a selling point, that their data meet the necessary standards. Additionally, given best practices proposed by, for example, the American Medical Association (AMA), it is hopeful that when physicians prescribe a mobile medical app or a wearable for a patient, they will also choose apps or wearables that meet the standards.

This proposal is not without its own concerns. Notably, as a centralized pathway, it will likely become an appealing target for malicious hackers. And even though privacy concerns will likely make the data anonymous, it will nevertheless require persistent identifiers across devices for the data to be usable by downstream users. With enough data from enough devices, it is conceivable that the data could be deanonymized. Further, best practices may not be practical for all users, and the demands by the system may be too high or not easily or practically implemented by many consumers. Or some devices manufacturers may not respond to the suggested market forces and prioritize consumer usability of the device over the safety and efficacy of the data.

Further, the clearinghouses are not intended to assess the overall efficacy of any particular app, nor will they prevent the continued generation of ineffective (at best) applications that exploit the weak to nonexistent barriers to entry. Not that this oversight is not necessary; a notoriously inaccurate app spent the better part of a year as a top mHealth app on both Apple's and Google's sites.[64] However, there are other efforts that may be better suited to this task, both from the public sector, such as the AMA[65] and the UK's National Health Service,[66] or from the

---

[63] Stephen S. Intille et al., New Horizons in Sensor Development, 44(1 Suppl. 1) *Med. Sci. Sports Exerc.* S24 (2012); Ty Ferguson et al., The Validity of Consumer-Level Activity Monitors in Healthy Adults Worn in Free-Living Conditions: A Cross-Sectional Study, 12(1) *Int'l J. Behav. Nutrition Physical Activity* 42 (2015).

[64] Satish Misra, Blood Pressure App Study Shows That Top Health App Was Highly Inaccurate, iMedicalApps (March 2, 2016), available at www.imedicalapps.com/2016/03/instant-blood-pressure-app-study/# [https://perma.cc/94QT-GFLR].

[65] American Medical Association, AMA Adopts Principles to Promote Safe, Effective mHealth Applications (November 16, 2016), available at www.ama-assn.org/ama-adopts-principles-promote-safe-effective-mhealth-applications [https://perma.cc/MV4K-2AL8].

[66] Health Apps Library, NHS (October 16, 2015), available at www.nhs.uk/pages/healthappslibrary.aspx [https://perma.cc/2FMU-855C].

private sector.[67] Alternatively, app stores benefiting from economies of scale as well as extensive experience are arguably better suited to prevent ineffective apps from getting to consumers.[68]

9.7 CONCLUSION

With mHealth growth far outstripping government agency regulatory abilities and continued growth and inherent variability in the mobile device market, there is an urgent need for a useful and flexible solution to many of the ethical and legal concerns associated with mHealth. I propose a clearinghouse solution that funnels all mHealth data through a centralized location that can provide usability, safety, and interoperability through, among other applications, enforced standards, encryption, and other technical measures to ensure that consumers' health data are safe and useful.

---

[67] Stephen Armstrong, Which App Should I Use?, *BMJ: Br. Med. J.* (Online) 351 (2015); Stovan Stoyanov et al., Mobile App Rating Scale: A New Tool for Assessing the Quality of Health Mobile Apps, 3(1) *JMIR mHealth uHealth* e27 (2015).

[68] Iltifat Husain, Apple Will Now Start Screening Medical and Health Apps More Closely, iMedicalapps (September 2, 2016), available at www.imedicalapps.com/2016/09/apple-screening-medical-health-apps/# [https://perma.cc/4XCF-SH33].

10

Data Policy for Internet of Things Healthcare Devices

Aligning Patient, Industry, and Privacy Goals in the Age of Big Data

Marcus Comiter

10.1 INTRODUCTION

While the healthcare Internet of Things (IoT) holds much promise, regulating consumer-grade healthcare data not covered under existing healthcare data regulations, such as the Health Insurance Portability and Accountability Act (HIPPA), is a substantial policy challenge of the present day.[1] As a first step toward regulating the healthcare IoT, I introduce the concept of "third-party data auditors" (TPDAs). TPDAs are specialized, highly technical third-party actors hired by individuals to audit the collection and use of their healthcare data with the goal of giving users control over and understanding of their data.

TPDAs present a novel regulatory framework: rather than advocating top-down policies at this early point in the development of the healthcare IoT, TPDAs empower individuals to take control of their data and its use while allowing for necessary innovation in this rapidly developing field, as well as help to inform regulators to create more effective policy by illuminating the now-hidden world of data use. TPDAs reflect the Federal Trade Commission's (FTC's) current strategy of "giving consumers information and choices about their data" in regulating the IoT.[2] Specifically, this new TPDA-mediated framework will accomplish these goals by enshrining the following policy goals, inspired by the 2012 Consumer

---

[1] US Federal Trade Commission, FTC Spring Privacy Series: Consumer Generated and Controlled Health Data 1–2 (2014), available at www.ftc.gov/system/files/documents/videos/spring-privacy-series-consumer-generated-controlled-health-data/ftc_spring_privacy_series_-_consumer_generated_and_controlled_health_data_-_transcript.pdf [https://perma.cc/M7C3-QQFK].

[2] US Federal Trade Commission, Internet of Things Privacy and Security in a Connected World, FTC Staff Report, vii (2015), available at www.ftc.gov/system/files/documents/reports/federal-trade-commission-staff-report-november-2013-workshop-entitled-internet-things-privacy/150127iotrpt.pdf [https://perma.cc/XQR9-HRUV].

Privacy Bill of Rights,[3] within the healthcare IoT: individual awareness, accountability through transparency, enforcement of existing laws, and protection of innovation.

10.2 CONSIDERATIONS IN DESIGNING POLICY FOR THE HEALTHCARE IOT

Before describing TPDAs, I first highlight leading considerations in current policy thought in regulating the IoT and their applicability to the healthcare IoT. I will demonstrate how TPDAs embody these leading considerations in the fourth section of this chapter.

"Fair information practice principles" (FIPPs) have formed the basis of modern privacy protection.[4] According to an Obama White House report, "[T]he FIPPs articulate basic protections for handling personal data. They provide that an individual has a right to know what data is collected about him or her and how it is used."[5]

In 2012, the Obama administration released *Consumer Data Privacy in a Networked World*, an updated privacy framework largely in line with the principles espoused by FIPPs.[6] The mainstay of the report is a "Consumer Privacy Bill of Rights" (CPBR), which embodies the same spirit of the FIPPs by advocating individual control over data collection and use, transparency in use, respect for the context in which the data were collected, security in handling data, consumer access and ability to correct inaccuracies, focused collection, and accountability.[7]

10.2.1 *Concept I: Individual Awareness*

I define "individual awareness" as the ability of individuals to be aware of what data are being collected, when data are being collected, how data are being used, and when data are being used. Two elements of the CPBR address individual awareness: "individual control," defined as "the right to exercise control over what personal data companies collect from [users] and how they use it,"[8] and "respect for context," defined as "the right to expect that companies will collect, use, and disclose personal data in ways that are consistent with the context in which consumers provide

---

[3] White House, Consumer Data Privacy in a Networked World: A Framework for Protecting Privacy and Promoting Innovation in the Global Digital Economy 47–48 (2012), available at https://obamawhitehouse.archives.gov/sites/default/files/privacy-final.pdf [https://perma.cc/RQ2V-3CCB].
[4] Ibid.
[5] Ibid.
[6] Ibid.
[7] Ibid., at 10.
[8] Ibid., at 47.

the data."[9] This principle is perhaps the cornerstone of the CPRB, "assuring consumers that their data will be collected and used in ways consistent with their expectations."[10] This concept was derived from two principles codified as a part of the FIPPs: specifying the purpose of using collected data and limiting the use of those data.[11]

The structure of the healthcare IoT presents new challenges to individual awareness because the physical nature of IoT devices makes surreptitious data collection and dissemination easy. To see this, consider, for example, that IoT devices may collect nonrelevant data incidentally, such as location information, due to their connection to the Internet via a cell phone. As a further example, consider a fitness-tracking device with an end-user license agreement (EULA) that stipulates permission to share collected data with other third parties. Because many users do not read EULAs,[12] this scenario constitutes an example in which the individual may be aware that data are being collected by the device but may not be fully aware of the extent of how these data are used and shared. As a result, users may be unaware of what data are collected and how they are shared.

10.2.2 Concept II: Accountability through Transparency

Accountability and transparency[13] regarding the practices of firms operating in the healthcare IoT will enable both the public and regulators to hold these firms accountable for their practices. The CPBR enshrines these elements in three pillars: "transparency," defined as "a right to easily understandable and accessible information about privacy and security practices"[14]; "accountability," defined as "a right to have personal data handled by companies with appropriate measures in place to assure they adhere to the CPBR"[15]; and "access and accountability," defined as "a right to access and correct personal data in usable formats in a manner that is appropriate to the sensitivity of the data and the risk of adverse consequences to consumers if the data is inaccurate."[16]

---

[9] John Podesta, Big Data: Seizing Opportunities, Preserving Values 19 (2014), available at https://obamawhitehouse.archives.gov/sites/default/files/docs/big_data_privacy_report_may_1_2014.pdf [https://perma.cc/A2N4-GV72].

[10] Ibid., at 20.

[11] White House, Consumer Data Privacy in a Networked World, at 16.

[12] Aleecia M. McDonald & Lorrie Faith Cranor, The Cost of Reading Privacy Policies 17 (2008), available at http://lorrie.cranor.org/pubs/readingPolicyCost-authorDraft.pdf [https://perma.cc/LV46-TTAW].

[13] US Federal Trade Commission, Data Brokers: A Call for Transparency and Accountability 1 (2014), available at www.ftc.gov/system/files/documents/reports/data-brokers-call-transparency-accountability-report-federal-trade-commission-may-2014/140527databrokerreport.pdf [https://perma.cc/4HTH-ZHX7].

[14] Podesta, Big Data, at 19.

[15] Ibid.

[16] Ibid.

Accountability is needed in the healthcare IoT to protect users from data-inflicted harms. In other consumer data-driven industries, there is little or no accountability or transparency regarding firms that use or collect data. For example, on the Internet, the firms collecting, selling, and using the data of a particular individual do not necessarily have a relationship with that individual.[17] In this respect, many individuals are completely unaware even of the existence of these firms, let alone do they understand how their data is being used.[18] This precipitates a fundamental lack of accountability in the system, as individuals have little if no recourse with which to hold firms responsible for harms their actions may inflict.

Such firms, including data brokers, have already emerged, combining and selling anonymized healthcare data.[19] However, the structure of the IoT itself makes transparency more difficult. Firms that may have traditionally relied on explicit consent mechanisms to achieve transparency in their data-collection actions cannot do so in the IoT because this would require consent prompts possibly "hundreds or thousands of times a day."[20]

10.2.3 Concept III: Accordance with Existing Laws and Norms

Policy must ensure that existing laws, such as antidiscrimination laws, are followed and enforced in the healthcare IoT. The existence of complicated machine learning and Big Data inference algorithms complicate enforcement abilities drastically: these algorithms, which largely function as a "black box," have the danger of producing unlawful behavior possibly unbeknown to the firms operating these algorithms. As a way to combat this, the CPBR prescribes "focused collection," defined as "a right to reasonable limits on the personal data that companies collect and retain."[21] Under this concept, data that are not relevant and could be used for discrimination either directly or indirectly by algorithms should not be collected.

In the context of the healthcare IoT, the potential for discrimination and other unlawful behavior poses serious threats. Firms may hide behind complicated algorithms that are able to create discriminatory or harmful behavior automatically. For

---

[17] Ibid., at 56.
[18] This further supports the previous claim regarding the lack of individual awareness. FTC, Data Brokers, at i.
[19] Adam Tanner, How Data Brokers Make Money Off Your Medical Records, Sci. Am., February 1, 2016, available at www.scientificamerican.com/article/how-data-brokers-make-money-off-your-medical-records/ [https://perma.cc/JQ4R-FF3T].
[20] Christopher Wolf & Jules Polonetsky, An Updated Privacy Paradigm for the "Internet of Things" 4 (2013), available at www.futureofprivacy.org/wp-content/uploads/Wolf-and-Polonetsky-An-Updated-Privacy-Paradigm-for-the-%E2%80%9CInternet-of-Things%E2%80%9D-11-19-2013.pdf [https://perma.cc/7QK5-P69P].
[21] Ibid.

example, healthcare IoT data, such as the items in a family's smart refrigerator, may be a de facto indicator for race or religion. However, discriminatory behavior in this context is difficult to observe because it occurs behind an algorithmically obscured wall and may even be done unbeknown to the firm by an algorithm automatically learning this discriminatory behavior. A White House report has already found examples of algorithmic discrimination on the Internet.[22]

10.2.4 *Concept IV: Protecting Innovation*

For all its potential pitfalls, the healthcare IoT holds great promise in promoting progress and advancing civilization in the context of healthcare. As such, regulatory policy must not be prohibitively burdensome as to discourage this innovation.

However, to protect innovation, consumer confidence in the healthcare IoT itself must be maintained, for example, through taking proper security protections. The CPBR supports this with its "security element," defined as "a right to secure and responsible handling of personal data."[23] The FTC has further supported this, suggesting data minimization, security audits, and testing as ways to prevent security lapses.[24]

10.3 THIRD-PARTY DATA AUDITORS: A NEW SOLUTION

In this section I introduce the concept of "third-party data auditors" (TPDAs). In the following section I examine how TPDAs embody the guiding policy principles outlined in the preceding section and then discuss potential limitations and considerations of TPDAs.

10.3.1 *What Are TPDAs?*

TPDAs are a class of highly technical, skilled organizations that are hired by individuals to monitor and audit the collection and use of their data. After collecting all the data that have been collected on their clients or purchased by firms, TPDAs analyze the data that were collected, how the data were collected, and how they were used. Once finished with this analysis, the TPDAs present their findings to the client in an easy-to-comprehend report, as well as alerting the client to potentially harmful, unscrupulous, or unlawful collections or uses of data. By empowering individuals, TPDAs will allow the public to regain control of their data.

---

[22] Podesta, Big Data, at 7.
[23] White House, Consumer Data Privacy in a Networked World, at 48.
[24] FTC, Internet of Things Privacy and Security, at iii.

TPDAs as the mainstay of healthcare IoT regulatory policy offer a number of benefits:

- **TPDAs are entirely devoted to protecting the citizenry's healthcare IoT data.** In their capacity, TPDAs act as trusted third parties for their clients – their charters are solely to audit on behalf of their clients, and they have no institutional or proprietary loyalties. To formalize this, TPDAs will hold a distinction from a government agency to certify their practices and enforce the formal duties the TPDA has to its clients. In this respect, TPDAs are essentially instantiating permanent citizen advocates for consumers' healthcare data.
- **TPDAs will embody policy goals without top-down regulation.** TPDAs are an effective first step in advancing current policy goals, as discussed previously, but will do so without potentially difficult or ineffective top-down regulation that is difficult to create while the industry is developing at this early stage.
- **TPDAs' structure allows them to address the rapidly changing technology sector.** As TPDAs seek to inform individuals and society about data use, they are well suited as a regulatory tool in this rapidly changing field because they can continue to inform users and policy makers as the field develops.

With these thoughts in mind, we now examine how TPDAs will function. I envision TPDAs operating as follows:

Step 1: The TPDA Obtains Certification

TPDAs will first obtain an official certification. This certification will hold them to predetermined legal requirements and conduct, such as not selling their clients' data and upholding set security standards, and establish the TPDA as an agent working on behalf of its clients.

Step 2: The TPDA Completes Initial Setup

After the TPDA is created, it immediately begins the preparations necessary to operate, creating the software and tools it will use to perform its job. As a first step, the TPDA chooses which firms (i.e., which device manufactures, data brokers, insurance firms, etc.) it will offer as part of its auditing services, and writes software to be able to interact with those firms' data systems. This will allow the TPDA to work with the data it receives on its clients from the firms (see step 4).

Second, the TPDA will begin creating the software it will use to analyze and audit its clients' data. Using highly technical data-processing, machine learning, and statistical techniques, each TPDA will design its own proprietary methods to understand how data are used. With this preliminary work completed, the TPDA is now ready to accept clients.

Step 3: Client Hires a TPDA

The first step in the client-TPDA relationship is the hiring of a particular TPDA. TPDAs can compete on a number of potential issues, including price, level of services offered, reputation, capabilities, and purpose. Once the client has hired the TPDA, the client provides the appropriate level of identification, as well as authorization to request his or her data from firms. This identification and authority will allow the TPDA to access the client's data from firms (see step 4).

Step 4: The TPDA Requests Data

After the client and TPDA have established a formal relationship, the TPDA uses the identification and authorization provided by its client to "pull," or request, the client's data from all firms with which the TPDA offers auditing services. This mechanism is similar to the manner in which a patient going to a new doctor may authorize the new doctor to request a copy of his or her chart from the previous doctor. In response to the request, each firm responds with the client's data.

Step 5: The TPDA Parses and Analyzes the Data

Once the data are received, the software the TPDA has already developed parses the data in order to transfer them into its system. Once the data are in a usable form, the substantive work begins. Using the proprietary algorithms and methods it has previously designed (step 2), the TPDA begins analyzing how the client's data have been used. By searching for common patterns, understanding use cases, and tracking data flow between all the firms being audited, the TPDA attempts to find all the relevant information regarding the collection and use of the client's data.

Step 6: The TPDA Formulates a Report

Following this analysis, the TPDA produces a detailed report for each of its clients. Each report contains information regarding how the client's data have been collected, used, and sold. The report, like the algorithms used to generate the analysis, is a product of each particular TPDA. It is at each TPDA's discretion how best to represent the data, focus the client's attention, and discover any potential sensitive, illegal, or abusive uses of the data. This report may also make suggestions to the client as to changes in use of technologies, tracking opt-out opportunities not currently used, and other potential suggestions of importance.

Step 7: The TPDA Formulates Aggregate Reports

TPDAs will also create aggregate reports studying the use of data across society at large. To formulate these reports, TPDAs will use the data they have collected across all clients (which will be provably anonymized and subject to client opt-in). The idea behind aggregate reports is to enable larger-scale analysis of how firms use healthcare data – information that can be useful, for example, to regulators and policymakers. TPDAs are in the perfect position to complete this task. Given their skills and the algorithms already developed, they have the ability; given the data they have collected on behalf of their clients, they have the means; and given their certification and statutory obligations to not work in their own or any competing interest, as well as strict anonymization and opt-in controls, they have the trust. The levels of ability, means, and trust are levels perhaps no other entity possesses, rendering TPDAs singularly worthy and capable of examining this extremely large and powerful data set.

10.4 TPDAs ADDRESS IMPORTANT CONSIDERATIONS IN DATA POLICY

In the second section I discussed a number of considerations that should influence the design of policy for the healthcare IoT. We will now explore how TPDAs embody these principles.

10.4.1 Promoting Individual Awareness

The cornerstone of TPDAs is in providing individual awareness as a service. Through the reporting and advisory roles TPDAs play, individuals are empowered to understand what data have and are being collected and how those data are being used, shared, and sold within the industry.

10.4.2 Promoting Transparency and Accountability

TPDAs create an accountability mechanism by creating a window through which consumers may examine firms' use of their data. Because of the light shined on the industry through the TPDAs' analysis and report-writing process, firms will no longer be able to operate in obscurity, therefore bringing important transparency to the industry. Illegal data practices will be swiftly brought to the attention of regulators. Further, legal yet misleading or potentially harmful data practices will be revealed to consumers and subsequently tried in the court of public opinion (e.g., consumers may stop buying products from firms shown to have unscrupulous practices).

Further, TPDAs are a meaningful way to create transparency and accountability for this highly technical field. Rather than attempting to enumerate precise rules governing data use, which would be an impossible and unrealistic goal in the current complicated landscape while the field is still rapidly developing, TPDAs empower consumers to understand how their data are being used and then enable consumers to rectify potentially harmful situations.

10.4.3 Promoting Accordance with Existing Laws

TPDAs will become an important tool in the fight to uphold law and order in the healthcare IoT. On an individual level, consumers can now see what information has been collected and shared with particular organizations, as well as the data-based inferences made from it by firms such as data brokers. Once empowered with this information, consumers, either by their own impetus or on recommendation of their TPDA, may further examine potential misuses of data if they feel unlawful behavior has occurred. On a societal level, aggregate reports can play an important role in discovering potential misuses of data, as discussed in the preceding section.

10.4.4 Promoting the Protection of Innovation

While TPDAs are an effective regulatory structure for the healthcare IoT, this regime also happens to minimize the regulatory impact on firms themselves. There is little, if any, burden placed on firms. The policies that will precipitate TPDAs, as discussed in the final section of this chapter, do not force substantial changes to the operation and behavior of healthcare IoT firms beyond the current trajectory of regulation in this area. After the proliferation of TPDAs, the information gained by consumers and regulators will identify areas that need more specific regulation rather than proscribing specific actions prior to the industry's development to the potential harm of innovation in the industry.

10.5 LIMITATIONS AND CONSIDERATIONS OF TPDAS

I now discuss a number of limitations and considerations with the use of TPDAs.

10.5.1 Economic Disenfranchisement

One potential problem with TPDAs is that economically marginalized individuals, the group perhaps requiring the greatest protection, may be unable to afford the services of the TPDA. In this case, there are three possible solutions:

- **Government subsidies.** The government may subsidize TPDA service for these groups. Just as the government subsidizes access to the Internet

for certain segments of the population,[25] this service may be subsidized as well in conjunction with access.
- **TPDAs subsidize their own services.** TPDAs themselves may wish to provide reduced-fee or complimentary service to these disadvantaged groups in an effort to improve the quality of the firm's own aggregate reports, which will help the TPDA deliver better services to all of its clients and society at large.
- **The emergence of free, self-service TPDAs.** Free, self-service online TPDAs may come into existence. Free services very similar in nature to TPDAs have already come into existence.[26]

These ideas are realistic because TPDAs operate at economies of scale: after initial setup, the cost of producing an additional report is negligible, allowing TPDAs to quickly scale and provide subsidized service.

10.5.2 *Expanding Amounts of Relevant Data*

As discussed earlier, much of the healthcare data relevant to the IoT resemble those of consumer-grade technologies, such as the Internet, more than that of traditional sources of healthcare data. This is partially due to the fact that consumer-grade technology data, such as web search history, can themselves have use in the healthcare decisions made by relevant parties. This expanding amount of relevant data presents a unique challenge to the feasibility of TPDAs because it directly increases both the amount and types of data that TPDAs must be able to process.

To address this issue, TPDAs must focus on the data that are *most relevant* to healthcare decisions, where relevancy can be determined by the data that are being used most frequently by parties of interest (e.g., insurance providers). It is of note that these parties of interest consuming this broad set of data must similarly find ways to acquire, parse, and meaningfully use these data. As such, these parties are similarly limited in the amount of data that can be meaningfully consumed.

However, it is important to note that TPDAs need not be all encompassing to have practicality and meaningful relevancy to their customers. A recognition of the impossibilities of all-encompassing policy solutions in this complicated environment is in fact enshrined within FTC policy itself: the FTC's "harm-based approach" to regulation specifically hinges on an ability to recognize and then rectify harms

---

[25] US Federal Communication Commission, E-Rate: Schools and Libraries USF Program (2017), available at www.fcc.gov/general/e-rate-schools-libraries-usf-program [https://perma.cc/N7G7-YRDQ].
[26] About, Data Selfie, available at http://dataselfie.it/#/about [https://perma.cc/PEL5-KMRN] (last visited April 1, 2017).

rather than relying on a fully consent-driven regulatory approach.[27] In this regard, TPDAs will help to bring data-based harms to regulators' attention.

10.5.3 Technical Practicality

TPDAs will naturally be limited by the lack of interoperability between and similarity of data sources, which will pose great operational challenges in successfully parsing and using data. However, this also can be mitigated in a manner similar to that discussed in the preceding subsection (to meet the challenges posed by the large amounts of relevant data). Further, certain policy interventions may help in increasing the technical practicality of TPDAs. In the United States, a lack of interoperability between electronic health record (EHR) systems currently plagues digital healthcare data systems.[28] As a solution, government regulations from the US Department of Health and Human Services are targeting interoperability as a requirement by the year 2024,[29] which will aid TPDAs in consuming this source of data. However, while this policy is limited in scope to EHRs, the European Union has taken interoperability a step further with Article 20 of the General Data Protection Regulation (GDPR), which creates a right to data portability, guaranteeing the right for users to "receive the[ir] personal data ... in a structured, commonly used and machine-readable format, and to transmit them to another data controller."[30] Future US policy may similarly dictate interoperability or clear data layouts for sources of data that are treated as relevant healthcare data, where relevancy is defined as data being sold or used specifically for healthcare, using the same logic that governs the interoperability requirement of EHRs and Article 20 of the GDPR.

10.5.4 Security

Because the data TPDAs monitor are highly sensitive, the collection and pooling of these data present a valid concern, potentially creating new avenues for security and data breaches. However, this concern is of a similar nature to the concern created

---

[27] US Federal Trade Commission, Protecting Consumer Privacy in an Era of Rapid Change: A Proposed Framework for Businesses and Policymakers, 9–10 (2010), available at www.ftc.gov/sites/default/files/documents/reports/federal-trade-commission-report-protecting-consumer-privacy-era-rapid-change-recommendations/120326privacyreport.pdf [https://perma.cc/CHW4-MHEW].

[28] Office of the National Coordinator for Health Information Technology, Connecting Health and Care for the Nation: A 10-Year Vision to Achieve an Interoperable Health IT Infrastructure 4 (2014), available at www.healthit.gov/sites/default/files/ONC10yearInteroperabilityConcept Paper.pdf [https://perma.cc/U4M2-JYT5].

[29] Ibid., at 2–3.

[30] European Commission, Guidelines on the Right to Data Portability 3 (2016), available at http://ec.europa.eu/information_society/newsroom/image/document/2016-51/wp242_en_40852.pdf [https://perma.cc/V3C3-YPFL].

by the existence of electronic data themselves, especially the sensitive electronic healthcare data stored in EHRs. Further, there are a number of reasons why TPDAs' collection of data is not unprecedented. Over the past twenty years, the collection and pooling of sensitive data have become commonplace in both companies that take collection and pooling actions as their main business (e.g., data brokers) and companies that pool data (including healthcare data[31]) over many services into one main account. Importantly, while the FTC generally has suggested data minimization as a way to mitigate security risks, it explicitly notes that innovative uses sometimes require large amounts of data and, as such, offers flexibility in this recommendation.[32] In this respect, the collection of data performed by TPDAs is not unprecedented and has already received thought from regulatory bodies such as the FTC.

Beyond existing examples, there are regulations that can be put in place to further protect data in this sensitive field. Already, the FTC has taken stringent action against security and privacy transgressions committed by EHR companies.[33] The FTC should play a similarly strict role in its oversight of TPDAs. Further, because TPDAs will be chartered by the FTC or other appropriate regulatory body, the FTC can require stringent security and privacy regulations of TPDAs as a precondition for certification, affording regulators an opportunity to ingrain the best security practices before the creation of these entities and providing an opportunity to set a "gold standard" for the data industry in general.

10.5.5 *User Education*

TPDAs rely heavily on user education, which has been unsuccessful in some facets of security policy.[34] However, in the context of regulating the healthcare IoT, this education-centric approach aligns with two major facets of regulatory thought. First, policies aimed at informing users underscore the current FTC approach to regulating the IoT. In its most recent report on IoT privacy policy, the FTC takes as its position that, in consideration of the unique regulatory aspects presented by the IoT, "giving consumers information and choices about their data ... continues to be the

---

[31] Aaron Brown, An Update on Google Health and Google PowerMeter, Google Official Blog (June 24, 2011), available at https://googleblog.blogspot.com/2011/06/update-on-google-health-and-google.html [https://perma.cc/7KQY-AACU].
[32] FTC, Internet of Things Privacy and Security, at iv.
[33] US Federal Trade Commission, Electronic Health Records Company Settles FTC Charges It Deceived Consumers about Privacy of Doctor Reviews (2016), available at www.ftc.gov/news-events/press-releases/2016/06/electronic-health-records-company-settles-ftc-charges-it-deceived [https://perma.cc/C5GT-FGVZ].
[34] Bruce Schneier, On Security Awareness Training, Dark Reading (March 19, 2013), available at www.darkreading.com/risk/on-security-awareness-training/d/d-id/1139381 [https://perma.cc/SH7Z-8LCH].

most viable [approach for regulation] for the IoT in the foreseeable future."[35] Second, TPDAs support the harm-based model that the FTC has had great success in using over the past decade. Under the harm-based model, the FTC focuses on "specific consumer harms as the primary means of addressing consumer privacy issues ... [r]ather than emphasizing potentially costly notice-and-choice requirements for all uses of information."[36] TPDAs, through educating users specifically about potential harms of how their data are being used, as well as through their role in creating aggregate reports for regulators to use, specifically will help to enable this harm-based model in the healthcare IoT.

10.6 POLICY RECOMMENDATIONS FOR PRECIPITATING TPDAS

I now briefly introduce the regulatory policies needed to bring about TPDAs.

10.6.1 Recommendation 1: Mandate Data Access with a Focus on Interoperability

Congress should mandate that all healthcare IoT and healthcare data-using firms must oblige consumer requests for access to any data held on them by a firm, regardless of whether that firm collected or purchased those data. Data include both facts directly collected on an individual and inferences made about that individual via machine learning algorithms or other means. Further, these data should be given in a structured machine-readable format, similar in nature to Article 20 of the GDPR.[37]

This regulation will directly enable TPDAs to operate by allowing them to collect all the necessary data on behalf of their clients in order to perform their analysis. This policy is largely in line with existing policy thought. In the FTC's May 2014 data broker report, a main legislative recommendation is, "[T]he Commission unanimously recommends that Congress should consider enacting legislation that would enable consumers to learn of the existence and activities of data brokers and provide consumers with reasonable access to information about them held by these entities."[38] Further, if needed, the scope of this regulation can apply only to data used in healthcare decisions to reduce the scope of the regulation in general.

10.6.2 Recommendation 2: Create TPDA Regulations and a Certification Process

Congress should create a task force to create the necessary regulations regarding the legal responsibilities of TPDAs or task the FTC with this responsibility.

---

[35] FTC, Internet of Things Privacy and Security, at vii.
[36] FTC, E-Rate, at 9.
[37] European Commission, Guidelines on the Right to Data Portability, at 3.
[38] FTC, Data Brokers, at 49.

Following this, Congress should task the FTC with setting up the mechanism to create the TPDA certification process.

The legally binding relationship between a client and his or her TPDA forms the cornerstone of the trust that supports the work the TPDA conducts. Strong legal protections, rivaling the legal requirements dictating doctor-patient and lawyer-client relationships, should be clearly established and sufficiently clear for the lay citizen to understand. In this respect, citizens will feel sufficiently confident in using TPDAs, just as the idea of doctor-patient/lawyer-client confidentiality is clear enough that a patient or client feels confident in confiding sensitive information.

After establishing these regulations, the FTC should create a process by which new TPDAs may obtain their official certification. The certification process, while essential in creating the trust and embodying this trust within legal guarantees, should attempt not to dissuade new potential TPDAs from entering the market. Especially as the TPDA marketplace emerges, the FTC should take special care to help the first firms successfully obtain certification.

10.6.3 Recommendation 3: Educate the Citizenry

Congress should create a task force to educate the citizenry regarding the existence of TPDAs and the services they offer in the context of the healthcare IoT.

10.6.4 Concluding Thoughts on Policies

As these policy recommendations demonstrate, the policy regime needed to support the emergence of TPDAs is quite light. There is no need for systematic overhauls nor unreasonable changes posed to disrupt any industries.

Further, there is little downside to the creation of these policies. The first policy, regarding data access, has tremendous benefits beyond those it potentially provides to TPDAs because it will, at a minimum, help users to better understand their data. The second policy, needed to establish the laws and certification process regarding TPDAs, although specific to TPDAs, is not onerous for regulators to create. Further, the research, discussions, and rules that emerge from this process can be applied to other sectors of data regulation and therefore are useful exercises in and of themselves. Finally, the third policy, advocating citizenry education regarding data use and TPDAs, will inform the citizenry about the healthcare IoT itself in addition to TPDAs.

10.7 CONCLUSION

The healthcare IoT holds promise through its ability to increase the health of the nation and build a strong twenty-first-century healthcare system. However, with this power comes a responsibility to protect users from data-driven harms. To this end, regulatory policy should aim not only toward protecting society from potential harmful uses of data but also toward empowering individuals to understand and operate meaningful control over their data. TPDAs, by creating a regulatory avenue that will succeed largely on its ability to empower individuals, accomplishes this explicitly. Given the means, knowledge, and ability to exercise control over their digital lives, citizens will be able to make the most of the great opportunities the healthcare IoT presents.

PART IV

Protecting Health Privacy in the World of Big Data

INTRODUCTION

Effy Vayena

Big Data and privacy are an inseparable pair. The pairing, however, is one that is assumed to be so deeply antithetical that it is often put in mortal terms. Either part ought to be dead, and usually the death penalty goes to privacy. Big technology company executives were among the first to deliver such a verdict, causing spine-tingling excitement among the dreamers of the new data economy and bloodcurdling reactions in those fearing total surveillance.[1] The chorus of mortal exclamations about privacy has only grown and was recently joined by bioethicist Art Caplan, who opined that health privacy too must die. "It is time to grudgingly say goodbye to privacy – we hardly ever knew ye,"[2] says Caplan after some quick reference to recalcitrant problems of health data security and the potential public health benefits of easier access to health data. Death and loss are sad events, especially in the case of privacy, which is arguably an important moral value, a human right to be enjoyed by all, and a legal right inscribed to most legal systems in the world. It is premature to wipe out all of these with the click of a mouse.

The mortal talk, however, still needs to be taken seriously insofar as it illustrates where the tensions and new vulnerabilities of privacy are. It can serve as a call to rethink privacy, something that the United Nations Human Rights Council[3] has formally taken onboard by appointing a special rapporteur to examine the status of

---

[1] Amitai Etzioni, Privacy Isn't Dead Yet, *New York Times*, April. 6, 1999, available at www.nytimes.com/1999/04/06/opinion/privacy-isn-t-dead-yet.html.

[2] Art Caplan, Why Privacy Must Die, The Health Care Blog (December 19, 2016), available at http://thehealthcareblog.com/blog/2016/12/19/goodbye-privacy-we-hardly-knew-ye/ [https://perma.cc/3CU3-MVBX].

[3] United Nations Human Rights Office of the High Commissioner, The Right to Privacy in the Digital Age, available at www.ohchr.org/EN/Issues/DigitalAge/Pages/DigitalAgeIndex.aspx [https://perma.cc/QRE8-ZFFZ] (last visited May 31, 2017).

the human right to privacy in the digital era. Privacy is notoriously difficult to define, especially in its contemporary context. It is often conflated with autonomy; it is sometimes argued as an absolute right. There is an urgent need to understand what the scope of privacy is today in order to protect it effectively and proportionally.

The chapters in this section engage precisely with the rethinking of privacy by exploring privacy challenges from the disciplinary angles of law, philosophy, and empirical bioethics. Two of the chapters focus on genomics not only because genomic research produces vast amounts of data but also because genetic and genomic data have been treated as worthy of exceptional privacy protections. Yet even the high expectations on genomics are powered by the potential of linking them with other data sets. It is therefore all health data that are at stake. The chapters treat different aspects of privacy by shedding light on three fundamental and interdependent issues at the root of the privacy problem in Big Data: relationality, temporality, and uncertainty. It is at the intersection of these issues that several salient ethical challenges emerge. If they are properly understood and addressed, they can point to a conceptualization of privacy and its protection that is better suited to the Big Data era.

Big Data analytics, especially in the domain of health, show how we are all related. We share genes, environmental exposures, habits, and behaviors. Data collected from some people can predict health and disease patterns for their relatives and others with similar traits. But how can those individuals about whom information is inferred through data of others protect their privacy? This is especially relevant in the context of scientific research, where regulatory and ethical frameworks still treat privacy as a matter of individual control typically exercised through the research participant's informed consent.

Donna Gitter explores this issue of relationality starting from deCODE Genetics' fascinating claim regarding its capacity to accurately predict genetic information of individuals who were never genotyped or ever participated in a genetic study. The claim, which made waves in 2015,[4] is a powerful demonstration of how Big Data analytics can reveal how we relate to each other, without us as individual agents exercising control over such revelations. This case illustrates a widely shared sentiment that Big Data analytics and genomics are a lot more than meets the "I." Gitter's concern is precisely with the "I" who did not consent to having her information inferred because she never was a study participant. She extends her claim beyond genetics to argue that inferring information about people without their permission violates both their privacy right and their right not to know, if information about them is returned to them. Gitter argues that following the alluring path of using deidentified data without consent does not pay due respect to individual

---

[4] Antonio Regalado, Genome Study Predicts the DNA of the Whole of Iceland, *MIT Tech. Rev.*, March 25, 2015, available at www.technologyreview.com/s/536096/genome-study-predicts-dna-of-the-whole-of-iceland/ [https://perma.cc/6Q2E-VAEV].

autonomy. And it is this interesting distinction that is important to note here, along with the fact that privacy and autonomy are two distinct values that occupy some overlapping moral space. Gitter proposes to extend the informed-consent requirement for anonymized and estimated data uses. While acknowledging the impracticalities of her proposal, she still considers consent as the key protection mechanism.

Relationality shakes up the notion of individual control of privacy, especially through consent, as an effective method of protection. And this is the case due to both the dilated temporal dimension that is fundamental to Big Data uses and the uncertainty about such uses. In fact, in that constellation, I am more concerned about the illusion of control creating a fertile ground for poor privacy protections. As I have argued elsewhere, while consent has a role to play in privacy protection, it is unlikely that it can do all the moral work.[5]

Laura Beskow et al. present qualitative data from interviews probing the perspectives of thought leaders on confidentiality and privacy risks in precision medicine research. The findings reinforce what is well discussed in the literature, namely, that the risks span a wide spectrum. Notably, however, they also reveal some shifts within the typical understanding of privacy risks, at least as these are usually presented and communicated to participants in consent documents. One such interesting shift is from understanding privacy risks mainly in terms of individual harm to considering group harm as a fundamental dimension of privacy. Individual risk of harm is the dominant conceptualization of risk in health research as well as in the respective protections and remedies that have evolved over time. The group risk of harm is little understood and even less addressed in current protection mechanisms. In the Big Data environment, risks are exacerbated by at least two factors: first, the never-ending uses of multiple data sets and, second, the difficulty in predicting how data will be used and what they will yield. The uncertainty about what will emerge makes it virtually impossible to assess resulting risks a priori.

Brent Mittelstadt calls these mostly algorithmically created groups "ad hoc groups," which "provide unanticipated ways of viewing and inferring information about the individual." In his chapter (Chapter 12), he goes beyond acknowledging the increasing weight of ad hoc group privacy harms in Big Data research, advancing the case for a *group privacy right*. Mittelstadt's attempt to establish this moral right is rooted in an understanding of the right to privacy as the right to inviolate personality. On this account, informational privacy allows the constitution of one's informational identity. Privacy harms thus include any intrusions that interfere with the formation and evolution of identity. This theory of privacy, first proposed by Luciano Floridi, is applied by Mittelstadt to ad hoc groups created by Big Data analytics. The claim is that grouping on the basis of shared characteristics and subsequently attributing such characteristics to individuals simply by their ad hoc

---

[5] Effy Vayena & Alessandro Blasimme, Biomedical Big Data: New Models of Control over Access, Use and Governance, *J. Bioeth. Inq.*, October 5, 2017, doi: 10.1007/s11673-017-9809-6.

group membership can interfere with identity constitution at both the group and individual level. Therefore, to better protect privacy, Mittelstadt argues, simply focusing on protecting the individual right to privacy is not enough. He proposes to add a group right to privacy in the ethical framework for Big Data uses. This appears to be an innovative move. Yet it still faces the usual objections to any claim of "group rights," for example, that a group right dissolves quickly into an individual right.

Protecting health privacy – and privacy more broadly – in the Big Data era will remain a challenging issue. One approach for addressing it is to keep strengthening existing mechanisms (consent, for example); another is to devise entirely new mechanisms. For the latter, some further normative investigation of the value of privacy is required. One thing is clear: while privacy protections in health thus far have focused mainly on individual control even prior to generation of the data, the action is now downstream, namely, in the infinite and uncertain uses of data that affect groups and individuals. It is there that privacy protections need to be added. Privacy protection is a complex challenge that is unlikely to have a simple solution. Arguably, multiple mechanisms and approaches will have to be developed and act synergistically. It won't be an easy ride, but privacy must not die on us.

11

Thought-Leader Perspectives on Risks in Precision Medicine Research

Laura M. Beskow, Catherine M. Hammack, Kathleen M. Brelsford, and Kevin C. McKenna

11.1 INTRODUCTION

Large-scale gene-environment interaction studies, such as the Precision Medicine Initiative,[1] are capitalizing on advances in mobile health technologies, widespread adoption of electronic health records (EHRs), and increasingly sophisticated data science approaches. These offer unparalleled opportunities to learn more about human health and disease but raise significant concerns about privacy and confidentiality. A range of potential solutions has been proposed, but how best to proceed in this era of Big Data is not known.

We conducted empirical research on the scope of confidentiality risks and protections applicable to genome research, as well as how these are and should be described to prospective participants. Here we report key findings from in-depth interviews conducted with a diverse group of thought leaders – prominent individuals uniquely positioned to identify critical issues in the swiftly changing environment of genome research. Specifically, we focus on their perspectives on the risks associated with precision medicine research.

11.2 METHODS

11.2.1 *Participants*

We interviewed recognized individuals representing a range of perspectives, including

- **Ethical, legal, and social issues research (ELSI).** Scholars who study ethical, legal, and social issues in genome science.
- **Ethics (Ethics).** For example, directors of centers for bioethics.

---

[1] See Francis S. Collins & Harold Varmus, A New Initiative on Precision Medicine, 372 N. Engl. J. Med. 793 (2015).

- **Federal government (Government).** Individuals in relevant positions in the federal government.
- **Genome research (Research).** Bench science and medical genomics researchers.
- **Health law (Law).** For example, directors of centers for health law.
- **Historically disadvantaged populations (Historically disadvantaged).** Scholars who study issues related to historically disadvantaged populations.
- **Human subjects protections (Human subjects).** For example, leaders of national organizations related to human subjects protections.
- **Informatics (Informatics).** Bioinformatics, clinical and medical informatics experts.
- **Participant-centric approaches (Participant-centric).** Leaders in participant-centric approaches to research.

We used stratified purposive sampling to interview at least six thought leaders per group, the minimum expected to detect saturation.[2] Prospective participants were identified based on leadership positions in prominent organizations, institutions, and studies and authorship of influential papers on relevant topics, as well as through referral sampling.

11.2.2 Data Collection

We developed a semistructured interview guide centered on a hypothetical "Million American Study" (available on request) – that, like the All of Us Research Program,[3] involved extensive characterization of biospecimens (including whole-genome sequencing), ongoing collection of information from EHRs, and real-time monitoring of lifestyle and behavioral information via mobile devices. Here we report responses to this question:

> Imagine that your family members and close friends are all at a gathering together. The conversation turns to the "Million American Study" that has been in the news recently. Everyone is eager to hear your thoughts about whether they should consider signing up to be in this study.
>
> 4. How would you describe to your family and friends the primary risks of participating in the Million American Study?

The Duke University Health System Institutional Review Board deemed this research exempt under 45 C.F.R. § 46.101(b)(2) (2009). Experienced research staff (CMH, KCM, KMB) conducted the interviews by telephone between September

---

[2] See Greg Guest et al., How Many Interviews Are Enough? An Experiment with Data Saturation and Variability, 18 *Field Methods* 59 (2006).

[3] See National Institutes of Health, All of Us Research Program (2016), available at www.nih.gov/research-training/allofus-research-program [https://perma.cc/295Z-ZG23].

2015 and July 2016. Participants received a study information sheet, a description of the hypothetical study, and an outline of the interview topics in advance and were offered $100 compensation for their time.

11.2.3 Data Analysis

We uploaded transcribed interviews into the qualitative research software NVivo 11 and developed a codebook via a standardized iterative process capturing structural and thematic codes. Research staff independently applied these codes to the transcripts, regularly checking intercoder agreement to ensure that it remained at a minimum of 80 percent.

Next, we systematically generated summaries of the structural and content codes to explore the range of thematic responses and to identify additional subthemes. All summaries were reviewed by at least one other team member, who independently read the code report to identify and confirm agreement with subthemes identified and the summary itself.

11.3 RESULTS

11.3.1 Participant Characteristics

We interviewed sixty thought leaders, representing a wide array of perspectives and demographic diversity (Table 11.1).

11.3.2 Views on Risks in Precision Medicine Research

When we asked thought leaders how they would describe the primary risks of participating in our hypothetical Million American Study, four broad categories of responses emerged: unintended access to identifying information, permitted but potentially unwanted use of information, risks based on the nature of genetic information, and risks associated with the longitudinal study design.

Unintended Access to Identity

Nearly three-fourths of interviewees mentioned unintended access to identifying information as a risk. Many expected that despite data security measures, it could be relatively easy to identify research participants:

> With enough informatics and somebody who wanted to, even in something that doesn't have your name attached to it, it can be traced back to you without a huge amount of effort and energy and cost. [11, ELSI]

> Even really secure systems sometimes get cracked. Now, there will be lots of protections around this, and some of the best minds in the business will be working

TABLE 11.1 *Participant Characteristics* (n = 60)

	n	(%)
Perspective		
ELSI research	6	(10.0)
Ethics	7	(11.7)
Federal government	7	(11.7)
Genome research	7	(11.7)
Health law	6	(10.0)
Historically disadvantaged populations	7	(11.7)
Human subjects protections	7	(11.7)
Informatics	6	(10.0)
Participant-centric approaches	7	(11.7)
Gender		
Female	31	(51.7)
Male	29	(48.3)
Race		
American Indian or Alaska Native	2	(3.3)
Asian	5	(8.3)
Black or African American	3	(5.0)
Native Hawaiian or Other Pacific Islander	1	(1.7)
White	49	(81.7)
Ethnicity		
Hispanic or Latino	2	(3.3)

on it. But it is possible that at some point your identity could be disclosed. Or someone could figure it out, despite all the protections against it. [53, Informatics]

A few interviewees, however, thought the ease with which participants can be meaningfully identified is often overestimated:

Some people say, "Oh, it's almost inevitable. It's trivially easy to identify people." You see that kind of language a lot. I think that is overhyped ... A lot of re-identification methods are resource-intensive. They can be very technical. They can take a lot of time. They don't yield all that much ... Then you have to think about: well, what do I now know about these people? So much of genetic information is highly probabilistic. It's not something that you know really. [54, Ethics]

Still others described the ability to identify participants as a moving target – hard to quantify but likely to increase over time as technical capabilities expand and data accumulate. As one interviewee predicted:

As time goes on, that's going to be more and more likely to happen. You need to be comfortable with the fact that what you have in there may eventually come out. There is some risk of that. It may not happen for a number of years, but there is some risk of that. [55, Government]

Regardless of how easy or difficult it might be to identify research participants, many interviewees assessed the risk to individuals as low, distinguishing between the possibility of identification and the likelihood of harm:

> I know we talk a lot about the potential harm, but in the grand scheme of things, when individuals contribute their DNA and it's de-identified and they're not getting information back, as long as the security mechanisms are in place, I really don't see harm coming back to the individual in the way that we worry it could. [10, Historically disadvantaged]

> The likelihood that the information could be accessed inappropriately and used to their detriment is quite low, although not zero, since we can't guarantee that data breaches won't occur ... But the actual impact of such a disclosure at present would not seem to have substantial risks. [58, Research]

Some described the risks as low particularly compared with those associated with daily life (e.g., through credit cards, financial records, shopping trails) and routine clinical care:

> We take risks all the time, every day, and most of those risks are things we don't even think about ... The difference with this is that it's not an everyday activity. So we scrutinize it and agitate about it in ways that we don't with daily risks that we take. But, really, when it comes down to risk assessment, you have to bring it back to the statistical likelihood being a lot less than these things that we do all the time without worrying about it. [24, Government]

Overall, skepticism concerning intent or motive to target individuals was apparent in interviewees' assessments of the risks associated with identification:

> The risk that someone is going to search specifically for you, that risk is low ... Unless, I don't know, you're running for office or whatever. [45, Participant-centric]

A few noted that, to date, the primary motivation seems to have been among academic researchers attempting to demonstrate that identification is possible:

> The rates of re-identification are a lot lower than the media sometimes reports. In addition to that ... almost all of this is coming from academic researchers. They have an incentive to do this ... I mean, they've made careers literally on this. [54, Ethics]

> You have some people out there who like to play with this data ... researchers, for example, who research anonymization, like to get their hands on this data and embarrass the organization that's holding it to show that it's not really de-identified. [55, Government]

Still, because the possibility of identification is real, some interviewees highlighted individual-level factors that prospective participants might consider when gauging the risks:

> I would emphasize that it's not just genomic data. You think about your electronic health record, too, because that might be much more likely to immediately be embarrassing to you or harmful to you if it were made public. But that depends on you: do you have anything embarrassing in your record? And, are you the kind of person who finds things embarrassing? [54, Ethics]

> My personal opinion is that no one really cares about individuals unless they do care about the individual. If you have your own sort of personal enemy – or your nemesis – then they're gonna find ways to harm you. But globally, no one really cares about each individual. So, it's unlikely that they'll actually see any adverse results for themselves. [48, Law]

Among interviewees who discussed unintended access to identifying information in general, nearly all mentioned specific ways this could occur, including *breach* or *hacking* and *triangulation*. Some thought the likelihood of such occurrences was high, given the depth of data collected and visibility of the study:

> When there is a reason for an entity to get their hands on information ... there is every reason to think they can. China getting government security information is a great example, and we've seen breaches in health information, credit cards, etc. The real question is, will anyone want to do it? Is the information useful enough to a malevolent third party that they'd be motivated to do it? If they are sufficiently well motivated, I think they can do it. [08, ELSI]

> You should just assume that sooner or later ... somebody's going to hack into it. The more prominent the study is, the more likely it is to happen, because it makes such a good political target for hackers. [20, Research]

> Collection of all this rich data in one repository is like a candy store. To me, it's probably not a question of whether it will be breached; it's a question of when it will be breached. [55, Government]

More interviewees, however, thought the likelihood of breach/hacking or triangulation was low, assuming that "cutting edge" or "gold standard" security measures were in place, as well as a "rigorous oversight system" and "strong terms" in material transfer and data access agreements. Several pointed to lack of historical examples of actual harm:

> I'm not aware frankly of harms having come from the hundreds and thousands of studies that people have been conducting already in this area. I think the numbers of times when people have been harmed by a breach are vanishingly small. Although we identify it as a risk, it remains largely a hypothetical risk. [26, Human subjects]

Notably, throughout the discussion of unintended access to identities, several interviewees suggested that the major consequences would accrue to the study itself:

> The consequences for the research community would be terrible, because it would really decrease faith and people's willingness to trust researchers. That would be the biggest problem. [02, Government]

Permitted but Unwanted Use of Information

Over half of interviewees highlighted the risk that information might be used in ways that are permitted but potentially unwanted by some participants. Many described general loss of control over who would have access to biospecimens and data and for what purposes:

> The risks are almost entirely the dignitary risks, the privacy, confidentiality, misuse of information, and so on ... Many people, depending on their cultural beliefs and their personal feelings, really have a great attachment to their biological specimens, and want more control over what happens to it than is likely to be afforded them in a study such as this. [12, Law]

> What I would think should be most a matter of concern for people is: what is being done with really personal information ... by people whom you cannot see, and you don't know, and do not know the purposes ... I would describe that as a lack of control. It is a diminishing of agency when someone has ongoing access to your data. [45, Participant-centric]

Interviewees noted both research and nonresearch uses that some participants might find objectionable. With regard to research uses, they raised concerns about problematic topics and downstream implications of certain kinds of research:

> For example, we have developed all sorts of new screening tests that can be used prenatally ... There are people who have a family member with, say, Down's syndrome, who are very nervous about that, because they think if you can get a prenatal diagnosis from circulating fetal cells, at a time when terminating the pregnancy is safe and easy ... then substantial numbers of people are gonna do that. Then the remaining affected children and adults are going to be less tolerated in society. There's gonna be less research done to develop true cures for them, etc. You can see how even seemingly benign developments are not always viewed positively by people who are affected. [12, Law]

> It's possible that researchers ... might study it for something that you object to – like genetic contributions to violent tendencies, say. Even if you are never identified as having participated – it's not really a privacy/confidentiality thing; it's more of a complicity thing. You are contributing your data, literally pieces of your body, to a study that you might object to morally. [54, Ethics]

They also noted potential concerns about researchers, including their motives and incentives, as well as the places where they work:

> As much as I'd like to say [the study] would uphold the highest ethics, the law of the land and the Supreme Court says that once the tissue is in the hands of the

researcher they are owned by the researcher. Until ... the rights of the individual who participates are also included, there will always be a possibility of someone stepping outside of their ethical bounds for their personal gain. We've seen it time and time again – a population of any size could be stigmatized for the benefit of an individual career. [36, Historically disadvantaged]

My sense is that people would ascribe different risks if they thought a pharmaceutical company was doing the study versus the government versus academic researchers or a recognized entity, versus an unrecognized entity. [31, ELSI]

People need to understand what kind of researchers might have access to this information. We've seen instances ... where researchers that access health information had affiliations with health plans and other organizations that most consumers don't think of as being researchers. When they think of a researcher, they're thinking of usually an academic medical center research situation. [55, Government]

With regard to nonresearch use of biospecimens and data, interviewees identified several uses to which some participants might object, such as politics and law enforcement, marketing, and healthcare efficiency:

[Compared to a decade ago, risk is] higher because of the unstable nature of our congressmen. Congress's relationship to NIH is a clear risk portal. Because they are relatively uneducated and erratic around science and the pursuit of research ... Imagine [them] making decisions that all of the DNA data that's in federal repositories should be made available to the FBI as a part of their, I don't know, bad ideas about immigration. [05, Research]

That data is gonna look so attractive to a lot of companies that are gonna be there saying, "Well, we're here to use this information to help people make health improvements, so we should be able to get access to it." Unless there's a way for people to make a choice about that, it's highly likely that their information could be going to people that they would prefer it not go to. [19, Ethics]

Your healthcare providers and government are integrally involved in the project. It's very likely that they would see good uses for this information – and it is furthering their own interests rather than your health interests. From looking for ways to cut costs in the healthcare system, looking for ways to improve national security, etc. It's really the internal leaks ... and sharing of the information that I'd be more worried about than external breaches of data security. [37, ELSI]

Throughout this discussion of objectionable uses, both research and nonresearch, many interviewees pointed to the history of ill-conceived notions of superiority or inferiority of different populations:

As one who works on issues of race and identity, and recognizing how groups are perceived and treated in America, it's possible that information could be purposefully misused to either propagate ... negative perceptions about groups, or to initiate ideas about differences ... or use information to supposedly provide support or ideas about superiority, inferiority of groups. [25, Historically disadvantaged]

There's a lot of interest in using this information to try to do something about the healthcare disparities that show up between different groups ... But if a researcher took your information and used it to make the case that: "Well, the reason why our group has worse outcomes is because we're genetically inferior to other groups," then it only adds to whatever sort of social burden we're already dealing with. A lot of people would be upset to know that that contributed to a research project that ended up stigmatizing their community or their group. [37, ELSI]

And many also pointed to the history of other kinds of group harm more generally, such as studies that reinforce rather than address health disparities:

Scientific uses of data could have stigmatizing effects – especially non-health researchers using data to generate findings that were not intended by the people donating. Just as an example, the Havasupai tribe in Arizona: they donated their samples and they intended for those samples to be used for health research, and they ultimately were used for other purposes, and it was those other purposes that they tended to not approve of. [42, Ethics]

One of the major risks tends to be really stigmatizing research. It could be unintended. It could be we're going to do research to look at why African-American women die more from breast cancer. So we sit down and say, "Okay, well what are the differences?" We can find a genetic difference and so that's the thing we focus on. But by doing that, we overlook one of the main problems is that black women get treatment much later than white women ... When we're really focusing on the genetics ... we could be missing big things. [46, Historically disadvantaged]

Some interviewees commented on procedures to control unwanted use, which they tended to view as only partially effective:

Once this is in the databank, it could be used by just about anybody anywhere in the world for almost any purpose. They will have data access limitations. Those limitations will I guarantee not be perfect. Grad students and postdocs in one lab when they move to another lab are likely to take data with them no matter what NIH says, and you don't know what the data-access committee will approve of. So it could be that your information will be used for research you don't approve of ... That possibility is unavoidable once you join this databank. [14, Law]

I don't have confidence in the way data will be used and distributed. I don't have confidence it won't end up in the hands of people whose motivations I don't agree with. I don't think the NIH has a stellar track record of who gets access to data. [49, Research]

However, they recognized the need for balanced procedures that are neither too lax nor too strict:

> From my perspective the primary risk is that the control mechanism over the data [becomes] either unconscious, so it's not doing what the individual would have wanted – or alternatively, that the focus on the security of the data takes precedent over the individual's wishes, so that their data is not being used as broadly in order to advance as much research as they would hope for. [17, Participant-centric]

Nature of Genetic Information
Nearly half of interviewees described risks arising from the nature of genetic information. Familial implications were prominent among these:

> Genomic data is inherently familial. Anything I learn about myself from my genome says something about my first-degree relatives, says something slightly less salient about my second-degree relatives, and so on. I would just reiterate that there's really no such thing as: "Well, I'm gonna consent to do this even though you're not." It's more fluid than that. We can't draw sharp fences around our genome. [54, Ethics]

Interviewees noted that identification risks extend to other family members:

> One would probably quite easily be able to identify family members, if one was seeking to do that, very quickly ... But that's at the core of all research participation – it's an unsolved problem. [03, Informatics]

> Revealing a person's health information or their family history or their genomic information – all of those types of things could have implications for family members, for parents, for siblings. [42, Ethics]

More often, however, interviewees focused on the risks associated with the disclosure of individual genetic research results to participants, anticipating tensions among family members:

> Risk to a family of discrimination is low, but risk of tension in the family could be higher ... Tension or other emotions and feeling, such as the guilt a parent might feel if a child is determined to have something that they passed on to them, or if there are people in the family who don't want to know about the genetics of the family, but there are others in the family who are receiving information from the study and talking about it all the time. [10, Historically disadvantaged]

Several interviewees noted misattributed parentage as an example of a particularly concerning discovery:

> There might be paternity, familial relationship information that might come out that might be unexpected. Whether or not this is harmful, that's another question – it's just that this may be information that people did not necessarily want to know. [13, Informatics]

Beyond familial implications, interviewees spoke about other risks associated with genetic information, often featuring the theme of "the unknown":

It's this idea that ... we're putting out there into the world our genomic sequences, and we don't know how that information could be used to harm us in the future. Someone else is going to have access to our genetic information and understand it before we do. [10, Historically disadvantaged]

We really have no idea what the really gigantic break through benefits and risks are going to be from this study, because we've never had enough information to really use it. So the biggest risks and biggest benefits are in that unknown unknowns box. [23, Participant-centric]

Longitudinal Study Design
Over one-third of interviewees identified risks associated with the longitudinal study design. A few noted the burdens associated with long-term participation:

It's a burden of time and trouble ... Unless I'm assured that this study is actually going to work and it's being done appropriately, it's going to be funded for its entire life, etc., my fear would be people are gonna take time and trouble to participate in this and the result is not going to be significant and so why would anybody waste their time? [29, Human subjects]

More commonly, interviewees raised concerns about the open-ended nature of the study:

It's completely open-ended and Murphy's law probably is in effect here. Anything that can go wrong, will. If you are a very curious person and are really interested in being a research participant and like the idea of genomic research, and are willing to sign up for open-ended study with undefined risks, this is perfect for you. [20, Research]

They did so particularly in combination with the use of broad consent for future unspecified research:

The bottom line really is this – after you sign up, most likely you're going to forget about it, and you're going to have to be comfortable with the fact that researchers will be using your data, your samples, your information for lots of uses in the future for which you will not have any say. [02, Government]

Additionally, some identified limits on the ability to withdraw as a risk:

Now the genome doesn't change, and this information can be there for a very long time. You can ... quit from this study, but the information, if it was processed, will stay there. So there is the risk that you leave a digital footprint of your genome in a place. [07, Research]

You can never unparticipate, right? There's the immediate risks to the individual, which is that you are signing up for life and beyond. Kind of like the way that the HeLa cells continue on. [47, Historically disadvantaged]

Interviewees also discussed changes external to the research that could occur over time and affect perceptions of risk, including changes in participants' lives as well as in the sociopolitical environment:

> People have change of circumstances all the time. They get HIV, they have drug abuse problems, and maybe they're not happy about ... people having access to it even when their personal identifiers are removed. It's just too sensitive, too stigmatizing, too personal, and they would say no if they were [asked] later down the road. [12, Law]

> As a geneticist, I know quite a lot about what are the limitations and possibilities [for] what someone can infer from a genome, but I don't know what will happen thirty years from now [in terms of] how this country will evolve, how interpretation services will evolve. How the political climate will evolve that might create some harm. [07, Research]

Indeed, "uncertainty" was a common theme across interviewees' comments about study design–related risks, including significant challenges in even articulating the risks:

> There are risks and there are benefits and an honest discussion about such a study would say we don't really know what the magnitude or the severity of those will be. [20, Research]

> I would be really honest and say, "We don't know because we haven't done this before." [50, Human subjects]

Several interviewees specifically referenced "unknown unknowns":

> The unknown unknowns are the scary part, right? Not the thing that we know – but there's always something that can go wrong fifty years from now. [07, Research]

This lead some to acknowledge that participants would be asked to take a leap of faith and to help society understand the risks:

> Different people in such a study are going to have very different things happen to them. You don't know a priori if you're going to be one of the people who have this or that happen to them ... It all depends. Participants have to take a leap of faith ... [and be] willing to accept any nature of potential downstream risks as we go through this. [20, Research]

> The risks aren't known yet, and by participating in this, one of the biggest benefits to society is to help us understand those risks. But that means we'll be the first ones exposed to them. [23, Participant-centric]

11.4 DISCUSSION

Data-sharing practices, coupled with the informational richness of genome-scale information, challenge the ability to protect research participants' privacy and confidentiality while also ensuring appropriate and maximal use of the data they contribute for the greatest societal good. Many of the risks raised by our interviewees have been discussed in the literature, including the identifiability of genomic information,[4] objectionable use[5] and group harm,[6] the familial nature of genetic information,[7] and study design features such as broad consent,[8] controlled access,[9] and limits on discontinuing participation.[10] Our research illuminates this ongoing debate with several key findings.

First, even as technical capabilities to gain unintended access to identities expand, many interviewees explicitly distinguished between the likelihood of such access and the likelihood of harm to participants. Barring individual-level factors, such as celebrity status or a possibly damaging medical history, they generally described the risk of adverse consequences as low – comparing it favorably with risks regularly encountered in modern life and noting the lack of historical instances of actual harm. They expressed skepticism as to motivation to target particular individuals and instead identified the high visibility of our hypothetical Million American Study as a primary reason why some – including academic researchers – might want simply to demonstrate that study information *can* be breached, hacked, or triangulated. Importantly, several thought leaders viewed the research initiative as bearing the primary impact of such intrusion due to erosion of public trust and willingness to participate.

Second, risks that emerged as perhaps most pressing could be considered "internal" to the study, including those associated with permitted uses and users of data that participants might find objectionable. For example, in a notable departure from the traditional focus on individual risks in biomedical research, many interviewees volunteered that they would talk about risks to groups if friends or family

---

[4] See Laura L. Rodriguez et al., Research Ethics: The Complexities of Genomic Identifiability, 339 *Science* 275 (2013); Eric E. Schadt, The Changing Privacy Landscape in the Era of Big Data, 8 *Mol. Syst. Biol.* 612 (2012); Carol J. Weil et al., NCI Think Tank Concerning the Identifiability of Biospecimens and "Omic" Data, 15 *Genet. Med.* 997 (2013).
[5] See Tom Tomlinson et al., Moral Concerns and the Willingness to Donate to a Research Biobank, 313 *JAMA* 417 (2015).
[6] See Aaron J. Goldenberg et al., Patient Perspectives on Group Benefits and Harms in Genetic Research, 14 *Pub. Health Genomics* 135 (2010); Michelle M. Mello & Leslie E. Wolf, The Havasupai Indian Tribe Case: Lessons for Research Involving Stored Biologic Samples, 363 *N. Engl. J. Med.* 204 (2010).
[7] See Kathy L. Hudson & Francis S. Collins, Biospecimen Policy: Family Matters, 500 *Nature* 141 (2013); Susan M. Wolf et al., Returning a Research Participant's Genomic Results to Relatives: Analysis and Recommendations, 43 *J.L. Med. Ethics* 440 (2015).
[8] See Laura M. Beskow, Lessons from HeLa Cells: The Ethics and Policy of Biospecimens, 17 *Ann. Rev. Genomics & Hum. Genet.* 395 (2016); Christine Grady et al., Broad Consent for Research with Biological Samples: Workshop Conclusions, 15 *Am. J. Bioethics* 34 (2015).
[9] See Jane Kaye, The Tension Between Data Sharing and the Protection of Privacy in Genomics Research, 13 *Ann. Rev. Genomics Hum. Genet.* 415 (2012); Schadt, The Changing Privacy Landscape.
[10] See Kaye, The Tension Between Data Sharing and the Protection of Privacy.

asked them to describe the primary risks of participating in our hypothetical study. This included interviewees who revealed that, although their family members were not part of a vulnerable group, they would not want to contribute to research that stigmatized others. Pointing to examples such as the Havasupai case[11] and recent publications on topics such as the genetics of intelligence[12] and criminal behavior,[13] they saw these risks as concerning not only to particular groups, but to the research enterprise and thus future patients more broadly.

Other prominent examples of "internal" risks were those arising from procedures such as return of individual research results with unproven clinical utility and the use of broad consent for unspecified future research. The constellation of uncertainty created by future technological developments, genomic discoveries, and medical advances; the open-ended nature of the study; changes over time in the lives and health of participants and their families; and the evolution of the sociopolitical environment led many interviewees to describe the "unknown unknowns" as potentially the most conspicuous risk of participation.

The findings reported here represent just one part of a complex interview with a diverse group of prominent thought leaders. Even so, this glimpse suggests a potential shift in the kinds of risks typically highlighted during the informed-consent process for precision medicine research. It also suggests that the likelihood and severity of these risks cannot be assessed in isolation but rather require careful attention to the design, conduct, and oversight of the research, heightened awareness of a wide array of relevant contextual factors, and close monitoring of changes in the scientific and societal landscape over time.

---

[11] See Mello & Wolf, The Havasupai Indian Tribe Case.
[12] See Davide Piffer, A Review of Intelligence GWAS Hits: Their Relationship to Country IQ and the Issue of Spatial Autocorrelation, 53 *Intelligence* 43 (2015).
[13] See Niklas Långström et al., Sexual Offending Runs in Families: A 37-Year Nationwide Study, 44 *Int. J. Epidemiol.* 713 (2015); Jari Tiihonen et al., Genetic Background of Extreme Violent Behavior, 20 *Mol. Psychiatry* 786 (2015).

12

From Individual to Group Privacy in Biomedical Big Data

Brent Mittelstadt

12.1 INTRODUCTION

Mature information societies are characterized by mass production of data that provide insight into human behavior.[1] Analytics (as in "Big Data analytics") has arisen as a practice to make sense of the data trails generated through interactions with networked devices, platforms, and organizations.[2] Users are understood through small patterns or correlations with others in the system, by which individuals are clustered into meaningful groups (or classes) based on their behavior, preferences, and other characteristics.[3] Analytics informs immediate responses to the needs and preferences of users as well as longer-term strategic planning and development by the platform provider.[4] Decision making in areas such as research, risk stratification, credit scoring, search and media filtration, market segmentation, employment, policing, and criminal sentencing is now routinely informed by analytics.

Analytics allows persistent knowledge describing the behaviors and characteristics of people to be constructed over time, forming individuals into meaningful groups or classes. Individuals are linked according to offline identifiers (e.g., age, ethnicity, geographic location) and new identity tokens based on shared behaviors, allowing

---

[1] Luciano Floridi, Mature Information Societies: A Matter of Expectations, 29 *Philos. Tech.* 1 (2016).
[2] Peter Grindrod, *Mathematical Underpinnings of Analytics: Theory and Applications* (2014); Jenna Burrell, How the Machine "Thinks": Understanding Opacity in Machine Learning Algorithms, 3 *Big Data Soc.* 1 (2016).
[3] Mike Ananny, Toward an Ethics of Algorithms: Convening, Observation, Probability, and Timeliness, 41 *Sci. Tech. Human Values* 93, 101 (2016); Bart W. Schermer, The Limits of Privacy in Automated Profiling and Data Mining, 27 *Comput. L. Security Rev.* 45 (2011); Mireille Hildebrandt, Defining Profiling: A New Type of Knowledge?, in *Profiling the European Citizen* 17 (Mireille Hildebrandt & Serge Gutwirth eds., 2008). "Big Data" may be the wrong term to describe such data. Correlations can be found between "small amounts of densely connected metadata" that are not "big" in terms of volume.
[4] Grindrod, Mathematical Underpinnings of Analytics.

for predictions and decisions to be taken at a group rather than individual level.[5] These digital collective identifiers disrupt the long-standing link between the individual, identity, and privacy.

Algorithmically grouped individuals have a collective interest in the creation of information about the group and actions taken on its behalf. However, a theoretical framework to recognize ad hoc groups as holders of privacy rights does not yet exist. In this chapter, I examine the feasibility of granting algorithmically assembled (ad hoc) groups a right to privacy. As conceived here, a "right" is the formalization of protection for mutually valued interests. Rights are based on a type of interest deemed worthy of protection[6] and normally correspond with duties for other agents to respect the interests in question.[7] All rights thus have constituent interests that the right, and legal and moral mechanisms based on it, aim to protect. A distinction can also be recognized between moral and legal rights. Both types of rights establish duties for agents to respect the interests of the right holder. The two differ only in terms of their grounding: moral rights are based on moral norms or ethical theory, whereas legal rights have a basis in law. The categories are, of course, not mutually exclusive; a right can have both a moral basis and be legally enforceable.

This chapter does not define a general theory of group privacy but instead examines the case for granting a specific moral informational privacy right (the "right to inviolate personality") to ad hoc groups as opposed to the prevailing concern with identifiable individuals in privacy and data-protection law. Granting ad hoc groups a right to privacy would formally recognize the validity and importance of their privacy interests independent of the privacy interests of individual members. Doing so is necessary given the function of ad hoc groups in Big Data analytics. The argument made here is that ad hoc groups possess privacy interests that are sufficiently important to warrant formal protection through recognition of a moral (and perhaps, in the future, legal) right to group privacy.

In international law, groups are defined by a shared background (e.g., culture or collective purpose). Such purposeful collectives are granted rights, including the right to assemble.[8] In contrast, I argue that algorithmically constructed ad hoc groups lacking a shared background should also have their interests in privacy formally recognized by being granted a right to control the group's identity. Group privacy is proposed as a third interest to balance with individual privacy rights and the social, commercial, and epistemic benefits of analytics.

---

[5] Ibid.
[6] Christoph Grabenwarter, *European Convention for the Protection of Human Rights and Fundamental Freedoms: Commentary* (2014).
[7] Peter Jones, Group Rights, in *The Stanford Encyclopedia of Philosophy Archive* (2016), available at http://plato.stanford.edu/archives/sum2016/entries/rights-group/ [https://perma.cc/L5VV-EBT5].
[8] Corsin Bisaz, *The Concept of Group Rights in International Law: Groups as Contested Right-Holders, Subjects and Legal Persons* (2012); Edward J. Bloustein, Group Privacy: The Right to Huddle, 8 *Rutgers Camden L. J.* 219 (1976).

To begin to unpack the real-world applicability of a right to group privacy, the proposed right is examined in the context of biomedical Big Data. From data repositories and biobanks supporting aggregation of clinical trial and routine health data to support research[9] to personal health tracking and wellness platforms that provide feedback on a stream of real-time monitoring data, health and wellness data of uncertain value are increasingly collected in mature information societies. Various legal restrictions on processing and governance structures are in place to help, yet the prevailing ideals of informed consent, ownership, and control of personal data are proving inadequate in the face of Big Data analytics.[10] Numerous reforms have been proposed to "fix" governance of biomedical Big Data platforms through stewardship, altruism,[11] or solidarity.[12] To assess the potential for group privacy to serve a similar role, the potential impact of group privacy protections on medical research, medical insurance, and health and wellness monitoring services is examined.

This chapter is structured as follows: the second section describes the ethical significance of groups to how identity is formed through analytics. Advances in analytics methods and technologies create a need for a right to group privacy. The third section then introduces Floridi's approach to informational privacy and the right to "inviolate personality," which serves as a basis for group privacy, as defined in the fourth section. Theoretical challenges to this type of right are then considered, including an examination of what it means to be a rights holder and the case for ad hoc groups to be considered rights holders in parallel to the privacy rights of individuals. The fifth section then considers how the concept and protections of group privacy considered here could apply to biomedical Big Data analytics. The chapter concludes with reflections on future work required to develop real-world protections and the relevance of group privacy to the exercise of rights specified in the forthcoming EU General Data Protection Regulation.

12.2 THE ETHICAL SIGNIFICANCE OF GROUPS AND IDENTITY

Analytics involving algorithmic classification of humans can be considered a privacy-invasive practice not yet sufficiently regulated due to a prevailing focus on

---

[9] Nuffield Council on Bioethics, *The Collection, Linking and Use of Data in Biomedical Research and Health Care: Ethical Issues* 198 (2015), available at http://nuffieldbioethics.org/wp-content/uploads/Biological_and_health_data_web.pdf [https://perma.cc/A3RH-BWV8]; Tobias Schulte in den Baumen et al., Data Protection in Biobanks: A European Challenge for the Long-Term Sustainability of Biobanking, 31 *Law Human Genome Rev.* 31 (2009).

[10] Janet Currie, "Big Data" versus "Big Brother": On the Appropriate Use of Large-Scale Data Collections in Pediatrics, 131 *Pediatrics* S127 (2013); Stine Lomborg & Anja Bechmann, Using APIs for Data Collection on Social Media, 30 *Inf. Soc.* 256 (2014).

[11] Mark A. Rothstein & Abigail B. Shoben, An Unbiased Response to the Open Peer Commentaries on "Does Consent Bias Research?," 13 *Am. J. Bioethics* W1 (2013).

[12] Barbara Prainsack & Alena Buyx, A Solidarity-Based Approach to the Governance of Research Biobanks, 21 *Med. L. Rev.* 71 (2013).

the privacy interests of identifiable individuals. Data must normally contain identifiers (e.g., name, address) to be legally classified as "personal" and thus warranting additional controls on processing and exchange.[13] An individual's claim to manage data about himself or herself often ends once identifiers are removed from the data.[14] This approach incorrectly implies that privacy cannot be violated in isolation of identifiability.

Algorithmic classification systems raise a unique challenge for existing theories of privacy by creating groups defined by identity tokens not reducible to or owned by individual members of the group. In turn, traditional identifiers (e.g., name or address) are increasingly irrelevant in analytics to learn something about people. Individuals can be clustered according to behaviors, preferences, and other characteristics while remaining anonymous.[15] Such methods find individuals interesting only to the extent that they can be correlated with others in the system (i.e., as members of classification groups)[16]; advertisers care not who they are advertising to, but whether their advertisements reach a target market. Members of the group (e.g., a market segment) need not be *identified* but rather *classified* to be targeted. Connections between individuals revealing particular risks or behaviors are of interest, not the identifiable individual as such.[17] Algorithmic classification tells us something about individuals through their association with ad hoc, ephemeral, but insightful groups of allegedly similar people.

Algorithmic classification necessarily involves grouping of data subjects. Grouping can occur in two senses: either in the description of subjects or actions taken on the basis of probabilities and predictive analytics. For the former, data subjects must always be considered along a limited set of dimensions. Classifications are defined along these dimensions. A simplistic example will suffice: assume that we want to classify festival goers according to the festivals they have already attended (perhaps for the sake of predicting which festivals they will attend in the future). Further, assume that we are considering two previous festivals P and Q. Four possible groups emerge according to these dimensions (see Figure 12.1): festival goers can be PQ,

---

[13] Cf. European Commission, Regulation of the European Parliament and of the Council on the Protection of Individuals with Regard to the Processing of Personal Data and on the Free Movement of Such Data (General Data Protection Regulation) (2012), available at http://ec.europa.eu/justice/data-protection/document/review2012/com_2012_11_en.pdf [https://perma.cc/XLU9-LBXU].
[14] This is not entirely the case in the forthcoming EU General Data Protection Regulation. The definition of personal data has been modified in the draft regulation to include pseudonymized data, where a link to identifiers is maintained but held separately from the data set.
[15] Bart Van der Sloot, Privacy in the Post-NSA Era: Time for a Fundamental Revision? (2014), available at http://papers.ssrn.com/sol3/papers.cfm?abstract_id=2432104 [https://perma.cc/FJ7X-3VAN].
[16] Luciano Floridi, Open Data, Data Protection, and Group Privacy, 27 *Phil. Tech.* 1 (2014); Anton Vedder, KDD: The Challenge to Individualism, 1 *Ethics Info. Tech.* 275 (1999).
[17] Floridi, Open Data, Data Protection, and Group Privacy; Vedder, KDD: The Challenge to Individualism.

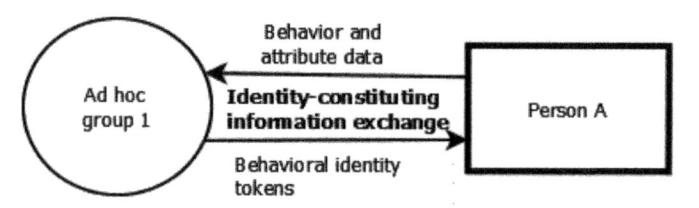

FIGURE 12.1 Information exchanged to create a profiling identity.

PnQ, nPQ, or *nPnQ*. While a certain group may remain temporarily empty; for instance, if we lack data on any festival goers that have not attended either festival in question, the number of possible groupings is limited according to the quantity of dimensions considered.

The same logic applies to descriptive and predictive classification; the number of possible groups will always be limited by the number of dimensions under consideration. For predictive analytics, dimensions can also refer to nondescriptive choices, for instance, the choice to deliver a certain advertisement due to observations of prior actions. In this case, each data subject will be understood through a series of probabilities in addition to observations; for instance, based on your attendance of festivals *P* and *Q* and your expressed musical interests, we predict with 75 percent confidence that you will attend festival *R*. At the point an action is taken on the basis of a probability, a group is formed of all data subjects receiving the action.[18] Once again, the possible range of actions and thus groups will be limited by the dimensions under consideration.

Identifiability operates at two levels here. The individual's "offline" identity consists of the types of identifiers currently protected under data-protection law (e.g., name, address, national insurance number, unique identifier). Offline identities always describe one and only one unique person; they are way to ensure a persistent record can be assembled over time and between different systems. The offline identity of the individual is irrelevant to the formation of an ad hoc group and learning things about it.

In analytics systems, individuals also possess a profiling identity constructed from connections with groups of other data subjects based on behaviors, attributes, and other factors identified by the system. A "profiling identity" consists of all the groups a data subject is placed into by the system (see Figure 12.2). These groups, referred to here as "ad hoc groups," are designed from connections between data subjects perceived by an analytics system (i.e., a classifier algorithm). The identifiers or information constituting the group and thus the individual's profiling identity are nonrandom behaviors and attributes that allow data subjects to be meaningfully

---

[18] Some may wish to argue that such probabilistic reasoning is not a type of grouping. However, probabilities are calculated to drive decision making or, at a minimum, learn something about the data subject, that is, to classify him or her for future decision making.

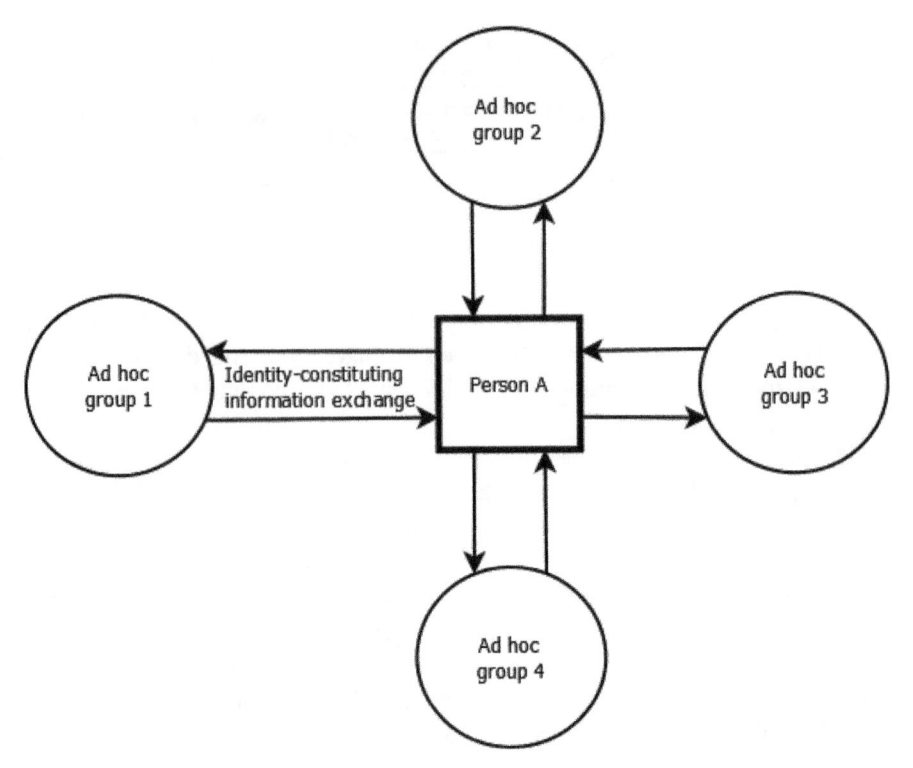

FIGURE 12.2 Profiling identity structure.

grouped, referred to here as "behavioral identity tokens."[19] Similar to some shared offline identifiers (e.g., culture, ethnicity, post code), ownership of behavioral identity tokens is distributed across members of the group (see Figure 12.3). Changes to the token (e.g., defaulting on a loan) and decisions based on it affect all members of the group, including members not yet observed by the analytics system.

Shared ownership of identity is largely ignored in the aforementioned data-protection policy. Existing legal protections reflect piecemeal responses to particularly egregious uses of shared offline identifiers in decision making, seen, for instance, in antidiscrimination law or the ban on personalized insurance premiums based on risk profiling in the European Union.[20] Case-based regulation and detection of discriminatory decision making are feasible when the set of shared identifiers remains small. The challenge now faced is that analytics produces shared identifiers (i.e., behavioral identity tokens) as a matter of course. Proxies for protected attributes

---

[19] Cf. Grindrod, Mathematical Underpinnings of Analytics.
[20] Sue Newell & Marco Marabelli, Strategic Opportunities (and Challenges) of Algorithmic Decision-Making: A Call for Action on the Long-Term Societal Effects of "Datification," 24 J. Strategic Info. Systems 3 (2015).

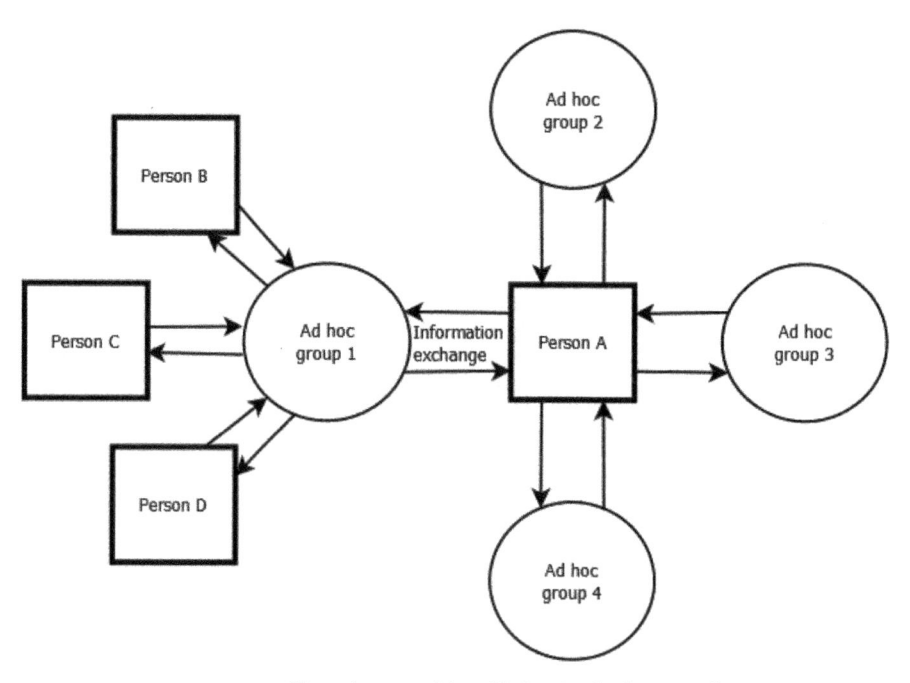

FIGURE 12.3 Shared ownership of behavioral identity tokens.

are not easy to predict or detect,[21] particularly when algorithms access linked data sets.[22] Profiles constructed from neutral characteristics such as postal code may inadvertently overlap with other profiles related to ethnicity, gender, sexual preference, and so on.[23] It is not clear from the outset what types of behavioral identity tokens and decision-making models can be produced and which of these are potentially ethically problematic.[24]

[21] Andrea Romei & Salvatore Ruggieri, A Multidisciplinary Survey on Discrimination Analysis, 29 Knowledge Engineering Rev. 582 (2014); Tal Zarsky, The Trouble with Algorithmic Decisions: An Analytic Road Map to Examine Efficiency and Fairness in Automated and Opaque Decision Making, 41 Sci. Tech. Human Values 118 (2016).
[22] Solon Barocas & Andrew D. Selbst, Essay: Big Data's Disparate Impact, 104 Cal. L. Rev. 671 (2016).
[23] Kevin Macnish, Unblinking Eyes: The Ethics of Automating Surveillance, 14 Ethics Info. Technol. 151–67 (2012); Schermer, The Limits of Privacy.
[24] A few examples to demonstrate the ethical relevance of classification: profiling can inadvertently create an evidence base for discrimination. Katja de Vries, Identity, Profiling Algorithms and a World of Ambient Intelligence, 12 Ethics Info. Technol. 71 (2010). Discrimination produced by algorithmic comprehension is not harmful or ethically problematic in principle; rather, it is the effects of discrimination that can be harmful and unjust. Personalization segments a population so that only some groups are worthy of receiving certain opportunities or information, reinforcing existing social (dis)advantages. Personalization systems create self-fulfilling behaviors and limit the opportunities available to users according to their classification within the system. Macnish, Unblinking Eyes; Matthias Leese, The New Profiling: Algorithms, Black Boxes, and the Failure of Antidiscriminatory Safeguards in the European

Algorithmic classification can be ethically problematic for a number of reasons. It can, for example, reduce individual control of identity. The identities of individual members are mediated by knowledge about the group. Groups are formed from observables chosen at a particular level of abstraction for a particular purpose.[25] Ad hoc groups are constructed from observables of interest to algorithmic classification systems, which produce a certain kind of knowledge (e.g., a recommendation, rank, classification). These groups are imperfect reflections of the individuals contained within, constrained by the types of questions they are designed to answer and the flaws of the observables (i.e., the data) from which they are constructed. The meaning given to a particular group, and thus imposed on the individual, will not necessarily reflect his or her self-understanding.[26] Ad hoc grouping provides unanticipated ways of viewing and inferring information about the individual. Algorithmic classification therefore must be considered a threat to data subjects' capacity to shape and control identity.

The fair and equitable treatment of individuals is also undermined by predictive analytics.[27] It is difficult for lay data subjects to notice and redress unfair or harmful decisions driven by analytics.[28] Systematic identification of the limitations of recorded data, or the set of observables that informs algorithmic classification, and how these limitations are reflected in models and decisions produced with analytics[29] are hindered by the opacity of analytics.[30] Algorithmic profiles are volatile[31]; the subject's representation in a classification scheme evolves over time, with new labels applied, tweaked, and removed as patterns are identified from new inputs.

"Privacy," conceived of as the right to control data about oneself, is an unrealistic ideal under these conditions. The scale of the behavioral data produced in

Union, 45 *Security Dialogue* 494 (2014). Personalization "involves unseen, categorical, computational judgments about which searches, articles, or purchases should *probably* come next." Ananny, Toward an Ethics of Algorithms, at 103. Discrimination or social, economic, and epistemic benefits of Big Data can inadvertently localize around groups that offer easy or interesting analysis opportunities. Kate Crawford et al., Critiquing Big Data: Politics, Ethics, Epistemology. Special Section Introduction, 8 *Int'l J. Commun.* 1663 (2014). Questions of the fairness and the distributive justice of such practices can be raised. Anthony Danna & Oscar H. Gandy, Jr., All That Glitters Is Not Gold: Digging Beneath the Surface of Data Mining, 40 *J. Bus. Ethics* 373 (2002); Alan Rubel & Kyle M.L. Jones, Student Privacy in Learning Analytics: An Information Ethics Perspective, 32 *Info. Soc.* (2016); I. Glenn Cohen et al., The Legal and Ethical Concerns That Arise From Using Complex Predictive Analytics in Health Care, 33 *Health Affairs* 1139 (2014).

[25] Cf. Luciano Floridi, The Method of Levels of Abstraction, 18 *Minds & Machines* 303 (2008).
[26] Deborah Lupton, The Commodification of Patient Opinion: The Digital Patient Experience Economy in the Age of Big Data, 36 *Soc. Health Illness* 856 (2014).
[27] Cf. Newell & Marabelli, Strategic Opportunities (and Challenges) of Algorithmic Decision-Making.
[28] Brent Daniel Mittelstadt & Luciano Floridi, The Ethics of Big Data: Current and Foreseeable Issues in Biomedical Contexts, 22 *Sci. Eng. Ethics* 303 (2016).
[29] Grindrod, Mathematical Underpinnings of Analytics.
[30] Cf. Burrell, How the Machine "Thinks."
[31] Leese, The New Profiling.

information societies, the complexity of methods to make sense of them,[32] and the shared ownership of behavioral identity tokens all undermine efforts to protect individuals' rights to privacy and identity with limits on processing of identifiable data. Protections are required that respond to the inherent uncertainty of algorithmic classification and the emerging capacities to learn about individuals through knowledge about the groups to which they are allocated.

12.3 INFORMATIONAL PRIVACY AND THE RIGHT TO INVIOLATE PERSONALITY

To develop privacy protections responsive to advances in data analytics, an approach to privacy is required that can address groups and shared identity. Group privacy as developed in the remainder of this chapter is based on Luciano Floridi's concept of an "informational identity,"[33] understood within his approach to informational privacy[34] and broader philosophy of information.[35] When referring to "group privacy," I am explicitly addressing the privacy of information that constitutes identity; a violation of informational privacy disrespects the agent's claim over information about itself.

This claim can be interpreted in several ways: to control, manage, own, or prevent access to information about the self. Traditionally, the damage caused by breaching privacy has been linked in reductionist theories to its undesirable consequences (e.g., distress or discrimination) or in ownership-based theories to the individuals' right to exclusive use of information. Problems exist with both approaches.[36]

The alternative approach adopted here to describe group privacy, of privacy as "identity constitutive,"[37] connects privacy to the integrity of information constituting one's identity.[38] While this is certainly not the only feasible theoretical basis for the development of "group privacy," it is adopted here due to its relevance to unpacking the effects of shared ownership of identity-constituting tokens on privacy.

According to this approach, identity is constituted by information describing the individual or group. Privacy is therefore a respect for the right to "inviolate personality"[39] or the "right to immunity from unknown, undesired, or unintentional

---

[32] Mittelstadt & Floridi, The Ethics of Big Data.
[33] Luciano Floridi, The Informational Nature of Personal Identity, 21 *Minds & Machines* 549 (2011).
[34] Luciano Floridi, The Ontological Interpretation of Informational Privacy, 7 *Ethics Info. Technol.* 185 (2005); Luciano Floridi, Four Challenges for a Theory of Informational Privacy, 8 *Ethics Info. Technol.* 109 (2006).
[35] Luciano Floridi, *The Philosophy of Information* (2013).
[36] For a discussion, see Luciano Floridi, Group Privacy: A Defence and an Interpretation, in *Group Privacy: New Challenges of Data Technologies* (Linnet Taylor et al. eds., 2016).
[37] Floridi, The Informational Nature of Personal Identity.
[38] Floridi, Group Privacy: A Defence and an Interpretation.
[39] Samuel D. Warren & Louis D. Brandeis, The Right to Privacy, 4 *Harv. L. Rev.* 193, 203 (1890).

changes in one's own identity as an informational entity, both actively and passively."[40] According to this view, identity itself, and the information constituting it, has value independent of the role it plays in decision making that produces harmful or beneficial effects. The integrity of the subject's identity is breached when data or information is added to subject's identity without consent. Breaches of identity are considered an attack on the person who is constituted by his or her information.

A right to inviolate personality protects against the tendency in mature information societies[41] to produce a longitudinal, semipermanent view of the individual through data analytics that would violate his or her right "to be allowed to experiment with one's own life, to start again, without having records that mummify one's personal identity forever."[42] Compared with "offline" decision making, algorithmic classification poses new restrictions on an individual's capacity to shape and alter identity over a lifetime, albeit with historical precedence. Breaches of the integrity of identity are not limited to the online world; rather, the description of a right to group privacy in relation to data analytics and automated decision making is a response to an issue of the scale and persistence of breaches rather than a fundamentally new type of breach of the integrity of identity. The difference is that analytics allow for the identities or beliefs at the basis of the choice architecture offered to the person not to be limited to a single third-party actor but rather something that persists over time, travels with the person between systems, and affects future opportunities and treatment at the hands of others. How a classification is reached is arguably irrelevant to the impact on the data subject's capacity to shape and alter identity over time and the power afforded to decision-making entities to externally shape his or her identity. The accuracy of a categorization does not affect its persistence; as long as the grouping is in place or the categorization applies to the subject, the subject retains an interest in the information constituting it, even if the grouping proves to be inaccurate.

Floridi compares this process to kidnapping: "the observed is moved to an observer's local space of observation (a space which is remote for the observed), unwillingly and possibly unknowingly. What is abducted is personal information, even though no actual removal of information is in question, but rather only a cloning of the relevant piece of personal information."[43] Analytics is precisely this: the individual's identity (as contained in the system's inputs) is temporarily kidnapped and modified through classifications that reveal something new about the person.[44] External identity construction breaches the individual's inviolate personality.

---

[40] Floridi, Group Privacy: A Defence and an Interpretation.
[41] Floridi, Mature Information Societies.
[42] Luciano Floridi, Four Challenges for a Theory of Informational Privacy, 8 *Ethics Info. Technol.* 109 (2006).
[43] Ibid., at 112.
[44] Cf. Hildebrandt, Defining Profiling.

The informational privacy right described by Floridi is a fundamental moral right, meaning that the starting point for any negotiation over privacy should start from a position of respecting this right.[45] As Floridi notes,[46] in contrast to reductionist theories, which allow for privacy to be overridden through consequentialist appeals, the identity-constituting approach starts from the position that the right should be respected. Fundamental rights cannot be negated as such by consequentialist appeals but can nonetheless be waived through negotiation or consent from the rights holder or breached due to overriding interests.[47] Grounds for justifiable breaches under special circumstances, of course, can be identified, but this does not alter the fact that a breach of privacy has occurred.[48]

12.4 THE RIGHT TO INVIOLATE PERSONALITY AS A BASIS FOR GROUP PRIVACY

Group privacy as a right to inviolate personality aims to protect the integrity of a group's identity, which is nonreducible to the identities of members. We can speak of the integrity of a group's identity being breached in two senses. Active breaches of identity involve replication and manipulation of the person's identity within a system. Passive breaches involve indirect pressure placed on the person to include newly generated information in his or her identity, caused by a failure to obtain meaningful consent for processing.[49] Passive breaches describe potential future effects on identity. A group member's self-perception will not necessarily be affected by information about the group due to a lack of self-awareness (i.e., the person does not know that he or she is a member) or a small effect size (e.g., the disturbance of a poorly targeted advertisement). The right to inviolate personality is nevertheless passively breached in both cases because information that will potentially affect the individual's or group's identity in the future has been generated.

Algorithmic classification primarily produces passive breaches of identity. Members of ad hoc groups will struggle to become self-aware regarding the group's existence due to the opacity, secrecy, and ubiquity of analytics in information societies.[50] It is for this reason that ad hoc grouping poses a different challenge to

---

[45] Floridi, Four Challenges for a Theory of Informational Privacy.
[46] Floridi, Group Privacy: A Defence and an Interpretation.
[47] This is not the same as the reductionist approach: where consent is not obtained, meaning "unknown, undesired, or unintentional" changes to identity occur, the subject's privacy right is breached.
[48] It is questionable, for example, whether agreement mechanisms governing many digital sources of data (e.g., privacy policies and "terms and conditions") grant meaningful consent. Similarly, consent does nothing to address the cumulative effects of knowledge generated through analytics on social and organizational decision-making processes (e.g., healthcare commissioning).
[49] Floridi, Four Challenges for a Theory of Informational Privacy.
[50] Cf. Leese, The New Profiling; Hildebrandt, Defining Profiling.

identity management than membership of offline collectives or ascriptive groups in which self-awareness and collective agency are possible. Pragmatically, third-party use of information that constitutes identity is unpredictable; a privacy right focused on the integrity of identity made up of this information, rather than the effects of its usage, is therefore required to ensure that privacy is protected independent of the capacity to observe and correct for the harmful effects of data processing.

Floridi's approach to the right to inviolate personality is preferred because it formalizes the harm to identity caused by third parties that process data to create (actionable) information about groups. An ad hoc group's identity consists of the classifications and rules constructed by an algorithmic classification system (i.e., why you are a member of this particular group), along with predictions of unobserved or future collective preferences and behaviors. This identity is viewed by the system itself and decision-making processes influenced by its outputs. Opportunities to protect identity require awareness of when, where, and how this identity is crafted. Both an individual's and a group's right to inviolate personality therefore can be violated when identity is crafted externally, without either's consent or awareness.

If group privacy is viewed as a way to correct the imbalance of power created by the proliferation of data analytics (i.e., the power to craft and manage identity), three interpretations come to mind. A strong interpretation would allow for rights holders to make claims over any data processing that generates identity-constitutive information via algorithmic classification.[51] A strong right would equate to control of third-party data controllers and algorithmic classification systems. This approach would create new conflict points for data controllers and subjects.

A weakened but practically feasible interpretation recognizes the claims of rights holders over identity-constitutive data processing as valid but limits their claims to oversight over these processes, not control. A duty thus would be created for data controllers to keep rights holders "in the loop." This moderate interpretation differs from existing rights and duties enshrined in EU data-protection law in the sense that it validates the individual's claim to information about the groups to which he or she nominally belongs, either as rights holder or as member of a rights-holding group.

A weak interpretation denies the rights holders any claim to control how third parties form views about him or her. On this view, a weak right to group privacy would be one of enhancement only, meaning that data controllers have a nonbinding duty to educate data subjects about how their "data trails" mediate their experiences within analytics-driven decision making.

Note that the term "rights holder" is preferred here to "group" or "individual" in recognition that it is possible to grant a right to group privacy to either. The nature and validity of group rights is a long-standing problem in political philosophy.[52]

---

[51] Irwin Altman, Privacy Regulation: Culturally Universal or Culturally Specific?, 33 J. Soc. Issues 66 (1977).
[52] Ibid.

Rights held by groups (i.e., a "group right") are not reducible to the rights of members; it is a right held by a group qua group. Members of the group can also be granted individual rights due to their membership in the group, seen, for instance, in rights and privileges granted to members of a social club. Such rights are not group rights as discussed here; rather, a group right is attributed to the group itself, not individual members.[53]

Concerning privacy, the loss of a particular member will not change the group's history or how it is understood externally. The possibility of a right to group privacy held by groups themselves is thus worth initial consideration, even if it turns out to be theoretically invalid or practically infeasible to enforce.

To establish ad hoc groups as legitimate holders of a right to group privacy, it is first necessary to examine in what sense groups themselves can have privacy interests and rights.[54] For our purposes, we can consider three types of groups as potential rights holders:

- **Collective.** A group intentionally joined due to collective interests, shared background, or other explicit common traits and purposes.
  Examples: Patient advocacy groups, labor unions.
- **Ascriptive group.** A group whose membership is determined by inherited or incidentally developed characteristic. Ascriptive groups cannot normally be intentionally joined or left without redefining the boundaries of the group.
  Examples: Ethnic groups, patient cohorts.
- **Ad hoc group.** A group whose membership is assembled for a third-party interest according to perceived links between members, often for a time- or purpose-limited period.
  Examples: Market segments, profiling groups (e.g., high-income parents in Wales aged forty to fifty-five likely to purchase a house in the next six months).

Collectives and incidental groups are already legally recognized as legitimate rights holders in some contexts.[55] Collective rights include the right to self-determination held by nations and legal rights granted to corporations.[56] Prior work on group

---

[53] Floridi, Group Privacy: A Defence and an Interpretation.
[54] The nature and validity of group rights are long-standing problems in political philosophy. See, e.g., ibid; Jones, Group Rights.
[55] Collectives and incidental groups can also be protected indirectly through individually held rights. Antidiscrimination law protects groups or "protected classes" from "disparate impact" in social and political decision making. See Barocas & Selbst, Essay: Big Data's Disparate Impact. However, in this case, protections are aimed at individual members of relevant groups; the group functions only as a vehicle or focal point to deliver protections to individuals. This type of arrangement is comparable to a right to group privacy held by individuals.
[56] Christian List & Philip Pettit, *Group Agency: The Possibility, Design, and Status of Corporate Agents* (2011).

privacy has established a right for labor unions, understood as collectives, to assemble.[57] Other examples include prohibitions on genetic discrimination[58] and protections of minority cultural and linguistic traditions. In contrast, ad hoc groups are not yet recognized as deserving of legally enshrined privacy rights.

Rights can be granted to groups on the basis of several characteristics. As suggested by the aforementioned examples of rights held by collectives and ascriptive groups, collective identity[59] and agency[60] are common minimal requirements for the possession of group rights.

Ad hoc groups appear to fail both requirements. They are assembled by algorithmic classification systems as "types" of individuals with common *characteristics*,[61] not common *intentions*, which suggests a lack of self-recognition, collective interests, and agency. To exist, ad hoc groups require only a third-party desire to group a set of individuals according to perceived similarities.[62] An identity can be imposed on members unaware that they are, in fact, members of the group. The third-party interests in the formation of ad hoc groups also need not be long term: ad hoc groups need last only long enough to answer a question posed by a data controller. Both characteristics undermine any ascription of collective agency or intentionality.[63] Ad hoc groups are thus a unique type of group insofar as they are externally crafted and lack the intentionality and self-awareness of existing protected groups.

Collective identity and collective agency are not absolute requirements for groups to hold rights. Instead, moral patienthood may prove sufficient. Groups must "possess a moral standing that is not reducible to the standing of its members" to

---

[57] Bloustein, Group Privacy: The Right to Huddle.
[58] Marvin R. Natowicz et al., Genetic Discrimination and the Law, 50 *Am. J. Hum. Genet.* 465 (1992).
[59] "Collective identity" can refer to both a reducible identity aggregated from the independent identities of members (such that the group's identity necessarily changes when members leave) and a nonreducible external identity held by the group itself. Institutions show how collectives can possess this latter type of nonreducible group identity; sports clubs, for instance, have an identity (e.g., history, norms) and interests independent of the identities and interests of their members, who change over time. For more, see Peter A. French, *Collective and Corporate Responsibility* (1984).
[60] Jones, Group Rights. "Collective agency" refers to the capacity to act to fulfill or protect the interests of the group. Needs and interests are shared between members insofar as "what benefits or harms any member must benefit or harm all." Agency requires self-awareness: groups cannot act in their best interests without first being aware that the group exists. All members of a collective will by definition possess self-awareness. However, for ascriptive groups, self-awareness is required only at the group level; genealogy, for instance, demonstrates quite clearly the extent of ignorance of inherited traits and cultural history.
[61] Floridi, Open Data, Data Protection, and Group Privacy.
[62] French, Collective and Corporate Responsibility.
[63] With that said, persistent profiling identities can be extremely valuable in analytics. The profiling identity, as a record of one's ad hoc group memberships, is akin to a digital "permanent record" that reflects one's identity within one or more linked algorithmic classification systems. An electronic health record linked across general practitioners, hospitals, and other facilities that describes a patient's personal health risks is but one example.

possess rights.[64] On all but a strict anthropocentric view, ad hoc groups can be moral patients on this basis.[65] Floridi[66] argues that groups can be right holders by the same logic that rights are attributed to individuals as long as the group itself is treated as an individual (as in corporate personhood). Groups serve the same role as individuals in interactions involving the exchange of information. Rights can simultaneously be held by the individual and the individual's group as long as identity-forming interactions exist at both levels. If these interactions constitute the group's identity (as is the case for individuals), then groups can be recognized as possessing an interest in controlling that identity. This interest can be formally recognized as a group right to inviolate identity,[67] even if the group cannot itself act to control that identity. Agency can be hypothetically attributed to ad hoc groups if third-party processors act to respect interests the group would presumably have if self-aware.[68]

In the case of ad hoc groups, identity-forming interactions involving the group and individual members intersect due to shared ownership of behavioral identity tokens (see Figures 12.1 through 12.3). The behaviors of individuals produce data used to define an actionable group. Actions taken by members affect the interests of the whole group due to the predictive power attributed to the algorithmic classifications; the group is actionable in the sense that members have been observed (or perceived) to be similar and are thus predicted to behave or respond to stimuli (e.g., advertisements) similarly in the future. As a result, the group as a whole has a claim to the tokens used to define it and guide future actions taken toward it. Individual members do not retain an exclusive claim to their data trails once they are algorithmically grouped. This dimension of ad hoc groups emphasises the existence of a separate group identity and privacy interests that are nonreducible to the identities and interests of individual members.

From this brief discussion, ad hoc groups can tentatively be treated as moral patients and thus as valid rights holders. This issue requires further contextualization within a theoretical framework of political and legal rights, which goes beyond the scope of this chapter. Furthermore, it may largely be a semantic point due to ad hoc

---

[64] Jones, Group Rights; Carl Wellman, *Real Rights* 75 (1995). Thresholds for patienthood vary. A strict anthropocentric view grants patienthood only to fellow moral agents. In contrast, the mere possession of a "reason to regard a group as an object of moral concern," such as the recognition of collective interests, may itself provide sufficient reason to treat an entity as a moral patient. Similarly, particular capacities can serve as a minimal threshold, for instance, the capacity to suffer (cf. Peter Singer, *Practical Ethics* [1993]), or be harmed by entropy as an informational object (Luciano Floridi, *The Ethics of Information* [2013]).
[65] Floridi, The Philosophy of Information.
[66] Floridi, Group Privacy: A Defence and an Interpretation.
[67] Ibid.
[68] Such attributed interests can be based on observed interests of individual members, for instance, the interest to be accurately classified according to their data. This is not to say the group's interests are reducible to the interests of members but rather that an educated guess can be made about what the group would value if given the opportunity to assemble and act collectively.

groups lacking self-awareness and collective agency, meaning that ad hoc groups cannot themselves act to protect their privacy interests enshrined in the right to group privacy. However, as discussed earlier, the establishment of a right creates concomitant duties for agents, in this case for data controllers to respect groups' interests in inviolate personality. Consideration is therefore required of how to enact formal protections of group privacy that do not require action from ad hoc groups themselves.

12.5 GROUP PRIVACY IN BIOMEDICAL BIG DATA

With a tentative right to group privacy held by ad hoc groups now sketched, we return to the context of biomedicine to begin to unpack the real-world implications of the right for analytics. "Biomedical Big Data" refers to the application of analytics methods (i.e., algorithmic classification) to diverse streams of biomedical data. Research repositories that aggregate disparate data sources and facilitate data exchange are a standout example of biomedical Big Data in practice.[69] However, analytics methods are also used beyond research, for instance, to inform medical insurance premiums, risk stratification, or as part of health and wellness tracking devices and services.[70]

A right to group privacy is applicable in principle to all types of biomedical Big Data. Genetics research provides an example where group privacy is clearly applicable, albeit to ascriptive groups (i.e., individuals with a particular genetic mutation). New research modifies how a group (i.e., people with a particular mutation) is perceived in future decision making, with potentially discriminatory effects for individuals.[71] Precisely this concern led to the adoption of the Genetic Information Nondiscrimination Act of 2008 in the United States. In this case, members of the group have a stake in how they are perceived and thus how research modifies the group's identity, which influences individual-level decision making about both current and future members.

The relative strength of a group's privacy interests will vary between data-processing contexts. While the right to inviolate personality is fundamental in principle, in practice, it must be balanced with individual privacy rights and the social, commercial, and epistemic benefits of medical data processing. It is thus not in principle an additional barrier to data processing but rather a third set of considerations for ethical assessment of biomedical Big Data projects and platforms. Group privacy could, for instance, ground changes to individualistic privacy and consent mechanisms with cohort consultations in research examining aggregate data.

---

[69] Edward S. Dove et al., Towards an Ethics Safe Harbor for Global Biomedical Research, 1 J. L. Biosci. 3 (2014); Mittelstadt & Floridi, The Ethics of Big Data.
[70] Cf. Brent Mittelstadt et al., The Ethical Implications of Personal Health Monitoring, 5 Int'l J. Technoethics 37 (2014).
[71] Crawford et al., Critiquing Big Data.

To implement group privacy in the context of biomedical Big Data, bargaining mechanisms are required between groups and data controllers. The social contract that exists for data sharing and medical research provides a starting point. However, explicit bargaining mechanisms are required in contexts where a strong social contract does not exist. In research, emerging digital epidemiological research methods introduce new ethical challenges due to the impracticality of obtaining consent from unknowing or unwilling digital research participants.[72]

In healthcare, applications of analytics methods to recommendation and clinical decision-support systems require further consideration. Patients may be less willing, for example, to submit to algorithmic classification for the sake of personalized risk stratification.[73]

The health insurance and health and wellness monitoring industries also increasingly employ analytics for customer personalization. Group privacy can ground claims to redress the informational imbalance between users and data controllers concerning the extent of data being collected and their strategic and commercial value to the processor.[74] For example, further restrictions can be justified for processing of anonymized health monitoring data to segment users for marketing and personalized feedback.

12.6 CONCLUSION

Advances in data analytics necessitate new protections for the privacy interests of ad hoc groups formed by algorithmic classification. While we may only care about harms of decision making informed by analytics insofar as individuals are the moral patients that ultimately experience the harm, it cannot be ignored that analytics produces knowledge addressing groups or "types" of persons over time. With Big Data analytics, we learn about and take actions based on types, here "ad hoc groups." Individuals are assigned a type, but the knowledge about this type preexists the persons being classified as such. This is why protection of groups is important, even if the group cannot experience harm directly.

Privacy protections are needed that are responsive to the ways we now make sense of people and take actions toward them. Mechanisms are required to protect the privacy interests of groups independent of the interests of their individual members. The privacy interests of ad hoc groups are not reducible to the interests of members

---

[72] Cf. S. D. Rhodes et al., Collecting Behavioural Data Using the World Wide Web: Considerations for Researchers, 57 J. *Epidemiol. Community Health* 68 (2003); Erin F. Kenneally & Kimberly Claffy, Dialing Privacy and Utility: A Proposed Data-Sharing Framework to Advance Internet Research, 8 IEEE *Security & Privacy* 31 (2010); Ulrike Schultze & Richard Mason, Studying Cyborgs: Re-Examining Internet Studies as Human Subjects Research, 27 *J. Info. Technol.* 301 (2012).

[73] Cf. Melanie Swan, Health 2050: The Realization of Personalized Medicine through Crowdsourcing, the Quantified Self, and the Participatory Biocitizen, 2 *J. Person. Med.* 93 (2012).

[74] Cf. Mittelstadt & Floridi, The Ethics of Big Data.

due to shared ownership of behavioral identity tokens. It is these tokens, as opposed to information about a unique individual, that mediate the individual's treatment within a given analytics system. Each individual thus has a valid claim to the tokens constituting the group's identity.

The group's identity is not, however, reducible to the identities of individual members, which are defined by a far greater set of identity tokens than those that define the group. If an ad hoc group possesses a nonreducible identity, interests can be ascribed to the maintenance of this identity. Protecting privacy by hiding the identity of the subject of processing does not therefore address how algorithmic classifiers make sense of individuals.

As suggested by the depth of philosophical work on group rights,[75] establishing ad hoc groups as valid rights holders is too complex a problem to fully explore here. My intention has not been to make this case in full but rather to argue that ad hoc groups possess a right to privacy not reducible to those of members despite lacking collective agency and self-awareness. If it is decided that ad hoc groups cannot hold rights, the protections described here would need to be linked or reduced to the rights of individuals or an ethical duty imposed on data controllers. This important theoretical issue requires further attention before group privacy protections can be designed.

The forthcoming EU General Data Protection Regulation includes provisions for data subjects to request information about the logic involved in automated algorithmic decision making.[76] This may prove a turning point for legal recognition of a right to group privacy. As shown by the difficulty of detecting group privacy violations, practical implementation of this right will be extremely difficult. Going forward, ad hoc groups should be formally recognized as moral patients in data-protection law and privacy theory. Legal mechanisms based on the identifiable individual will not limit the formation of knowledge about groups and actions taken toward individuals on its basis. The privacy interests of ad hoc groups must be recognized to ensure that legal and moral conceptions of privacy adapt to advances in the ways we make sense of each other through the data we create.

---

[75] For an overview, see Jones, Group Rights.
[76] Sandra Wachter et al., Why a Right to Explanation of Automated Decision-Making Does Not Exist in the General Data Protection Regulation (2017), available at https://papers.ssrn.com/sol3/papers.cfm?abstract_id=2903469 [https://perma.cc/Y9BU-Y2TQ].

13

Big Data and Informed Consent

The Case of Estimated Data

Donna M. Gitter

13.1 INTRODUCTION

The Icelandic biotech firm deCODE Genetics has pioneered a means of determining an individual's susceptibility to various medical conditions with 99 percent accuracy by gathering information about that person's relatives, specifically the person's genealogical records.[1] Of course, inferences have long been made about a person's health by observing and gathering information about his or her relatives. What is unique about deCODE's approach in Iceland is that the company uses the detailed genealogical records available in that country in order to estimate genotypes of close relatives of individuals who volunteered to participate in research[2] and extrapolates this information in order to make inferences about hundreds of thousands of living and deceased Icelanders who have not consented to participate in deCODE's studies.[3] DeCODE's technique is particularly effective in Iceland, a small island nation that, due to its largely consanguineous population of just 333,000 citizens and detailed genealogical records, is highly suitable for genetic research.[4]

Just as Iceland's detailed genealogical records enable the widespread use of estimated data in Iceland, a large enough US database could potentially allow researchers to make similar inferences about individuals in the United States. While the United States lacks a national database similar to Iceland's, private companies such as 23andme and Ancestry.com have created rough gene maps of several million people, and the National Institutes of Health (NIH) plans to spend millions of

---

[1] Jocelyn Kaiser, Agency Nixes deCODE's New Data-Mining Plan, 340 *Science* 1388, 1388–89 (2013).
[2] In this chapter, the term "estimated data" is used to refer to inferred genetic data for people who never participated in a genetic study but whose relatives did participate.
[3] Kaiser, Agency Nixes deCODE's New Data-Mining Plan, at 1389.
[4] David E. Winickoff, Genome and Nation: Iceland's Health Sector Database and Its Legacy, *Innovations: Tech., Governance & Globalization* 80, 84–86 (Spring 2006).

dollars in the coming years sequencing full-genome data on tens of thousands of people.[5] Such databases could allow the development of estimated data on countless US citizens.

DeCODE recently planned to use its estimated data for an even bolder new study in Iceland. Having imputed the genotypes of close relatives of volunteers whose DNA had been fully catalogued, deCODE intended to collaborate with Iceland's National Hospital to link these relatives, without their informed consent, to some of their hospital records, such a surgery codes and prescriptions.[6]

When the Icelandic Data Protection Authority (DPA) nixed deCODE's initial plan in May 2013, deCODE agreed that it will generate for only a brief period a genetic imputation for those who have not consented and then delete that imputation from the database. The only accessible data would be statistical results, which would not be traceable to individuals. The DPA approved this approach in November 2013.[7]

The solution deCODE proposed to the DPA, to delete the individual-level imputation, is premised on the idea that individuals whose data have been deidentified do not face a serious risk of reidentification, a notion that has been called into question. Professors Yaniv Erlich and Arvind Narayanan, experts in computational biology and computer information systems, mention deCODE's efforts in an article describing various "genetic privacy breaching strategies" that have become increasingly common in the last few years as the range of techniques to carry out such privacy breaching "attacks" has expanded.[8] In particular, they term deCODE's method a "completion technique," meaning the use of known DNA data "to enable the prediction of genomic information when there is no access to the DNA of the target."[9] There have been several high-profile breaches of privacy whereby an "attacker" has been able to infer the genomes of relatives of an individual whose genome is known.[10]

Erlich and Narayanan note that deCODE's approach is an advanced version of the completion technique, given that deCODE has access to the genealogical and

---

[5] Antonio Regalado, Genome Study Predicts DNA of the Whole of Iceland, *MIT Technology Review* (March 15, 2015), available at www.technologyreview.com/news/536096/genome-study-predicts-dna-of-the-whole-of-iceland/ [https://perma.cc/CTE7-VFWW].

[6] Kaiser, Agency Nixes deCODE's New Data-Mining Plan, at 1389.

[7] E-mail message from Thordur Sveinsson, Iceland Data Protection Authority, to Donna M. Gitter, Professor of Law, Baruch College (October 20, 2014, 11:53 AM) (on file with author).

[8] Yaniv Erlich & Arvind Narayanan, Routes for Breaching and Protecting Genetic Privacy, 15 *Nat. Rev. Genet.* 409 (2014). Erlich and Narayanan note that although most of these techniques are currently not accessible to the general public, they can be carried out by those trained in the field. Ibid., at 409.

[9] Ibid., at 416.

[10] See, e.g., Mathias Humbert et al., Addressing the Concerns of the Lacks Family: Quantification of Kin Genomic Privacy, in Proceedings of the 2013 Association for Computing Machinery (ACM) Special Interest Group on Security, Audit and Control (SIGSAC) Conference on Computer & Communications Security 1141 (2013) (noting that the uploading of the genome of Henrietta Lacks, a famed but unwitting research subject, violated the privacy of her surviving descendants).

genetic information of several relatives of the target, and permits genotypes of distant relatives to be inferred. The company explains that it is possible to develop an algorithm that finds relatives of a "target" who donated their DNA to the reference panel and who share a "unique genealogical path that includes the target, for example, a pair of half-first cousins when the target is their grandfather," and that "a shared DNA segment between the relatives indicates that the target has the same segment."[11] By studying more pairs of relatives that are connected through the target, it is possible to collect more genomic information on the target without any access to his or her DNA.[12] This raises the question: are the individuals from who estimated data are gathered entitled to informed consent, given that their data will be used for research, even if the data are putatively unidentifiable?

There is evidence, based on a proposed Human Subjects Research Notice of Proposed Rulemaking (NPRM)[13] and current NIH policy, that policymakers are paying increased attention to the requirement of informed consent for the use of nonidentified data.[14] The question then arises whether there is a meaningful distinction between nonidentified data and estimated data in terms of the need for informed consent for the use of such data. It should be noted that neither nonidentified nor estimated data require any direct interaction with the individual about whom data are gathered. Indeed, the US regulations specify that human subject research occurs when an investigator obtains data either through intervention or interaction with the individual or obtains identifiable private information.[15] They further provide that "[p]rivate information must be individually identifiable (i.e., the identity of the subject is or may readily be ascertained by the investigator or associated with the information) in order for obtaining the information to constitute research involving human subjects."[16] It is this condition of individual identifiability that deCODE seeks to avoid when it declares to the Icelandic DPA that the data will be individually identifiable only for a brief period and then deleted from the computer memory.[17] This argument fails, however, if data are as easily identifiable as Yaniv and Erlich have described.[18] The main difference between nonidentified and estimated data is that the latter are not accurate at the individual level but only at the group level.[19]

[11] Erlich & Narayanan, Routes for Breaching and Protecting Genetic Privacy, at 416.
[12] Ibid.
[13] See notes 24–27 and accompanying text.
[14] See infra notes 20 for an explanation of the terms 'de-identified' and 'non-identified'.
[15] 45 C.F.R. § 46.102(f) (2009).
[16] Ibid.
[17] See note 7 and accompanying text.
[18] See notes 9–13 and accompanying text.
[19] For example, as noted by Craig Venter of the biotechnology firm Celera, Inc., which published the complete sequences of his genome in 2007, although his genomic data indicate an increased statistical risk of developing Alzheimer's disease, he was not surprised that his brain scan results were negative for early signs of the disease. "What works statistically for a population with genomics does not work statistically for individuals. Either you have something or you

13.2 INFORMED CONSENT AND PRIVACY UNDER US LAW

In the United States, consideration of the application of the law of informed consent to estimated data must take into account not only the need for privacy enshrined in the federal law of informed consent but also the right of autonomy, which empowers individuals to decline to participate in research. Although estimated DNA sequences, unlike directly measured sequences, are not very accurate at the individual level, but rather at the group level, individuals may nevertheless object to research participation for moral, ethical, and other reasons. A competing principle, however, is beneficence, and any impediment to deCODE using its estimated data can represent a lost opportunity for the complex disease genetics community.

It is worthwhile to consider what US law has to say about privacy in such a context. The federal legislation enacted to protect human research subjects, known as the "Common Rule," was established in 1991 mainly in order to prevent physical harm to vulnerable populations, ensuring that no human being would be required to participate in physically risky research against his or her will. This legislation, titled the "Federal Policy for the Protection of Human Subjects," was set forth in the *Code of Federal Regulations* (C.F.R.).[20] In brief, federally funded research involving identifiable human biological specimens generally is considered human subjects research for the purposes of the Common Rule. In contrast, federally funded research is not considered human subjects research where the samples have been decoupled from their identifying information or were never associated with identifying information; such samples are referred to as "de-identified and non-identified, respectively."[21] While the physical risks involved in genetic and genomic research are typically minimal, the potential harms generally derive from the potential for misuse of information, which could lead to employment or insurance discrimination, stigmatization, psychological harm, and familial discord.

The potential for such harms is certainly raised by the use of estimated data, even though the Common Rule does not address the need for informed consent for their use, given that the development of estimated data was not possible at the time of the Common Rule's enactment, which was before the advent of computational genomics. The Common Rule clearly suggests that the use of biospecimens and personal information from research participants themselves in order to gain information about their relatives raises privacy issues. Indeed, the Common Rule provides that

---

don't. You don't have 30 percent of Alzheimer's." Liza Gross, The First Individual Genome: One is the Loneliest Number, *PLOS Biol.* (October 21, 2013), available at http://blogs.plos.org/biologue/2013/10/21/the-first-individual-genome-one-is-the-loneliest-number/ [https://perma.cc/WA89-TPEP].

[20] US Department of Health and Human Services, Protection of Human Subjects, 45 C.F.R. §§ 46.101–46.124 (1991).

[21] Gail H. Javitt, Take Another Little Piece of My Heart: Regulating the Research Use of Human Biospecimens, 41 *J. L. Med. Ethics* 424, 426 (2013).

research participants are entitled to "[a] description of any reasonably foreseeable risks or discomforts to the subject."[22] These risks include privacy breaches due to possible reidentification or other losses of confidentiality and the fact that information about participants in some cases might extend to relatives or identifiable populations or groups, contributing to potential discrimination or stigmatization.[23] For this reason, the Common Rule requires "a statement describing the extent, if any, to which confidentiality of records identifying the subject will be maintained."[24] One might argue that if potential research participants have a right to informed consent relating to the possible revelation of their relatives' personal health information and data, then those relatives, who were not knowingly part of the study at all, certainly have a right of informed consent.

Since the Common Rule was enacted, advances in technology, combined with the increasing volume of data, mean that much of what is considered deidentified data is potentially identifiable. For this reason, the US Department of Health and Human Services proposed changes to the Common Rule in its September 8, 2015, Notice of Proposed Rulemaking (NPRM).[25] The NPRM would have treated biospecimens as "intrinsically identifiable because of the information imbedded in them"[26] and would therefore have required informed consent for research using all existing biospecimens, whether clinical or from prior research, even those that had been stripped of identifiers. As noted earlier, US law does not presently require informed consent for deidentified biospecimens and personal information. This rule change, had it been enacted, would have applied prospectively to biospecimens collected after the effective date of the new rules.[27] Instead, in January 2017, federal officials dropped controversial language in the law that would have required written consent for broad future use of deidentified samples. Nevertheless, one former NIH official who helped draft the revised rule still believes that it "was and is the right and respectful thing to do" and commented, in a personal rather than an official capacity, that the NIH can now collect evidence in order to demonstrate whether is it feasible to collect broad consent for samples.[28]

---

[22] 45 C.F.R. § 46.116 (2009).
[23] National Human Genome Research Institute, National Institutes of Health, Informed Consent for Genomics Research: Special Considerations for Genome Research (2015), available at www.genome.gov/27559024 [http://www.chcf.org/~/media/MEDIA%20LIBRARY%20Files/PDF/PDF%20H/PDF%20HeresLookingPersonalHealthInfo.pdf].
[24] 45 C.F.R. § 46.116 (2009).
[25] Federal Policy for the Protections of Human Subjects, 80 *Fed. Reg.* 53,942 (September 8, 2015), available at www.gpo.gov/fdsys/pkg/FR-2015-09-08/pdf/2015-21756.pdf [https://perma.cc/BEV7-G9SN] (hereinafter Human Subjects Research NPRM).
[26] Barbara J. Evans, Why the Common Rule Is Hard to Amend, 10 *Ind. Health L. Rev.* 365, 378 (2013).
[27] See, generally, Human Subjects Research NPRM, at 53,936.
[28] Jocelyn Kaiser, Update: U.S. Abandons Controversial Consent Proposal on Using Human Research Samples, *Science* (January 18, 2017), available at www.sciencemag.org/news/2017/

This proposed rule change clearly contemplated that the use of even deidentified biospecimens raises privacy concerns, given researchers' ability to extract identifying information from such samples. While the NPRM did not address estimated data, a broad reading of the NPRM would suggest that the use of estimated data to extrapolate information about individuals gives rise to the need for informed consent so as to protect the privacy of individuals who have not expressly agreed to participate in research.

It should be noted that one special case that the NPRM singled out is treatment of genomic sequencing data. Under the main NPRM proposal, the treatment of deidentified (or nonidentified) data was no different than under the current Common Rule. As noted by the NIH National Human Genome Research Institute, "Research with non-identified data does not constitute human subjects research and is not covered under the regulations." This is true regardless of the source (e.g., biospecimen or medical record).[29] Thus "genomic sequencing data from clinical encounters could be stripped of identifiers and used without consent (if not originally anticipated for research use)," and "secondary users of previously generated genomic data could conduct research on non-identified data without the data security safeguards" proposed in the NPRM.[30]

The NPRM also proposed an "Alternative Proposal B," however, that would have expanded the definition of human subjects to include research produced using a technology that creates information unique to an individual. This alternative proposal, which was broader than the main proposal, would have required consent for not only whole-genome sequencing but also genomic sequencing of even a small portion of a person's genome, as well as other technologies that might be developed in the future that similarly generate biounique information.[31] In this way, Alternative Proposal B would have provided the same high level of protection of the right of informed consent for research participants as was recently implemented by the newly revised NIH Genomic Data Sharing (GDS) Policy.

The NPRM noted that the NIH has already changed its policies regarding genomic research so as to express the expectation that researchers funded by the NIH obtain the informed consent of study participants for the potential future use of

---

01/update-us-abandons-controversial-consent-proposal-using-human-research-samples [https://perma.cc/NR6F-C37B].

[29] National Human Genome Research Institute, National Institutes of Health, The Notice of Proposed Rulemaking (NPRM) for Revisions to the Common Rule: Summary of Proposed Changes Relevant to Genomics Research (2015), available at www.genome.gov/27563327#al-3 [https://perma.cc/AZB3-R8L4].

[30] Ibid.

[31] Human Subjects Research NPRM, at 53,945–46. It should be noted the NPRM also included an Alternative Proposal A that is narrower than the main proposal, in that it would expand the definition of human subjects research to include "only specifically whole genome sequencing data, or any part of the data generated as a consequences of whole genome sequencing, regardless of the individual identifiability of biospecimens used to generate such data." Ibid., at 53,945.

their nonidentified data.[32] The purpose of the NIH's GDS Policy is to encourage researchers to inform study participants that their data will be broadly shared for future research, given that the NIH requires data sharing as a condition of its funding. The NIH expects research subjects to be asked for their informed consent not just for genomic data but also for cell lines or clinical specimens such as tissue samples, even when these cell lines or specimens are stripped of information that directly identify the source.[33] Thus the NIH has stated that for NIH-funded studies initiated after January 25, 2015, "NIH expects investigators to obtain participants' consent for their genomic and phenotypic data to be used for future research purposes and to be shared broadly" with other researchers and that the "consent should include an explanation about whether participants' individual-level data will be shared through unrestricted- or controlled-access repositories."[34] Furthermore, "[f]or studies proposing to use genomic data from cell lines or clinical specimens that were created or collected *after* the effective date of the Policy, NIH expects that informed consent for future research use and broad data sharing will have been obtained even if the cell lines or clinical specimens are de-identified."[35] The NIH explained that the reason it "expects consent for research for the use of data generated from de-identified clinical specimens and cell lines created after the effective date of the Policy is because the evolution of genomic technology and analytical methods raises the risk of re-identification."[36] In addition, "requiring that consent be obtained is respectful of research participants, and it is increasingly clear that participants expect to be asked for their permission to use and share their de-identified specimens for research."[37]

13.3 INDIVIDUALS' PERSPECTIVES ON INFORMED CONSENT AND PRIVACY

Survey research indicates that the public does not recognize the regulatory distinction between identifiable and nonidentified samples and information currently enshrined in US law. One survey published in 2008 included 1,193 patients recruited from general medicine, thoracic surgery, and medical oncology clinics at five US

---

[32] Ibid., at 53,939.
[33] Richard Van Noorden, U.S. Agency Updates Rules on Sharing Genomic Data, *Nature*, September 1, 2014, available at www.nature.com/news/us-agency-updates-rules-on-sharing-genomic-data-1.15800 [https://perma.cc/V9B8-FK9B].
[34] National Institutes of Health, NIH Genomic Data Sharing Policy: Notice Number NOT-OD-14-124 (August 27, 2014), available at http://grants.nih.gov/grants/guide/notice-files/NOT-OD-14-124.html [https://perma.cc/4J3P-6KVY] (hereinafter NIH, GDS Policy). Some commentators have asserted that the policy does not go far enough to protect against the misuse of data and should use the language "required" rather than "expected" with regard to the responsibilities outlined in the document, as well as set forth penalties for noncompliance. Ibid.
[35] Ibid.
[36] Ibid.
[37] Ibid. (citations omitted).

academic medical centers from 2002 to 2003. Most respondents stated that it was moderately to very important for them to be informed that research would be performed on their samples: 72 percent when the data were anonymous versus 81 percent when identifiable. Only 23 percent of respondents differentiated between the two scenarios, including 17 percent who felt that it was moderately or very important for them to know about the identifiable scenario and not about the anonymous scenario – which tracks the requirements of the Common Rule – and 6 percent felt the reverse was true.[38] Of those who wanted to be informed about either or both scenarios, as many as 57 percent would require their permission to be sought before their samples were used, whereas the other 43 percent would accept notification only. For anonymous samples, neither is required under the current Common Rule.[39] The authors of this study concluded that "[f]ew patients expressed preferences consistent with the regulatory distinction between non-identifiable and identifiable information," which should "cause policy-makers to question whether this distinction is useful in relation to research with previously collected" samples.[40]

There are many reasons that individuals may object to the use of their nonidentified data, even if they are estimated data. First, they may decline on ethical, religious, or other personal grounds to participate in certain controversial forms of research, such as somatic nuclear cell transfer, stem cell research, and germ-line gene therapy. In addition, individuals may reject research that purports to establish a genetic link between the members of a specific ethnic group and a particular medical problem. As noted in the Human Subjects Research NPRM, "a more participatory research model is emerging in social, behavioral, and biomedical research, one in which potential research subjects and communities express their views about the value and acceptability of research studies."[41] Second, research participants may object to commercial exploitation of discoveries developed through the use of their nonidentified data. Largely in response to some highly publicized lawsuits in which research participants have sued researchers for revenue earned from using their information and biospecimens, it has become common for researchers to present research participants with informed-consent documents that disclaim any economic interest in possible commercial applications flowing from the research. Research using nonidentified records is highly problematic in that there is no informed consent and therefore no disclaimer.[42] Since past legal cases

---

[38] Sara Chandros Hull et al., Patients' Views on Identifiability of Samples and Informed Consent for Genetic Research, 8 Am. J. Bioethics 62, 65–66 (2008).

[39] Ibid., at 66.

[40] Ibid., at 69.

[41] Human Subjects Research NPRM, at 53,938. According to the NPRM, "This participatory model has emerged alongside a broader trend in American society, facilitated by the widespread use of social media, in which Americans are increasingly sharing identifiable private information and expect to be involved in decisions about how to further share [it], including health-related information that they have voluntarily chosen to provide." Ibid.

[42] Mark A. Rothstein, Is Deidentification Sufficient to Protect Health Privacy in Research?, 10 Am. J. Bioethics 3, 7 (2010).

contesting researchers' commercial interests in biological materials involve the use of actual biospecimens, not nonidentified data,[43] it is not clear whether allegations of commercial exploitation would lie where researchers make use without consent of nonidentified health records and data without corresponding biological specimens.[44]

Indeed, it can undermine trust in the medical establishment when individuals learn that their data, whether nonidentified or estimated, are used without their consent. As noted by Rothstein, in discussing the need for informed consent for nonidentified data, individuals are likely to conflate their healthcare providers and researchers, particularly "when the providers and researchers work for the same institution and patient based clinical records and specimens are used in the research."[45] He mentions, among the list of possible consequences of denying informed consent with respect to nonidentified data, individuals delaying or foregoing treatment, seeking care only at institutions that do not conduct research, refusing to participate in clinical trials, and declining to support public expenditures for health research.[46] The Human Subjects Research NPRM stated that "the failure to acknowledge and give appropriate weight to this distinct autonomy interest in research using biospecimens could, in the end, diminish public support for such research, and ultimately jeopardize our ability to be able to conduct the appropriate amount of future research with biospecimens."[47]

Just as there are many valid arguments in favor of expanding informed-consent protections for research participants, and even to those from whom estimated data have been gleaned, there are numerous legitimate concerns voiced by the research community in their opposition to the extension of research protections, whether for nonidentified or estimated data. First, it is not feasible to contact each individual from whom data have been deidentified or estimated in order to request that person's informed consent. Even if it were possible, it would be very time-consuming and costly. Each individual's contribution to the research is so small, perhaps as to be dispensable, yet would require the full process of informed consent. Most important, and flowing from these reasons, the necessity of such informed consent might delay and perhaps even preclude altogether the development and introduction of medical advances.[48] Furthermore, it is not only researchers but also

---

[43] See, e.g., *Moore v. Regents of the Univ. of Cal.*, 793 P.2d 479 (Cal. 1990) (treating physician failed to disclose a commercial interest in biological materials); *Greenberg v. Miami Children's Hosp. Research Inst., Inc.*, 264 F. Supp. 2d 1064 (S.D. Fla. 2003) (researcher failed to disclose an interest in biological materials); *Wash. Univ. v. Catalona*, 490 F.3d 667 (8th Cir. 2007) (research institution asserted ownership claims over specimens in a way that contradicted the claims of the principal investigator and the informed-consent agreement).
[44] Rothstein, Is Deidentification Sufficient to Protect Health Privacy in Research?, at 8.
[45] Ibid. (citations omitted).
[46] Ibid., at 8–9.
[47] Human Subjects Research NPRM, at 53,942.
[48] Rothstein, Is Deidentification Sufficient to Protect Health Privacy in Research?, at 10.

patient advocacy groups who warn of these dangers. As noted by these critics, in the context of requiring informed consent for the use of nonidentified data, requiring such consent "might inappropriately give greater weight to the ... principle of autonomy over the principle of justice, because requiring consent could result in lower participation rates in research by minority groups and marginalized members of society," though "most of the comments from individual members of the public strongly supported consent requirements for use of their biospecimens, regardless of identifiability."[49]

13.4 FURTHER IMPLICATIONS: THE CHALLENGE TO THE RIGHT NOT TO KNOW

The work of Jeffrey Skopek presented herein takes comfort in this safety-in-numbers approach, claiming that numbers might facilitate privacy.[50] Skopek distinguishes between privacy losses and privacy violations, stating his view that nontransparent data-mining techniques will not constitute privacy violations because they will be based on mere inferences rather than discoveries of fact. However, Skopek explains that in order to violate someone's privacy, one must not only obtain new knowledge about the person but also do so in a way that breaches a privacy norm. DeCODE's use of certain hospital records for individuals, such as surgery codes and prescriptions, to deduce information about individuals is just such a breach because individuals do have a reasonable expectation of privacy in such documents. Moreover, deCODE is able, through the use of this imputation technique, to use the full genomes it has for about 10,000 Icelanders and the partial genetic information on 150,000 more to generate a report for genetic disease on every person in Iceland. For example, the firm claims that it can identify every person with the well-known BRCA2 mutation, which raises the risk of breast and ovarian cancer, even if the individual herself has not submitted to genetic testing.[51] Currently, this information is withheld from Icelanders, though deCODE's founder, Kari Steffanson, feels strongly that "[i]t's a crime not to approach these people."[52] Clearly, this scenario raises significant privacy concerns regarding the "right not to know."

The right not to know genetic information about oneself was traditionally a generally accepted principle.[53] As noted by one commentator, however, the "right not to know" has become more controversial in recent years due to evolving

---

[49] Human Subjects Research NPRM, at 53,943–44.
[50] See Chapter 2.
[51] Carl Zimmer, Snapshot of Icelandic DNA Shows New Gene Mutations Tied to Disease, *New York Times*, March 26, 2015, at A6.
[52] Ibid.
[53] See, e.g., Council of Europe, Convention on Human Rights and Biomedicine Oviedo (ETS 164), Article 10.2 (1997) ("Everyone is entitled to know any information collected about his or her health. However, the wishes of individuals not to be so informed shall be observed").

professional practice guidelines.[54] In 2013, the American College of Medical Genetics and Genomics (ACMG) issued a highly controversial recommendation that when a report is issued for clinically indicated genome sequencing, "a minimum list of conditions, genes, and variants should be routinely evaluated and reported to the ordering clinician."[55] The ACMG advised these incidental findings be reported "even without seeking preferences from the patient and family."[56] The ACMG acknowledged that this approach "may be seen to violate existing ethical norms regarding the patient's autonomy and 'right not to know' genetic risk information" but emphasized its view that "clinicians and laboratory personnel have a fiduciary duty to prevent harm by warning patients and their families about certain incidental findings and that this principle supersedes concerns about autonomy."[57] This recommendation was very surprising because it not only imposes on the medical establishment a "duty to hunt" but clearly moves from a regime that respects the "right now to know" to one that imposes the obligation to learn one's genetic risks.

The ACMG reversed its position the following year due to criticism from many groups, including a federally appointed bioethics panel. Now the ACGM recommends that patients having their genome sequenced consult with their doctors to decide whether they want genetic testing for an array of genetic disorders.[58]

Despite the ACMG's reversal, its original viewpoint seems to be shared by many IRB members and staff, according to the first extensive national survey of IRB professionals, published in 2015.[59] An overwhelming majority of respondents, 96 percent, endorsed the right of research participants not to know their genetic incidental findings. However, when asked about a case where a specific patient has chosen not to receive clinically beneficial incidental findings, only 35 percent

---

[54] Benjamin Berkman, Should a Patient Have a Right Not to Know Genetic Information about Him or Herself?, Bill of Health (November 19, 2015), available at http://blogs.harvard.edu/billofhealth/2015/11/19/should-a-patient-have-a-right-not-to-know-genetic-information-about-him-or-herself/ [https://perma.cc/8V5D-DUUZ]; see also Effy Vayena & John Tasioulas, Genetic Incidental Findings: Autonomy Regained?, 15 Genet. Med. 868 (2013).

[55] Robert C. Green et al., ACMG Recommendations for Reporting of Incidental Findings in Clinical Exome and Genome Sequencing, 15 Genet. Med. 565, 573 (2013).

[56] Ibid. The ACMG chose conditions for which diagnoses could be confirmed; preventive measures and/or treatments were available; and individuals with pathogenic mutations might be asymptomatic for long periods of time. Ibid., at 567.

[57] Ibid., at 568.

[58] Rina Shaikh-Lesko, The Right to Not Know, The Scientist (April 2, 2014), available at www.the-scientist.com/?articles.view/articleNo/39614/title/The-Right-to-Not-Know/ [https://perma.cc/BSC2-6XWM]. It should be noted that one critique of the right not to know is that it disproportionately affects the disenfranchised, by permitting doctors to skip important testing for those who may need it but not advocate for themselves. Ibid. One way of dealing with this issue might be better informed-consent policies, which offer and explain testing to individuals who may need it, as opposed to mandating such testing and return of its results to individuals who may prefer not to undergo it.

[59] Catherine Gliwa et al., IRB Perspectives on Obligations to Disclose Genetic Incidental Findings to Research Participants, 18 Genet. Med. 705 (2016).

indicated that the individual's right not to know should absolutely be respected, and 28 percent responded that they would "probably" honor the request not to know. The percentage of respondents who do not support the RNTK increased from 2 percent at baseline to 26 percent when presented with the specific case, and the percentage of people who are unsure likewise increased from 1 to 11 percent.[60] As noted by one of the principal investigators, "These data demonstrate that the support for a strong RNTK is soft; while autonomy and the RNTK may seem sancrosanct in isolation, forcing people to confront the tradeoffs inherent in real world cases changes many minds."[61]

In their chapter in this volume, Beskow et al. note that in their interview of thought leaders in the field of genomics, the return of research results is considered a primary risk in precision medicine research. Risks include the potential for researchers to uncover things about members of a research subject's family that the research subject or their family did not necessarily want to know or the potential that inaccurate or uncertain information would be returned and acted on.[62]

The application of the right not to know becomes even more complex with the estimated data gleaned from individuals who are not research participants. The potential limitation of this right raises the specter of individuals who have given consent neither for the use of their information nor for the return of incidental findings to them, having their estimated data used for research and then being contacted with researchers' incidental findings. This paternalistic approach conflicts deeply with long-standing norms of biomedical ethics.

13.5 CONCLUSION

Further policies must be developed to protect research participants from a system that would conscript them into research and then foist the results on them. There are many reasons, whether emotional, religious, cultural, or even pragmatic (i.e., avoidance of discrimination), that individuals reject participation in genomic research and the incidental findings that it might provide to them about their own health. These individual choices not to participate and not to learn incidental findings deserve legal protection, whether the data are accessed conventionally or via advanced computational methods. The fundamental precepts on which informed consent rest, including the Nuremberg Code, suggest that human dignity requires no less.

---

[60] Ibid.
[61] Berkman, Should a Patient Have a Right Not to Know Genetic Information about Him or Herself?
[62] See Chapter 11.

PART V

Oversight of Big Data Health Research

Proposals for Improvement

INTRODUCTION

Holly Fernandez Lynch

"Data has become the most valuable commodity of the twenty-first century." So claims Margaret Foster Riley in Chapter 17 in this part, and she is right. Everyone collects data, from Internet service providers and social media sites to grocery stores and pharmacies. Data have financial value to marketers – and, of course, to hackers. And data can bring substantial social value when used by policymakers, healthcare providers, and researchers. Data from individuals can be independently valuable depending on the context, but data are most valuable in aggregate, when data from multiple people and sources are combined and analyzed. It is this Big Data that can answer big questions, predicting patterns, behavior, and outcomes. But when the data relate to health, how should their use be regulated – and is there something unique about health-related data (or data used for health-related questions) that suggests unique regulatory considerations are needed? These are the fundamental questions motivating the chapters in this part, examined through both ethical and legal lenses.

Facilitating data use is important given the value just described. But also important is protecting the interests of data sources. Data sources may claim interests in both consent and control regarding how and by whom data derived from them are used. Indeed, some may intuitively feel that health data are more demanding of the protections offered by consent and control than other types of data given concepts related to both medical autonomy and confidentiality. However, contributors to this part argue that consent to Big Data health research is, in many circumstances, neither required nor desirable.

I. Glenn Cohen in Chapter 14 suggests that electronic health records should be made available for healthcare improvement research regardless of whether or not patients consent to such use. In fact, Cohen suggests that patients have a duty to permit such research and that seeking their consent is unnecessary given their lack of any property interest in the data and that (in general) we all benefit from improved healthcare outcomes. That said, Cohen recognizes several caveats, such as when privacy is not adequately protected, subjecting data sources to risks, or when reciprocal social benefit is less likely to accrue to particular populations.

Laura Odwazny in Chapter 15 explores several different regulatory pathways by which Big Data health research may be conducted without obtaining consent from the data source, offering regulatory support for Cohen's ethical vision. And Liza Dawson in Chapter 16 takes the argument one step further by arguing that not only is consent not necessary but indeed that it can offer a false sense of protection against the key risk of Big Data health research: breach of privacy.

With regard to privacy, both Dawson and Riley rail against exceptionalism when it comes to Big Data health research. Dawson takes issue with the idea that research use of data should be treated differently from other, nonresearch uses as it is at present given application of the Common Rule (as described in more detail in Chapter 15). While the Common Rule fails to adequately protect data privacy, in Dawson's estimation, she contends that "a distinct set of privacy regulations for *research* with data are not needed; rather, all uses of data from individuals should be regulated to some extent to protect privacy while allowing legitimate and valid activities."

For her part, Riley argues that data derived from healthcare interactions are really not much different from other personal data and, moreover, that health-related data may be generated from a variety of interactions outside the healthcare sphere, such as grocery store loyalty cards, fitness wearables, ancestry websites, and the like. Thus the focus of the Health Insurance Portability and Accountability Act (HIPAA) on healthcare settings as the exclusive locus of privacy risks is misplaced: "It is both overregulatory because it makes it very difficult to use data that may have little informational risk and underregulatory because it does not apply to a great deal of data that fall out of the definition of [protected health information]."

In other words, neither research use of data nor health data are special, and thus the Common Rule and HIPAA leave much to be desired. Instead, the chapters in this part support the premise that in an age of Big Data, broader and better privacy protections are needed for all sorts of personal data, period. And this is precisely what Riley recommends: more comprehensive and uniform protections of privacy.

An essential set of questions, then, is whether such protections should and could be adopted and implemented and, if so, whether privacy protections would really be a panacea for the concerns associated with data research and Big Data in particular. I have my doubts, given two potentially divergent considerations.

First, while privacy has been an important concern, cultural shifts suggest that it is becoming less so. Even in the quintessential context of HIPAA, patients seem to blindly sign authorizations for disclosure and sharing of records within piles of other forms and paperwork pushed in front of them at doctors' offices around the country, often without reading them or truly understanding their scope and parameters. And HIPAA is often decried as a tremendous pain, sometimes being used as a shield against any sort of request that a "covered entity" prefers to decline, from reporters' questions to – anecdotally – patient requests for their own medical records or information. While the law and its implementing regulations have become synonymous with health privacy, perhaps things have gone too far.

Beyond HIPAA, one need only look at the world of social media to realize that privacy mores are breaking down, in particular, among the millennial generation. We are increasingly posting personal information on public websites for all to see – photos, location information, emotions, memories, and the like. We have invited Amazon Echos and Google Homes into our living rooms to silently listen to our conversations and to chime in when asked. We allow our purchases to be tracked for "rewards points," our GPS locations to be tracked in case we lose our iPhones or need directions, and our children to be monitored by video cameras over their cribs. It may be an overstatement to suggest that privacy is dead, but many of us have clearly demonstrated a willingness to trade privacy for access to various benefits we deem more important.

This suggests that what really matters when it comes to Big Data health research is not consent, control, or privacy, but rather information – knowledge about how information about us is being collected, aggregated, and used, by whom, and for what purpose and awareness of how that information is protected or not. It is precisely lack of this sort of information that can sometimes make Big Data research in general feel "creepy" or invasive when we eventually learn what is going on.

Importantly, information about how a lot of our data could or will be used is available to us now, through terms of use and other disclosures. Nonetheless, inevitably there are stories of surprise – customers who didn't realize 23andMe is selling access to their genetic information[1] or patients who didn't realize how their health insurance data can be mined. Thus, it seems, we need a two-pronged solution: a greater recognition on the part of data sources of the need to avail themselves of available information and disclosures and a stronger responsibility on the part of data users to provide information in a usable and understandable format.

In this regard, the 2017 revisions to the Common Rule seem to head in the right direction.[2] The new rule (slated to take effect in January 2018, although a delayed date is currently under review) includes requirements for improved disclosures as part of the informed-consent process for how data (and biospecimens) collected for research may be used and shared with others (§ ___.116(b)). It also adds a new option for "broad consent" that may be used for data collected in the clinical,

---

[1] Marcy Darnovsky, 23andMe's Dangerous Business Model, *New York Times*, March 2, 2015, available at www.nytimes.com/roomfordebate/2015/03/02/23andme-and-the-promise-of-anonymous-genetic-testing-10/23andmes-dangerous-business-model-17 [https://perma.cc/9BU9-FJR8].

[2] Department of Homeland Security et al., Final Rule: Federal Policy for the Protection of Human Subjects, 82(12) *Fed. Reg.* 7149 (January 19, 2017).

nonresearch setting, which would include disclosures regarding the types of research that may be conducted sufficient for a reasonable person to understand what is contemplated, the data that may be used, the types of institutions and researchers with whom data may be shared, for how long data may be stored and maintained, and the like (§ ___.116(d)).

While not suggesting that consent is actually necessary, these disclosures may be a fruitful step for Big Data health research. Indeed, assessing how best to inform data sources of how their data will be used – providing education and facilitating understanding – may be the most important aspect of regulating Big Data health research going forward and one that has received woefully little attention to date. Before we can shift our focus, however, there are several preliminary battles that must be won, including moving away from claims to consent to research use of one's data when the risks of such use are exceedingly low, shoring up privacy protections and avoiding negative repercussions for data sources, and treating Big Data health research and other data uses differently only when there is good reason to do so. The chapters that follow in this part make important strides toward achieving these goals.

14

Is There a Duty to Share Healthcare Data?

I. Glenn Cohen*

14.1 INTRODUCTION

As many of the chapters in this book make clear, the future of healthcare will depend heavily on access to patient-level data, in aggregate or more individual-level form. One important source of these data is electronic health records (EHRs), which are increasingly the norm in the United States and even more so in many other countries.

Should those who want to use the data from EHRs for healthcare improvement purposes (including drug development and monitoring) be required to obtain the consent of the patients whose EHRs are used? I argue that such use should be permitted without seeking consent in many circumstances. I offer a normative (more than legal or technical) analysis of this issue.

To the extent that this issue is debated in the current literature, it is typically framed as whether the data *user* has a *duty* to ask for consent from the data source. I want to reframe the question about whether the data *source* has a *duty* to provide it. I will call this the "duty to share healthcare data" and offer two very different argumentative "paths" in favor of such a duty. These paths may be self-reinforcing – one may appeal to those with one set of prior beliefs but not another – and I think, most important, the argument one adopts will control the scope of the duty and the implications of endorsing it.

14.2 CLARIFICATIONS AND CONDITIONS

Before I offer my arguments, let me offer a few clarifications. The first is that this is about the duty to share *healthcare* data, not other kinds of data. By "healthcare data," I mean the kind of data typically stored in EHRs regarding our bodies and our health.

---

* I thank Tim Caulfield, Timo Minssen, and participants at "Global Genes, Local Concerns: A Symposium on Legal, Ethical and Scientific Challenges in International Biobanking" at the University of Copenhagen for helpful comments.

This move seems intuitive, but it is worth expressing why it may not be wholly correct. As several of the chapters in this book suggest, much of the data about one's health come from nonhealthcare sources, the anecdote about Target using purchasing data to predict pregnancy being a good example.[1] Thus one may reasonably question whether it makes sense to draw the line at "healthcare data" instead of "data about one's health." For my argument here, I will focus on the smaller category of "healthcare data" because my argument partially trades on the physician-patient relationship as data coproduction and because the larger category contains data of such variety for which special arguments or interests may apply. If the argument I offer succeeds, though, it may be possible to extend it to some parts of the larger category.

The second clarification is as to who the "user" of the data will be. I focus on two "ideal types." The first is a governmental agency committed to improving healthcare (be it diagnosis, workforce management, surgery, pharmaceutical, etc.) for the people it serves. The second is a hospital system that has similar goals. In both instances, the use is at least largely aimed at the public good. An argument for a duty would be weaker, for example, if the user was a for-profit genomic testing company such as 23andMe in part because one of the argument paths I rely on depends on reciprocity between the patient contributing data and being a potential beneficiary. But I do not further develop this distinction in this chapter.

I will also assume that both of my ideal-type data users have strong data security processes that will help repel potential hacking and malicious reidentification of data sources' identities.[2] "Strong" does not mean impregnable, and as several of the chapters in this book detail, such breaches pose a real risk as to all the data we share with governments and other entities. At the same time, though, we should not assume that any piece of data shared with the users I envision will necessarily be hacked or used for reidentification. Instead, what I imagine is, to use a nonhealth comparison, that the risk is on par with the risk we currently experience when our tax information is used or stored by a government or a large employer. This assumption helps to distinguish concerns related to privacy (related to risk of reidentification) from concerns with autonomy (relating to rights to control information that I understand largely in property terms).[3] If my argument succeeds with

---

[1] Charles Duhigg, How Companies Learn Your Secrets, *New York Times*, February 16, 2012, available at www.nytimes.com/2012/02/19/magazine/shopping-habits.html?pagewanted=all&_r=0 [https://perma.cc/H7MA-MA4S].

[2] Here I ally myself with Jeff Skopek in Chapter 2, distinguishing invasions of privacy from the use of data to draw *inferences* about your likely behavior, a sort of profiling. If Skopek is right that the drawing of inferences is not a *privacy* violation, my argument for a duty to donate becomes stronger still. Another way of putting the point is that Skopek leaves open the question about whether violations of informed consent for data use might be a separate moral violation from any purported privacy violation, and this chapter argues against that proposition.

[3] A similar distinction was made by the drafters of the new revisions to the Common Rule governing human subjects research in the United States as to biospecimen research – distinguishing privacy concerns against reidentification from autonomy concerns in terms of what

this assumption in place, it may require us to determine how much this assumption could be relaxed before the argument fails.

One final clarification pertains to how the duty would be effectuated – specifically the permission steps needed for the user to access the source's data. There exists a spectrum of options. On one end would be an immutable duty that admits of no consent requirement whatsoever. In the case of a hospital, this would, for example, mean access to health data as a condition of getting nonemergency treatment at that hospital. In theory, this would mean a patient could seek to go to a competing hospital without such a requirement, but that might depend on whether the patient's socioeconomic and geographic reality permits that other option and whether competing hospitals themselves adopt the same requirement. In terms of government access, one imagines a mandate put in place to share health information akin to the mandate to buy health insurance in the Affordable Care Act.[4]

On the other end of the spectrum would be a requirement that the patient has affirmatively opted in to specific uses of the data, which would be essentially a denial of a duty in an enforceable sense. This is slightly too quick – perhaps we could speak of a *moral* duty in such a case, but it would be more like one's duty to serve in the military in time of national security threat under current American law (volunteer army) as opposed to such service under a regime of conscription. Such a moral duty certainly would be something, but not what I am driving at in this chapter. If the argument fails, one might consider an argument for this kind of duty as a sort of second best.

In between are several intermediate possibilities, such as (1) "broad opt in" (when a patient joins a medical practice, he or she is asked to broadly consent to giving access to all his or her EHR data for all uses) or (2) "specific opt in" (when a patient joins a medical practice, he or she is asked to consent to give access to specific uses of his or her data or to general use of specific subsets of his or her data). Patients may be periodically asked to update and expand the access they have granted as new data uses come into fruition. Then there is possibility (3) "opt out" (variations of (1) and (2) where the default is to treat the patient as having granted permission for data use unless the patient specifically opts out).

Largely for expositional reasons I am going to focus on the strongest form of the duty in this chapter. The regime I have in mind might include the *informed* part of "informed consent" – the need to educate patients that their data are being used

---

uses biospecimens are put to. See Federal Policy for the Protection of Human Subjects, 82 *Fed. Reg.* 7149, 7260 (January 19, 2017).
[4] That mandate was upheld in *NFIB v. Sebelius*, 132 S.Ct. 2566 (2012). In the US context, attempts to mandate sharing of health information might implicate not just the constitutional question of Commerce Clause authorization but also the question of whether other constitutional rights are violated. In part in an attempt to avoid being too parochial, this chapter focuses on the ethics of imposing such a duty more generally and not these jurisdiction-specific legal questions.

and for what reason and with what security measures and remedy – but not the *consent* part in any meaningful way. This regime would involve notice and patient education but not opt out or opt in; everyone's data would be included without exception. If my argument fails for such a duty, it nonetheless may justify one of the intermediate forms of the duty. If it succeeds, it likely justifies all the less demanding forms a fortiori.

In the next section I consider two separate but related argumentative paths for defending a duty to share health data.

14.3 TWO ARGUMENTATIVE PATHS TO REACH A DUTY TO SHARE DATA

Why should we have a duty to share our health data? I believe that there are two families of argument – or, as I prefer to call them, "paths" – to reach this conclusion. Neither is airtight, and I consider objections to each, as well as ways in which each path might limit the kinds of data that might be shared or circumstances under which sharing may not be a duty. I do, however, ultimately believe that some combination of them provides a good foundation for the duty. The paths are (1) healthcare data are not the patient's property and (2) sharing healthcare data fulfills obligations of reciprocity.

14.3.1 *Do Patients Have a Property Right in Their Data?*

The first path is to dispute what seems like a premise of those who would reject a duty to share health data – that the data "belong" to the individual patient who has the privilege to share or not share. To say that you must *ask* me to share X thing with you is for me to claim in some loose form a property right (or, more accurately, a particular stick in the property bundle relating to alienability) in X. Importantly, in our case, the X is informational and is nonrivalrous, so it might be more helpful to analogize to intellectual property rather than real property. Do patients have strong property claims in their health data?

Intuitively, it seems that the answer is yes – the data came from the patient and are about the patient, but we should go beyond intuition. One prominent set of theories for property is Lockean, focused on the mixing of labor and sweat equity. I *deserve* an entitlement in my data. But why do I deserve that? Desert is often thought to be a function of effort: I deserve my paycheck and you do not because I have worked for it. The same is not true about my health data at first glance; how have I worked to produce it?

The same problem is evident when the theory is framed in economic rather than moral terms, as is familiar in intellectual property discourse, using entitlement as an economic incentive for productive labor. Unlike with copyright in a novel, for example, there does not seem to me much productive labor to incentivize here when it comes to producing health data; the facts about my health are not creations

I need to be motivated to bring into existence. And, as I suggest below, while these facts do require as a but-for cause my encounters with medical professionals, my motivation for those encounters is improving my healthcare, not producing the data.[5]

But perhaps we do not need labor, desert, or incentives here. One might instead argue for the allocation of the entitlement from a starting point of self-ownership – that my body is my property. John Locke begins with a thesis that "every man has a property in his own person" and from this derives his theory that an individual also can claim property in whatever he mixes his labor.[6] But even if we grant the Lockean postulate of self-ownership, it does not clearly resolve the cases that interest us. The observations about my health and body in my EHR are not in a real sense the *product* of my labor. At best, we might think of them as a kind of *coproduction*, wherein I am the subject being observed by a physician, nurse, etc., who uses his or her medical knowledge to record and transform those observations into something that is useful.[7] So the EHR data seem to have two elements in tension with the recognition of a property right: (1) the data are a *by-product* of my seeking healthcare, the data are a kind of *dual-use* good, usable for both the particular healthcare need of the patient and for Big Data use, and (2) the data are not produced *by the patient* but instead are a description *of the patient*.

Let me say something about this second feature. In some ways one might, oddly, think about this as being similar to art. Suppose that as I walk down the street in the public square, an artist is taken by me (unlikely, but you never know!). A week later, when the artist begins a new art project of a man eating an orange, she thinks of me and draws on that memory as inspiration. It bears some resemblance to me, but of course it is not a perfect likeness – it is certainly not my person, just an observation of it; it is the result of both me and the artist's artistic temperament, powers of observation, and so on. Under American law, that artist

---

[5] This seems generally right to me, but one caveat and one worry. The caveat is that there may be healthcare data on the research/care line where this is not true – if the physician asks in addition to the blood drawn for my diagnosis to draw another syringe worth for biospecimen bank purposes, for example. That latter *is* a form of productive labor we may need to incent, although, interestingly, the current regime typically does not. The worry is that some individuals would reduce their frequency of doctors' visits if they believed their EHR data were used in this way. This seems farfetched to me, and whatever losses occur through this effect are probably outweighed, from the social perspective, by the gains of having large data sets of EHR data for use, but if evidence suggested a large effect, this would be a relevant consideration.

[6] John Locke, *Second Treatise of Government* § 27, at 19 (C. B. Macpherson ed., Hackett Publishing Co. 1980) (1690) ("[E]very man has a property in his own person."); see also I. Glenn Cohen, The Right Not to Be a Genetic Parent?, 81 S. Cal. L. Rev. 1115, 1148, 1151–55 (2008) (examining ownership claims in genetic material).

[7] This train of thought might take us to an unexpected direction that is *not* the subject of this chapter or really much discussed in the literature. That is whether the consent right, should it exist, belongs to the *physician* who is the one who actually enters the data into my EHR in whole or in part – the analogy would be to coinventors or tenancy in common.

owes me no duty of consent or to share in the proceeds of the sale of the work. Why are the data in my EHR so different?

You might push back here, to accuse me of going from the "is" of American law to the "ought "of generalizing to a new case. You might suggest that I am right on a Lockean theory of property but not on a theory of property and personhood, where it is the reflection of my personhood in the *res* that justifies my property interest, not the labor; as Radin puts it, some property is closely bound up with personhood and thus deserves special treatment because it is "part of the way we constitute ourselves as continuing personal entities in the world" and gives the examples of a wedding ring, heirloom, portrait, or house.[8] You might object to the fact that in my initial hypothetical I went into the public square as opposed to seeing a trusted fiduciary at my most vulnerable. Surely if my physician were to paint me in a hospital robe without my consent and sell that painting, matters would be different!

Fair points, but this may just mean that we need a more precise set of analogies. When a physician who is a textbook author writes up a case study of a disease, say prosopagnosia (face blindness), that is a composite of what he has learned from the twenty patients he has seen with the disorder, must he specifically ask each of the patients for his or her consent? Imagine that it is not twenty patients, but at the end of his career, it is every patient he has ever treated, thousands or tens of thousands; must he seek consent from each individual patient in order to use the knowledge he has gleaned? In terms of "is," in current practice, the answer is certainly "No."[9] And if pressed for the "ought" that justifies this convention, I think it would be very similar to the arguments offered here – it is a by-product of the health encounter, it is a description of the patient not work by the patient, it is used in a way that is aggregated and not easily reidentifiable, and the patient needs no economic incentive to provide this information.

Indeed, forget about the write-up. My primary care physician is in his midforties. He has undoubtedly seen thousands of patients in his career so far and what has worked in his clinical experience for particular patients with particular presentations of the disorder, lifestyles, etc. When he treats me, it is not only my expectation but indeed *my fervent hope* that he uses that prior experience in helping to treat me. If I were to say to him, "Thank you very much for the help on the bronchitis today, doctor, but I want your solemn pledge that you will forget everything you learned in

---

[8] Margaret Jane Radin, Property and Personhood, 34 *Stan. L. Rev.* 957, 959 (1982); see also Sonia M. Suter, Disentangling Privacy from Property: Toward a Deeper Understanding of Genetic Privacy, 72 *Geo. Wash. L. Rev.* 737, 776 (2004).

[9] Even when writing up the case study of a single case, there is some disagreement in the literature about whether informed consent is required, and the discussion often connects it to how identifiable the patient may be, even to themselves, from the write-up. For a good discussion, see Ronald Pies & Judy L. Kantrowitz, Case Studies and the Therapeutic Relationship, 13 *Virtual Mentor* 425 (2011).

this encounter and never use that knowledge to help another patient," I know of no physician who would agree to this, were it even possible.[10]

But if this is true about health "little data" – the cumulative experience physicians have from the patient experiences of their years of practice, plus their learning from the cumulative experience of other physicians in training, publications, and so on – why is it not true for health Big Data? Indeed, if anything, the argument is stronger not weaker for the Big Data version. Why? The more individual patient observations are mixed together to generate information, guidance, and so on, the less any individual patient's experience constitutes the key contributor and the weaker their claim for desert or control.[11]

What this tells us, I think, is that what is really worrying us is *not* that "my data are being used for the healthcare system in a way I disagree with" (a property or autonomy kind of claim) but instead that "my data might lead back to me" (a privacy claim).

This, then, puts pressure on the question of how much protection from malicious reidentification (a privacy concern) we can offer. Or to put the claim in a positive form, there is no need to require individual consent from patients *as long as* we can reduce the risk of reidentification. We may also have additional duties if and when reidentification occurs – to offer assistance with identity theft or recompense for damages sustained, for example – but perhaps only if we have been negligent in the way we stored the information.

Now if one accepted this argument, perhaps one might be tempted to think "but wouldn't it be nice – perhaps supererogatory – to ask people for their consent nonetheless, especially if they prefer to be asked?" Indeed, even if I am right as a normative matter that individuals have no property right claim in their data, they may *feel* incorrectly as though they do. I shy away from recommending that for two reasons: first, asking is not costless. When it was proposed by federal regulators to require affirmative opt-in consent for research use of biospecimens (the matter was finally dropped with regard to nonidentified biospecimens, at least for now), it was estimated that this would cost at least $1.2 billion in the United States annually to

---

[10] This line of thought bleeds into the reciprocity argument I offer later. Notice how this again illustrates a difference from my initial artist hypothetical – the gain from the recording is not primarily to the doctor but to his future patients, including to me as one of his potential future patients.

[11] This, I think, makes the case easier than other famous cases in bioethics about the use of biospecimens such as Henrietta Lacks, the children with Canavan's X, or even the Havasupai tribe. See *Greenberg v. Miami Children's Hosp. Research Inst., Inc.*, 264 F. Supp. 2d 1064, 1074–76 (S.D. Fla. 2003); Rebecca Skloot, *The Immortal Life of Henrietta Lacks* (2010); Katherine Drabiak-Syed, Lessons from *Havasupai Tribe v. Arizona State University Board of Regents*: Recognizing Group, Cultural, and Dignitary Harms as Legitimate Risks Warranting Integration into Research Practice, 6 *J. Health Biomed. L.* 175 (2010). In each of these cases, the research turned on individual features of those patients that made them "special."

implement, roughly 4 percent of the NIH budget.[12] Requiring consent here also may be expensive. To be fair, though, some of these costs nonetheless would be present in a regime of informing without consenting, which I do recommend.[13] Second, asking and honoring the opt outs may result in gaps in the data, making generalizability more difficult and actually in some ways degrading the value of those who provided the data – a topic covered in part in Chapter 7. In particular, one might worry that patients who say "Yes" when asked and say "No" when asked are different in important ways such that a data set comprised of only the former will not be generalizable to the whole population, and if forced to get true informed consent, some institutions may just decide not to bother, creating other gaps in the larger data set.

In sum, if this argument were accepted, it would suggest that patients have no right to refuse to provide the data from their EHRs as long as deidentifiabiltiy was relatively achievable with some recourse in cases of malicious reidentification. This argument nicely demystifies the Big Data element of the normative discussion with a strong comparison with the "little data" patients are constantly cogenerating with their physicians in every clinical encounter and that are by-products of those clinical encounters. If we do not require consent to add to the physician's knowledge base in those quotidian "small data" encounters, we should not require it here where the individual patient's contribution is much lower and the social value of the aggregate knowledge is much greater.

14.3.2 Data Sharing as Reciprocity

Those who benefit from Big Data analytics derived through EHRs have a duty to contribute. This is the basic logic of the second argumentative path, one from the principle of reciprocity. This benefit comes in both an indirect form – to the extent Big Data allows us to better bend the cost curve, all boats rise in paying lower healthcare costs – and a more direct one – to the extent new therapeutics or refinements of existing therapies I use or will use are the result of patients like me contributing their EHR data, I have an obligation to contribute myself.

In an article aimed at making a much stronger claim – that individuals have an obligation to participate in research that includes such things as blood draws and that coercing participation may be justified – the late Alan Wertheimer sketches the basic argument well. He notes that the United States already requires participating

---

[12] Council on Governmental Relations, Analysis of Public Comments on the Common Rule NPRM 9 (2016), available at http://www.cogr.edu/sites/default/files/Analysis%20of%20Common%20Rule%20Comments.pdf [https://perma.cc/ 7NRH-33NM]. The same report also noted that "[t]his does not include the significant costs of documenting and tracking permissible uses of biospecimens" and thus underestimated the cost "by a factor of at least ten." Ibid. (internal quotation marks omitted).

[13] Some of the intermediate-duty options discussed earlier, it is worth noting, might be less costly.

"in a form of social and behavioral research – the Census – on pain of being fined for refusal."[14] This comparison is particularly apt for our purposes in that the Census also uses aggregated data about individuals to further the public good.[15] In a similar vein, we might analogize the obligation to provide health information to the obligation to pay taxes,[16] which is a well-accepted requirement imposed on citizenry. One might think that the case for the duty discussed here is *easier* to ground than the duty to pay taxes in that the information is nearly costless for the patient to generate (it is already being generated from the health encounter for EHRs) and nonrivalrous as opposed to paying taxes, which individuals give up money they would rather use on many other things.

Commenting on the work of Ruth Faden et al. on the "learning health system," Wertheimer writes:

> They maintain that patients have an obligation "to contribute to the common purpose of improving the quality and value of clinical care and the health care system." The authors note that "Securing these common interests is a shared social purpose that we cannot as individuals achieve" and that those goals may require something like "near-universal participation in learning activities through which patients benefit from the past contributions of other patients whose information has helped advance knowledge and improve care." This argument does not claim that current patients have such obligations because they have benefitted from the past contributions of other patients. Rather, it argues that a learning health care system will provide benefits to prospective patients in which they will come to benefit from the contributions of other patients.[17]

Wertheimer considers a series of objections, some of which may apply to my argument as well – though I believe that because the "ask" is so much more minimal in this case (access to *already* collected EHR data to be used in aggregate and in a largely deidentified way), the responses are also easier.

First, one might object that this treats the individual as merely a means in violation of the Kantian interdiction – understood as treating an individual in a way to which no individual could rationally consent.[18] Of course, if this is true, so

---

[14] Alan Wertheimer, (Why) Should We Require Consent to Participation in Research?, 1 J.L. Biosci. 137, 144 (2014).
[15] Ibid.
[16] Ibid., at 143.
[17] Ibid., at 145 (quoting Ruth R. Faden et al., An Ethics Framework for a Learning Health Care System: A Departure from Traditional Research Ethics and Clinical Ethics, 43 *Hastings Ctr. Rep.* S16 [2013]).
[18] Immanuel Kant, *Grounding for the Metaphysics of Morals* 429 (James W. Ellington trans., 3d edn, 1981) (1785); see Wertheimer, (Why) Should We Require Consent to Participation in Research?, at 148 (citing Rieke van der Graaf & Johannes J. M. van Delden, On Using People Merely as Means in Clinical Research, 26 *Bioethics* 76 [2012]); see also Christine M. Korsgaard, The Reasons We Can Share: An Attack on the Distinction between Agent-Relative and Agent-Neutral Values, 10 *Soc. Philos. Pol'y* 24 (1993).

does the Census data and taxation, so if one believed this, those practices would have to go as well. But the response might be "all the better" and again accuse me of moving from "is" to "ought" with that reply. So here is a different response: the objection makes a category error. The kind of work we are discussing uses a person's *data* not *the person* as a means.[19] There is absolutely nothing wrong with treating individuals' data as a means – for example, looking at traffic patterns when deciding whether to place a stop sign at an intersection. This is especially true when the data are largely deidentified and aggregated – when that happens, it is even further from treating the person as a means, in that the data become more *de*personalized.

Second, and more specifically, one might argue that participating in research without one's consent is a violation of one's autonomy, regardless of any harm that results.[20] I do not think this will work for several reasons. Unlike forced participation in interventional research, this does not seem to me like being conscripted into research in the morally relevant sense. Once again, it is not the person but that person's data that are being used for analysis – and once deidentified and aggregated, it is hard to see it as research with human subjects, either formally[21] or normatively. It is not violating my bodily integrity or requiring me to do anything. When the data are deidentified and aggregated, it seems hard to think that it is even about *me* participating. Nor can I claim a property kind of right here being violated for the reasons discussed in the prior section.

Third, one might object that the conditions of reciprocity are not met. Unlike the tax dollars that pay for the roads on which I drive, the police that save me from crime, and so on, I may not myself benefit from the use of my EHR data in this way. I think this objection has more bite. My contribution to the tax base is maximally fungible – once the taxman collects the funds, they go into the general pool and

---

[19] One might also retort that it is not using the person as a *mere* means because the point of the reciprocity argument is that the individual benefits from the data access. I make a similar point later in a non-Kantian frame.

[20] Cf. Alexander M. Capron, Legal and Regulatory Standards of Informed Consent in Research, in *The Oxford Textbook of Clinical Research Ethics* 613, 620 (Ezekiel J. Emauel et al. eds., 2008); Wertheimer, (Why) Should We Require Consent to Participation in Research?

[21] Under the pre-2018 version of the Common Rule governing federally funded research, a "human subject" was defined as "a *living* individual about whom an investigator (whether professional or student) conducting research obtains (1) Data through intervention or interaction with the individual, or (2) Identifiable private information." 45 C.F.R. § 46.102(f) (emphasis added). Under the revision set to take effect on January 19, 2018 (which may be delayed further, as postponement is under review as of press time), the term is defined as "a living individual about whom an investigator (whether professional or student) conducting research: (i) Obtains information or biospecimens through intervention or interaction with the individual, and uses, studies, or analyzes the information or biospecimens; or (ii) Obtains, uses, studies, analyzes, or generates identifiable private information or identifiable biospecimens." Federal Policy for the Protection of Human Subjects, 82 *Fed. Reg.* 7149, 7260 (January 19, 2017). Under either definition, Big Data analysis of already-collected EHR data will not qualify as human subjects research – it is not "identifiable private information," and there is no "intervention or interaction" with the individual by the researcher.

are interchangeable with all other dollars. I cannot track my dollars and which community they did or did not benefit. In a real sense, every dollar collected by the taxman supports every government program. This is not quite true of EHR data, which are not always interchangeable and are much more conceptually "taggable." For example, imagine that a research project using EHRs is aimed at improving cardiac care for women. Imagine that my (male) EHR data are used as part of the training set for a predictive algorithm. Can I complain of a failure of reciprocity – I contributed data but only women (and therefore not me) benefited?

The force of this objection may depend on the level of generality of the analysis. While I may not benefit directly in this example from whatever intervention for women is developed, I do reap several indirect benefits. For example, if women suffer less from cardiac disease thanks to my data, I may benefit in several ways – the cardiologist has more time and resources to devote to me as a male, my (hypothetical) wife and daughter will live longer and be healthier, my female employees may be more productive, and so on.

Moreover, as data are deidentified and aggregated, the line between "mine" and "yours" breaks down, and one might think it becomes as fungible as other comparable cases. Take the example of conscription for national defense during World War II. Not everyone benefited equally from it – imagine that perhaps because of where I lived in the country or my ethnic heritage, I still would not have been at substantial risk had we lost the war. But the fact that the reciprocity is not perfect does not for that reason make the practice morally problematic; we seem to tolerate a relatively broad definition of "people like you" in the claim "it was permissible to demand your sacrifice because it protects people like you." And there are a host of other benefits to all citizens of living in a free country, regardless of whether each benefit is used or accessible to each citizen.

But these examples (all citizens, all men) involve fairly large and disparate communities who are asked to "give." Things might look somewhat different when the community is small and also "thick" in terms of its cohesion and identity. So, for example, if one were to take the EHR data of a rare disease group – say patients with Canavan's X – and use it to develop interventions for those *without* that disease, this argument may not justify the no-consent use. More generally, what would be worrisome would be (to borrow from legal language) a discrete minority who are always the "givers" asked to provide data but not reaping their benefit. The precise line where a community becomes "thick" enough is uncertain,[22] and indeed, it is uncertain whether the judgment depends on the views of the community itself (self-definition), the views of those outside, or some objective factors (size, amount of communication between members, etc.).[23]

---

[22] One interesting test case is classing by insurance type. If Medicaid data were used to develop an intervention that was largely unavailable to Medicaid populations, for example.

[23] These issues have long been at the core of most communitarian kinds of arguments, and I don't think I will improve much on that which has already been said.

The upshot of all this, though, is that it imposes a constraint on using this argumentative path to generate a duty to share data: where the benefit of the data use will not inure, even in an inexact way, to a community that is the data source; then it may not be justified to impose a duty to share on them. This requires at least three bits of unpacking:

1. Much of the work undertaken with EHR data has only speculative benefit. It may be that many of these projects never benefit any patient. Of course, this is true with other collectivized investments – when the NIH funds research using tax dollars, for example, or even defense spending. While we should not spend collective resources on activities likely to fail, the constraint I have in mind does not require that every bet pan out either. Instead, the question is whether those who contribute have the chance to benefit should it come to fruition. What would be problematic is a case where benefit arises and we know that the contributors will not share in it.
2. It seems to me that the condition is more easily met the more socialized the medical system is and at its zenith in a universal healthcare system. The reason is because in such systems the minority community usually benefits from cost reduction through health research using data, even if it may not benefit as much as other communities. By contrast, it might suggest that this argument path is weaker when we move away from my ideal types to, for example, a private for-profit drug manufacturer that will not ensure affordable posttrial access or other mechanisms of ensuring that data providers can access benefits.
3. One might think that this reciprocity requirement is proportionate to the "ask" being made in terms of benefit and burden. The analogy is to cases of "easy rescue" in ethics. Where rescue is costless or at least low cost, we might be more comfortable imposing the duty even on a group that we believe is less likely to be rescued themselves. Where the benefit is small and the burden is great, requiring stricter reciprocity and proportionality seem more justified. Allowing deidentified and aggregate use of EHR data poses a relatively low "ask" on the data source, especially in a world of good data protection. Where the chance of a data breach is low such that the risk of malicious reidentification is low and/or when there is a commitment to recompense patients who suffer such harms, I think one can tolerate less fit between the data providers and those who benefit.[24]

---

[24] I have not really said anything about conscientious objection in this context. One can imagine a case equivalent to the famous Havasupai tribe controversy involving EHRs. See, e.g., Drabiak-Syed, Lessons from Havasupai Tribe v. Arizona State University Board of Regents. There is a vast bioethics and legal literature on conflicts of conscience and complicity. See,

This is a way in which this argumentative path is more demanding than the first. However, it is possible that this argument is more compatible with an increased risk of reidentification than the first argument. Both taxation and conscription do involve significant sacrifices from those on whom they are imposed. It thus may be justifiable to demand that individuals "sacrifice" a risk of reidentification if the benefits to EHR use in this way are both significant and the burdens and benefits are fairly well matched.

14.4 CONCLUSION

I offered an argument for not imposing a consent requirement for the contribution of EHRs to research and other social endeavors when certain conditions are met. But who should determine whether such conditions are met? It seems to me the answer should *not* be the researcher seeking to use the data – he or she may be, at least implicitly, biased into thinking that these conditions are met. At the same time, an institutional review board (IRB) or research ethics board (REB)– the usual go-to in human subjects research – may not be the best fit. On the one hand, the kind of review I am imagining leaves out much of what the IRB/REB normally does (consider the informed consent, risk and benefit, and local community conditions). On the other hand, meaningful review may require things for which the IRB/REB is not particularly well trained to do – understand the risk of reidentifiability and the extent to which the benefits of the research may inure to the population who is the data source. Finally, the fact that the data will likely pool EHRs from multiple healthcare institutions may make the local IRB a poor fit, and single IRB review through reliance agreements may become complex. Instead, my recommendation would be that there be "Big Data review boards" set up that might be regional or even national. It may also make sense to divide them not by region but by kind of Big Data research if we think the questions pertinent to deidentification and reciprocity cluster. In my ideal world, such boards would also include patient representatives in their governance. Of course, we are all patients at some point in our lives and thus all potential data sources, but as the community becomes thicker

e.g., Holly Fernandez Lynch, *Conflicts of Conscience in Healthcare* (2008); Amy Sepinwall, Conscientious Objection, Complicity, and Accommodation, in *Law, Religion, and Health in the United States* (Holly Fernandez Lynch, I. Glenn Cohen, & Elizabeth Sepper eds., 2017). My own feeling is that the use of one's EHR data in this context is most similar to the use of one's tax dollar for a purpose to which one was imposed (say, the Iraq war) more than the use of a biospecimen. That said, as we saw in the case of the controversy over the contraceptive mandate, some have and have endorsed very strong theories of complicity. One who was concerned about honoring those theories of complicity could create carve-outs for religious or other kinds for EHR data use and allowing limited opt outs or requiring consent for studies that are particularly controversial in this way. I would not be inclined to go there, especially if the costs of implementing such a system and maintaining registries of preferences/objections was high, but others may prefer this kind of approach.

(like a disease group), patient representation may be helpful in informing in particular whether the reciprocity requirement is met. There may also be a pragmatic reason to include patients, as a trust-building opportunity.

I have sketched – and given the length of this chapter, I don't think it is fair to call it more than a sketch – two argumentative paths for arguing against imposing a consent requirement on the use of EHR data. Each argument has a boundary condition. The argument from "no property right" depends on being able to achieve a reasonable amount of deidentification and providing recourse for malicious reidentification. The argument from "reciprocity" requires that those whose data are used have some reasonable chance of benefiting from the use, though the strength of that fit will depend on such things as how much risk is being imposed on the data source from the use, how socialized is the healthcare system in which this takes place, and so on. When the conditions for both arguments are met, the two arguments work in tandem and establish the strongest case for such a duty.

15

Societal Lapses in Protecting Individual Privacy, the Common Rule, and Big Data Health Research

*Laura Odwazny**

15.1 INTRODUCTION

The protection of individual privacy is a growing concern in the era of Big Data collection. The use of sensitive information available from accessing, combining, and manipulating Big Data can have an impact on the privacy of individuals, and scholars have theorized that this information should be protected under a new legal scheme.[1] Because health data almost invariably contain sensitive information, the impact of Big Data health research on individual privacy, and whether additional structures need to be created to protect the individuals to whom the data pertains, is the legitimate object of a wide-ranging social conversation.

While the development of additional structures to protect individual privacy is debated, research institutions may struggle with how to provide appropriate protections to individuals whose data are used in Big Data health research. As explained in detail in this chapter, much Big Data health research is not regulated as "human subjects" research under the jurisdiction of the US federal Common Rule because the information obtained is either not "private" or not "individually identifiable" or both, and researchers do not obtain data through interaction or intervention with living individuals.[2] Yet institutional review boards (IRBs) routinely are presented with Big Data health research for review and approval as though it were human subjects research governed by Common Rule standards. This may be in part because no alternative legal structures exist to protect the privacy of the individuals to whom the health and other data pertain and due to a belief that this societal lapse needs to be

---

* The views expressed in this chapter are those of the author and are not necessarily those of the Office of the General Counsel or the US Department of Health and Human Services. Thanks to Dave Wendler and Ivor Pritchard for their helpful comments on a previous draft of this chapter.
[1] Paul Ohm, Sensitive Information, 88 S. Cal. L. Rev. 1125 (2015).
[2] US Federal Policy for the Protection of Human Subjects, 45 C.F.R. part 46 (1991).

addressed even for research use of data that are not private or not individually identifiable.[3] IRB review also may serve as a default method of privacy protection because of legitimate uncertainty as to whether health Big Data actually ought to be treated as private and individually identifiable or whether health Big Data research can qualify for a regulatory exemption from the Common Rule's substantive requirements.

Revisions to the Common Rule were published on January 19, 2017, and are scheduled to become effective on January 19, 2018.[4] However, the Common Rule regulatory scheme still poorly fits the Big Data research context. If an IRB treats Big Data health research as involving human subjects, unless the research is determined to qualify for a regulatory exemption,[5] the Common Rule generally requires that researchers obtain the informed consent of subjects, which may be impossible in the Big Data research context due to the thousands or millions of subjects that would need to be contacted. The alternative is for an IRB to approve a waiver of informed consent, which requires determining that the research presents no more than minimal risk to subjects (among other conditions). Identification and assessment of research risk appear to be sticking points for Big Data research: because privacy and Big Data may be viewed as incompatible,[6] it may prove challenging for an IRB to find Big Data health research to present minimal risk to subjects due to the

---

[3] Helen Nissenbaum, *Privacy in Context: Technology, Policy, and the Integrity of Social Life* (2009).

[4] US Federal Policy for the Protection of Human Subjects, 82 *Fed. Reg.* 7149 (January 19, 2017).

[5] Big Data research may qualify for exemption from the current Common Rule under 45 C.F.R. § 46.101(b)(4) (1991), which applies to research using existing data if the researchers record data such that subjects cannot be identified. As SACHRP recognized, using this exemption may prove difficult in practice, however, because after obtaining, combining, and using data sets, researchers would need to destroy all identifiable information, which may not be desirable or adequate for ensuring research integrity. Letter from Jeffrey R. Botkin, Chair, SACHRP, to Honorable Sylvia M. Burwell, Secretary of Health and Human Services (April 24, 2015) (hereinafter SACHRP 2015 Letter), available at https://www.hhs.gov/ohrp/sachrp-committee/recommendations/2015-april-24-letter/index.html [https://perma.cc/S4SA-XFJV]. The revised Common Rule contains additional exemptions for secondary-use research, for which researchers obtain information or biospecimens collected from an individual for another purpose. One of these exemptions could apply to Big Data research if the Big Data obtained is "publicly available." US Federal Policy for the Protection of Human Subjects. The utility of this exemption when applied to Big Data research remains to be seen because the existing difficulty for IRBs in determining whether Big Data is "private" may extend to the assessment of whether Big Data is "public." Another of these exemptions could apply to Big Data health research conducted at an institution regulated under the Health Insurance Portability and Accountability Act (HIPAA) Privacy Rule if the secondary research use of information would be considered under HIPAA to be research, healthcare operations, or conducted for public health activities and purposes. Ibid., at 7194. Because some health Big Data is not public, such as aggregated medical records, and some health Big Data research is not regulated under HIPAA, the addition of these exemptions likely will not allow all Big Data research to be exempted from the Common Rule's requirements.

[6] Solon Barocas & Helen Nissenbaum, Big Data's End Run around Anonymity and Consent, in *Privacy, Big Data, and the Public Good: Frameworks for Engagement* 44 (Julia Lane et al. eds., 2014).

inherent threat to individual privacy. Moreover, IRBs vary widely in determining whether research presents minimal risk,[7] and there is no published guidance from US federal regulatory agencies as to how IRBs should apply the Common Rule minimal risk standard to Big Data research.

In response to this perceived (and understandable) confusion, the US Department of Health and Human Services (HHS) Secretary's Advisory Committee on Human Research Protections (SACHRP), which is charged with advising the Secretary of HHS regarding issues pertaining to human subjects protection, has recommended that, to aid IRB deliberations, the HHS Office for Human Research Protections (OHRP) should clarify application of the Common Rule minimal risk standard to Big Data research and that compliance with existing data security regulations and best practices may allow an IRB to conclude that Big Data research presents minimal risk to privacy.[8]

The Common Rule was not designed to address the research use of data that are not individually identifiable or private. This chapter demonstrates, however, that although they are ill fitting, the Common Rule requirements need not prove an obstacle to the use of Big Data in health research. A uniform application of the Common Rule's minimal risk standard – which, in pertinent part, is tied to the risks of daily life – permits IRBs to find Big Data health research to present no more than minimal risk. Even if a reviewing IRB is uncomfortable with this assessment of the baseline daily life risks, as per SACHRP's recommendations, the IRB may consider data privacy and information protections applicable to the research to reduce the risks of Big Data health research to below the minimal risk threshold.[9] Either approach provides a pathway for the IRB to access the regulatory flexibility to waive the subject's informed consent, which may be necessary for Big Data health research to be conducted consistent with the Common Rule.

15.2 IS BIG DATA RESEARCH DIFFERENT FROM OTHER RESEARCH USES OF INFORMATION?

While challenges posed by the Common Rule are not exclusive to the Big Data research context, aspects of Big Data research create added tension when considering application of the regulatory requirements. First, Big Data research may use gigantic amounts of data from a variety of sources and combine the data such that patterns and trends become evident, either descriptively or predictive of future

---

[7] Jon Mark Hirshon et al., Variability in Institutional Review Board Assessment of Minimal-Risk Research, 9 *Acad. Emerg. Med.* 1417 (2002); Seema Shah et al., How Do Institutional Review Boards Apply the Federal Risk and Benefit Standards for Pediatric Research?, 291 *JAMA* 476 (2004).
[8] SACHRP 2015 Letter.
[9] Ibid.

individual or group behavior. Information that would not be considered sensitive or identifiable per se may transform into individually identifiable private information through combination of several data sets and by matching characteristics that may serve to uniquely identify an individual (e.g., zip code + date of birth + sex).[10] As identified by Evans in Chapter 1 of this volume, traditional mechanisms for protecting subjects, such as obtaining informed consent or deidentifying research information, may be insufficient to protect against privacy and dignitary risks related to Big Data analysis. Although Big Data researchers may not purposively pick individuals out of the shielding obscurity of the crowd of metadata, individual protections may best be accomplished by focused safeguards for the group to which data pertain – a premise that appears inconsistent with the Common Rule's focus on individualized protections.[11]

15.2.1 Does Big Data Health Research Involve "Human Subjects"?

The Common Rule applies to "research" with "human subjects" that is either conducted or supported by a US federal department or agency that has adopted the regulations. Big Data health research that does not involve intervention or interaction with living individuals to obtain their data specifically for purposes of the research at hand will be regulated under the Common Rule only if researchers obtain information about living individuals that is both "individually identifiable" and "private."

Individually Identifiable
The Common Rule defines "individually identifiable" to mean that the identity of the subject is or may readily be ascertained by the investigator or associated with the information.[12] Often, a Big Data set is composed of aggregate information and will not contain individual identifiers linking information directly to living individuals. However, it has been demonstrated repeatedly that individuals may be reidentified from supposedly anonymous or deidentified data sets: the structure of one's social network,[13] Internet search terms,[14] purchase

---

[10] Latanya Sweeney, Simple Demographics Often Identify People Uniquely, Carnegie Mellon University, Data Privacy Working Paper No. 3 (2000), available at http://dataprivacylab.org/projects/identifiability/paper1.pdf [https://perma.cc/7PM5-8X93].
[11] Luciano Floridi, Open Data, Data Protection, and Group Privacy, 27 *J. Philos. Tech.* 1 (2014).
[12] US Federal Policy for the Protection of Human Subjects 45 C.F.R. § 46.102(f)(2) (1991); see also US Federal Policy for the Protection of Human Subjects, 82 Fed. Reg. 7149, 7163 (January 19, 2017).
[13] Kevin Lewis et al., Tastes, Ties, and Time: A New Social Network Dataset Using Facebook.com, 30 *Soc. Networks* 330 (2008).
[14] Michael Barbaro & Tom Zeller, Jr., A Face Is Exposed for AOL Searcher No. 4417749, *New York Times*, August 9, 2006, available at www.nytimes.com/2006/08/09/technology/09aol.html [https://perma.cc/P7KU-URV6].

habits,[15] or movie ratings on Netflix[16] may uniquely identify an individual. A question for contemplation is whether, given the demonstrated ability to reidentify individuals from anonymized or aggregated data, identifiability offers a meaningful decision point for regulatory applicability? Regardless, IRBs must consider this standard as part of the regulatory framework.

The revised Common Rule maintains the central role of identifiability in the "human subjects" definition and further emphasizes identifiability as a gatekeeper concept through a new mandate for Common Rule agencies. Common Rule agencies will be required to regularly engage in two types of expert consultation regarding interpretation of the regulatory standard of identifiability. The revised rule requires expert consultation, including experts in data matching and reidentification, to reexamine the terms "identifiable private information" and "identifiable biospecimen." This consultation may, but need not, lead to alterations in the agencies' interpretation of these terms (e.g., through guidance). Moreover, the agencies must consult with appropriate experts to assess what analytic technologies or techniques generate identifiable private information or an identifiable biospecimen. A draft list of such technologies or techniques will be published for notice and public comment, and the final list will be publicly available.[17]

These self-imposed requirements for Common Rule agencies allow a responsive application of the regulatory standard of identifiability in light of evolving analytic techniques that increase the ability to reidentify data sets and generate identifiable data from nonidentified information or biospecimens. By highlighting the importance of the identifiability assessment, this may provide added certainty for the regulated community if an end point is the development of clear and consistent guidance. In the absence of such guidance, in assessing whether a subject whose data are part of a Big Data set might be readily identified by an investigator, an IRB might consider the investigator, including his or her relationship to the subject and access to a mechanism for identification (e.g., the Federal Bureau of Investigation fingerprint database); the potential or partial identifiers contained in the information; and the likelihood of reidentification of individuals by correlating deidentified data sources with external data sets that link to an individual's identity (and not just whether this is theoretically possible). In the absence of published guidance from the US federal Common Rule agencies on how to apply the definition of human subject, IRBs likely arrive at inconsistent determinations regarding whether Big Data health information is "individually identifiable."

---

[15] Charles Duhigg, How Companies Learn Your Secrets, *New York Times*, February 16, 2012, available at www.nytimes.com/2012/02/19/magazine/shopping-habits.html [https://perma.cc/ZJ2F-CE7H].

[16] Arvind Narayanan & Vitaly Shmatikov, Robust De-Anonymization of Large Sparse Datasets, in *Proceedings of the 2008 IEEE Symposium on Security and Privacy* 111 (2008).

[17] See US Federal Policy for the Protection of Human Subjects, 82 *Fed. Reg.* 7149 (January 19, 2017).

Private

Even if information is individually identifiable, Big Data health research using publicly available information does not involve "human subjects" if the information is not also "private" under the Common Rule standard, which dictates that "[p]rivate information includes information about behavior that occurs in a context in which an individual can reasonably expect that no observation or recording is taking place, and information which has been provided for specific purposes by an individual and which the individual can reasonably expect will not be made public."[18]

Collecting already-generated information that is presumptively public in which an individual has no reasonable expectation of privacy does not involve human subjects for purposes of the Common Rule. For example, an IRB may consider research analyzing publicly accessible tweets or accessing publicly available health claims data sets not to involve human subjects for this reason. Yet IRBs must make a judgment call as to how to interpret the regulatory phrases "reasonably expect that no observation or recording is taking place" and "reasonably expect will not be made public." Recognizing that the regulatory standard of "reasonable" does not depend on an individual subject's own expectation of privacy, an IRB considering what expectations of privacy in the information are "reasonable" might obtain information about the research context and the potential subjects in that context and review any relevant terms of service or site policy (e.g., for Internet sites) or applicable data use agreement. For example, information accessed via a social media site may not necessarily be considered by an IRB to be presumptively public if the site's terms of service indicate that user-posted information may not be used for research purposes.[19] Further, not all health Big Data will be presumptively public (e.g., a health system's aggregated medical records). Again, in the absence of federal agency guidance on how to apply the definition of "human subjects," IRBs likely arrive at inconsistent determinations regarding whether Big Data health information is "private."

15.2.2 Why Do IRBs Apply the Common Rule to Big Data Health Research?

In line with the preceding regulatory analysis, SACHRP has advised the Secretary of HHS that Big Data research generally does not trigger the Common Rule's substantive requirements, in that Big Data research typically does not involve "human subjects" under the Common Rule definition or could qualify for exemption.[20]

---

[18] 45 C.F.R. § 46.102(f)(2) (1991).
[19] SACHRP, Considerations and Recommendations Concerning Internet Research and Human Subjects Research Regulations, with Revisions (2013), available at www.hhs.gov/ohrp/sachrp-committee/meetings/2013-march-12-13-presentation/index.html [https://perma.cc/BX8P-U9VR].
[20] SACHRP 2015 Letter.

Nonetheless, research institutions may ask IRBs to review Big Data health research as human subjects research.

Health Information Is Sensitive

One reason research institutions and IRBs may want to define Big Data health research as involving human subjects (and therefore subject to regulatory oversight under the Common Rule) is because health information is traditionally considered highly sensitive. This has to do with the nature of the information as being about the inner workings of the individual and the private and privileged physician-patient relationship context within which the information is disclosed and developed, as well as the possibly detrimental social or legal consequences of revealing certain types health information.[21] Health Big Data has been used for reidentification and reidentification-like demonstrations to illustrate that privacy protections in the era of Big Data are insufficient. For example, researchers have demonstrated that it is possible to use non-DNA-based information to infer a DNA-based code that can resolve an individual's identity out of hundreds of millions of individual genotypic profiles obtained in a completely different context.[22] The heightened awareness of the potential to identify individuals from a supposedly deidentified or anonymized data set has been brought about by the publicity surrounding "proof of concept" projects such as Latanya Sweeney's reidentification research involving the information held by the Personal Genome Project[23] and the identification of five individuals (and their male family members) by surname in the 1000 Genomes Project data set by triangulating base pairs on the Y chromosome with user profiles on a genealogy website and Google searches.[24] The publicity surrounding these same reidentification demonstration projects likewise has affected the IRB landscape by calling into question the notion of a truly deidentified or anonymized data set. Indeed, it appears that many and perhaps most purportedly deidentified or anonymized data sets will not remain so when challenged. Given this idea, the most conservative course for an IRB in applying the "readily ascertainable" or "associated with the information" tests within the regulatory definition of "individually identifiable" is to determine that health information contained within such a data set is *potentially* identifiable. The revised Common Rule mandate for expert consultation (explicitly requiring inclusion of deidentification experts) regarding

---

[21] Paul Ohm, Response: The Underwhelming Benefits of Big Data, 161 *U. Pa. L. Rev. PEN-Numbra* 339 (2013).

[22] Eric E. Schadt, Sangsoon Woo, & Ke Hao, Bayesian Method to Predict Individual SNP Genotypes from Gene Expression Data, 44 *Nat. Genet.* 603 (2012).

[23] Latanya Sweeney, Akua Abu, & Julia Winn, Identifying Participants in the Personal Genome Project by Name (Harvard University Data Privacy Lab White Paper) (2013), available at http://dataprivacylab.org/projects/pgp/1021-1.pdf [https://perma.cc/AA3A-FUXH].

[24] Melissa Gymrek et al., Identifying Personal Genomes by Surname Inference, 339 *Science* 321 (2013).

how Common Rule agencies ought to assess identifiablity may release some such pressure on the IRB's consideration of presumptively deidentified data sets.[25]

The "Wild West" flavor of reidentification demonstrations and the continued persistence of such projects may cause research institutions and IRBs to reason that without a formal system outside the scope of the Common Rule to rely on for appropriate information protections, considering Big Data research to be individually identifiable private information and applying the Common Rule standards are the best option.

Societal Lapse in Privacy Protections
When discussing how to design a schema to protect an individual's privacy in information, Nissenbaum[26] asserts that a public-private dichotomy is insufficient to understand the basis on which use of presumptively "public" data is considered objectionable. Considering the outcry surrounding the "Tastes, Ties, and Time" Facebook social networking study, in which researchers obtained arguably public information from a shared social network without consent,[27] it is apparent that individuals care about the use of information they deem to be "public" or "private." Further, as Evans postulates in Chapter 1 of this volume, consent may be a less effective model to protect privacy of subjects of Big Data health research given the interconnectedness of twenty-first-century data environments.

The desirability and current unavailability of a protective framework other than the Common Rule may propel IRB consideration of Big Data research into a regulatory quagmire: Big Data by its nature often may not appear readily identifiable to an individual, and if an IRB accepts that Big Data is not individually identifiable private information, the Common Rule requirements do not attach, and no mandatory set of standards may provide equivalent protections to the Common Rule. But, if IRBs apply the Common Rule requirements, triggering the need to obtain informed consent of the subjects, it may pose a barrier to conducting the research. What is a reasonable IRB to do?

15.2.3 Assessing the Risks of Big Data Health Research

Risks of Big Data Research
Big Data research in general is recognized as presenting primarily informational risk,[28] although the potential of dignitary harm is gaining larger recognition.[29]

---

[25] See US Federal Policy for the Protection of Human Subjects.
[26] Nissenbaum, Privacy in Context.
[27] Michael Zimmer, "But the Data Is Already Public": On the Ethics of Research in Facebook, 12 J. Ethics Info. Technol. 313 (2010); Lewis et al., Tastes, Ties, and Time.
[28] SACHRP 2015 Letter.
[29] "Dignitary harm" is a tort law concept allowing redress for harms to a person's dignity. Like an invasion of privacy, this is considered harmful per se in that "it is defined as that which injures

Informational risks stem from the unauthorized or inappropriate use or disclosure of information in ways that could be harmful to research subjects. For instance, disclosure of illegal activities, a contagious disease, substance abuse, or chronic illness might jeopardize the current or future employment of subjects, injure their reputation within the community, or cause emotional or psychological harm. In general, informational risks are correlated with both the nature of the information and the degree of identifiability of the information.

Determining Minimal Risk
The Common Rule defines "minimal risk" as meaning that "the probability and magnitude of harm or discomfort anticipated in the research are not greater in and of themselves than those ordinarily encountered in daily life or during the performance of routine physical or psychological examinations or tests."[30] Application of the definition of minimal risk involves a comparison of the risk level presented by the research with the risk level of daily life activities or routine physical and psychological examinations. The risks of daily life activities, or the risks of routine examinations, represent a range of risks because some daily life activities or examination procedures are more risky than others. SACHRP recommended that the minimal risk threshold – the upper boundary of the range of daily life risks – is fixed at the harms and discomforts ordinarily encountered, reflecting familiar and routine background risks for the average person in the general population.[31] Therefore, the risks of research must be not greater than the risks of the riskier activities of daily life.[32] This analysis need not involve a determination that the research procedures themselves actually are activities experienced in daily life but rather an assessment of the risks presented by the research compared with the risk level of daily life – for example, an MRI administered without sedation may reasonably be considered to present no more than minimal risk to research subjects, even if an MRI procedure is not a routine daily life activity, if the level of risk presented by the MRI procedure is considered to fall below the upper boundary of the range of daily life risks.

Minimal risk is used as a gateway to many of the flexibilities available in the Common Rule, including waiver or alteration of informed consent, which is permitted under the Common Rule if the IRB finds that the research presents minimal risk to subjects; waiver will not adversely affect the rights and welfare of subjects; the research could not practicably be carried out without waiver; when

social personality" and thus a plaintiff need not prove actual injury. Robert C. Post, *Constitutional Domains: Democracy, Community, Management* (1995).
[30] 45 C.F.R. § 46.102(i) (1991).
[31] Letter from Samuel Tilden, Chair, SACHRP, to Honorable Michael O. Leavitt, Secretary of Heath and Human Services (January 31, 2008) (hereinafter SACHRP 2008 Letter), available at www.hhs.gov/ohrp/sachrp-committee/recommendations/2008-january-31-letter/ [https://perma.cc/Q7D6-N8LF].
[32] David Wendler et al., Quantifying the Federal Minimal Risk Standard: Implications for Pediatric Research without a Prospect of Direct Benefit, 294 *JAMA* 826 (2005).

appropriate, subjects will be provided with additional pertinent information after participation; and under the new criterion added in the revised Common Rule, for research using identifiable private information or identifiable biospecimens, the IRB must find that the research could not practicably be carried out without using them in an identifiable format.[33] If no other law requires subject consent to Big Data health research, an IRB reasonably could determine that waiver of consent will not adversely affect the rights and welfare of subjects; as Big Data research uses information from a subject population that could number in the millions, an IRB likely would determine that the research could not practicably be conducted without waiving consent[34]; and if the Big Data research involves correlating data sets and matching characteristics in a way that could result in identification of an individual, the IRB reasonably could find that the research could not practicably be carried out without using the information in an identifiable format because otherwise the intended correlation could not be achieved. However, regarding the minimal risk assessment, IRBs have difficulty implementing the minimal risk concept, and the extreme variability with which IRBs review minimal risk research is well documented.[35]

Application of the Uniform Daily Life Risks Standard

The regulatory definition of minimal risk embodies two separate comparator tests to assess risk: the "daily life risks standard" and the "risks of routine physical or psychological examinations" standard. Some bioethicists both view the comparator of the risks of the research with the level of risk of experiences ordinarily encountered in daily life to be ambiguous[36] and assert that this aspect of the definition has led to the demonstrated great variation in the way different IRBs evaluate minimal risk.[37] One extreme critique concludes that the most ethical approach is to eliminate, or read out of the regulatory definition, the daily life standard for assessing minimal risk and apply only the comparator standard of routine examinations.[38] Notwithstanding these criticisms, it is within the IRB's discretion to choose which standard to apply to a given research project. Because the procedures involved in Big

---

[33] US Federal Policy for the Protection of Human Subjects.
[34] SACHRP recognized that IRBs consider administrative burden and cost in assessing practicability of conducting the research with consent and recommended that scientific validity be considered because studies involving very large populations likely will have a significant number of unreachable subjects. See SACHRP 2015 Letter.
[35] Jon Mark Hirshon et al., Variability in Institutional Review Board Assessment of Minimal-Risk Research; Seema Shah et al., How Do Institutional Review Boards Apply the Federal Risk and Benefit Standards for Pediatric Research?
[36] Loretta M. Kopelman, Moral Problems in Assessing Research Risk, 22 IRB: Ethics Hum. Res. Risk 3 (2000).
[37] Seema Shah et al., How Do Institutional Review Boards Apply the Federal Risk and Benefit Standards for Pediatric Research?
[38] D. B. Resnik, Eliminating the Daily Life Risks Standard from the Definition of Minimal Risk, 31 J. Med Ethics 35 (2005).

Data health research appear to be less like the procedures in routine physical or psychological examinations, the daily life risks standard may align better with the Big Data health research context.

The uniform, or objective, interpretation of minimal risk provides the same standard for all research subjects by reference to the daily life risks of an average healthy person.[39] SACHRP has aligned with the uniform standard for minimal risk and endorsed a "fixed" notion of minimal risk, recommending that the minimal risk threshold remains fixed as the harms and discomforts ordinarily encountered and that reflects familiar background risks that are part of the routine experience of life for the average person in the general population, while recognizing that research risks themselves are procedure specific and population dependent.[40]

How should IRBs assess minimal risk for Big Data research in a background environment in which information sharing is becoming the norm and privacy less and less protected, allowing for elevated informational and dignitary risks? Should these be considered elevated background risks irrelevant to where the minimal risk threshold is set, like risks presented to a community by civil unrest and natural disaster,[41] or uniform daily life risks? SACHRP, in discussing how to identify the harms and discomforts ordinarily encountered in daily life, recommended that an ethically meaningful notion should reflect "background risks" that are familiar and part of the routine experience of life for the "average person" in the "general population."[42]

One proposal is to view the risks relating to the unauthorized sharing and use of the kind of personal information accessed and analyzed in Big Data health research to be so prevalent that the risks have transcended the experiences of the subject population and are better conceived of as general risks of daily life for healthy individuals living in safe environments. The National Research Council recognized that "[t]here is so much information that is freely and openly available about individuals that informational risk is ubiquitous in society. In many respects, informational risk is an everyday aspect of life in the twenty-first century."[43] Even with widespread recognition of the risk of unauthorized use of their personal information, people still choose to routinely and voluntarily use the technologies that generate Big Data and lead to the attendant informational risks and potential

---

[39] David Wendler, Protecting Subjects Who Cannot Give Consent: Toward a Better Standard for "Minimal" Risks, 33(5) *Hastings Ctr. Rep.* (September–October 2005), at 37; Robert M. Nelson, Editorial, Minimal Risk, Yet Again, 150(6) *J. Pediatr.* (June 2007), at 570.

[40] SACHRP 2008 Letter.

[41] Ibid.

[42] Ibid.

[43] Committee on Revisions to the Common Rule for the Protection of Human Subjects in Research in the Behavioral and Social Sciences, National Research Council, Proposed Revisions to the Common Rule for the Protection of Human Subjects in the Behavioral and Social Sciences (2014) (hereinafter National Research Council Proposed Revisions).

dignitary harms. Thus, under a uniform application of the daily life risks standard, Big Data health research permissibly can be deemed to present no more than minimal risk to subjects.

Critics of the relative standard of daily life risks risk have asserted that "daily life risks must first be deemed ethically acceptable before they can be used to normalize research risks,"[44] and a similar criticism could be levied against the proposal to allow application of a uniform standard to determine Big Data health research to present no more than minimal risk. A response is that the daily life risks of healthy individuals living in safe environments are not static and need not remain set at the comparators for daily life risks of 1991, when the Common Rule was first promulgated, and recognition of changing social norms about the use of information may alter the assessment of what today are daily life risks.

Further consideration is needed as to whether an ethical framework can be developed for assessing whether a risk ought to be considered a daily life risk under the uniform standard. The activities of daily life and the risks of those activities against which the risks of research are evaluated must change over time with new and different social and technological developments, and the approach to quantifying the risks of daily life and identifying the appropriate comparison with the risks of research warrants additional discussion (e.g., if daily life activities become substantially safer for all average healthy individuals, this could result in the risks of even low-risk research exceeding daily life risks, with the end point that all research would be considered to present more than minimal risk).[45]

Mediating Risk to Below Minimal through Privacy Protections

The National Research Council indicated that research data may involve informational risk that is potentially more than minimal because they include (1) highly sensitive, private information that could lead to civil or criminal liability or economic, social, or psychological harm or (2) information that could increase the likelihood of reidentification.[46] It seems likely that much health Big Data appears to meet these criteria. If an IRB considering waiver of consent for subjects of Big Data health research agrees with the National Research Council's view and rejects application of a uniform daily life risks standard that encompasses informational risks, the IRB may request that the researcher add such protections in order to reduce the risk to below the minimal risk threshold such the IRB can permissibly waive consent. This aligns with OHRP's long-standing position that individual research procedures can serve to lower the overall risk level that research presents to subjects. A plan for confidentiality protections of research data can serve to

---

[44] Seema Shah, The Dangers of Using a Relative Standard for Minimal Risk, 6 Am. J. Bioethics 22 (2011).
[45] Thanks to Dave Wendler for this comment on a prior draft of this chapter.
[46] National Research Council Proposed Revisions.

decrease the risk of a more than minimal risk study to below the minimal risk threshold – as advocated by the SACHRP recommendations on minimal risk and on Big Data research[47] and the National Research Council's recommendation to incorporate practices for reducing informational research risk.[48]

15.3 OPTIONS FOR POLICYMAKERS TO AID THE RESEARCH COMMUNITY

The National Research Council recommendations pertaining to the regulatory definition of "minimal risk" are very relevant to the context of Big Data research.[49] The council identified the need for further research targeted at understanding the risks of daily life and how practically to implement research procedures and reduce risk to below minimal. Further, the council recommended grounding the minimal risk definition by developing standards for assessing probability and magnitude of harm, with recognition that regulating to the worst-case scenarios presented by reidentification "proof of concept" projects is undesirable. SACHRP recommended that OHRP clarify how the minimal risk and informed-consent waiver requirements apply to Big Data research and that adherence to data privacy protections may reduce the level of risk to privacy to minimal and proposed addition of an exemption to the Common Rule for Big Data research conducted in conformance with identified data security and privacy protections.[50] In response, the Common Rule agencies could publish guidance endorsing a specific IRB review structure for Big Data research, including guidance on application of the definition of minimal risk to big data research.

Even if the risks of big data health research are minimal, addressing the protection of individual privacy in big data research remains a priority. Possible solutions are addressed elsewhere in this volume: in Chapter 1, Evans suggests a data commons approach may satisfy the needs presented by big data research; in Chapter 13, Gitter presents an argument for consent for big data research regardless of applicability of the Common Rule; and, in Chapter 16, Dawson asserts that robust ethical guidelines could better serve to protect individual privacy interests than application of the Common Rule. A larger evaluation of these and other suggested approaches might alleviate the responsibility currently being carried by the Common Rule and the applying IRBs with regard to ensuring privacy protections for the individuals to whom Big Data pertains. The tension between the societal lapse in privacy protection in the Big Data context and the resulting application by IRBs of the Common Rule regulatory structure – designed to apply to the research use of individually

---

[47] SACHRP 2008 Letter; SACHRP 2015 Letter.
[48] National Research Council Proposed Revisions.
[49] Ibid.
[50] SACHRP 2015 Letter.

identifiable private information – could be relieved with the advent and application of viable alternative protective models.

15.4 CONCLUSION

Big Data health research does not involve "human subjects" under the Common Rule if the health information accessed is either not private or not identifiable to a living individual. If an IRB does apply the Common Rule regulatory requirements, a pathway exists by which an IRB may determine that the research presents minimal risk to subjects (1) under a uniform daily life risks standard, determining that informational risk is a daily life risk for healthy individuals living in the same environments and comparing the risks of Big Data health research with the daily life informational risk to determine that the research presents minimal risk to subjects or (2) using data security protections and other research procedures designed to reduce informational risk and dignitary harm to reduce the research risk to below the minimal risk threshold. Under either assessment, the IRB may determine it permissible to waive the informed consent of subjects. The challenge for the IRB is to consider what approach is ethically defensible to protect individual privacy in the context of Big Data health research.

16

The Common Rule and Research with Data, Big and Small

*Liza Dawson**

16.1 INTRODUCTION

Recently, concerns about the use of Big Data approaches in health research have led to several commentaries urging greater privacy protections and control over research. Rapid technological advances and increases in electronic communication in all forms have outpaced efforts to provide privacy protections for average citizens in daily transactions as well as in potential Big Data research. The advent of new and complex technologies for gathering, transmitting, disseminating, and analyzing data provides a new opportunity to think through the ethical rationale for regulation. This chapter argues that the Federal Policy for the Protection of Human Subjects, the "Common Rule" – both as it existed before the 2017 regulatory revisions and thereafter[1] – *should not* govern research with Big Data and that alternative oversight mechanisms are needed.[2] Furthermore, Big Data research and its challenges expose the inherent flaws in our current system of regulating research with "small data" more generally; the advent of Big Data has brought the inherent unsuitability of Common Rule regulation of research with data into clearer focus. A new and conceptually distinct standard is needed for regulation of *all* types of research

---

* This chapter represents the views of the author alone and does not represent any viewpoint, policy, or position of the National Institutes of Health or the Department of Health and Human Services or any of its components. Sections of this chapter were included in a master's thesis submitted to the George Washington University Department of Philosophy in March of 2017.
[1] The Common Rule was revised in January 2017; see Federal Policy for the Protection of Human Subjects, 82 *Fed. Reg.* 7149 (January 19, 2017), for description of the response to public comments, the revised rule, and regulatory citations of signatory agencies.
[2] This chapter does not address actual interpretation by federal regulators with regard to the question of whether the Common Rule does or does not apply to Big Data research but rather the normative question of whether it should apply. For the former, see Chapter 15 by Laura Odwazny.

involving data collected for other purposes (i.e., secondary-use research), whether or not the research is Big Data research.

This chapter consists of four sections. First, it addresses the historical rationale for the Common Rule, arguing that the rule should never have been applied to research involving secondary use of data derived from private records. Next, it describes several controversies in application of the Common Rule to research with data that demonstrate conceptual flaws in the Common Rule approach. These examples also show how deidentification of data has been used as a massive workaround to avoid regulation. Then the chapter describes how Big Data research makes this workaround impossible and how the increasingly blurred lines between public and private information also create difficulties for application of the rule. None of these problems have been resolved in the Common Rule's 2017 revisions.

Finally, the chapter discusses an alternative approach to oversight of Big Data research that would be feasible under the 2017 Common Rule. Given that the new rule was issued after years of debate and numerous delays, it is unlikely that any new regulatory standard will emerge soon. Therefore, conceptual difficulties in applying the rule to Big Data research will need to be addressed. The proposed alternative oversight framework could be adopted by professional societies, institutions, and research funders as a voluntary ethical guideline and thus have practical and normative value, even in the absence of incorporation into regulatory standards. The aim of such guidelines would be to maintain transparency about research processes, as well as to support efficient, ethical, and scientifically rigorous research.

16.2 RATIONALE FOR THE COMMON RULE'S APPROACH TO REGULATION OF RESEARCH WITH DATA

16.2.1 *The National Commission and the Distinction between Research and Clinical Care*

The National Commission for Protection of Human Subjects of Biomedical and Behavioral Research was an independent federal advisory commission set up in 1974 via the National Research Act[3] to develop an ethical framework for the oversight of research with human subjects; this ethical framework formed the basis of the Common Rule. The National Commission had been tasked with delineating the difference between research and medical care for the purpose of regulating research; therefore, the commission carefully laid out a definition of research to distinguish research activities from clinical practice while recognizing that sometimes physicians offer experimental treatments to individual patients solely in pursuit

---

[3] Pub. L. 93-348, 88 Stat. 342 (1974), available at www.gpo.gov/fdsys/pkg/STATUTE-88/pdf/STATUTE-88-Pg342.pdf [https://perma.cc/H3AK-URTG].

of clinical benefit for that individual.[4] The commission's definition of research – "systematic investigation designed to produce generalizable knowledge" – reflects the idea that a physician conducting research may depart from acting in the best interest of the patient, at least in part, in the pursuit of knowledge.[5]

Arguably, the distinction between research and clinical care is important for the regulation of biomedical research involving direct interventions on human subjects because departures from standard clinical practice may threaten subjects' interests. In contrast, in research involving only secondary use of human subjects data, without direct intervention on subjects, this definition of research fails to inform any meaningful distinction regarding risk. Research with data is not inherently riskier or more morally suspect than other nonresearch activities with data and in many ways is less so.

16.2.2 *Privacy Concerns in Research with Human Subjects Data*

Traditionally, the biggest ethical concern in research with secondary use of data is protection of privacy, because no physical risks are entailed. Therefore, the scope of the Common Rule includes only research with data that are both private and individually identifiable. Privacy concerns could arise in two ways: breaches (inappropriate or inadvertent release or disclosure of information) or researcher misconduct. Absent either of these occurrences, remaining privacy concerns may relate to general interest in privacy protection rather than specific threats. Individuals might be concerned about lack of individual control over data or about government interference or about embarrassment or discomfort knowing that others are privy to intimate details of one's life. Out of all of these concerns, only researcher misconduct involves any kind of unique association with research as an activity compared with others. In other words, the distinction between research uses versus nonresearch uses of individually identifiable private data fails to demonstrate a unique need for privacy regulation in the context of research. Nonresearch activities with private identifiable data – such as the transmission of health records used for payment of insurance claims, or quality control testing for individual clinical laboratory tests, or records of prescription drug purchases – involve private identifiable health information, and any of them could be misused or leaked inappropriately. Concerns about privacy of identifiable data exist, independently of whether the data are used for research.[6] So why is research use regulated differently?

---

[4] Tom L. Beauchamp & Yashar Saghai, The Historical Foundations of the Research-Practice Distinction in Bioethics, 33 *Theoretical Med. Bioethics* 45 (2012).

[5] National Commission for the Protection of Humuman Subjects of Biomedical and Behavioral Research, *The Belmont Report: Ethical Principles and Guidelines for the Protection of Human Subjects of Research* (1979).

[6] For further discussion of risks of data breaches in daily life and the definition of minimal risk in human subjects research, see Chapter 15 by Laura Odwazny.

The National Commission tied research consent for use of identifiable private information to the same standard used for interventional biomedical research, in part because during that time period privacy concerns had come to the forefront of political discourse. Civil rights movements of the 1960s and 1970s motivated a number of unsavory government actions in tracking and surveillance of citizens' groups; the need for protection of the rights of citizens to self-expression and freedom from government intrusion were common themes.[7] At the same time, the advent of computer technology in the 1970s put the creation and reproduction of larger data sets within reach, again raising concerns about possible misuse of data or privacy risks, particularly with regard to data about individual citizens held by the federal government.[8] Against this backdrop, a rigorous approach to the protection of individual privacy interests was politically desirable.[9]

The Privacy Act of 1974 was aimed at addressing some of these concerns. The act mandated that the federal government could collect or share data with other agencies only for legitimate agency purposes and required agencies to provide individuals access to the government-held information about them on request.[10] The National Commission viewed the movement to protect privacy of individual private data as consistent with, and part of, its overall mission to protect the rights of subjects in research. However, in extending the provisions of informed consent and institutional review board (IRB) review – the key elements of the Common Rule – to research with data (rather than with people themselves), the commission did not tailor oversight specifically to privacy concerns. Informed consent does not guarantee subjects' privacy and may provide only an illusion of protection; review boards that handle biomedical research may lack tools and procedures to address the technicalities of data research.

The Common Rule's approach to regulating research with data differently from nonresearch uses of data might make sense if research posed a greater risk to privacy than other data-related activities. However, there is no clear evidence that this was, or is, the case. There are few sources of systematic evidence about the extent (incidence and severity) of data breaches in research with human subjects data, but available sources seem to indicate that breaches are rare. In addition, there is little evidence that the harms from data breaches in research are more likely than from breaches in other settings. For example, a list of breaches in the Institute of Medicine (IOM) 2009 report on health information privacy noted that no misuse or other harm resulted from the breaches

---

[7] Alan F. Westin, The Current Impact of Surveillance on Privacy, 66 *Colum. L. Rev.* 1003 (1966).
[8] US Department of Health, Education and Welfare, *Records, Computers, and the Rights of Citizens* (Willis H. Ware ed., 1973).
[9] Arthur R. Miller, Personal Privacy in the Computer Age: The Challenge of a New Technology in an Information-Oriented Society, 67 *Mich. L. Rev.* 1089 (1969).
[10] Pub. L. 93–579, 88 Stat. 1896 (1974) (codified at 5 U.S.C. § 552a).

reported.[11] There is little empirical support for the idea that research exposes human subjects to more privacy risks than do other activities with their private identifiable data, especially as breaches from other data uses have, unfortunately, become more common.[12]

Of course, privacy should be protected in research as well as nonresearch activities. But a distinct set of privacy regulations for research with data is not needed; rather, all uses of data from individuals should be regulated to some extent to protect privacy while allowing legitimate and valid activities – as will be proposed later.

16.2.3 *Is Some Research with Human Subjects Data Morally Suspect?*

Perhaps there are other, nonprivacy concerns in research with data that distinguish research from nonresearch activities. Some commentators suggest that there are cases in which the purpose of the research activity itself is objectionable to some parties, if they are deemed offensive or morally objectionable. Yet the Common Rule is not oriented around this concern because there is no method for individuals to express disapproval of research with deidentified data, which might be just as objectionable but which falls outside the rule. (If research with deidentified data were regulated, researchers would need to at least obtain IRB approval of any research projects proposed, even if individual consent was not required.) By limiting its scope to identifiable private information, the Common Rule only allows subjects the right to decline research that might potentially affect their privacy interests – at which point they may also express a view about the nature of the research itself. In short, with its focus on identifiable private data, the National Commission prioritized privacy over other issues with regard to human subjects oversight of data research.

The revised version of the Common Rule, published January 19, 2017, likewise maintains a demarcation between identifiable and nonidentifiable data while acknowledging the increasing difficulty in ensuring that reidentification cannot occur.

---

[11] Sharyl J. Nass et al. eds., *Beyond the HIPAA Privacy Rule: Enhancing Privacy, Improving Health through Research* 95, table 2.2 (2009).

[12] For example, see these recent news reports: Alison Diana, Montana Health Department Hacked, InformationWeek (June 25, 2014, 5:20 PM), available at www.informationweek.com/healthcare/security-and-privacy/montana-health-department-hacked/d/d-id/1278872 [https://perma.cc/C34N-RU7F]; John Woodrow Cox et al., Virus Infects MedStar Health System's Computers, Forcing an Online Shutdown, *Washington Post*, March 28, 2016, available at www.washingtonpost.com/local/virus-infects-medstar-health-systems-computers-hospital-officials-say/2016/03/28/480f7d66-f515-11e5-a3ce-f06b5ba21f33_story.html [https://perma.cc/YMB6-T3CQ]; US Office of Personnel Management, Cybersecurity Resource Center: Cybersecurity Incidents, available at www.opm.gov/cybersecurity/cybersecurity-incidents/ [https://perma.cc/2Y9P-23F8].

16.3 PROBLEMS WITH THE COMMON RULE'S REGULATION OF RESEARCH WITH DATA

16.3.1 The Problem of Sweeping Data Research into the Common Rule: Big Net, Too Many Fish

Even at the time of the National Commission's work, experts recognized that an unreasonably large number of activities with identifiable data would be swept up in the scope of the Common Rule. A commissioned paper addressed use of identifiable information in a range of research activities, noting that the existing regulation in Public Law 93–348, the National Research Act, included in its scope research with identifiable private information.[13] The authors commented:

> There is general agreement that these areas of research are and should be covered by PL93–348 and other rights-of-subjects legislation. Probably 99% of such research already is conforming to such standards in the sense of not violating the rights-of-subjects specified. There are essentially no publicized cases of violations in these areas. The problem raised by PL93–348 is the monstrous bureaucratic burden of requiring this vast area of low-risk research to go through formal institutional review processes.[14]

Even in the earliest framing of the new oversight standards being considered by the National Commission, a list of activities involving certain private identifiable data was exempted from the rule.[15] These activities were recognized as legitimate and necessary for the functioning of federal institutions, agencies, and private organizations; posed low risk to human subjects; and were well established and accepted. Therefore, imposing a new regulatory burden, requiring IRB review, informed consent (or waiver) seemed an unreasonable and unjustified burden. The list of exemptions was designed to remove several classes of activities from the purview of the rule. The difficulty, both then and now, is that there is no conceptual boundary between activities that were exempted and activities that were not. In an

---

[13] Pub. L. 93–348, 88 Stat. 342 (1974), available at www.gpo.gov/fdsys/pkg/STATUTE-88/pdf/STATUTE-88-Pg342.pdf [https://perma.cc/H3AK-URTG].

[14] Donald T. Campell & Joe Shelby Cecil, Protection of the Rights and Interests of Human Subjects in the Areas of Program Evaluation, Social Experimentation, Social Indicators, Survey Research, Secondary Analysis of Research Data, and Statistical Analysis of Data from Administrative Records, in *The Belmont Report: Ethical Principles and Guidelines for the Protection of Human Subjects of Research* app. II (1979).

[15] Ibid. at 8. After describing how operational monitoring within an institution would not constitute research, the authors go on to state: "These proposed regulations have obvious ambiguities, but rather than suggest specific refinements, it seems better to wait, allowing operating agencies to define their activities as they choose until specific problems emerge. We must remember that there are Rights-of-Participants issues in every social institution and profession, public and private, whether doing research or not, and this Commission must avoid taking on this whole responsibility." Ibid.

effort to determine the appropriate boundaries of regulated activity, commentators and regulators have focused on the regulatory definition of research: systematic investigation designed to produce generalizable knowledge.[16] This approach has done little to clarify the situation. Many putatively nonresearch activities, such as quality improvement (QI), are systematic, just like research, but the distinction between "generalizable" and "not generalizable" findings does not imply greater risk or greater need for protection of privacy. The preamble to the revised Common Rule alludes to debates about the boundary between research activities and other activities such a QI or program evaluation but avoids defining a category of exempt activities in these areas, in part because of the difficulty in establishing a bright line between exempt and nonexempt activities for regulatory purposes. Many of these activities consist of secondary uses of data collected for other purposes. The 2017 revised Common Rule also carves out a longer list of activities involving secondary use of data for which Common Rule oversight is not required.[17] For activities in national security or criminal justice, there is a rationale to avoid inclusion in the Common Rule because other regulatory standards apply. However, for other activities, the rationale for inclusion or exclusion is unclear. For example, the discussion of clinical data registries illustrates the problem of manufactured boundaries between regulated and nonregulated activities that pose identical privacy risks. The preamble states that "the creation of a clinical data registry designed to provide information about the performance quality of institutional care providers, and whose design is not influenced or altered to facilitate research, is not covered by this rule even if it is known that the registry will be used for research studies," whereas "[i]n contrast, if investigators receive funding from a Common Rule department or agency to design a clinical data registry for research purposes and the registry includes identifiable private information, or involves interacting with individuals (for example, a research survey), then such an activity involves human subjects research, but may be exempt of it meets one or more of the exemption categories under § __.104(d)7."[18]

While the Common Rule applies to identifiable private data, researchers have continued to conduct large volumes of research using deidentified data, an activity that falls outside the Common Rule's scope. Even the seemingly simple solution

---

[16] Under 45 C.F.R. § 46.102(d), "research" means "a systematic investigation, including research development, testing and evaluation, designed to develop or contribute to generalizable knowledge. Activities which meet this definition constitute research for purposes of this policy, whether or not they are conducted or supported under a program which is considered research for other purposes. For example, some demonstration and service programs may include research activities." See also US Department of Health and Human Services, Quality Improvement Activities FAQs (2017), available at www.hhs.gov/ohrp/regulations-and-policy/guidance/faq/quality-improvement-activities/index.html [https://perma.cc/42MH-W3RR].
[17] See Federal Policy for the Protection of Human Subjects, 82 *Fed. Reg.* 7149, 7184–86 (January 19, 2017).
[18] Ibid., at 7200.

of deidentification has its problems, however. Deidentification can detract from scientific quality because important variables may be lost and cannot be used in the analysis. It also becomes impossible to link individual records from different data sets unless a third party holds a key to identifiers.

Along with these problems, new regulatory challenges have emerged. In 2004, the Office of Human Research Protections (OHRP), the federal office within the Department of Health and Human Services responsible for enforcing the Common Rule, issued new guidance stating that when the holder of a data set containing identifiers releases deidentified data to a research team, OHRP would not consider the resulting project to be human subjects research under the Common Rule as long as the data holders agree not to release identifiers to the researchers.[19] While this approach seems reasonable, questions emerged about whether the holders of the identifiers are considered part of the research team if they collaborate on design or analytical plans. Where does the boundary between "engaged in research" and "not engaged" lie? And again, the lack of a clear rationale for regulatory oversight over secondary data research has hampered efforts to find a coherent boundary between regulated and nonregulated activities.

In sum, the National Commission advocated sweeping data research into the human research oversight system, focusing on privacy rights of individuals and distinguishing research from nonresearch activities for the purpose of regulation. But the process of constructing the Common Rule neglected two key conceptual elements: (1) what distinguishes the types of activities with private identifiable data that require oversight from those that do not? and (2) for activities that require oversight, what kind of oversight is needed?

16.3.2 *Informed Consent, Confidentiality, and Control in Research*

The Common Rule's twin pillars of human subjects protection are informed consent and approval of research protocols by IRBs. Is informed consent needed to protect the rights of human subjects whose data are used in research? Norms and expectations have been determined for the last forty years by the Common Rule and other associated regulations. Often the claim is made reflexively that informed consent is needed for research use if the data are identifiable and previous consent was not given. What is the ethical underpinning of this standard?

Informed consent does not protect subjects if investigators use inadequate data-protection measures, allowing breaches to occur. A 2009 IOM report on the Health Insurance Portability and Accountability Act (HIPAA) Privacy Rule and health research argues that consent is obsolescent as a protective standard, pointing out

---

[19] US Department of Health and Human Services, *Coded Private Information or Specimens Use in Research, Guidance* (2008), available at www.hhs.gov/ohrp/regulations-and-policy/guidance/research-involving-coded-private-information/index.html [https://perma.cc/DY48-X36H].

that individuals do not have sufficient time, expertise, and access to background information to evaluate every potential use of their private information.[20] Informed consent offers the chance for control only by declining to give consent. But those who do consent should have their private information well protected, and consent does not guarantee this.

Regulatory and ethical standards for appropriate handling of data provide better protection. Review committees can assess whether privacy and data security protections are adequate. However, IRBs may not be the bodies best suited to this task because most are not constituted with experts in data security. An alternative oversight mechanism would be review by a scientific committee that can examine methodology, data security, and appropriate qualifications of researchers for these tasks.

The second point is that interests of those whose data are used lie not only in the protection of their private information; like others whose data are not used, individuals have a general interest in receiving the benefit of advances in healthcare, biomedical science, and public health. Research projects that produce valuable findings benefit society at large, including those whose data are used and those whose data are not used. These benefits may not be obvious at the outset of every research project. Offering every individual the opportunity to agree or decline to use of his or her data would be reasonable if use of the data posed an unreasonable burden or risk of harm on some individuals. But secondary research with existing data poses no burden at all and minimal risk, provided data security measures are in place. The case has not been made that individuals have the right to decline such research in virtue of a privacy right, and those who do not consent to research and benefit from research activities might be viewed as free-riders on the consent of others.

Public health law authorizes use of identifiable data in some cases without express notification or consent of individuals in order to address important public health concerns.[21] And as noted, a wide range of nonresearch activities are conducted with identifiable data without consent, such as quality improvement/quality control (QI/QC) programs in hospitals, program evaluations, and many types of health services research.

A third reason for rejecting consent as a default procedure for research with data is the burden on the research itself – not only monetary costs and time but also scientific quality. A number of articles document detrimental effects on registry data when consent is required, for example.[22] When some individuals decline to consent for use of their data, a population sample may no longer be representative

---

[20] Nass, ed., *Beyond the HIPAA Privacy Rule*.
[21] Lawrence O. Gostin et al., The Public Health Information Infrastructure: A National Review of the Law on Health Information Privacy, 275 *JAMA* 1921 (1996).
[22] Jack V. Tu et al., Impracticability of Informed Consent in the Registry of the Canadian Stroke Network, *N. Engl. J. Med.* 1414 (2004); Julian Peto et al., Editorial: Data Protection, Informed Consent, and Research, 328 *BMJ* 1029 (2004).

of the larger population or capture all the relevant information to inform clinical practice or public health policy.

In sum, health research with private identifiable data poses no risks to human subjects when adequate privacy protection and data security procedures are in place, and such research helps to advance public health and medical science, which benefit individuals and society as a whole. Data of public health importance ought to be made available systematically for use in research, with appropriate controls, without a default requirement for consent.

16.4 BIG DATA'S CHALLENGE TO THE COMMON RULE

Big Data research has brought the various weaknesses of the Common Rule approach described earlier to the breaking point. We are now confronted with research that can no longer be carved out of the Common Rule's purview because it is increasingly difficult to ensure nonidentifiability of individuals given very large databases derived from multiple sources and powerful analytical techniques.[23] Furthermore, there is little clarity about what data are public versus private.[24] In essence, Big Data research pushes the boundaries of the previous workaround solutions for conducting research outside the scope of the Common Rule. It is no longer straightforward to carve out massive data projects by stripping identifiers from data sets, nor is it easy to claim that data accessed through different commercial entities is publicly available information. Gray areas abound. It is this present situation that increases the urgency of a reexamination of the regulatory approach. The conceptual work needed now is what should have been done in 1974 – or in the regulatory revision process culminating in a new Common Rule published in 2017 – to define the threshold and type of regulatory oversight needed for research with private identifiable data.

Another ethical concern in Big Data research is the practice of notice and consent in the context of electronic communication. This illustrates the erosion of the original meaning and intent of informed consent. Agreement to terms and conditions is not well informed, and no other viable choices exist for most users of electronic communication except to click "I agree" or to avoid using that service. This is a Hobson's choice – it is a choice in name only, because no alternatives are offered. Furthermore, most users do not have time or expertise to critically evaluate privacy practices among highly technical Internet-based services. The many hundreds of such transactions that occur within a week and the level of legal detail would make it prohibitively time-consuming and burdensome to evaluate and

[23] Solon Barocas & Helen Nissenbaum, Big Data's End Run around Anonymity and Consent, in *Privacy, Big Data, and the Public Good: Frameworks for Engagement* 44 (Julia Lane et al. eds., 2014).
[24] Katherine J. Strandburg, Home, Home on the Web and Other Fourth Amendment Implications of Technosocial Change, 70 *Md. L. Rev.* 614 (2011).

choose meaningfully among providers. This does not mean that the interests of individuals should be discounted or denied – it merely means that the practice of individual notice and consent in these electronic transactions is not a reasonable way to protect the interests of members of the public in maintaining confidentiality of their information.

16.5 A DIFFERENT APPROACH

16.5.1 *The Value of Ethical Guidelines for Research with Human Subjects Data*

A pragmatic reader might question the value of analyzing the Common Rule's structure and approach given that the 2017 revisions to the rule mean that further regulatory change is unlikely in the near future. Despite these developments, this exercise is useful for four reasons.

First, the Common Rule has considerable flexibility with regard to oversight of data research – yet there is uncertainty about the ethical appropriateness of implementing flexible approaches such as waivers of consent with identifiable data or use of exemptions. Conceptual clarity is needed about the ethical rationale for regulation; then regulatory flexibility can be used with greater assurance of ethical acceptability.

Second, there are issues (described below) that are not currently addressed in the Common Rule the must be thought through systematically and could be addressed via voluntary ethical standards. A proactive approach to sensitive issues could help to stave off controversy and lead to a more balanced approach to future guidelines and regulatory change.

Third, a more robust ethical exploration of data research ethics will help regulation in various arenas, not only the Common Rule, because there are commonalities across data activities that should lead to harmonized standards. For example, protection of data confidentiality in program evaluation, healthcare, and educational settings is also important. Professional standards should be developed or existing standards strengthened for data security measures, for responsible and limited sharing of data, and for training of researchers in appropriate practices. While there are some regulatory standards addressing data privacy, such as HIPAA, a consistent ethical framework for use of all data would instill a culture of responsible conduct across diverse areas of programmatic and research activity, including Big Data research in which future identifiability is uncertain.

Fourth, and perhaps most important, public trust is a key element of maintaining an effective research enterprise. Individual informed consent is not the optimal means to promote public trust due to the limited amount that the public actually learns about the conduct of research. Ethical guidelines need to not only take a principled approach to addressing privacy concerns and research needs but also need to include transparency and communication standards to enable public awareness, discussion, and debate about research.

16.5.2 Revisiting the Rationale for the Regulation of Research with Data

The ethical concerns related to research with data, including Big Data, can be divided into three categories: those related to privacy of individuals, those related to group harms from research, and those related to larger social processes, for example, effects on public trust or cooperation with research institutions. Privacy concerns are the only category directly addressed in the Common Rule, yet, as noted, these ethical tensions are not unique to research with data and arise in diverse activities with data. Moreover, the existing requirements for consent and IRB review do not necessarily secure privacy for individuals whose data are used. Therefore, the regulation of data use ought to be systematically organized according to rational criteria that address (1) reducing likelihood of breach, (2) ensuring that responsible practitioners are the only ones with access, (3) ensuring that projects are designed with sound methodology addressing socially valuable goals, and (4) ensuring a level of transparency and communication appropriate to the activity.

A new set of ethical guidelines for data research, including Big Data studies, could address the full array of ethical responsibilities related to the design, conduct of, and communication about research studies. A set of standards was proposed by the IOM committee addressing research and HIPAA,[25] which addressed health research and made the following recommendations:

- All researchers should be required to follow the same set of privacy rules.
- Whenever possible, information-based research should be done using health data with direct identifiers removed.
- Access to personally identifiable health data without patient consent should require impartial, outside scientific, and ethical review that considers
  ○ Measures taken to protect the privacy, security, and confidentiality of the data;
  ○ Potential harms that could result from disclosure of the data; and
  ○ Potential public benefits of the research.
- Researchers should identify and document research objectives to justify the data they wish to use and/or collect.
- Researchers, institutions, and organizations that store personally identifiable health data should establish security safeguards and set limits on access to data.
- Researchers who violate individuals' privacy should be penalized.

[25] Nass, ed., *Beyond the HIPAA Privacy Rule*.

Each of these points is perfectly valid in the Big Data context and could be incorporated into ethical guidelines for Big Data research regardless of whether or not the research is deemed to fall within the scope of the Common Rule.[26] In addition, due to the critical issues of public trust involved in the use of digital data from novel and diverse sources, researchers should develop good communication plans regarding their research objectives, the potential value of the research activity, the implications of research findings, and opportunities for discussion and clarification with relevant stakeholders. These activities will also help to address the potential for group harms from data research. In sum, a new ethical framework for handling research with Big Data may help to address the fundamental flaws in the current system of regulation of data research under the Common Rule.

With Big Data research, the impossibility of true anonymization, along with the challenges of inadequate notice and consent, means that traditional research protections will not suffice. Also, in most cases, traditional requirements such as individual informed consent are simply impossible. In the increasingly complex research environment, fundamentally, the secondary use of individual-level data for research projects and nonresearch uses should be subject to the same basic ethical requirements: (1) each project should have a defined purpose and methodology that serves a socially valuable goal, as determined by well-informed experts in the same field, (2) data-protection measures should be in place for all instances of data access, analysis, or transfer, (3) data obtained for a project should never be transferred to or shared with unauthorized parties, (4) investigators should make no attempts to reidentify individuals in the course of the research project, (5) investigators or other practitioners must be adequately trained in both scientific methods and ethical safeguards for use of data, (6) information about the process and outcomes of research (or other activity) should be reasonably accessible to the public through publicly available websites, and (7) when research process or research findings have the potential to raise public concern due to the nature of the topic or research question, public consultation and community engagement should be instigated prior to initiating the project. Note that informed consent and IRB review are not part of this scheme. These proposed protective measures should be more effective than the Common Rule in addressing the most salient concerns in the Big Data environment. It is also significant that determinations about identifiability of data sets or whether data are truly public versus private would no longer be pertinent to the ethical oversight process because uniform protections would apply in all cases.

The value of having a uniform set of standards for research and nonresearch activities with data that are identifiable or may become identifiable at some point through analytical procedures is that there will be no incentive to skirt the research

---

[26] Similar recommendations were made in Charles Safran et al., Toward a National Framework for the Secondary Use of Health Data: An American Medical Informatics Association White Paper, 14 *J. Am. Med. Inform. Assoc.* 1 (2007).

regulations, and an increase in transparency of the process will serve to allay public fears about misuse of data. This approach will also allay fears of regulators that allowing Big Data projects will result in researchers posing new types of risks to members of the public. Research sponsors could institute this kind of policy as terms and conditions of awards; institutions or professional societies could likewise adopt these standards. This oversight scheme could help to advance important scientific inquiry while maintaining the highest ethical standards and enhancing public trust.

17

Big Data, HIPAA, and the Common Rule

Time for Big Change?

Margaret Foster Riley

17.1 INTRODUCTION

The Health Insurance Portability and Accountability Act (HIPAA)[1] was a laudable attempt to get in front of developing issues with health privacy and the networking of data. But it was too early, now out of date, and way too complicated. We now operate in a world of networked medicine, ideally combining social networks, disease networks (human disease associations, especially those based on genomic characteristics), and pathophysiologic networks (physiologic and biochemical characteristics of disease). A tremendous amount of useful data may come from sources outside the typical health record. For example, pharmaceutical and laboratory research and development (R&D) data and patient behavior and preferences may be found outside the HIPAA firewall. Those data may be more actionable than the medical record.

Fundamental characteristics of Big Data challenge the structure of how we regulate human subjects research, the impact of HIPAA, and how we think of healthcare itself. The analysis of Big Data related to healthcare is often for a different purpose than the purpose for which the data were originally collected. This challenges notions of meaningful consent – or even what consent might mean. The volume of data used for Big Data purposes means that it comes from many sources, often outside the purview of any oversight. In addition, none of the current regulations deal with issues of ownership. These data have rapidly increasing commercial use, and individuals assign ownership of their data to commercial entities without much thought. At the same time, regulations impose inconsistent and sometimes onerous obligations on researchers.

Big Data really begs for a comprehensive, nonsectoral approach. HIPAA imposes a tangled web of regulation that hampers the use of healthcare data, especially their use with data from other sources. This requires us to fully examine the question: are

---

[1] Pub. L. No. 104–191, 110 Stat. 1936 (1996) (codified as amended in scattered sections of the US Code).

data derived from healthcare interactions really different from other personal data? How can or should we move beyond HIPAA to both protect individuals from risk borne by improper use of healthcare data and make those data more freely available for research?

17.2 BIG DATA IN HEALTHCARE RESEARCH

Traditional health research is conducted through controlled clinical trials. Researchers start with a hypothesis and develop a protocol to prove – or disprove – it. The population involved, the interventions, and the timing are all set in the protocol. While the trial may involve many sites, even the largest clinical trials involve only thousands of people. This is still the "gold standard" for medical research. For example, Food and Drug Administration (FDA) drug approvals generally require at least two adequately controlled trials.[2] Even larger projects that are designed to answer big questions in medicine often involve researchers working in parallel, not together. Of course, clinical trials have never been the only kind of health research; we have a long history of epidemiologic research involving large cohorts. But even those are small by Big Data standards.[3]

This changes significantly with Big Data. Much of the data used in Big Data research were generated for some other purpose. "Big Data" has been defined as "large volumes of high-velocity, complex, and variable data that require advanced techniques and technologies to enable the capture, storage, distribution, management and analysis of the information."[4] In the context of health data, much of those data are expected to come from expanded use of electronic health records (EHRs) – and scholars speak instead of "longitudinal health records" (LHRs), which track an individual's health encounters over time with disparate parts of the health system, and "longitudinal population health data" (LPHD), which combine the data of many LHRs.[5] Such data sets are themselves challenging.

So how does Big Data change health research? One way is in the volume of data involved. Big Data is ... bigger. Big Data means working together – not just across institutions, but perhaps across nations. Some studies may involve the data of hundreds of thousands – or even millions – of people. In addition, the type and sources of data that may be involved are potentially much broader. Such data include conventional types of health data – electronic medical records, medical

---

[2] See Federal Food, Drug, and Cosmetic Act, 21 U.S.C. §§ 505(d), 355(d) (2012).
[3] See, e.g., *The Framingham Heart Study: A Project of the National Heart, Lung, and Blood Institute and Boston University* (2017), available at www.framinghamheartstudy.org/participants/original.php [https://perma.cc/E9CR-6KGL].
[4] Wullianallur Raghupathi & Viju Raghupathi, Big Data Analytics in Healthcare: Promise and Potential, 2 *Health Info. Sci. Syst.* (2014), available at https://hissjournal.biomedcentral.com/articles/10.1186/2047-2501-2-3 [https://perma.cc/JRU2-TCT3].
[5] See Barbara J. Evans, Much Ado about Data Ownership, 25 *Harv. J.L. Tech.* 69, 91 (2011).

images, and clinical biospecimens – but they might also go much further. In fact, Big Data's true potential is likely to be realized by combining traditional health data with new forms of data.[6] Thus such data would likely also include pharmaceutical R&D data, including data amassed prior to clinical trials or data amassed in prior clinical trials. They might also include data acquired by outside laboratories through decades of testing. They might include claims and cost data acquired by payers and insurers. Census data and Social Security data can be particularly powerful. They might include data relating to individuals' education, social media indicators of patient behavior and sentiment, data in consumer outlets such as Ancestry.com, environmental data, retail purchases, and most recently, data amassed by wearable technology. Much – in fact, most – of these data reside with entities that are *not* covered by federal privacy law governing health data. But they are certainly actionable health data. In fact, just grocery loyalty cards and wearable technology may well have far more actionable data than a typical EHR.

More than $300 billion in savings in healthcare expenditures per year could be realized via Big Data, through comparative effectiveness research and evidence-based medicine, better targeting of R&D in the drug pipeline, better clinical trial design, improved public health tracking and response, genomic analysis as part of the individual medical record, targeted patient analysis to determine needs for preventive care or behavioral changes, and safety monitoring and adverse-event prevention through real-time device monitoring.[7] And of course, those results have significant value – namely, improved population health – which is even more important than cost savings.

17.3 CHALLENGES FOR BIG DATA USE IN HEALTHCARE RESEARCH

There are, however, significant challenges in gathering and using healthcare Big Data. Even the most obvious data sources are not standardized. For example, there are a number of EHR platforms, and these platforms are not readily compatible, even when offered by the same provider. Similarly, only some data held in the biopharmaceutical industries are readily available for open research use, and it may not be in the interests of individual companies to make those data immediately usable. There are issues of how to develop appropriate analytical platforms and whether such platforms will be open source or proprietary.[8] Nonetheless, because of

---

[6] Basel Kayyali et al., *The Big-Data Revolution in US Health Care: Accelerating Value and Innovation* (2013), available at www.mckinsey.com/industries/healthcare-systems-and-services/our-insights/the-big-data-revolution-in-us-health-care [https://perma.cc/5DTT-PHHJ].
[7] See Raghupathi & Raghupathi, Big Data Analytics in Healthcare; James Manyika et al., *Big Data: The Next Frontier for Innovation, Competition, and Productivity* (2011), available at www.mckinsey.com/business-functions/digital-mckinsey/our-insights/big-data-the-next-frontier-for-innovation [https://perma.cc/K48J-7W9Z].
[8] See Raghupathi & Raghupathi, Big Data Analytics in Healthcare.

the value of these data, new players have arisen in the commercial sector to gather, aggregate, and standardize health data. For example, major health insurers have created analytics divisions that provide data analytics to outside entities. In 2012, ten pharmaceutical companies formed TransCelerate Biopharma, a nonprofit consortium that has established some best practices in clinical trial design and implementation and is developing industry-wide data standards.[9] IMS Health is well known as having amassed the largest repository of physician prescribing data, but IMS is also involved in data mining social media, EHRs, and multiple other sources in its health data aggregation processes.[10] IBM has recently made a robust move into the Big Data healthcare space with Watson Health, which combines personal, academic, and industry data to provide new insights into care options.[11]

One of the biggest challenges for Big Data in this context is linking data from multiple sources so that data describing an individual located in one source are linked with data about the same individual in other sources. This is difficult to do in the context of traditional health records located in multiple institutions; it is even more difficult to link different kinds of data. Such linkages require some identifiers to prevent errors, but use of identifiers may increase privacy concerns. There are no consistent rules about appropriate use of identifiers and security across data sources.

Through healthcare Big Data, it may be possible to reveal information about individuals that they and their healthcare providers do not know themselves. For example, aggregated data may reveal increased risks for developing certain diseases or conditions. While there are legal restrictions on how such knowledge may be used by an insurance company or a healthcare provider,[12] there is relatively little protection for information amassed by other commercial sectors. In fact, the Supreme Court likely limited potential protections that might have been placed on commercial sectors when it ruled that the acquisition of such data did not pose significant privacy risks and was protected speech under the First Amendment.[13] But because it is so difficult – and expensive – to gather these data, the larger projects are taking place in the commercial sector rather than in traditional research frameworks. Much of these data can be accumulated without an

---

[9] Dalvir Gill, Re-Inventing Clinical Trials through TransCelerate, 13 *Nat. Rev. Drug Discovery* 787–88 (2014), available at www.nature.com/nrd/journal/v13/n11/full/nrd4437.html [https://perma.cc/2QLV-9E3A].

[10] Adam Tanner, This Little-Known Firm Is Getting Rich Off Your Medical Data, *Fortune*, February 9, 2016, available at http://fortune.com/2016/02/09/ims-health-privacy-medical-data [https://perma.cc/CC3Y-7ZLT].

[11] Laura Lorenzetti, Here's How IBM Watson Health Is Transforming the Health Care Industry, *Fortune*, April 5, 2016, available at http://fortune.com/ibm-watson-health-business-strategy [https://perma.cc/VN6N-8HGD].

[12] See, e.g., National Association of Insurance Commissioners, NAIC Privacy of Consumer Financial and Health Information Model Regulation: Frequently Asked Questions (2001), available at www.naic.org/documents/prod_serv_legal_pcf_op.pdf [https://perma.cc/7PQQ-TQCR].

[13] *Sorrell v. IMS Health Inc.*, 564 U.S. 552 (2011).

individual's consent, and even where technical consent is sought, there is little evidence that consumers are paying close attention.[14]

In the meantime, Big Data means that more individuals' health information may be compromised. As the framers of HIPAA correctly anticipated, while a paper record can be kept behind lock and key, networked data can be hacked. But the issues exceed those that were envisioned at the time the legislation was passed. With Big Data, sufficient data can be acquired so that it may possible to identify the source of the data even when much of the data have been stripped of identifiers.[15] Moreover, the acquisition of such data has itself become "big business," and there is also a significant black market. In fact, on the black market, health data are more valuable than credit-card data because they are just as valuable for fraudulent purposes but less likely to be detected.[16] Most of these data are obtained through hacking vulnerable medical systems that have not kept up with the latest security protections. It is important to recognize, however, that the motivation for such hacking seems not to be the nature of the data but the identifiers that can be obtained. Most hacking is motivated by financial fraud; the hackers seek that information so that they can file false health claims.[17] But they are relatively uninterested in what the individual whose record is hacked might consider private or confidential health information.[18]

17.4 HISTORY OF HIPAA AND BIOMEDICAL RESEARCH

The Privacy Rule commonly known as HIPAA was passed in 1996.[19] At that time, the Internet was just taking off, but electronic transmission of health information was already occurring. The original goal of HIPAA was to create uniform electronic healthcare transaction codes. But as electronic transmission of data was contemplated, the growing risks to privacy were already apparent. The Privacy Rule was part

---

[14] University of California Berkeley School of Information, KnowPrivacy 11 (2009), available at http://knowprivacy.org/report/KnowPrivacy_Final_Report.pdf [https://perma.cc/ U36J-TJUA].
[15] See, e.g., Paul Ohm, Broken Promises of Privacy: Responding to the Surprising Failure of Anonymization, 57 *UCLA L. Rev.* 1701 (2010); Khaled El Eman et al., A Systematic Review of Re-Identification Attacks on Health Data, *PLoS ONE*, December 2011, available at http://journals.plos.org/plosone/article?id=10.1371/journal.pone.0028071 [https://perma.cc/ ZP5W-ZEK8].
[16] Caroline Humer & Jim Finkle, Your Medical Record Is Worth More to Hackers than Your Credit Card, Reuters (September 24, 2014), available at www.reuters.com/article/us-cybersecurity-hospitals-idUSKCN0HJ21I20140924 [https://perma.cc/5DW5-C76V].
[17] Ibid.
[18] The exception, of course, is celebrity health records, which are improperly accessed frequently. See, e.g., Charles Ornstein, Celebrities' Medical Records Tempt Hospital Workers to Snoop, NPR (December 10, 2015, 10:20 AM), available at www.npr.org/sections/health-shots/2015/12/10/458939656/celebrities-medical-records-tempt-hospital-workers-to-snoop [https:// perma.cc/4SPP-XTSJ].
[19] Pub. L. 104–191, 110 Stat. 1936 (codified as amended in scattered sections of the *US Code*).

of that. On the one hand, the drafters of HIPAA were remarkably prescient: the HIPAA Privacy Rule anticipates the existence of new privacy concerns that would develop through electronic communication. At the same time, the drafters of HIPAA could not know what was to come, and they therefore could not anticipate the character of those concerns or the best way to deal with them. It is worth remembering the state of the Internet in 1996. Amazon was just starting, and it sold only books. The primary use of the Internet by most people – and most people did not have access to the Internet – was e-mail. The "cloud" did not exist. Even when the Privacy Rule regulations were developed a few years later, the Internet was still in relative infancy. Google had just been incorporated; it had not yet become a public company. It took thirteen years to map the human genome, culminating in 2003. Big Data was not yet a "thing."

In addition, most medical records in 1996 existed as paper records. Physicians and hospitals had large chart rooms where they stored patient records. Those records were not digitized, and for most healthcare institutions, the concept of extended EHRs was still in the future.[20] There were aspects of what was to come that could be anticipated by the existing state of the technology. It was already apparent that the quantity of data that could be amassed, and therefore the quantity of data that could be breached, would grow exponentially. It was also apparent that data that heretofore would likely have been out of the reach of anyone other than someone who physically had (or took) access to the files could now be readily accessible by anyone who could access (or breach) the network. It was even apparent that health data would become ever more commercially valuable.

But what was less apparent was how these new technologies, the Internet, and the related ability to create huge integrated data sets might change our notions of privacy. Professor Fred Schauer warned of this possibility in 1998:

> It is easy to explain the rush to erect new legal protections in light of perceived new threats to our privacy. If the new threats are not only to our privacy but also to our concept of privacy, however, then it may be important to know what this transformed concept of privacy turns out to be before we too quickly put in place new laws to protect what may turn out to be yesterday's concept of privacy.[21]

Unfortunately, this is exactly what HIPAA does. While the legislation and implementing regulations address very real issues,[22] for example, the need to provide individuals with more access to and control of their health information and to improve trust in the health systems by bolstering privacy protections – and attempts

---

[20] See Institute of Medicine, *The Computer-Based Patient Record* (1997).
[21] Frederick Schauer, Internet Privacy and the Public-Private Distinction, 38 *Jurimetrics J.* 555, 564 (1998).
[22] These purposes are stated in the implementing regulations, 45 C.F.R. §§ 160, 164, which went into force in 2003.

to do so by creating a national framework that should arguably improve efficiency – they do so in the context of 1996 concepts of health privacy. The definition of what constitutes health information is far narrower than we would conceive of such information today. It includes information about an individual's health, provision of healthcare, or payment for healthcare that is held by a healthcare provider or healthcare payer (a "covered entity") or a business associate of a covered entity.[23] For example, masses of data are collected through wearable technology such as Fitbits, but those data are usually not subject to HIPAA. A great deal of genomic data is held by laboratories and also by entities such as Ancestry.com. Similarly, data held by insurance companies that are not health insurers are not covered by HIPAA. HIPAA's focus is on information collected in traditional medical charts and encounters with healthcare providers in medical contexts. Moreover, the regulations add a complexity that limits rather than enhances efficiency. From the start, this has hampered efforts to use health information for research and quality improvement while leaving commercial use of actionable health data outside the HIPAA confines largely unprotected. Thus HIPAA provides individuals with an appearance of control of their health data, but it is not clear that it actually enhances their privacy interests.

Prior to the implementation of HIPAA, the Common Rule,[24] which governs much of human subjects research conducted in the United States, imposed (and continues to impose) some requirements on the use of health information in research through its risk-mitigation requirements, but there are no specific regulations relating to informational risk in the Common Rule. This does not mean that privacy interests are unprotected under the Common Rule. Privacy risks have always been part of the risk assessment in human subjects research.[25] HIPAA, however, created an overlay on top of the Common Rule that set new rules for the use of protected health information (PHI). But HIPAA does not function as a risk assessment. It imposes rules for accessing and using specific types of information and assumes that if those rules are followed, an individual's health privacy needs will be protected. It is both overregulatory because it makes it very difficult to use data that may have little informational risk and underregulatory because it does not apply to a great deal of data that fall out of the definition of PHI.

While the HIPAA regulations were theoretically designed with research in mind, there is little evidence that there was extensive consultation with actual researchers

---

[23] 42 U.S.C. § 1320d(4) (2012) (defining "health information").
[24] 45 C.F.R. § 46.101 (2016) (Basic HHS Policy for Protection of Human Research Subjects: To What Does This Policy Apply?); ibid. § 46.124 (Basic HHS Policy for Protection of Human Research Subjects: Conditions). See also Federal Policy for the Protection of Human Subjects, 82 Fed. Reg. 7149, 7168–69 (January 19, 2017) (to be codified at 45 C.F.R. part 46).
[25] Ibid. § 46.111(a)(7) (Basic HHS Policy for Protection of Human Research Subjects: Criteria for IRB Approval of Research).

prior to promulgation of the regulations. And the new regulations caused trouble from the beginning. Potentially significant penalties (although at the outset limited funds for enforcement) made institutions very wary, and regulatory guidance was fairly rigid. Soon reports of negative consequences mounted. For example, the American Association of Medical Colleges (AAMC) found that HIPAA regulations had a negative effect on recruitment to clinical research because subjects were confused by an additional and complicated consent demanded by HIPAA, beyond that required for research participation itself.[26] HIPAA requirements made multi-center collaborative research more difficult and weakened data integrity by introducing errors through required deidentification procedures. Researchers worried that these requirements added selection bias and limited data use in the long term.[27] Moreover, accompanying guidance was so confusing that there were plenty of opportunities for procedural error, and the complexity of the regulations meant that there was broad uncertainty about how the regulations should be applied. Even after that confusion was alleviated, the regulations have always required considerable expertise and considerable regulatory burden.[28] Even just accounting for waivers adds significant cost to research. Few researchers are able to find their way through the regulations without significant help from administrators at institutional review and privacy boards.

Finally, HIPAA creates serious barriers for researchers who try to aggregate data across unrelated entities. While HIPAA permits sharing PHI between one or more institutions through "organized healthcare arrangements" (OHCAs), those institutions must be clinically or operationally integrated to qualify. This would not necessarily occur across coordinating research sites. In the absence of OHCAs, aggregating data across sites requires either specific authorization for research use by the source of the data or deidentification of PHI, which makes those data much less useful because it is impossible to track the same individual's data over time or between entities. Moreover, even with the more relaxed rules of the HIPAA Final Rule, which makes secondary research activities using databases feasible,[29] researchers are required to describe the PHI that will be used and give a description of the intended recipients of that PHI. At the same time, the regulations permit those recipients to be unknown. This no longer feels like an authorization, but a notification. The individual whose PHI is being obtained has very limited information about who will use it and how. So it is a notification

---

[26] National Committee on Vital and Health Statistics: Hearing before the Subcommittee on Privacy and Confidentiality, 108th Congress (2003) (statement of Susan Ehringhaus on behalf of the Association of American Medical Colleges).

[27] See, generally, Institute of Medicine, *Beyond the HIPAA Privacy Rule* 199–240 (Sharyl J. Nass et al. eds., 2009).

[28] See ibid.

[29] Until the HIPAA Final Rule, HIPAA regulations required individual authorizations for each specific study. 45 C.F.R. § 164.508(b)(3)(i) and (iii).

that imposes considerable burdens on the researcher but does little to further the privacy interests of the individual involved.

17.5 ATTEMPTS TO AMELIORATE THE REGULATORY BURDEN

Recently, there has been renewed interest in addressing some of the privacy issues in human subjects research. After five years, several attempts, and considerable controversy, the Department of Health and Human Services (HHS) issued a final rule revising the Common Rule at the end of the Obama administration in January 2017.[30] This rule does add some important provisions that address Big Data issues. For example, because the rule's applicability to research with existing data depends on whether the data are private and identifiable, the 2017 revisions add a new process by which agencies must reassess reidentification risks as technology advances and require that the agency determine whether new security and privacy protections are warranted as previously deidentified data become technologically identifiable.[31] The rule also allows a broad consent to be used for secondary research involving information or biospecimens collected for some other activity, under certain conditions.[32] This limits some of the burdens on the researcher while at the same time bringing into question exactly how "informed" a broad consent actually is. The new rule thus does too much and too little. It weakens the individual's scope of consent to use of PHI but does not reduce the regulatory burdens on research use of PHI significantly.

While the Common Rule was being revised by HHS, Congress was simultaneously engaged in its own efforts to reduce the regulatory burden on researchers. There is, however, very little evidence of thoughtful coordination between the agency and legislative endeavors. The House version of the bill that became the Twenty-First Century Cures Act[33] would have allowed largely unfettered research use of PHI by reclassifying research as "operations," thus removing research use of PHI from HIPAA authorization requirements. This certainly would have made research use of PHI much simpler, but it would have done so by ignoring the privacy interests of the individuals whose data were being used. This provision was dropped from the final version of the bill, but no middle ground was proposed in its stead. There were no new attempts to address the problems with HIPAA in a way that would have preserved privacy interests. The final version of the law addresses privacy interests with a renewed focus on certificates of confidentiality

---

[30] Federal Policy for the Protection of Human Subjects, 82 *Fed. Reg.* 7149, 7168–69 (January 19, 2017) (to be codified at 45 C.F.R. part 46).
[31] Ibid., at 7191.
[32] Ibid.
[33] H.R. 6, 114th Congress (2015).

that do not seem to add any protections to existing law and that may even encourage greater burdens on researchers.[34]

17.6 A PATCHWORK SYSTEM OF PRIVACY LAWS

There are no overarching privacy laws that apply to data in the United States. Federal regulation, to the extent that it exists, is largely sector specific. The best known of these regulatory structures is probably HIPAA. For financial data, the Fair Credit Reporting Act[35] and the Gramm-Leach-Bliley Act[36] add privacy protections. In education, the Family Educational Rights and Privacy Act of 1974[37] (FERPA) applies. A patchwork of laws that cover specific issues, for example, the Telephone Consumer Protection Act of 1991,[38] also exists. For most of these, the Federal Trade Commission (FTC) is the major regulator, but there are overlapping authorities. In addition, other laws, such as those governing employment, for example, the Americans with Disabilities Act of 1990[39] (ADA) and Title VII of the Civil Rights Act of 1964,[40] may have implications for data use and protection. Finally, there are many state laws that apply, which may or may not be preempted by federal law depending on the circumstances.

This means that meaningful Big Data health research implicates many different laws that have different requirements. For example, health information in educational records would be covered by FERPA; employment records that may include health data may be covered by the ADA. Health information acquired directly from consumers may be governed only by state law. A quick examination of just the different requirements of HIPAA versus FERPA – regulations that cover data that might be extremely useful if combined in a Big Data project – demonstrates the complexity. For example, FERPA applies just to educational entities that receive funds from the Department of Education; HIPAA applies to any health provider, plan, or clearinghouse that transmits health information electronically. Thus HIPAA is at once broader and narrower than FERPA. HIPAA has a public health exception; FERPA does not. FERPA and HIPAA have different deidentification requirements: FERPA specifically states that deidentified data cannot be possible to reidentify through combination with other data sources. HIPAA and FERPA have different rules for the control and security of the data maintained by the affected entities. While this may be good for the lawyers who are hired

---

[34] 21st Century Cures Act, Pub. L. No. 114–255 (2016).
[35] 15 U.S.C. §§ 1681–1681x (2012).
[36] Pub. L. No. 106–102, 113 Stat. 1338 (1999) (codified in scattered sections of 12 and 15 U.S.C.).
[37] 20 U.S.C. § 1232g (2006 & Supp. V 2011).
[38] 47 U.S.C. § 227 (2012).
[39] 42 U.S.C. § 12,101 (2012).
[40] Ibid., § 2000e–2000e-17.

to navigate through this tangled web of laws, there is little evidence that it enhances privacy, and it certainly stymies research use of the data.

17.7 SOLUTIONS TO ENHANCE BIG DATA USE IN RESEARCH

Any rational data privacy scheme includes three considerations: ownership, control that does not have ownership characteristics,[41] and protection from the consequences of a breach or attempted breach. Common law and federal and state antidiscrimination laws are focused on the latter, but it is not clear that individuals are fully protected by those laws. Most American and European law on data privacy focuses on control but does not confer true property rights on the individual described by the data.[42] Those laws require notice or warnings that an individual's data are being gathered and how they might be used, but the property rights are usually conferred on the entity that holds the data once those notice requirements are met. In most cases, the individual is permitted to opt out of having his or her data used, but the price of that opt out is often that the person then cannot use a service or product that is far more valuable to him or her than his or her concern about privacy at that moment. Few people read the ubiquitous and lengthy privacy statements that abound on so many websites; most users happily click "agree" with no knowledge of what they are giving away.[43] Those same people, however, may be very wary when asked to share their healthcare data for a research study. It feels to them like they are giving away much more – and in those situations, the rules require not just notice but consent. But this differential approach is not consistent with the privacy issues that are actually at stake.

HIPAA was created to foster the confidential relationship between a patient and his or her physician. The data acquired through that relationship were largely contiguous with the potential actionable health information that described that individual. By protecting those data, one could assume that an individual's health information was protected and that, in turn, there was improved trust between patient and physician. But, as we have noted, in the era of Big Data, what a patient tells his or her physician and the data acquired during a conventional healthcare encounter are now a fragment of the full data profile of any individual's health. HIPAA underprotects privacy interests because it does not protect much of the data that describe any individual. Worse, it creates an illusion of protection.

---

[41] The FTC describes this process as "Notice/Awareness" and "Choice/Consent." Fred H. Cate, Protecting Privacy in Health Research: The Limits of Individual Choice, 98 *Cal. L. Rev.* 1765, 1768 (2010).
[42] Ibid.
[43] US Federal Trade Commission, Protecting Consumer Privacy in an Era of Rapid Change 8–9 (2010), available at www.ftc.gov/os/2010/12/101201privacyreport.pdf [https://perma.cc/7T3M-YMQ4].

What we need now is a solution that protects privacy, fosters confidentiality, and allows the free flow of data for public good. We should unbundle privacy and confidentiality solutions; privacy and confidentiality are not the same. Confidentiality focuses on the health provider–patient relationship. It can be promoted best by focusing rules around that relationship. In contrast, privacy concerns are how to protect the collection, storage, and use of intimate data.[44] HIPAA protects neither well.

Professor Barbara Evans has broached the notion of treating health data as a public good and has argued for appropriate use of the state's police power to create national or regionally scaled data networks that would include nonconsensual health data access for public use.[45] But even though Evans' argument is already controversial, it does not go far enough. As we have already demonstrated, the lines between what constitutes health data and other personal information are increasingly blurred. Instead of having HIPAA, FERPA, literally hundreds of specific state laws, and others, we need a national system that at least imposes similar rules for similar contexts.

Data have become the most valuable commodity of the twenty-first century. It makes sense to make data generated with the help of public funds more available for public use. We already do this for some public health information, but vast amounts of useful health, education, and financial data are buried behind complex and out-of-date privacy laws. Those laws were created with the best of intentions. They were designed to protect individuals from privacy incursions that might injure them and to promote trust in the systems involved. But the data uses of those systems have merged, and the privacy protections have not.

What might make more sense would be to separate the responsibility to maintain confidentiality within those systems and the responsibilities to collect, store, secure, and determine appropriate uses of personal information. Thus, for example, healthcare providers would continue to have an obligation to maintain confidentiality and secure data that are kept for the healthcare needs of their patients, but collection, storage, and use determinations for secondary use of data would be turned over to separate trusted entities, which could be private or government based and which would make data available for public research use. Those trusted entities could develop repositories that combine all sorts of personal information from many sources and use standardized formats that would allow greater interoperability. They could develop data-protection plans that are based on actual risk stratification – and amend those plans as risks change. As experts in the field, they can also develop better and more nimble technological solutions for securing the data than are currently available.

---

[44] See Institute of Medicine, Beyond the HIPAA Privacy Rule, at 199–240.
[45] Barbara J. Evans, Congress' New Infrastructural Model of Medical Privacy, 84 *Notre Dame L. Rev.* 585, 596–97 (2009); Evans, Much Ado about Data Ownership, at 120–30; see also David Blumenthal, Characteristics of a Public Good and How They Are Applied to Healthcare Data, in Institute of Medicine, *Clinical Data as the Basic Staple of Health Learning* 139 (2010).

For individuals to trust such a system, we would also need more robust antidiscrimination laws. For example, people would need to be assured that the data shared could not be used against them in contexts such as obtaining affordable healthcare, employment, or education. Since we also know that some individuals do not wish to share their data even when provided privacy guarantees, those people should be provided with the ability to opt out.

Big Data has a great deal of promise, but it can only realize that promise if large public multifactoral functional databases can be created. At the same time, we need to make sure that certain individuals are not harmed for the greater good, especially when they are ill equipped to predict those harms. Our current system of separate sectoral privacy laws is no longer working. It is time for Big Change.

PART VI

Big Data, FDA, and Liability Considerations

INTRODUCTION

Jerry Avorn

The dramatically increasing availability of "Big Data" – terabytes of information on all aspects of healthcare delivery and outcomes – is transforming medicine on many fronts: outcomes research, clinical decision making, program management and evaluation, regulation, and litigation. The evolution began when each item of medical care, from prescriptions to devices, office visits to intensive-care-unit stays, began to be recorded digitally. This was not done to meet the needs of researchers, economists, doctors, patients, or lawyers; it was done primarily for billing purposes, to make sure that all goods and services delivered were paid for efficiently. Eventually, the data became available for all the secondary uses one could imagine. The following three chapters examine three different facets of this transformational change.

Sarpatwari et al. in Chapter 18 consider the foundational issues related to privacy in this all-digital environment. They address key questions of how identifiable a given data element is and what risks its use poses to patients whose privacy was hitherto shrouded in impenetrable masses of hard-to-track paper records. The chapter comprehensively addresses the epistemological puzzle of what "identifiable" means and what can be done to protect confidential information. This is vital because we as doctors, patients, policymakers, and citizens truly need all the data we can legitimately get our hands on to better define the benefits, risks, comparative effectiveness, and costs of different therapeutic interventions, from diabetes drugs to pacemakers to artificial hips. Much attention is appropriately devoted, in the chapter and in the world it describes, to the security of various strategies for the protection of privacy and what safeguards are needed to preserve confidentiality. This is essential work because it is clear that at the time of approval of a new drug or device, there is often not enough information about rare or long-term risks, for which such observational research is not just the best but often the only means of discovery. And head-to-head comparisons of similar treatments, long ago abandoned as a core research agenda of the federal government, are now most likely to be conducted by such epidemiological research on very large data sets.

Keeping such data secure is vital, but in the strange new world of healthcare policy we have entered, it is also useful to ask which presents the greater threat to patients' privacy: implausible attempts at "re-identification" of peoples' names and addresses by rogue epidemiologists, or health insurance companies seeking to ferret out evidence of a preexisting condition whose costly care may not have to be covered?

Senger and O'Leary in Chapter 19 tackle a separate but no less fascinating aspect of Big Data: the evaluation and regulation of computer-based decision-support systems that draw on this massive information to make recommendations about clinical care decisions. Will the software-computer packages that are increasingly offering up such recommendations best be regulated as a kind of device or left unregulated as compendia of expert opinion? In this regard, they resemble the "singularity" that futurists and technophiles love to tell us about: the acceleration of computing capacity that will transform everything and leave our mere human minds behind in the dust, unless they're equipped with a USB port. We're not there yet, but at a time in which a computer has been able to beat the best players not just of chess but also of the far more complex game of Go, that future is likely coming at us fast.

To the extent that such clinical advice comes from identifiable algorithms built on knowable sets of data and probabilities, algorithms can be evaluated by actual people for accuracy and utility. But when the day comes (and it will soon) that the box is truly and opaquely black, this will raise important regulatory challenges. The authors point out the various strategies that public health authorities such as the Food and Drug Administration (FDA) could apply to determine whether these information interventions, like their metal and molecular cousins, are truly safe and effective. Again, current events intrude: at a time when the administration and Congress are calling for less and less regulation of drugs and devices by the FDA, what are the prospects for thoughtful assessment and control of this new kind of "doc-in-the-box"? The politically popular but inane recommendation made by some recent contenders for the job of FDA Commissioner – to allow new products to enter into widespread use with few barriers and then let the market decide what works and what doesn't – will be just as problematic for decision-support tools as it would be for drugs and devices.

Inevitably, even in the best of all worlds, problems will occur following the recommendations made by these new "electronic doctors." And then what? Price considers the legal similarities and differences between decisions made by Big Data/black-box algorithmic care versus those made by flesh-and-blood doctors. Who would be responsible for vetting the accuracy of machine-generated clinical decisions and who would be to blame if they go wrong? The logic underlying many basic clinical decision-support systems at present is knowable and auditable. But if we enter an era in which (as IBM assures us we will) "the computer" will draw on all known medical knowledge as well as all of a patient's medical history and genetic makeup and then prescribe a treatment plan, who's responsible for any adverse consequences? And conversely, who will be liable if adverse consequence could have been avoided if such computational tools were used in the first place? At a time when it's still often difficult to get to see the results of a cardiogram taken a month ago at another hospital across the street, such worries may seem premature. But change is proceeding at an exponential pace, and the issues that Price raises in Chapter 20 will be upon us before you can say "Watson."

Taken together, these three chapters provide a solid and provocative grounding in the legal, clinical, policy, and ethical issues that we are beginning to face as medical care becomes increasingly immersed in a nearly incomprehensible abundance of data. Fasten your safety belts.

18

Data Sharing that Enables Postapproval Drug and Device Research and Protects Patient Privacy

Best Practice Recommendations

Ameet Sarpatwari, Bradley A. Malin, Aaron S. Kesselheim, Joshua J. Gagne, and Sebastian Schneeweiss*

18.1 INTRODUCTION

The rise of Big Data has created an unprecedented opportunity for near-real-time research on prescription drugs and medical devices. Aggregation of data from such high-variety, high-volume, and high-velocity informational assets as insurance claims, electronic medical records (EMRs), and wearable devices can enable more powerful, accurate, and representative studies of therapeutics to guide decision making by physicians and patients.

Turning this promise into reality nevertheless has proved challenging. Federal privacy regulations promulgated under the Health Insurance Portability and Accountability Act (HIPAA)[1] and the Health Information Technology for Economic and Clinical Health (HITECH) Act[2] limit what individually identifiable ("protected") health information (PHI)–covered entities – healthcare providers, insurers, and administrators – and their business associates may share for research purposes without patient authorization (often impractical for high-volume data) or institutional review board (IRB) waiver of patient authorization (potentially time-consuming and conditional on protocol alterations). Important questions persist over how data sharing for prescription drug and medical device research can be accomplished with minimal risk to patient privacy under these rules.

This chapter lays out in greater detail the promise of enhanced data sharing in observational studies of prescription drugs and medical devices, the ways in which

---

* This work is partially derived from Ameet Sarpatwari, Aaron S. Kesselheim, Bradley A. Malin, Joshua J. Gagne & Sebastian Schneeweiss, Ensuring Patient Privacy in Data Sharing for Post-Approval Research, 371 N. Engl. J. Med. 1644 (2014). Used with permission.
[1] Health Insurance Portability and Accounting Act, Pub. L. No. 104–191, 110 Stat. 2033 (August 21, 1996).
[2] Health Information Technology for Economic and Clinical Health Act, Title XIII of Division A and Title IV of Division B of the American Recovery and Reinvesment Act of 2009, Pub. L. No. 111–5, 123 Stat. 227 (February 17, 2009).

HIPAA and HITECH Act rules limit such data sharing, and the ethical justifications for and against these restrictions. It concludes by proposing an initial set of best practice recommendations that are compliant with the existing regulatory framework.

18.2 THE PROMISE OF BIG DATA IN PHARMACOEPIDEMIOLOGY

Postapproval research on prescription drugs and medical devices is essential to investigate aspects of safety and effectiveness that are not elucidated in the pivotal trials leading to regulatory approval of these products by the Food and Drug Administration (FDA). Preapproval studies cannot answer all safety and effectiveness questions for several reasons, including their frequent exclusion of key segments of the population (e.g., the elderly)[3] and their inability to detect rare but life-threatening adverse events.[4] For example, the Crohn's disease and multiple sclerosis treatment drug natalizumab (Tysabri) was only linked to progressive multifocal leukoencephalopathy, a rare but fatal neurologic condition unseen in two Phase III trials of 942 and 1,171 patients,[5] following FDA approval.[6]

Big Data is poised to enhance postapproval observational research by increasing the breadth, depth, and timeliness of information with which to perform analyses. Repositories of such data include insurance claims, electronic medical records (EMRs), disease registries, and social media.[7] The technical ability to combine these assets presents an opportunity for investigators to study a greater number of individuals with exposures and outcomes of interest, as well as a broader spectrum of potentially relevant contextual variables. Combining insurance claims across multiple payers, for example, can dramatically increase available sample sizes. Similarly, merging EHRs with insurance claims, which poorly capture what transpires during a hospital stay, can help to ensure the uninterrupted patient follow-up necessary for accurate assessments. Multiple institutions have already succeeded in coupling their EHRs with claims data, and a wider effort by the FDA's Sentinel Program

---

[3] Donna M. Zulman et al., Examining the Evidence: A Systematic Review of the Inclusion and Analysis of Older Adults in Randomized Controlled Trials, 26 *J. Gen. Intern. Med.* 783, 786 (2011).
[4] Jonathan J. Darrow, Crowdsourcing Clinical Trials, 98 *Minn. L. Rev.* 805, 810 (2014).
[5] FDA approves Tysabri, Drugs.com (November 23, 2004), available at www.drugs.com/newdrugs/tysabri-approved-multiple-sclerosis-162.html [https://perma.cc/W9YB-GYCR].
[6] Gert Van Assche et al., Progressive Multifocal Leukoencephalopathy after Natalizumab for Crohn's Disease, 353 *N. Engl. J. Med.* 362, 364 (2005); B. K. Kleinschmidt-DeMasters & Kenneth L. Tyler, Progressive Multifocal Leukoencephalopathy Complicating Treatment with Natalizumab and Interferon Beta-1a for Multiple Sclerosis, 353 *N. Engl. J. Med.* 369, 374 (2005); Annette Langer-Gould et al., Progressive Multifocal Leukoencephalopathy in a Patient Treated with Natalizumab, 353 *N. Engl. J. Med.* 375, 380 (2005).
[7] See, generally, Carrie E. Peirce et al., Evaluation of Facebook and Twitter Monitoring to Detect Safety Signals for Medical Products: An Analysis of Recent FDA Safety Alerts, 40 *Drug Safety* 317 (2017); Abeed Sarker et al., Utilizing Social Media Data for Pharmacovigilance: A Review, 54 *J. Biomed. Inform.* 202 (2015).

and the Patient-Centered Outcomes Research Institute is currently underway.[8] Such enhancements can improve statistical power, permit more rigorous confounding adjustment, and enable more detailed subgroup analyses to better understand treatment-effect heterogeneity.

The need for such rapid and robust postapproval research is acute. In recent years, the FDA has approved an increasing number of drugs via expedited review pathways. Some researchers have reported an inverse association between review time and subsequent spontaneous adverse-event reporting.[9] The FDA has additionally approved a greater number of drugs based on surrogate measures of clinical outcomes. However, experience with some widely used surrogate end points has shown that they can be poorly predictive,[10] resulting in exposure of patients to expensive, ineffective, and unsafe therapies. The recently enacted 21st Century Cures Act will only exacerbate this problem by allowing the FDA to accept additional lower-quality safety and efficacy evidence in the process of approving new drugs and medical devices.[11]

Efficient postapproval research through data sharing can also play a critical role in the timely development of individually tailored therapies. A high-value scientific opportunity targeted under the recently launched Precision Medicine Initiative is "the identification of determinants of individual variation in efficacy and safety of commonly used therapeutics,"[12] which will require exceedingly large patient cohorts for which a wide range of variables is available.

18.3 HIPAA PATHWAYS FOR BIG DATA SHARING FOR OBSERVATIONAL RESEARCH

Passed by Congress in 1996, HIPAA required the Department of Health and Human Services (HHS) to establish national privacy and security standards for the use of PHI, which were finalized in 2002 and 2003, respectively. The legislation was in part motivated by concerns over widespread access to PHI and the potential for direct harm to patients related to public disclosure. HIPAA required criminal fines and jail

---

[8] Mary K. Olson, The Risk We Bear: The Effects of Review Speed and Industry User Fees on New Drug Safety, 27 J. Health Econ. 175, 187 (2008).
[9] Joel Lexchin, New Drugs and Safety: What Happened to New Active Substances Approved in Canada between 1995 and 2010?, 172 Arch. Intern. Med. 1680, 1680–1 (2012).
[10] Staffan Svensson et al., Surrogate Outcomes in Clinical Trials, 173 JAMA Intern. Med. 611, (2013).
[11] Ameet Sarpatwari & Michael S. Sinha, The Current 21st Century Cures Act Is Still a Bad Deal for Patients, Health Affairs Blog (November 30, 2016), available at http://healthaffairs.org/blog/2016/11/30/the-current-21st-century-cures-legislation-is-still-a-bad-deal-for-patients/ [https://perma.cc/N3K6-KJAM].
[12] Precision Medicine Initiative Working Group, The Precision Medicine Initiative Cohort Program: Building a Research Foundation for the 21st Century (2015), available at www.nih.gov/sites/default/files/research-training/initiatives/pmi/pmi-working-group-report-20150917-2.pdf [https://perma.cc/37GY-57MP].

time for covered entities that obtained or disclosed PHI knowingly, under false pretenses, or with the intent to secure commercial gain or inflict harm. Civil fines were reserved for willful neglect and capped at $25,000 per year.[13] Although HIPAA enumerated penalties for noncompliance, it did not create a private right of action. Thus patients who believe that their PHI has been compromised cannot sue covered entities directly. Instead, they must file complaints with the government, which will conduct an investigation to determine whether enforcement action is warranted.

Enactment of the HITECH Act in 2009 resulted in three changes to this enforcement regime. First, it extended the reach of HIPAA to the business associates of covered entities, defined as an entity that "receives, maintains, or transmits" PHI on behalf of a covered entity. It additionally authorized state attorneys general to bring civil actions on behalf of their constituents. Finally, the HITECH Act significantly increased the range of possible civil penalties for a wider range of noncompliant actions, including unknowing HIPAA breaches, permitting fines up to $1.5 million per year.[14]

HIPAA permits covered entities to share PHI for research without patient authorization or institutional review board (IRB) waiver of authorization under two circumstances: use of a limited data set or deidentification of the data. Deidentification may be achieved by fitting under a "safe harbor" or obtaining an "expert determination." Under institutional policies, these pathways often still necessitate IRB review of the research protocols. However, the review is simplified, expediting the process and limiting the possibility of alterations. This potential is most promising for multicenter investigations, which are often plagued by "inconsistent or ambiguous interpretation of federal regulations, and inefficiencies of review," as well as by changes required by individual IRBs that can "jeopardize the scientific integrity of ... national studies."[15]

18.3.1 Limited Data Set

Under the "limited data set" pathway, covered entities can share PHI that has been stripped of sixteen enumerated types of identifiers, including unique device identifiers (UDIs) and patient-specific addresses having a greater specificity than a ZIP code, as seen in Table 18.1. Sharing must be accompanied by a data-use agreement (DUA) that names the individuals afforded access and the purposes of use. The agreement must also condition receipt of the data on the limitation of subsequent disclosures, existence of appropriate safeguards, notification of potential breaches of the secure data set, and agreement not to reidentify or to contact patients to whom

---

[13] Health Insurance Portability and Accounting Act.
[14] Health Information Technology for Economic and Clinical Health Act.
[15] Laura Abbott & Christine Grady, A Systematic Review of the Empirical Literature Evaluating IRBs: What We Know and What We Still Need to Learn, 6 J. Empirical Res. Hum. Res. Ethics 3, 5 (2011).

TABLE 18.1 *Limited Data Set: Prohibited Identifiers*

1. Names
2. Postal addresses more specific than ZIP code
3. Telephone numbers
4. Fax numbers
5. E-mail addresses
6. Social Security numbers
7. Medical record numbers
8. Health plan beneficiary numbers
9. Account numbers
10. Certificate/license numbers
11. Vehicle identifiers
12. Device identifiers
13. Web Uniform Resource Locators (URLs)
14. Internet Protocol (IP) addresses
15. Biometric identifiers
16. Full-face photographs

the data correspond.[16] Data shared through this pathway still constitute PHI and therefore must be limited to the amount reasonably required to achieve the research goals – the so-called minimum necessary standard.[17]

18.3.2 *Deidentification via Safe Harbor*

HIPAA deidentification of data may be achieved by a safe harbor, in which data are stripped of sixteen types of identifiers precluded from limited data sets as well as all "elements of dates (except year)" and any other characteristic, code, or number that could be used to identify an individual. In addition, the geographic information that can be shared is limited to the first three digits of a ZIP code. Covered entities must attest that they have no actual knowledge that the remaining data are individually identifiable.[18] Because the deidentified data are no longer PHI, they fall outside of the scope of HIPAA regulation and need not meet the minimum necessary standard.

18.3.3 *Deidentification via Expert Determination*

Data can also be deidentified by having an expert certify that "the risk is very small that the information could be used, alone, or in combination with other reasonably available information ... to identify an individual" and documents the

---

[16] 45 C.F.R. § 164.514(e).
[17] 45 C.F.R. § 164.514(d).
[18] 45 C.F.R. § 164.514(b)(2).

reasoning underlying the determination.[19] There are no formal requirements for what the data must exclude.

In guidance published in 2012,[20] the government specified that experts broadly include individuals with training in statistics, mathematics, or science who have experience using health information deidentification techniques. Their determinations are not required to be indefinite because experts must "assess the expected change of computational capability, as well as access to various data sources" to define the periods over which their determinations are valid. To ensure that the risk of identifying shared data is "very small," the government recommended adoption of an iterative process of risk evaluation and mitigation. If the information to be shared is highly unique, replicable, and traceable given the anticipated recipients and other reasonably available data, experts must work to reduce the risk of identification by recommending the implementation of such tools as data suppression (e.g., the removal of ZIP codes from a database), data generalization (e.g., the abstraction of five-digit ZIP codes to four-digit ZIP codes), and data-use agreements, as shown in Figure 18.1. As with safe harbor sharing, data shared under the "expert determination" pathway are deemed deidentified, removing covered entities from the constraints of the minimum necessary standard.

18.4 APPLICATION OF THE PATHWAYS FOR POSTAPPROVAL RESEARCH

The limited data set, safe harbor, and expert determination pathways have different strengths and limitations in their ability to facilitate postapproval drug and device research. The ideal pathway would maximize utility (i.e., enable efficient transfer of critical information for analyses) while minimizing the risk of reidentification.

18.4.1 Limited Data Set

The chief advantage of the limited data set pathway in conducting postapproval drug and device research is that it permits sharing of precise patient-specific dates of healthcare encounters. Specificity in the timing of events such as treatment initiation, device implantation, and morbidity is necessary to establish temporal relationships, which, in turn, facilitates causal inference.

There are, however, important limitations to limited data sets. Their inability to contain device identifiers could hamper a new and powerful method to trace the

---

[19] 45 C.F.R. § 164.514(b)(1).
[20] Office of Civil Rights, US Department of Health and Human Services, Guidance Regarding Methods for De-Identification of Protected Health Information in Accordance with the Health Insurance Portability and Accountability Act (HIPAA) Privacy Rule, available at www.hhs.gov/ocr/privacy/hipaa/understanding/coveredentities/De-identification/guidance.html [https://perma.cc/L9QA-HFKW] (last visited April 6, 2016).

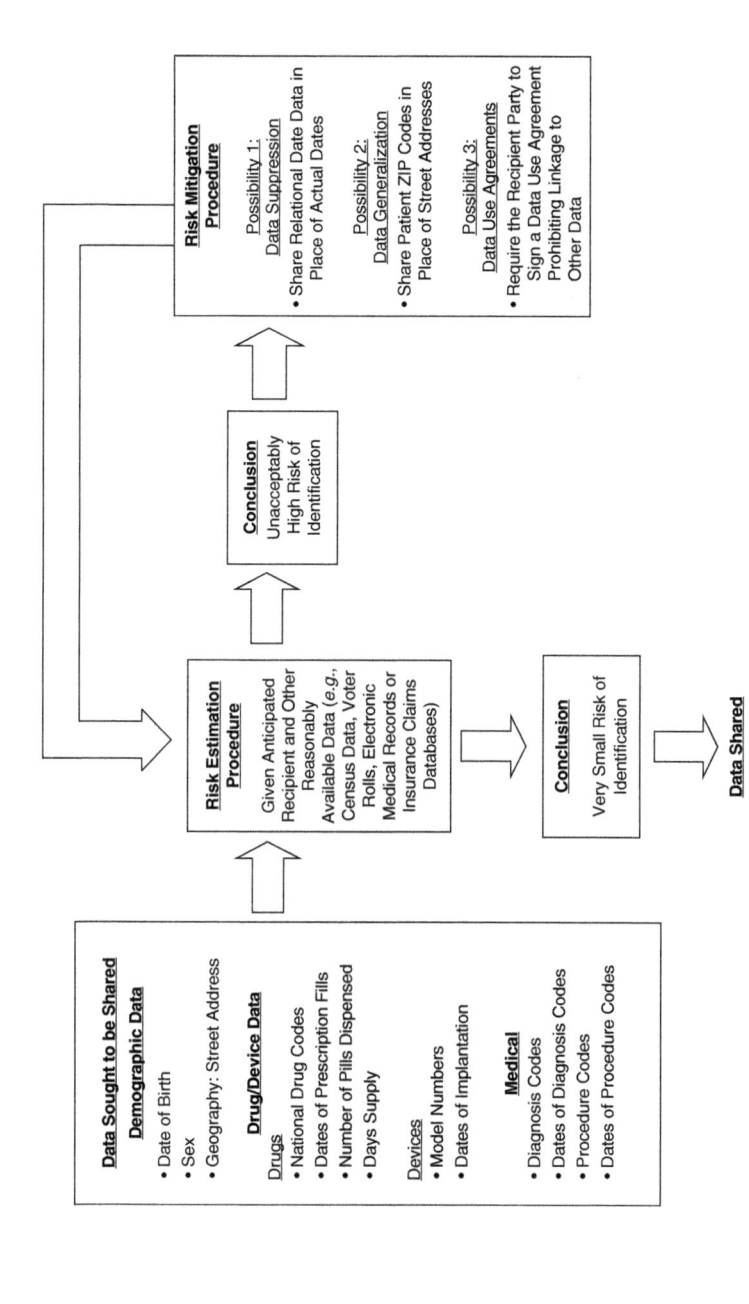

FIGURE 18.1 Illustration of the expert determination pathway in postapproval studies of drugs or devices. Demographic, drug or device, and medical data are necessary for most postapproval investigations. Under the expert determination pathway, an expert certifier will assess the risk of identification posed by data sharing given the anticipated recipient and other reasonably available information and recommend the adoption of risk-mitigation procedures until this risk is "very small."

origins of medical devices and thus to identify batch-specific manufacturing defects. In brief, most medical devices will soon be required to be affixed with a device identifier detailing the specific model or version of the device and a production identifier providing such information as the batch number, manufacturing and expiration dates, and serial number of the device.[21] While it is clear that sharing device serial numbers is precluded under the limited data set pathway, it is uncertain whether the prohibition extends to less unique batch numbers or even less unique model/version numbers supplied through the UDI system. Clarification is needed from HHS on how far the prohibition extends and thus how much it may hinder postmarket device safety studies.

In addition, the limited data set pathway's prohibition on providing patient-specific addresses more specific than a ZIP code prevents investigations of street-level disease burden and drug usage. Using a simulation model, Kamel Boulos et al.[22] visually demonstrated how data aggregation by Census tracts, which generally cover between 1,200 and 8,000 people,[23] can lead to poor spatial patterns of risk. Limited data sets therefore may prove suboptimal for postapproval studies involving narrow clustering of outcomes, such as with infectious diseases. The importance of using street addresses in observational research also extends to situations where socioeconomic confounding is a concern because addresses can serve as proxies for income,[24] which often cannot be directly ascertained from EMRs and insurance claims databases.

Because the information contained within a limited data set is still PHI, covered entities additionally face potential penalties under HIPAA for sharing more than the minimum amount of data necessary. The minimum necessary standard remains vague, with no case law and only minimal guidance explaining it. In the HITECH Act, Congress specified that all limited data sets would be deemed compliant with the minimum necessary standard until HHS provided additional clarification.[25] This guidance is overdue, but once issued, it may substantially affect the applicability of the pathway for postapproval drug and device research.

18.4.2 Deidentification via Safe Harbor

The safe harbor pathway, by contrast, places even greater restraints on postapproval research. Of primary concern is the prohibition on sharing patient-specific dates

---

[21] 78 Fed. Reg. 78:58817 (2013).
[22] Maged N Kamel Boulos et al., Using Software Agents to Preserve Individual Health Data Confidentiality in Micro-Scale Geographical Analyses, 39 J. Biomed. Inform. 160, 161 (2006).
[23] Department of Commerce Census Bureau, Geographic Terms and Concepts: Census Tracts, available at www.census.gov/geo/reference/gtc/gtc_ct.html. [https://perma.cc/N7UV-2N5M] (last visited December 1, 2016).
[24] John Glover et al., Unpacking Analyses Relying on Area-Based Data: Are the Assumptions Supportable?, 3 Int'l J. Health Geogr. 1, 7 (2004).
[25] Health Information Technology for Economic and Clinical Health Act.

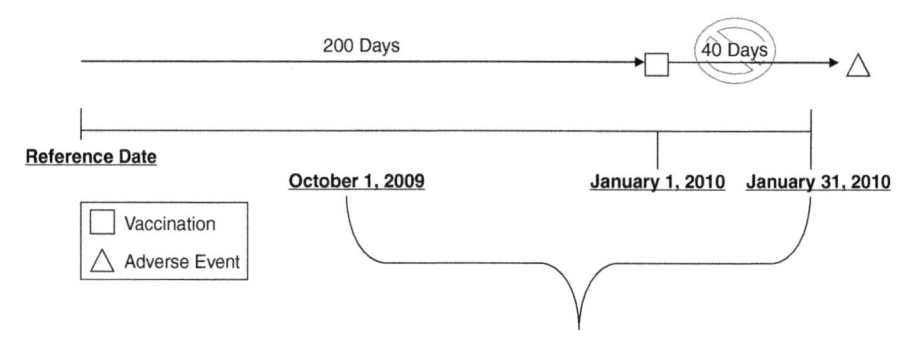

FIGURE 18.2 Example of a violation of the safe harbor pathway's date restriction. Given the study period of October 1, 2009 to January 31, 2010, if a physician informed researchers that Patient A was vaccinated 200 days after a randomly chosen, fixed reference date and experienced an adverse event 240 days after the reference date, the researchers would know that Patient A must have been vaccinated in the second half of 2009. Providing this information would violate the safe harbor, which prohibits covered entities from sharing all elements of patient-specific dates except the year

narrower than a year. In some instances, covered entities can mitigate the restriction by date shifting and truncation[26] or by sharing temporal data divorced from actual dates. For example, informing researchers that a particular patient experienced a myocardial infarction forty days after taking a newly approved drug is normally permitted. Such temporal data sharing is less feasible, however, for postapproval investigations of short duration or long-term collaborations involving routine data updates over short intervals because the recipient party will be able to use the supplied data to infer the date of occurrence of events with greater specificity than a year, violating the safe harbor.

Figure 18.2 illustrates such a scenario, modeling an early postapproval observational investigation of the safety of the influenza A (H1N1) monovalent vaccine (Focetria) in Italy from October 1, 2009, through January 31, 2010. Data for the study were collected from treating physicians in two periods: up to three weeks and between four and six weeks postvaccination.[27] Had patient-specific data been collected through date shifting, recipient researchers would know the date of vaccination with greater specificity than a year for many patients who experienced an adverse event in the second-follow-up period. For example, if a physician reported that a patient suffered acute respiratory failure forty days postvaccination, researchers could deduce that the patient was vaccinated in the latter half of 2009.

---

[26] George Hripcsak et al., Preserving Temporal Relations in Clinical Data While Maintaining Privacy, 23 J. Am. Med. Inform. Assoc. 1040, 1044 (2016).

[27] Silvia Candela et al., An Early (3–6 Weeks) Active Surveillance Study to Assess the Safety of Pandemic Influenza Focetria in a Province of Emilia-Romagna Region, Italy, Part One, 31 Vaccine 1431, 1432 (2013).

The safe harbor pathway would prohibit providers from sharing this time-to-event information in the United States, preventing accurate incidence-rate estimation.

While many current postapproval drug and device studies span a period of three years or more,[28] there is a growing impetus to harness Big Data assets to conduct more rapid investigations. Decreasing the duration of studies will increase the risk of temporal data sharing violating the safe harbor.

Finally, the safe harbor pathway imposes more restrictions on sharing patient-specific addresses than limited data sets. Under the safe harbor pathway, covered entities can only share the first three digits of a ZIP code and then only in circumstances in which the region they encompass has a population greater than 20,000 people. This heightened restriction can hinder production of descriptive information and confound adjustment. For example, under the safe harbor pathway, it would not be possible to perform a study similar to one conducted by Brownstein et al.,[29] who collected patient-specific drug use data within three-digit ZIP code regions – some with fewer than 20,000 inhabitants – to identify the geographic distribution of prescription opioid abuse in New Mexico.

18.4.3 Deidentification via Expert Determination

Deidentification via expert determination offers the most untapped promise for postapproval safety and effectiveness research on prescription drugs and medical devices. Under this pathway, covered entities can tailor the data they share to specific research needs, enabling the transfer of otherwise precluded identifiers. Evidence suggests that statistical certification can be as safe (i.e., less susceptible to identification) as the safe harbor,[30] which is generally safer than a limited data set.[31]

Widespread use of the statistical certification pathway, however, requires the development of currently lacking standards and experts who are willing to certify that the risk of identification is very small. Expert certifiers face no risk of liability under HIPAA. Although the HITECH Act expanded the requirements of HIPAA to the business associates of covered entities, expert certifiers would not fall under this

---

[28] Donnie Funch et al., A Prospective, Claims-Based Assessment of the Risk of Pancreatitis and Pancreatic Cancer with Liraglutide Compared to Other Antidiabetic Drugs, 16 *Diabetes Obesity Metab.* 273, (2014); Gerd R. Burmester et al., Safety and Effectiveness of Adalimumab in Patients with Rheumatoid Arthritis over 5 Years of Therapy in a Phase 3b and Subsequent Postmarketing Observational Study, 16 *Arthritis Res. Ther.* 1, 2 (2014); P. Michael Ho et al., Risk of Adverse Outcomes Associated with Concomitant Use of Clopidogrel and Proton Pump Inhibitors Following Acute Coronary Syndrome, 301 *JAMA* 937, 938 (2009).

[29] John S. Brownstein et al., Geographic Information Systems and Pharmacoepidemiology: Using Spatial Cluster Detection to Monitor Local Patterns of Prescription Opioid Abuse, 19 *Pharmacoepidemiol. Drug Safety* 627, 628 (2010).

[30] Bradley Malin et al., Never Too Old for Anonymity: A Statistical Standard for Demographic Data Sharing Via the HIPAA Privacy Rule, 18 *J. Am. Med. Inform. Assoc.* 3, 7 (2011).

[31] Bradley Malin et al., Evaluating Re-Identification Risks with Respect to the HIPAA Privacy Rule, 17 *J. Am. Med. Inform. Assoc.* 169, 176 (2010).

definition unless they received, maintained, or transmitted PHI. Expert certifiers could, however, face tort action for negligence under state laws because HIPAA implicitly imposes a duty of care on expert certifiers to patients whose data have been shared under the pathway. Given the infancy of the field, the standard of care required of an expert certifier when providing a certification and the cost of gauging the risk of identification incorrectly are unknown.

18.5 ETHICAL CONSIDERATIONS

Health privacy protections under the limited data set, safe harbor, and expert determination pathways vary but are generally strong. Recent high-profile instances of reidentification[32] have not involved HIPAA-limited or deidentified data. A systematic review of reidentification attacks in the published literature, moreover, uncovered only one case involving safe harbor deidentified data, yielding a 0.013 percent risk of reidentification.[33] While the technical ability to reidentify patients is greater with limited data sets, data sharing under the limited data set pathway is conditioned on execution of legally binding DUAs – a powerful risk-mitigation measure.

Such robust privacy protections are in many respects laudable. By granting a large measure of self-control over health information, they respect the moral status of patients as autonomous, rational actors. They also limit the potential for malfeasance – the use of PHI to the detriment of patients. Concern over such misuse is not simply hypothetical; in February 2016, the *Wall Street Journal* reported on the efforts of some companies to use third parties to obtain health information on their employees.[34] Additionally, without the assurance of anonymity, many patients may not feel comfortable disclosing sensitive information necessary for effective healthcare delivery. This reticence would likely result in less and more biased data from which to perform research.

HIPAA's privacy protections, however, are not without controversy. They create additional barriers for postapproval research, which can help to prevent exposure to ineffective or unsafe drugs and devices. The utilitarian justification for enabling efficient conduction of such research stands in inherent tension with the deontological basis for respecting health privacy.

HIPAA also raises equitable concerns. Of note, it leaves unregulated drug companies, data brokers (e.g., IMS Health), and contract research organizations

---

[32] Paul Ohm, Broken Promises of Privacy: Responding to the Surprising Failure of Anonymization, 57 *UCLA L. Rev.* 1701, 1717 (2010); Latanya Sweeney, Matching Known Patients to Health Records in Washington State Data, ArXiv (July 5, 2013), available at http://arxiv.org/abs/1307.1370 [https://perma.cc/Y4M5-P85R].

[33] Khaled El Emam, et al., A Systematic Review of Re-Identification Attacks on Health Data, 6 *PloS ONE* 1, 7 (2011).

[34] Rachel E. Silverman, Bosses Tap Outside Firms to Predict Which Workers Might Get Sick, *Wall Street Journal*, February 17, 2016, available at www.wsj.com/articles/bosses-harness-big-data-to-predict-which-workers-might-get-sick-1455664940 [https://perma.cc/V54S-RVSJ].

(e.g., HealthCore and RTI Health Solutions) that collect patient-level health information in collaboration with and independent of covered entities. One prominent example is so-called match backing, in which data brokers convert patient-level prescription records purchased from pharmaceutical benefits managers into numerical codes and match them with numerical codes of website users to enable targeted drug marketing.[35] In the absence of voluntarily assumed safeguards, it is possible that website owners could know what ads are being delivered to which online users and thus be privy to PHI through this process. It is unclear why noncovered entities should not be subject to the same health data stewardship responsibilities as covered entities.

At present, HIPAA is also rigid. To be effective, data-sharing schemes must be flexible. This is particularly true for observational research on approved drugs and devices because the value of variables differs substantially depending on the product(s) and outcome(s) under evaluation. Geographic data, for example, may be critical for mapping antibiotic use and resistance patterns but offer little value for investigations of the impact of statins on cardiovascular disease burden. The limited data set and safe harbor pathways impose strict rules on what information can be shared, offering no opportunity for study-specific tailoring. While such tailoring is theoretically possible under the expert determination pathway, additional steps are needed to make it more viable.

18.6 INITIAL BEST PRACTICE RECOMMENDATIONS FOR THE EXPERT DETERMINATION PATHWAY

Chief among these steps is the promulgation of additional deidentification standards. Even following 2012 HHS guidance,[36] considerable uncertainty remains over the threshold for a "very small" risk, proper risk ascertainment methods, and effective deidentification techniques. We accordingly propose four initial best practice recommendations.

First, in defining a "very small risk," we recommend that expert certifiers select a threshold that is proportional to the potential harm of reidentification. A recent review uncovered that state agencies in the United States and Canada have adopted a broad range of maximum risk values (i.e., 0.33–0.04) for the disclosure of health data.[37] This knowledge and the explicit statement in the 2012 HHS guidance that

---

[35] Jordan Robertson & Shannon Pettypiece, They Know You Buy Viagra and They Want to Sell You More, Bloomberg (December 10, 2014), available at www.bloomberg.com/news/articles/2014-12-10/they-know-you-buy-viagra-and-they-want-to-sell-you-more [https://perma.cc/HB3P-HQBP].

[36] See Office of Civil Rights, US Department of Health and Human Services, Guidance Regarding Methods for De-Identification of Protected Health Information.

[37] Khaled El Emam & Bradley Malin, Concepts and Methods for De-Identifying Clinical Trial Data, in *Sharing Clinical Trial Data* 231–32 (2015).

there "is no explicit numerical level of identification risk that is deemed to universally meet the 'very small' level indicated by the method"[38] suggest that expert certifiers have considerable discretion in determining what constitutes a very small risk. We believe that it is important for expert certifiers to anchor this discretion on the principle that not all risks are equal. Reidentification of the recipient of a statin, for example, raises on average less potential for harm than reidentification of a methadone user. For this reason, expert certifiers should adopt an equal or lower risk threshold for postapproval assessments of methadone products than of statin products.

To ascertain the risk of reidentification, we recommend that expert certifiers routinely model three so-called attack scenarios. Several factors may fuel reidentification efforts, including "financial interests, (pseudo-) ethical reasons, personal interests, or just curiosity."[39] This range of motivations can generally be accounted for by separately modeling the following types of attackers: prosecutors, who look to reidentify the record of a specific, known individual; journalists, who aim to reidentify any single record in the shared data set; and marketers, who seeks to reidentify as many records as possible.[40] Specifics as to how to model prosecutor, journalist, and market attacks are beyond the scope of this chapter but can be found in several other resources.[41] The expert-certified risk of reidentification should be a composite measure of the risks in each of these three attack scenarios.

Finally, we recommend that expert certifiers implement two complementary strategies to minimize the risk of reidentification. The first is a so-called k-map approach to anonymization, in which expert certifiers ensure that every record in a shared data set has $k - 1$ equal records (in which k represents a prespecified number) in the population from which the data were sampled. Thus, if $k = 10$ and the study entailed a random sample of elderly statin users from California, an expert certifier would be charged with confirming that there were at least nine elderly statin users in California with information that matched each record in the shared data set.

Other privacy protection methods exist. Some are ill suited to balance the competing goals of utility and privacy. The technique of k-anonymization, for

---

[38] Office of Civil Rights, US Department of Health and Human Services, Guidance Regarding Methods for De-Identification of Protected Health Information.
[39] Matthias Wjst, Caught You: Threats to Confidentiality Due to the Public Release of Large-Scale Genetic Data Sets, 11 BMC Med. Ethics 1, 2 (2010). See also European Medical Agency, External Guidance on the Implementation of the European Agency Policy on the Publication of Clinical Data for Medicinal Products for Human Use 41 (2016), available at www.ema.europa.eu/docs/en_GB/document_library/Regulatory_and_procedural_guideline/2016/03/WC500202621.pdf [https://perma.cc/5UDS-9QGY].
[40] Electronic Health Information Laboratory, FAQ, available at www.ehealthinformation.ca/faq/ [https://perma.cc/QRR2-6GAF] (last visited December 1, 2016).
[41] See, generally, Khaled El Emam, *Guide to the De-Identification of Personal Health Information* (2013); Khaled El Emam & Luk Arbuckle, *Anonymizing Health Data: Case Studies and Methods to Get You Started* (2013); Zhiyu Wan et al., A Game Theoretic Framework for Analyzing Re-Identification Risk, 10 PLoS Med. e0120592 (2015).

instance, demands that each record have at least $k-1$ equal records in the shared data set itself, enabling indefinite expert certifications. However, as El Emam and Dankar have demonstrated, k-anonymization "consistently over-anonymizes data sets," resulting in distortions that hinder the subsequently utility of the shared information.[42] Others, including differential privacy techniques showing spatial representation of individuals through controlled noise/randomization processes,[43] have not yet undergone sufficient testing to justify their adoption but are pushing the field forward at a relatively quick pace.

Data sharing under the expert determination pathway should additionally be contingent on execution of a DUA specifying the individuals who will have access to the data, mandating HIPAA-compliant security standards for storing the data, and precluding subsequent disclosure of the data. As demonstrated by the limited data set pathway, the imposition of such a contractual obligation would be a low-cost measure to mitigate unforeseen or emergent risks. Importantly, we do not believe it is necessary for the DUA to prohibit attempted reidentification of the data, which could be construed to prevent researchers from combining patient-level databases in a manner that does not expressly divulge the identity the individuals from whom the data were collected.

18.7 CONCLUSION

Although many long-term postapproval studies can be conducted with data shared through the safe harbor pathway, it is not conducive for investigations involving short follow-up or small-scale geographic variation in exposures, covariates, or outcomes. Furthermore, until HHS clarifies whether batch and model numbers are device identifiers under HIPAA, the utility of safe harbor data for postapproval research on devices remains uncertain. While limited data sets are better suited for postapproval research, data shared under the limited data set pathway are easier to reidentify and subject to the ambiguous minimum necessary standard. By contrast, the expert determination pathway is promising but requires additional standards to facilitate its uptake. To that end, we have proposed four initial best practice recommendations to guide its use, which we hope will foster robust discussion on their merits and other best practices to promote safe and effective sharing of Big Data assets to improve the assessment of prescription drugs and medication devices.

---

[42] Khaled El Emam & Fida Kamal Dankar, Protecting Privacy Using k-Anonymity, 15 J. Am. Med. Inform. Assoc. 627, 628 (2008).

[43] See, generally, Graham Carmode et al., Differentially Private Spatial Decompositions, IEEE (March 2011), available at http://ieeexplore.ieee.org/abstract/document/6544872/ [https://perma.cc/9AKE-XLWF]; Warbeh Quardaji et al., Differentially Private Grids for Geospatial Data, IEEE (June 25, 2013); Hao Wang & Zhengquan Xu, CTS-DP: Publishing Correlated Time-Series Data Via Differential Privacy, 122 Knowledge-Based Syst. 167 (2017).

19

Big Data and Human Medical Judgment

Regulating Next-Generation Clinical Decision Support

Jeffrey M. Senger and Patrick O'Leary

19.1 INTRODUCTION

Throughout the history of medicine, doctors have struggled with information deficits. Imperfect information about the causes of disease, emerging clinical and laboratory research, and patients' individual circumstances and characteristics have long impeded medical practice. Today, though many unknowns remain in medicine, practitioners increasingly confront a different problem. Doctors now confront having vast amounts of information but no way to use it all.[1] Indeed, the amount of information available to clinicians today is prodigious, and technological advances mean that doctors could soon have access not only to a patient's comprehensive medical history (including records from prior interactions with physicians, personal genomic data, and troves of behavioral and other data collected, wittingly or unwittingly, using mobile phones and wearable devices[2]) but also detailed environmental data and the world's cumulative medical knowledge, all instantaneously.

In considering how we can use this flood of information to improve healthcare, one answer that may be uncomfortable for some physicians is that computers will play an increasing role, including in the type of analytical and diagnostic work at the heart of the "practice of medicine."[3] The time approaches when algorithms, rather than oncologists, may take a lead role in deciding which combination of therapies

---

[1] See David W. Bates, Clinical Decision Support and the Law: The Big Picture, 5 *St. Louis Univ. J. Health L. Policy* 319 (2012) (noting evidence that access to more data, via EHRs, does not alone improve quality of care).
[2] See Alison M. Darcy et al., Viewpoint: Machine Learning and the Profession of Medicine, 315(6) *JAMA* 551 (February 9, 2016) (discussing potential integration of personal data collected from devices into individualized predictive models).
[3] See Isaac S. Kohane et al., Editorial: A Glimpse of the Next 100 Years in Medicine, 367(26) *N. Engl. J. Med.* 2538, 2528 (December 27, 2012).

is most likely to benefit a cancer patient.[4] Computers not only will calculate the appropriate dose for radiation treatment (a responsibility that humans have already abdicated) but also may be pivotal in determining whether to use radiation at all.

How we can take advantage of Big Data to support and improve on human medical judgment is a challenge with interrelated legal, ethical, and economic considerations. Whether we can ensure the safety and efficacy of the tools we develop to do so, such as Big Data–empowered clinical decision support (CDS) products and "next generation CDS," poses a particular challenge for the Food and Drug Administration (FDA).

As a public health agency, the FDA has much to be excited about here. Software that can intelligently prescribe a course of treatment based on a patient's genetic code and medical history, environmental information, and up-to-the-minute medical research and comparative data offers the potential of truly personalized medicine. Moreover, technology promises to expand access to the best care; when some of the world's top oncologists are algorithms, patients can receive the same caliber of medical advice at an understaffed rural clinic or a preeminent cancer center.

At the same time, these new products may demand a reexamination of the FDA's historical gatekeeper model of device regulation (established by statute in 1976, two years before Space Invaders made it into arcades). The application of this model to software is threadbare already, and the kind of complex, "black box" CDS coming down the pike will only further test the assumptions on which the model relies.

19.2 FDA REGULATION OF SOFTWARE

The FDA does not regulate the practice of medicine.[5] When a clinician exercises medical judgment, either in diagnosing a condition or in prescribing a treatment, federal law defers to that act of judgment. By contrast, the FDA does regulate medical devices – instruments, apparatus, implements, machines, and contrivances that are, among other things, "intended for use in the diagnosis of disease or other conditions, or in the cure, mitigation, treatment, or prevention of disease."[6]

Under this definition, a fundamental feature of devices is that they are "used" by people. They are, in a sense, tools intended to augment human abilities. Even complex devices generally fit this mold. An MRI machine, fundamentally, allows a doctor to see what is hidden to the eye. Robotic surgical tools give surgeons precision and control that they could not achieve with their own hands. These devices are sophisticated, but they are tools – they do not supplant the physician's judgment,

---

[4] Computers may have an important role even in the most human dimensions of healthcare. One recent study indicated that patients were more likely to reveal personal information in response to questions they believed were being asked by a computer than a live clinician. See Darcy et al., Viewpoint: Machine Learning and the Profession of Medicine, at 551–52.
[5] See 21 U.S.C.A. § 396 (2012).
[6] 21 U.S.C.A. § 321(h).

and their safety and effectiveness are measured against human intentions and expectations. The same is true of devices that complete analytical tasks that were once the domain of doctors. The analytical performance of a device that takes a measurement or makes a calculation (often much more quickly, accurately, and consistently than any human could) can be validated against its designer's intentions, just like the sharpness of a scalpel.

The tool-like character of most devices is reflected in the basic premise of device regulation, which is simply that devices should work as intended. Though there are countless complications involving old devices, new devices, Class II and Class III devices, and so on, the practical takeaway for most devices is clear: a manufacturer must be able to provide a reasonable assurance of a device's safety and effectiveness under the intended conditions of use.

In contrast, the FDA has long struggled with the application of this principle to devices that are meant to supplant human medical judgment. Indeed, the FDA historically has avoided the question of what it would mean to prove that a device can exercise judgment as well as a doctor. In part, it has been able to do so because, despite ambitious aspirations, such products have remained technologically infeasible.

To the extent that the FDA has grappled with this question, the first and most influential instance was the development of the agency's computer products guidance in 1987, in the wake of the Therac-25 radiation machine tragedy.[7] In the draft policy, the FDA explained that most products designed to assist in medical decision making were not even medical devices or were devices subject to only minimal regulation:

> FDA would not regard computer products used only for traditional "library" functions such as storage, retrieval, and dissemination of information – functions traditionally carried out through textbooks and journals – to be medical devices subject to regulation by the agency ... [M]any software products known as "expert" or "knowledge based" systems that are not used with existing medical devices and that are intended to involve competent human intervention before any impact on human health occurs (e.g., where clinical judgment and experience can be used to check and interpret a system's output) are exempt from registration, listing, premarket notification, and premarket approval requirements.[8]

The FDA revised the draft policy in the 1989 Draft Software Policy. The agency reaffirmed that "computer products (e.g., 'expert' or 'knowledge based' systems, artificial intelligence and other types of decision support systems) that are intended to involve competent human intervention before any impact on human health

---

[7] Software problems with the Therac-25 radiation therapy machine led to at least six patients receiving massive overdoses of radiation. See Nathan Cortez, The Mobile Health Revolution?, 47 U.C.D. L. Rev. 1173, 1218–19 (2014).

[8] Draft Policy Guidance for Regulation of Computer Products: Availability, 52 Fed. Reg. 36104–01 (September 25, 1987).

occurs, (e.g., where clinical judgment and experience can be used to check and interpret a system's output)" would be exempt from the FDA's general device controls.[9] Though the FDA withdrew this policy in 2005, its invocation of "competent human intervention" as a sufficient basis to avoid thorny questions about how to assess "artificial intelligence" systems has continued to influence the debate around FDA regulation of such products.

The FDA has occasionally confronted the limitations of the 1989 Draft Software Policy. We get a hint of this in the agency's 1999 guidance on "Off-the-Shelf Software Use in Medical Devices." There the Agency suggested – *contra* the 1989 Draft Software Policy then still on the books – that software intended to make informed, patient-specific recommendations to doctors would be subject to some kind of regulatory scrutiny, at least when incorporated into medical devices requiring a marketing application:

> OTS knowledge-based software (for example, artificial intelligence, expert systems, and neural net software) are being developed for a number of medical applications. A typical system accepts clinical findings (sometimes including imaging data) and generates probabilities of disease states and/or recommendations for subsequent data gathering or treatment. The clinician may order a surgical biopsy or other invasive tests or initiate therapy based on the system output. Such systems should be tested and reviewed in a manner consistent with both their safety and effectiveness of their direct effects (recommendations) and indirect effects (missed appropriate diagnostic testing and treatment).[10]

The FDA again flirted with the question of how to regulate such products in 2006 and 2007 when it issued draft and revised draft guidance addressing the regulation of so-called in vitro diagnostic multivariate index assays (IVDMIAs). Though the FDA subsequently abandoned its focus on IVDMIAs to address laboratory-developed tests (LDTs) more generally, the agency's IVDMIA draft guidance reflected a recognition that for certain tests intended to aid in clinical decision making, competent human intervention was not an available safeguard. The draft guidance noted that IVDMIAs provide "a result whose derivation is non-transparent and cannot be independently derived or verified by the end user" and that, accordingly, an "ordering clinician requires information from the test developer, rather than generally accepted information from the clinical community, in order to interpret the IVDMIA result for use in the management of the patient."[11]

---

[9] US Food and Drug Administration, FDA Policy for the Regulation of Computer Products (draft) (November 13, 1989) (unpublished).

[10] US Department of Health and Human Services. et al., *Off-the-Shelf Software Use in Medical Devices* (September 9, 1999), available at www.fda.gov/downloads/MedicalDevices/.../ucm 073779.pdf [https://perma.cc/4YK7-NEVP].

[11] US Food and Drug Administration, Draft Guidance, In Vitro Diagnostic Multivariate Index Assays 5 (July 26, 2007), available at www.fda.gov/MedicalDevices/DeviceRegulationandGui dance/GuidanceDocuments/ucm079148.htm [https://perma.cc/PS9W-L39V].

Interestingly, the draft guidance excluded from the IVDMIA category devices that simply facilitate the interpretation of multiple variables that physicians could otherwise interpret themselves. That is, even as the FDA grappled with how to regulate tests that are not amenable to competent human intervention, it reaffirmed that where such intervention is possible, this safeguard is sufficient. As for the opaque IVDMIAs, the FDA said in the draft guidance that it would take a risk-based approach to their regulation using traditional device authorities.

The FDA's 2014 draft guidance describing a "Framework for Regulatory Oversight of Laboratory Developed Tests (LDTs)" is the most recent sign that the notion of "competent human intervention" as a safeguard has continued to erode. It notes that many modern LDTs are "highly complex," characterized by features such as "automated interpretation, multi-signal devices, [and] use of non-transparent algorithms and/or complex software to generate device results."[12] The FDA proposes to take a risk-based approach to regulating LDTs using the standard tools of medical device classification and regulation.

As for standalone CDS products, the FDA has been essentially silent since it revoked the 1989 Draft Software Policy. A guidance document on the subject has been on the FDA's list of forthcoming guidance for several years, and there has been ongoing discussion among policymakers in recent years regarding where to draw the line between health information technology (IT) products (including CDS products) that the FDA will actively regulate and those toward which it will exercise enforcement discretion.[13]

Where does this leave us? In the absence of products that actually threaten to supersede physicians' medical judgment, the FDA has largely let its 1980s invocation of competent human intervention ride. At the margins, it has threatened to make manufacturers of some opaque LDTs comply with medical device regulations, but these threats have not come to full fruition and, in any case, have not been tested in cases where the opacity of the test's results is a function of the complexity of the algorithm.

This state of affairs – a tacit dependence on competent human intervention as a failsafe for many devices and a general idea that more complex or opaque systems will have to comply with traditional medical device rules – may not be sustainable. It has been as stable as it has only because several significant limitations have prevented CDS systems from reaching the full potential envisioned by artificial

---

[12] US Food and Drug Administration, Draft Guidance for Industry, Food and Drug Administration Staff, and Clinical Laboratories: Framework for Regulatory Oversight of Laboratory Developed Tests (LDTs) 8 (October 3, 2014), available at www.fda.gov/downloads/medical devices/deviceregulationandguidance/guidancedocuments/ucm416685.pdf [https://perma.cc/B32S-X27Z].

[13] See, e.g., FDASIA Health IT Report: Proposed Strategy and Recommendations for a Risk-Based Framework 26 (April 2014), available at www.healthit.gov/sites/default/files/fdasia_health itreport_final.pdf [https://perma.cc/FH4P-TJQB].

intelligence pioneers decades ago. These obstacles are rapidly disappearing, however, and recent developments challenge the assumption that interjecting a qualified human expert into a decision-making process necessarily improves the result. If and when next-generation CDS systems surpass human reviewers' ability to meaningfully second-guess their results, the FDA will have to confront what a reasonable assurance of safety and effectiveness for such systems looks like.

19.3 THE HISTORICAL FAILURE TO DEVELOP SOPHISTICATED CDS PRODUCTS

The FDA has been able to avoid directly addressing what it would take to demonstrate safety and effectiveness for a device intended to supplant human medical judgment because, simply, devices of this type have not been forthcoming. This is not for lack of effort. Researchers have sought to teach computers to exercise medical judgment for decades, and modern CDS systems, which apply medical knowledge to patient-specific data, "emerged from artificial intelligence and expert system research in the 1970s and 1980s that attempted to model the clinical diagnostician."[14] These early efforts proved overly optimistic.

Previous attempts at developing intelligent CDS systems failed largely for two reasons. First, the type of medical thinking that these systems seek to emulate is holistic, requiring knowledge of many relevant variables. It has traditionally been difficult to aggregate that information for a computer to analyze. Second, until recently, researchers struggled to enable computers to meaningfully engage and learn about complex, unstructured problems.

These limitations have challenged researchers working on complex problems such as medical diagnoses in a way that they have not for simpler problems such as chess. The universe of information necessary to play chess is closed: at any point in a game, there are a limited number of moves each player can make and a limited number of resulting "positions" on the board. A sufficiently powerful computer can apply predetermined rules about how to evaluate chess positions to these possibilities and thereby determine which is most favorable, that is, the "best" move.

In contrast with chess's closed universe and known rules, there is a theoretically infinite combination of factors that affect human health. While the relationships between illness and some factors are well understood, others remain mysterious, and few factors have been studied in terms of how they interrelate with one another, particularly in complex multivariable relationships. Simply put, chess is a less complex problem than medicine, and consequently, while computers have long since surpassed individual human chess players (as famously symbolized by Deep Blue's 1997 victory over Gary Kasparov), most CDS systems today remain comparatively unsophisticated.

---

[14] William R. Hersh, Medical Informatics: Improving Health Care through Information, 288(16) JAMA 1955, at 1956 (October 2002).

CDS systems are intended to provide users "with knowledge and person-specific information, intelligently filtered or presented at appropriate times, to enhance health and health care."[15] In practice, this means that many systems perform relatively simple functions such as providing computerized alerts and reminders, clinical guidelines, condition-specific order sets, focused patient data reports and summaries, documentation templates, diagnostic support, and contextually relevant reference information.

Some systems do go beyond decision support and actually engage in treatment independently, without physician review or prompting, but devices of this kind generally rely on rules that are well understood or else are intended for situations where waiting for additional human intervention is impossible. For example, when an implantable cardioverter defibrillator detects a heart rhythm that it is programmed to recognize as a dangerous arrhythmia, it does not wait for a physician's review before generating a corrective electrical pulse.

When it comes to complex medical decision making, however – generating diagnoses and treatment plans – most CDS products available today are not so different from those introduced decades ago and continue to leave the ultimate decision to the judgment of a human. These products may take the form of diagnosis checklists, for instance, employing patient demographic information and clinical observations (manually entered or drawn from an EHR) and generating a list of potential diagnoses, with relevant citations to reference volumes, clinical practice guidelines, and other resources intended to aid the ultimate (human) decision maker.

19.4 SIGNS OF CHANGE

Against this historical backdrop, there is now reason to believe that next-generation CDS will soon be more than science fiction. In particular, two recent developments have had the effect of weakening the barriers that historically limited the development of such software.

First, for several reasons, the amount of health-related information that can be ingested and processed by computers is now orders of magnitude greater than before. One reason is the increasing availability of genomic data. The cost of genomic sequencing has dropped dramatically in the past fifteen years as its speed and accuracy have increased. Whole-genome sequencing is now broadly accessible, and next-generation sequencing technologies allow for rapid sequencing that can

---

[15] Jerome A. Osheroff et al., A Roadmap for National Action on Clinical Decision Support, American Medical Informatics Association (June 13, 2006), available at www.amia.org/public-policy/reports-and-fact-sheets/a-roadmap-for-national-action-on-clinical-decision-support [https://perma.cc/GBC5-LJV2].

provide extensive and accurate genetic data. As a result, individual health records will increasingly contain personal genomic data. These advances also mean that doctors know more than ever before about diseases, through developments in fields such as cancer genomics and pathognomics. Expanded genomic testing also means that more population-level data are becoming available, against which a patient's genetic information can be compared.

Another reason for the flood of data available for analysis is the development of increasingly accurate and portable sensors and the emergence of the "quantified self movement." We are now constantly surrounded by products that collect information about us and our environment. Virtually anyone who carries a smartphone is already collecting activity and location data, and those who use a smart watch, smart scale, or other similar product may be collecting substantially more.

The digitization and standardization of medical records likewise helps to overcome the information deficits that have impeded CDS development. EHRs provide a convenient single location from which CDS systems can draw patient-specific information and mean that multiple streams of information – records from primary care physicians and specialists, from emergency rooms and urgent care clinics, and from different doctors a patient may have seen throughout a lifetime, as well as information about family medical history – can reside in one place.

The second development is the progress that artificial intelligence researchers are now making in replicating important and previously unattainable characteristics of human learning and analysis. Perhaps most notable are advances in the field of machine learning. Developments in this field were a large part of Google DeepMind's recent success in creating the first computer program capable of beating the best human players of the board game Go. Due to the number of potential moves and the nature of the game, Go is considerably more complex than chess as a problem for researchers, and until Google's success, many researchers believed that a program capable of beating professional-level players remained years away.[16] Google's program, AlphaGo, is notable in several respects. For one, the software is based on a general-purpose artificial intelligence that is capable of "learning" on its own. Whereas Deep Blue was programmed with chess-specific knowledge, AlphaGo learned how to play Go more or less by itself, beginning by analyzing a database of moves made by expert human Go players, and then playing thousands of games of Go against itself, adjusting its strategy in a process known as "reinforcement learning."[17]

---

[16] See Elizabeth Gibney, Google Masters Go: Deep-Learning Software Excels at Complex Ancient Board Game, 529 *Nature* 445–46 (2016), available https://ai.arizona.edu/sites/ai/files/resources/gibney_2016_google_masters_go.pdf [https://perma.cc/MX2J-V4DY].

[17] See Google, What We Learned in Seoul with AlphaGo (March 16, 2016), available at https://googleblog.blogspot.com/2016/03/what-we-learned-in-seoul-with-alphago.html [https://perma.cc/5B8G-PSQD]; Google, AlphaGo: Using Machine Learning to Master the Ancient Game of Go (January 27, 2016), available at https://googleblog.blogspot.nl/2016/01/alphago-machine-learning-game-go.html [https://perma.cc/HZ2A-JN2M].

19.5 NEXT-GENERATION CDS

Through these changes, which will make vast amounts of health-related data accessible to computers and allow for the development of increasingly sophisticated software capable of sifting and drawing inferences from these data, future CDS tools may eventually be better qualified to make a diagnosis or pick a treatment plan than the human doctors they are intended to "support."

This is not to say that CDS will replace human doctors; to the contrary, it is likely that computers and humans working in tandem will continue to provide the best care when complex decision making is required. The function of the human body, after all, is far more complex than either chess or Go, and computers will continue to benefit from human strengths, such as an expert's ability to draw on experience and intuition to help identify the right data sets to "train" software, to identify missing or potentially relevant information, to differentiate promising leads from dead ends in certain cases, and of course to take into consideration ethical or values-based aspects of medical decision making. A piece of software may be able to determine which treatment will extend life longest or even which treatment will maximize quality of life, but the personal dimensions of end-of-life decisions, for example, simply are not amenable to automation.

Nonetheless, even if humans continue to make valuable contributions along with next-generation CDS, they will not always add value as "competent human interveners" who can provide an independent assessment of the medical correctness of the software's recommendations. To the contrary, there may come a day when relying on a human's judgment second-guessing a CDS system would be tantamount to medical malpractice and even unethical. By analogy, if your life were somehow at stake based on the result of a chess game, you should follow the recommendations of the best computer rather than the best human player, even if you do not understand its reasoning.

In this regard, Nicholson Price has articulated a useful construct for thinking about these types of products as types of black-box software. Price draws interesting distinctions among several types of black-box software,[18] but the essential characteristic of such systems, and the one that confounds the idea of competent human intervention, is that they generate conclusions inscrutable to, and essentially unreviewable by, even knowledgeable human observers. In terms of next-generation CDS, this means that a CDS system's medical conclusions would be based on calculations that no human doctor could recreate and would reflect medical hypotheses that could not as a practicable matter be confirmed via conventional clinical trials.

19.6 A NEW REGULATORY PARADIGM

To experience the potential benefits of next-generation CDS products, we must have assurance of these products' safety and effectiveness. But how can we, if the

[18] See Nicholson Price, Black-Box Medicine, 28 Harv. J. L. Technol. 419, 433–34 (2015).

nature of these products belies the possibility of competent human intervention, and the FDA's traditional approach to assessing the effectiveness of medical products is likely to systematically result in the delay or denial of applications for products that work? While we do not presume to know how exactly next-generation CDS products should be regulated, certain features of the current regulatory regime may be particularly ill suited to the task of balancing the benefits of innovation against the need for assurances of safety and effectiveness in this case.

For instance, the logic these systems apply will not be characterized by easily stated relationships that can be tested in a controlled clinical trial. Rather, the logic may rely on relationships too complex to control for, or else on a form of knowledge, like AlphaGo's understanding of Go strategy, that cannot be articulated. Moreover, these products may not be amenable to prospective proof of safety and effectiveness for specific intended uses because their intended uses will undoubtedly be less narrowly defined than for conventional medical devices.

Given these concerns, the proof for these products ultimately may need to be found in the clinic rather than clinical trials (though premarket retrospective testing against databases may be able provide some assurance that the software will act predictably, at least). Nor is the problem avoided simply because some next-generation CDS products may aim only at recreating the level of judgment exercised by a well-informed human physician. Though we can conceive of study designs that would confirm whether such software is consistently capable of reaching the same conclusion as a human physician, human doctors will not always be the yardstick against which next-generation CDS products are measured; other products will, inevitably, be designed to process types and volumes of information human doctors cannot and to push the boundaries of well-understood medical practice. These tools, moreover, will learn and evolve with each new patient. When next-generation CDS comes to fruition, the fact that the software reaches a different conclusion than a human doctor could as likely be an indictment of the doctor's judgment as the computer's.

It should be noted that relying on postmarket data rather than large premarket pivotal trials is a strategy already used in places by the FDA, though the idea of continuously reviewing the effectiveness of an evolving product would be unprecedented. For example, the FDA's Center for Devices and Radiological Health (CDRH) has issued guidance recognizing that a "balance of premarket and postmarket data collection facilitates timely patient access to important new technology without undermining patient safety."[19] The CDRH even recognizes that there are circumstances when it "may be possible to approve a new device . . . based on bench data with postmarket confirmatory clinical data."[20]

---

[19] US Food and Drug Administration, Guidance for Industry and Food and Drug Administration Staff, Balancing Premarket and Postmarket Data Collection for Devices Subject to Premarket Approval (April 13, 2015), available at www.fda.gov/downloads/MedicalDevices/DeviceRegulationandGuidance/GuidanceDocuments/UCM393994.pdf [https://perma.cc/9D7J-4EQC].

[20] Ibid., at 13.

Existing approaches that rely on postmarket data are nonetheless premised on the assumption that a device itself is static – the device subjected to bench testing before approval will be the same as the device used on patients afterwards. The FDA is largely comfortable relying on postmarket data collection about a device when the device is already generally well understood, such as where a device has already been approved for other indications or where additional clinical trial data are needed only relating to rare adverse events.

Another challenge is how to conduct sufficiently rigorous postmarket monitoring and testing of these products to identify errors and adverse events and resolve them. The challenge of even identifying adverse events is not to be understated for devices that adapt with each new patient, are designed to identify novel diagnostic and therapeutic possibilities, and are often intended for use in patients who are very sick. Indeed, our ability to identify mistakes made by these systems is likely to be limited in proportion to how successful they generally are: once we have faith in the ability of a piece of software to think creatively, we run the risk of trusting it too much, even when it recommends a treatment that might otherwise raise red flags. The converse concern, of course, is potential underregulation. It is important to recall that when we place our trust in doctors' judgment, we rely on an elaborate system of controls – educational and licensing requirements – that ensure that physicians are qualified. Formal regulation by the FDA is one source of similar quality assurance for a medical product (though other informal forms of regulation exist, such as tort liability and insurance coverage determinations).

Given the complexity of next-generation CDS systems and the potentially high cost of errors, one class of requirements that may make sense to retain is those – such as human factors and usability studies – that ensure that doctors are able to use these systems as intended. After all, even as computers become increasingly sophisticated, there will always be challenges at the human-computer interface, where unintended "friction" between human and machine can rapidly defeat the potential benefits of such high-tech systems. Computer-generated instructions for a lifesaving treatment plan do not benefit the patient if they are misapplied.

19.7 CONCLUSION

We are at the beginning of a new era in medicine, defined by the convergence of two unprecedented developments. First, the information deficit that has long frustrated the medical profession is rapidly being turned on its head and replaced with a new and wholly different problem, a surplus of accessible data, including genomic, behavioral, and environmental information, as well as the aggregate of all human medical and scientific knowledge. As this incredible volume of data becomes accessible to physicians at the click of a button, the amount of potentially relevant information available to doctors in making a diagnosis or treatment decision exceeds what even the best human mind is capable of processing, understanding, or exploiting. Second, and just as important, developments in computer science now enable computers to digest massive troves of disparate data and "learn" from those data in ways that have never before been possible, identifying complex patterns and relationships that would elude even the most brilliant human analysts.

While we are not there yet, this convergence of new data and new tools ultimately may lead to a new generation of medical products that make patient-specific medical diagnoses and treatment recommendations that account for an unprecedented number of factors and are, to humans, inscrutable.

Next-generation CDS products promise not only to improve the practice of medicine by unearthing new medical insights from data but also to democratize cutting-edge medical knowledge. As a public health agency, the FDA should welcome these products, and perhaps it will. Yet these products will also pose a challenge to the FDA. Black-box software that is intended to supplant and surpass human medical judgment bears little resemblance to the medical devices Congress had in mind when it established the FDA's medical device authorities in 1976. Policymakers must examine whether an attempt to fit these products into the existing device framework by insisting on conventional assessments of their safety and effectiveness could unnecessarily delay the advent of lifesaving technologies. Now is the time to begin to confront the thorny question of how to regulate devices when they cease being simply tools and begin to encroach on what has long been the exclusive province of human physicians, the exercise of medical judgment.

20

Medical Malpractice and Black-Box Medicine

W. Nicholson Price II*

20.1 INTRODUCTION

The explosive proliferation of health data has combined with the rapid development of machine-learning algorithms to enable a new form of medicine: "black-box medicine."[1] In this phenomenon, algorithms troll through tremendous databases of health data to find patterns that can be used to guide care, whether by predicting unknown patient risks, selecting the right drug, suggesting a new use of an old drug, or triaging patients to preserve health resources. These decisions differ from previous data-based decisions because black-box medicine is, by its nature, opaque; that is, the bases for black-box decisions are unknown and unknowable.

Black-box medicine raises a number of legal questions, ranging from how to shape incentives for its development to how to regulate its growth and quality.[2] One key question is how black-box medicine will influence the medical malpractice liability of healthcare providers. How should tort liability apply to providers who cannot know the mechanistic underpinnings of the treatment they recommend? Must they learn as much as they can about the way algorithms are developed and verified? Or can they rely on the assurances of the developer without more knowledge?

This chapter explores the medical malpractice implications of black-box medicine. It briefly introduces the phenomenon and then considers how the tort system does, can, and should regulate the behavior of providers and healthcare facilities using black-box medical techniques. It concludes that while providers and facilities are ill suited to evaluate the substantive accuracy of black-box medical algorithms,

---

* Many thanks to Nicholas Bagley, Ana Bracic, Sherman Clark, Rebecca Eisenberg, Roger Ford, Jessica Litman, Margo Schlanger, Kayte Spector-Bagdady, and Effy Vayena for helpful conversations and advice. All errors are my own.
[1] For a detailed description of black-box medicine, see W. Nicholson Price II, Black-Box Medicine, 28 *Harv. J.L. Technol.* 419 (2015).
[2] See W. Nicholson Price II, Big Data, Patents, and the Future of Medicine, 37 *Cardozo L. Rev.* 1401 (2016).

they could and perhaps should be required to exercise due care to evaluate procedural quality – the expertise of the developer and the availability of independent external validation – when implementing black-box algorithms in a healthcare facility or using them to care for patients.

20.2 BLACK-BOX MEDICINE

Black-box medicine is a response to the immense complexity of biological relationships. Although we are constantly developing tools to plumb that complexity, our explicit understanding of those biological relationships is necessarily slow to develop. Putting our understanding of complex relationships into medical practice is similarly slow and cumbersome because clinical trials and traditional drug development take many years and cost hundreds of millions of dollars.

Black-box medicine seeks to exploit the tremendous amount of data being generated in healthcare to find and use these underlying relationships even without understanding them and without undergoing the expense and delay of clinical trials. Health data are proliferating rapidly and becoming newly accessible. Clinical records, long kept on paper in doctors' offices, are shifting to electronic form, as are pharmacy records and medical test results.[3] Newer systemic analyses, especially genomic sequencing, are creating large volumes of patient-specific data. These data can be combined into individual, group, or population-wide collections, whether by insurers, provider networks, or government entities like the United States' newly formed $215 million Precision Medicine Initiative.[4]

These collections of data can be used to test and develop explicit hypotheses about the biology of the body and medical implications. But the data also contain patterns that are too complex or concealed for such explicit hypothesis testing. Machine-learning algorithms, using approaches such as deep learning and neural networks, can find that sort of complex underlying pattern in the data – but cannot explain or even state what those patterns are.[5] Just as Facebook's DeepFace algorithm can match faces in a set of digital images without explicitly classifying the features it uses for recognition,[6] medical algorithms can (for instance) predict tumor

---

[3] Julia Adler-Milstein et al., Electronic Health Record Adoption in US Hospitals: Progress Continues, But Challenges Persist, 34 *Health Affairs* (published online November 2015), available at https://www.healthaffairs.org/doi/abs/10.1377/hlthaff.2015.0992 [https://perma.cc/6RQZ-LTW4].

[4] Francis S. Collins & Harold Varmus, A New Initiative on Precision Medicine, 372 N. Engl. J. Med. 793 (2015).

[5] See Joseph A. Cruz & David S. Wishart, Applications of Machine Learning in Cancer Prediction and Prognosis, 2 *Cancer Inform.* 59 (2007).

[6] DeepFace: Closing the Gap to Human-Level Performance in Face Verification, Research at Facebook (June 24, 2014), available at https://research.facebook.com/publications/480567225375/deepface-closing-the-gap-to-human-level-performance-in-face-verification/ [https://perma.cc/TNT3-JSUR].

response to a particular drug based on allelic patterns among thousands of genes or predict lung cancer prognosis by analyzing microscopic images[7] – all without understanding or identifying why or how those patterns matter.[8] This opacity is not deliberate, though some secrecy by developers could compound it.[9] Instead, the opacity is unavoidable. Sometimes patterns are opaque because they are too complicated; that is, even if the computer could state the set of, for example, thousands of genes and interacting patient-history factors, we could not understand it. Other times the opacity is a result of the machine-learning techniques used to find patterns; a trained neural network (one such technique) typically cannot output the artificial neurons' "connections" in any meaningful sense and thus does not demonstrate how it reached its result. To be clear, this opacity is also not desirable; it would be preferable to know and understand the relationships being used. And there are some machine-learning methods that are more transparent. But opaque black-box methods open up for use a broad swath of nuanced biological patterns currently too complex or hidden for explicit understanding and are the focus of this chapter.

Black-box medicine accordingly has tremendous potential benefits. Most important for the context of this chapter, it can direct care, predicting a patient's risk profile, helping choose between a selection of known interventions, or suggesting an off-label use of an approved intervention. A doctor might feed the genetic sequence of a patient's tumor into a black-box algorithm, for instance, and receive a recommendation as to what drug is most likely to treat the tumor effectively.[10] Alternatively, an opaque algorithm could continuously evaluate a trauma patient's electronic vital signs and sound an alarm at the earliest sign of trouble, perhaps even before trained providers could observe the need.[11] Black-box medicine can also be used to allocate scarce healthcare resources by suggesting which patient might benefit most from an organ transplant, a hospital bed, or the attention of the first available healthcare provider.[12] In addition, black-box medicine could potentially generate hypotheses for traditional biomedical research that might eventually uncover and understand the underlying mechanisms; that is, the box need not stay black forever. While all

---

[7] Kun-Hsing Yu et al., Predicting Non-Small Cell Lung Cancer Prognosis by Fully Automated Microscopic Pathology Image Features, 7 *Nat. Commun.* 12474 (2016).

[8] See, e.g., Hojin Moon et al., Ensemble Methods for Classification of Patients for Personalized Medicine with High-Dimensional Data, 41 *Artificial Intelligence Med.* 197 (2007).

[9] For a description of deliberately secret algorithms, see Frank Pasquale, *The Black Box Society: The Secret Algorithms That Control Money and Information* (2015).

[10] See Moon et al., Moon et al., Ensemble Methods for Classification of Patients for Personalized Medicine; Michael P. Menden et al., Machine Learning Prediction of Cancer Cell Sensitivity to Drugs Based on Genomic and Chemical Properties, 8 *PLoS ONE* e61318 (2013).

[11] See Nehemiah T. Liu et al., Development and Validation of a Machine Learning Algorithm and Hybrid System to Predict the Need for Life-Saving Interventions in Trauma Patients, 52 *Med. Biol. Eng. Comput.* 193 (2014).

[12] See, e.g., I. Glenn Cohen et al., The Legal and Ethical Concerns that Arise from Using Complex Predictive Analytics in Health Care, 33 *Health Affairs* 1139 (2014).

these possibilities are significant, this chapter focuses on the first: using black-box medicine to direct patient care.

As black-box medicine becomes increasingly capable of predicting patient outcomes and suggesting interventions, it will – and should – become an important part of patient care. Among many implementation issues, a key question for healthcare providers and facilities is the legal obligation of a provider or facility under the standards of medical malpractice. What must providers and facilities legally know and do when practicing black-box medicine?

20.3 LIABILITY FOR THE USE OF OPAQUE MEDICAL ALGORITHMS

Medical liability law, like tort law in general, typically serves at least two purposes: first, to compensate injured parties for their injuries and, second, to deter unreasonably dangerous behavior. To accomplish these goals, injured patients may recover from providers who provided substandard care. Patients may also sometimes recover from the healthcare enterprises involved in the provision of care, including hospitals and clinics, either vicariously based on the actions of the relevant professional or directly based on the enterprise's own duties to the patient.

Negligence actions are not the only possibility for patient recovery. In other contexts, patients can recover under a strict liability theory for injuries arising from products that are defective due to manufacturing defects, design defects, or failure to warn of risks. However, neither healthcare providers nor healthcare facilities are typically held strictly liable for defects in the products they provide, sell, or use.[13] Such cases might be brought against black-box medicine developers.[14] Patients may

---

[13] See *Hollander v. Sandoz Pharm. Corp.*, 289 F.3d 1193, 1217, n. 22 (10th Cir. 2002) ("[A]n overwhelming majority of jurisdictions have refused to apply strict liability principles to claims against hospitals and physicians involving the distribution of allegedly dangerous drugs or medical devices"); see also Randolph A. Miller & Sarah M. Miller, Legal and Regulatory Issues Related to the Use of Clinical Software in Health Care Delivery, in *Clinical Decision Support* 423, 426 (Robert A. Greenes, ed., 2007) (arguing against the application of strict products liability for clinical decision-support software to providers and hospitals).

[14] Potential liability for black-box medical algorithm developers could be conceived of under a product liability framework, typically based on strict liability – that is, liability for injury without any determination of fault. However, such liability is complicated by several doctrines, including the learned intermediary doctrine (limiting recovery against manufacturers where doctors prescribe drugs or devices to patients; see Timothy Hall, Reimagining the Learned Intermediary Rule for the New Pharmaceutical Marketplace, 35 *Seton Hall L. Rev.* [2005]); for the longtime immunity of software to product liability suits, see Frances E. Zollers et al., No More Soft Landings for Software: Liability for Defects in an Industry that Has Come of Age, 21 *Santa Clara Computer High Tech. L. J.* 745 (2004); to see whether software is properly classified as a good or a service, see Michael D. Scott, Tort Liability for Vendors of Insecure Software: Has the Time Finally Come, 67 *Md. L. Rev.* 425, 436–42 (2007); for the difficulty of proving causation and the possibility of preemption by regulatory regimes, see *Riegel v. Medtronic*, 552 U.S. 312, 330 (2008) (finding preemption of common-law tort claims against makers of medical devices requiring FDA preapproval).

also recover from providers who fail to obtain informed consent before undertaking a treatment that results in the patient's injury.[15] Both of these complex situations are outside the scope of this chapter, which focuses on malpractice liability against providers and against healthcare enterprises.

20.3.1 Medical Malpractice by Providers

Jurisdictions vary, but in general, providers must treat patients with due expertise and care. Typically, this means that the provider must provide the level of care that would be expected of relevant members of the profession. In most jurisdictions, courts insist on a national reference group for this comparison; in a minority, a provider is held, instead, to the level of care offered by those practicing in the same locality.[16] The care required may be modified based on the provider's specialized credentials or on the facilities available to the provider; a physician practicing in a small rural hospital will not be required to use the same specialized equipment available to the most well-resourced urban medical centers. Hornbook law is that adhering to customary practice will typically shield a provider from liability. The reality is more complicated, however; one observer has noted that "judicial deference to physician customs is eroding. Gradually, quietly and relentlessly, state courts are withdrawing this legal privilege."[17] Moreover, what tort law requires can be explicitly modified, for instance, to encompass a certain type of care or to immunize provision of some type of care from liability regardless of common medical

---

[15] Black-box medicine raises nuanced informed-consent issues. At an intuitive level, it is hard to imagine precisely what "informed" means in the context of a recommendation where no one knows exactly how it works. But informed consent aims to facilitate treatment decisions made in the context of a relationship between the trained doctor and the lay patient and recognizes that many things need not be disclosed. Providers must disclose to the patient information that a reasonable provider (in some jurisdictions) or a reasonable patient (in others) would find material and must give the patient a choice about accepting the treatment. See Jaime S. King & Benjamin Moulton, Rethinking Informed Consent: The Case for Shared Medical Decision-Making, 32 Am. J.L. Med. 429, 493–501 (2006) (appendix) (finding that about half of the United States follows a patient-based standard, about half a physician-based standard, and two a hybrid standard); see also Canterbury v. Spence, 464 F.2d 772 (D.C. Ct. App. 1972) (rejecting a physician-based standard and developing a patient-based standard). It is entirely possible that in most circumstances neither a reasonable provider nor a reasonable patient would find information about black-box medicine's development or opacity material to disclose, just as patients need not be informed about the strength of clinical trial evidence for most interventions recommended today.

[16] See Hall v. Hilbun, 466 So.2d 856 (Miss. 1985) (discussing the locality-based standard of care and adopting a modified nationally based standard of care); Michelle H. Lewis et al., The Locality Rule and the Physician's Dilemma: Local Medical Practices vs. the National Standard of Care, 297 JAMA 2633, 2635 (2007) (tallying which states follow various versions of the locality rule).

[17] Philip G. Peters, Jr., The Quiet Demise of Deference to Custom: Malpractice Law at the Millennium, 57 Wash. Lee L. Rev. 163, 164 (2000).

practice.[18] In outlier cases, judges have held that failure to provide a specific type of care, even if uncommon, is tortious.[19]

Providers thus could be held liable for harmful use of black-box medical algorithms depending on the prevailing customary practice and the extent that custom is considered dispositive. As with medical innovation more generally, there is a risk of liability during this transition phase,[20] which presents an opportunity to consider how tort law might encourage the most beneficial medical practices.

The closest useful analogy is clinical decision-support software, designed to help providers diagnose and treat patients.[21] This software can, for instance, provide relevant patient information, collate test results, and suggest diagnoses or treatments based on well-known explicit relationships. Clinical decision-support software has been analyzed as an aid to physicians exercising independent judgment when directing care; it merely "augments the physician's existing knowledge by providing further information."[22] Under this logic, a trained provider should be subject to the exact same standard of negligence irrespective of whether clinical decision-support software is used because any treatment decisions are ultimately his or her own. Software provides information, but the knowledgeable provider intervenes to make the final choice.

This knowledgeable intervention, however, is precisely what is different about black-box medicine. Because neither providers nor developers know the relationships underlying the recommendations of black-box medicine, the physician cannot stand as merely the final step in a sequence of care. Once he or she has decided to use a particular black-box algorithm – itself a complex choice[23] – he or she cannot understand and thus verify the algorithm's recommendation against his or her body of substantive expertise; the physician can only accept what the algorithm

---

[18] See, e.g., 18 Vt. Stat. § 5281 (immunizing physicians for civil liability for prescribing life-ending medication in compliance with certain statutory provisions).

[19] See *Helling v. Carey*, 83 Wn.2d 514 (Wash. 1974) (holding that ophthalmologists must test for glaucoma in patients under age forty as well as those over age forty, although under-forty testing was not common practice). On the impact of Helling, which was controversial and soon countermanded by state statute, see Jerry Wiley, The Impact of Judicial Decisions on Professional Conduct: An Empirical Study, 55 S. Cal. L. Rev. 345 (1982).

[20] See Anna B. Laakmann, When Should Physicians Be Liable for Innovation?, 36 *Cardozo L. Rev.* 913 (2015).

[21] See Miller & Miller, Legal and Regulatory Issues Related to the Use of Clinical Software in Health Care Delivery, at 424.

[22] Ibid., at 433; see also Randolph A. Miller, Kenneth F. Schaffner, & Alan Meisel, Ethical and Legal Issues Related to the Use of Computer Programs in Clinical Medicine, 127 *Ann. Intern. Med.* 842 (1985).

[23] A physician might choose an algorithm based on the recommendations of a professional society, the scholarly literature, or the choices of his or her hospital, as discussed below. The mechanics of approving, validating, ranking, and selecting black-box algorithms are outside the scope of this chapter. For an exploration of these issues, see Roger A. Ford & W. Nicholson Price II, Privacy and Accountability in Black-Box Medicine, 22 *Mich. Telecomm. Tech. L. Rev.* 1 (2016); W. Nicholson Price II, Regulating Black-Box Medicine, 116 *Mich. L. Rev.* 421 (2017).

recommends or not. In some instances, this is unlikely to make a difference: where black-box algorithms suggest an increased risk to be managed with closer monitoring, the provider's actions take over from there. But where black-box algorithms suggest taking an unrelated drug based on previously unknown secondary effects or changing a drug's dosage or schedule without conforming to existing medical knowledge, the resulting care is fundamentally different from care not directed by black-box algorithms. Imposing the same standard of negligence would make little sense.

So what should medical malpractice law require of providers? Ordinarily, medical malpractice law responds to medical practices developed by providers (although the law may indirectly shape those practices). As long as a set of reasonable providers follows a certain practice, that practice will not typically lead to liability.

But when a practice is too innovative to have many adherents, it runs significant liability risk. Such is the situation of black-box medicine. So right now, in this period of early development, legislative action and practice guidelines set by professional organizations could be particularly influential.[24] These types of interventions could incorporate different levels of skepticism associated with the severity of different interventions.[25] For minimal-risk interventions, such as otherwise unindicated testing, increased monitoring, or taking widely used low-side-effect drugs such as aspirin, the standard of care might require no particular inquiry of the recommendations of a black-box algorithm. For riskier interventions, such as taking higher doses of a powerful drug or avoiding such a course when otherwise suggested, providers might require some validation before relying on a black-box algorithm. The form of validation would differ from traditional evidence because it would likely need to be based on procedural checks or independent computation by third parties, not clinical trials.[26] Professional societies, the FDA, and other intermediaries might serve a role in that validation to make it more feasible for an individual physician to reasonably check an algorithm's quality.[27] Such a process suggests the exercise of

---

[24] See Michelle M. Mello, Of Swords and Shields: The Role of Clinical Practice Guidelines in Medical Malpractice Litigation, 149 U. Penn. L. Rev. 645 (2001).

[25] This structure parallels the risk-based framework the FDA applies to preapproval for medical devices; low-risk devices are subject only to agency notification, high-risk devices to rigorous clinical trials, and intermediate-risk devices to an intermediate standard of evidence. See, e.g., Aaron V. Kaplan et al., Medical Device Development from Prototype to Regulatory Approval, 109 Circulation 3068 (2004). Ex ante classification raises its own challenges, including who would classify the devices. See, e.g., "Software as a Medical Device": Possible Framework for Risk Categorization and Corresponding Considerations, International Medical Device Regulators Forum 13–15 (September 18, 2014), available at www.imdrf.org/docs/imdrf/final/technical/imdrf-tech-140918-samd-framework-risk-categorization-141013.pdf [https://perma.cc/GK54-UGVB] (describing potential risk classification of software). Ex post classification, whether tiered or not, raises risks of chilling physician adoption.

[26] See Price, Black-Box Medicine, at 440–42 (discussing computational validation of black-box medicine).

[27] See Price, Regulating Black-Box Medicine (discussing potential roles for the FDA and collaborating healthcare actors in validating black-box algorithms).

intervening procedural judgment, even if substantive judgment is impossible. In somewhat analogous situations, courts have been willing to treat the use of an outdated information source as evidence of substandard care.[28] For the riskiest and most counterintuitive interventions – for instance, prescribing high doses of thalidomide to a pregnant woman – it is possible that under current standards, no black-box verification could be strong enough to overcome the presumption of harm under a reasonable standard of care. Such validation and reliability concerns could also be incorporated into potential liability for choosing a poor-quality algorithm against, for instance, the recommendations of a professional society.

Using a risk-based approach to evaluate the recommendations of black-box medicine brings with it challenges of implementation, overcaution, and undercompensation. First, a risk-based approach might be hard to implement efficiently, requiring expert testimony about the appropriate level of procedural assurance required for a particular intervention's risk. This real concern is, unfortunately, an unavoidable aspect of defining negligence based on a practitioner-based standard of care. Demonstrating adequate procedural care does not on its face appear to raise substantially greater evidentiary challenges than substantive standards for non-black-box care.

Second, providers might be too cautious, avoiding beneficial interventions out of concern for potential liability. This concern is true about new medical interventions in general, but to the extent that opaque algorithms seem to have a higher risk of causing harm, it may be more salient. Notably, however, some of the limited work done on diagnostic aids suggests that juries are less likely to punish doctors who act in accordance with such aids[29]; similar patterns might occur for black-box medicine, easing adoption. Eventually, liability concerns might actually help drive adoption as black-box medicine graduates from its current status of untested innovation, becoming sufficiently prevalent to get the protection of the ordinary medical malpractice deference rules or even sufficiently dominant that *non*adherence is deemed unreasonable. Like other medical advances, once black-box medicine becomes a more routine and better-accepted tool for medical care, providers not incorporating it could be liable for negligence if patients sustain reasonably avoidable injuries.[30]

Third and finally, a risk-based standard of care might undercompensate patients if observing failures to follow the standard of care were particularly difficult. In medical malpractice in general, identifying errors and demonstrating causation raise

---

[28] See, e.g., *Boswer v. Craig Ranch Emergency Hosp.*, No. 05-14-00501-CV, 2015 WL 3946371, at *4–5 (Tex. App. Jun. 29, 2015) (finding that a hospital's use of an outdated textbook to establish its policy could imply a "failure to promulgate policies and procedures regarding the standard of care").

[29] Hal R. Arks et al., The Influence of a Physician's Use of a Diagnostic Decision Aid on the Malpractice Verdicts of Mock Jurors, 28 Med. Decision Making 201, 204–5 (2008).

[30] See Miller & Miller, Legal and Regulatory Issues Related to the Use of Clinical Software in Health Care Delivery, at 346 (making a similar argument in the context of clinical decision support software).

substantial challenges. Observing failures to evaluate the riskiness of a black-box algorithm's recommendation might be similarly challenging. However, limited observability and compensation are a long-term reality of medical malpractice in any context, not just black-box medicine.

In sum, liability for providers using black-box medicine is both familiar and quite novel, like black-box medicine itself. Providers will typically be held to the level of care of other comparable providers, which will develop over time as black-box medicine enters care. However, choices might best be shaped – judicially, legislatively, or professionally – to rely on risk-based procedural validation as the touchstone for practice and liability because the underlying physiologic cause of injury will be both unavoidably opaque and unevaluable by the expertise of the provider.

20.3.2 *Liability of Healthcare Enterprises*

In addition to providers, larger healthcare enterprises such as hospitals and clinics owe a duty of care to patients, especially in modern medical settings involving coordination of complex care. Hospitals may be vicariously liable for the negligence of healthcare providers who are actual or apparent agents of the enterprise but may also have duties directly to patients that are especially relevant for black-box medicine. In particular, hospitals have been held to have a duty to provide adequate facilities for patient care, including well-functioning equipment necessary for adequate care.[31] In some jurisdictions, hospitals have other direct duties to patients, including a duty to coordinate care and sometimes a nondelegable duty to actually provide care for patients.[32]

Under these theories, hospitals could be liable for negligently choosing, implementing, and using black-box medical systems. As with liability for providers, hospitals are typically held to the standard of a reasonable hospital; also as with providers, this means that a hospital's responsibilities can evolve as industry custom does. But policymakers could try to move hospitals' standard of care for implementing black-box algorithms toward one that would involve procedural tools to make sure that algorithms are well validated and competently developed before implementation.

Although hospitals are typically not liable for defects in the products they provide and/or sell, they may have a duty to nonnegligently evaluate the quality of those products and may be liable for failures of products that they fail to evaluate.[33]

---

[31] See *Washington v. Washington Hospital Center*, 579 A.2d 177 (D.C. Ct. App. 1990) (finding that a hospital could be directly liable for failure to provide carbon dioxide monitors in operating rooms).

[32] See *Thompson v. Nason Hospital*, 427 Pa. 330 (Penn. 1991).

[33] See *Parker v. St. Vincent Hospital*, 122 N.M. 39, (N.M. Ct. App. 1996) (finding that a hospital is not strictly liable for defects in a physician-selected implant but acknowledging potential liability for negligently failing to examine the safety of the implant before provision).

Thus hospitals might reasonably be held liable for failing to ensure that the algorithms they make available to providers and patients are, as a whole, high quality and safe. Because substantive validation may be impossible in many cases – given the opaque nature of black-box medicine – procedural validation could be required instead. Parallels could be drawn to a more familiar responsibility of hospitals: their requirement to adequately credential the physicians who work in them to ensure that patients are seen by high-quality, well-trained doctors.[34] While a hospital cannot ensure that each decision of its doctors is correct, it can ensure that the doctors it brings through its doors are reasonably proficient. Applying a similar duty to black-box medicine would recognize the inherent opacity of the technology while leaving some responsibility on hospitals to take care in selection and implementation.[35]

20.4 RECOMMENDATIONS AND CONCLUSIONS

The development and adoption of black-box medicine are complex processes that will naturally evolve over time. But black-box medicine is coming fast. Knowing the risks of legal liability under current law is important, but perhaps more important is the opportunity to shape that liability as black-box medicine becomes increasingly powerful and prevalent. Liability for the developers of black-box medicine is important and complicated and demands careful study to set incentives for development and validation. But providers and healthcare facilities will be the crucial frontline of black-box medicine, choosing and implementing algorithms and interfacing directly with patients. Correct liability rules for providers and facilities could help to ensure that they will exercise due care in that task; they could also direct compensation for patients injured by the absence of such care.

Setting the right standards of liability for providers and facilities may require more than just waiting for the professions to eventually evolve the proper standard of care. To reiterate, the baseline grounding of the standard of care in customary practice privileges hewing to tradition and may therefore slow the adoption of new technologies. Deliberate standard setting could provide a different path. This is not to suggest that deliberate standard setting is especially *likely* to occur; the shield of deference to customary practice has deep roots. But it remains worth considering whether medical malpractice could have a role in the responsible adoption of black-box medical algorithms and what that might look like.

Standards must tread a careful middle ground between two extremes. On the one hand, overly lax liability rules could result in potentially haphazard application of new algorithms that may be insufficiently validated. While this might speed

---

[34] See Torin A. Dorros & T. Howard Stone, Implications of Negligent Selection and Retention of Physicians in the Age of ERISA, 21 Am. J.L. Med. 383, 396–97 (1995).
[35] Hospitals could also potentially be involved in developing their own black-box algorithms, as custodians of substantial amounts of patient data. In such circumstances, they would potentially incur liability as algorithm developers, a topic outside the scope of this chapter.

adoption of black-box medicine, it could also insufficiently protect patients and would create fewer incentives for algorithm developers to demonstrate the quality of their products. On the other hand, overly stringent liability rules, such as strict liability for providers or facilities for injuries or requirements that they comprehend the inherently incomprehensible mechanisms of black-box algorithms, would stymie adoption and the benefits that black-box medicine could bring.

A potentially workable middle ground would require providers and facilities to exercise due care in procedurally evaluating and implementing black-box algorithms. Providers and facilities should evaluate black-box algorithms for hallmarks of careful development, including independent validation of algorithmic results and the qualifications of the developers. Facilities are best suited to evaluate algorithms at the point of implementation and should ensure that algorithms – as a whole – are high quality according to measurable characteristics. Providers are able to measure the risk associated with a particular intervention and should accordingly measure the level of validation and confidence against the risks entailed. Such a duty would help facilitate the development of independent private or regulatory mechanisms for developing and providing that type of validation.[36] Finally, these duties or individual determinations should not remain static; black-box medicine will develop and evolve rapidly, and the appropriate role for providers and healthcare facilities should evolve with it.

---

[36] See Price, Black-Box Medicine, at 457–62.

PART VII

Intellectual Property Rights for Health Big Data

INTRODUCTION

Rachel E. Sachs

The scholarly literature on Big Data, including many of the chapters in this book, has asked a range of questions about its promises and perils. What might scientists and physicians accomplish with Big Data that we currently can only imagine – or is the science already here? How might we manage privacy concerns or ensure appropriate oversight of such research? However, much of the literature ignores a key first-order question and its corollary: how do we encourage incentives to produce Big Data frameworks in the first instance? And once we have them, how do we promote access to these frameworks and their products?

Questions such as these have long been the domain of intellectual property law and particularly patent law because scholars and policymakers take seriously the Constitution's statement that patent law serves to "promote the progress of Science."[1] Most (although certainly not all) scholars therefore take a largely consequentialist view of patent law. Its purpose is to encourage inventors to develop and commercialize inventions. As such, we provide government-granted monopolies in exchange for the disclosure of those inventions to the public, allowing inventors to reap monopoly profits now so that after the expiration of the patent term the invention may be produced and sold more cheaply.

Yet few scholars have specifically applied these aspects of intellectual property law theory – the incentive to innovate on one end and the promotion of access on the other – to new technologies involving Big Data. On its face, at least in the United States, the two would not necessarily seem to be an easy fit. There is no patent protection available for collections of information, and copyright protection in

---

[1] U.S. Constitution, Article I, § 8, cl. 8.

databases is thin at best.[2] After a series of recent Supreme Court rulings,[3] it has also become more difficult to obtain protection over the algorithms used to analyze the relevant data sets.

Despite these apparent surface obstacles to traditional intellectual property protection, at the same time we are certainly observing an explosion in Big Data research. It is very likely true either that researchers are discovering other ways to protect their investments or that traditional intellectual property rights are not truly necessary for investment in this space. In either case, we might become concerned about the ability of other researchers and of patients to both access and benefit from these technologies because other intellectual property levers (such as trade secrecy) do not come with the same social bargain for public disclosure and future access that patent law does.

The chapters in this section take up these questions at the intersection of intellectual property law and Big Data, investigating both the strengths and weaknesses of intellectual property as a mechanism for promoting innovation into Big Data technologies and the potential difficulties this intellectual property may create from a social welfare perspective. Chapter 21, by Timo Minssen and Justin Pierce, considers the ways in which different intellectual property rights may be useful in protecting investments into Big Data technologies while also illustrating a set of emerging tensions between Big Data and some of these intellectual property rights. Chapter 22, by Ted Sichelman and Brenda Simon, first identifies a species of patents – those the authors refer to as "data-generating patents" – that have the potential to be socially problematic and then evaluates remedies for these problems.

Increasingly, scholars have sought to place new and different policy tools into the same bucket as traditional intellectual property rights such as patents and copyrights, considering the ways in which these additional policy tools may function – purposefully or not – to replicate the functions of those traditional rights. Minssen and Pierce contribute to this literature. They first argue that although in the United States patents and copyrights may not protect the full range of investments inventors may make in Big Data technologies, other policy tools may be available instead. The European Union has created special protections for databases. Trade secrecy may be available, although its indefinite duration and inherent secrecy may pose access concerns. And periods of regulatory exclusivity awarded by pharmaceutical regulators may similarly provide rewards for Big Data's use in the pharmaceutical space.

Yet Minssen and Pierce go on to pay close attention to the challenges posed at the intersection of Big Data and intellectual property rights. Some of these challenges are subject specific in nature. For instance, these authors highlight the increasing development of systems biology and note its similarities to many information

---

[2] *Feist Publ'ns, Inc., v. Rural Tel. Serv. Co.*, 499 U.S. 340 (1991); see also 17 U.S.C. § 103(b) (2012).
[3] See, e.g., *Alice Corp. v. CLS Bank Int'l.*, 134 S. Ct. 2347 (2014).

technologies, suggesting that some of the lessons learned in that field about the role of standard-essential patents might be similarly applicable here. Other challenges are more general. Chiefly, the authors express concern about the role of antitrust law and the use of Big Data resources in anticompetitive ways, including by Big Data companies who refuse to license their resources to others for their use.

Sichelman and Simon share some of these concerns about the potential social costs of using intellectual property rights to protect Big Data resources, but they do so through a new phenomenon they dub "data-generating patents." These are "patented inventions that by design produce valuable data through their operation or use," with Myriad Genetics' patents on genes coding for increased risk of breast cancer providing perhaps the most memorable example in the healthcare space. Myriad's patents on these genes allowed the company to develop a large database of genetic and phenotypic information about the women who received its test – a database that it continued to protect using trade secrecy even after its patents were invalidated in the courts. In the authors' view, patents such as these create harms both in terms of access to the resulting technologies and in terms of stifled sequential innovation downstream.

As such, the authors present a framework for identifying potentially problematic patents and suggest possibilities for remedying the social harms they may create. In terms of identification, the authors propose to use two factors in discovering such patents – the patents' potential to preempt competition in generating data and the potential for expansion into unforeseeable data markets. Patents with both high preemptive potential and high degrees of unforeseeability are likely to be socially problematic, whereas relaxing one or both assumptions decreases the likelihood of such problems. For the set of socially problematic patents, the authors evaluate solutions both internal and external to patent law that would help to remediate some of the concerns both for encouraging access and for promoting innovation.

21

Big Data and Intellectual Property Rights in the Health and Life Sciences

Timo Minssen and Justin Pierce

21.1 INTRODUCTION

As the other chapters in this book detail, Big Data plays a crucial role in the ongoing evolution of healthcare and life science sector innovations. In recent years, US and European authorities have developed public platforms and infrastructures providing access to vast stores of healthcare knowledge, including data from clinical trials and chosen patient information. In light of these developments and rapid technical advances, which have significantly facilitated the collection and analysis of information and knowledge from multiple sources, the protection of such data but also the access thereto have become ever critical to the innovation narrative.[1] The vast prospects of Big Data and the gradual shift to more "personalized," "open," and "transparent" innovation models highlight the importance of an effective, efficient, and well-calibrated regulation, governance, and use of biological and personal data.

The intersection between the Big Data narrative and intellectual property rights (IPRs) raises a significant challenge, especially when questions of ownership rights of data arise and where ownership is challenged by potential users seeking access to data becomes a consideration. Data analytics or data mining will often involve the copying of, or references to, information or databases, all of which might be protected by various forms of IPRs in relevant jurisdictions. Where data are not owned or licensed, the user will need to rely on an exception to IPR infringement to use data. This has given rise to fierce controversies between data "owners," data researchers, and entities that provide enabling technologies, large research infrastructures, and standardization platforms. These tensions at the interface of Big Data and IPRs involve complex considerations relating to innovation economics, ownership, licensing, and exceptions to IPRs.

---

[1] See, e.g., Michael L. Katz & Carl Shapiro, Product Introduction with Network Externalities, 40 J. Indust. Econ. 55, 55–83 (1992); Mark A. Lemley & Ziv Shafir, Who Chooses Open-Source Software?, 78 U. Chi. L. Rev. 139, 139–64 (2011); Michael A. Carrier, *Innovation in the 21st Century: Harnessing the Power of Intellectual Property and Antitrust Law* (2011).

This chapter offers general insights into challenges resulting from the intersection between the Big Data narrative and IPRs. It first provides a brief summary of the most relevant IPRs for data-based life science research. Due to space constraints, we concentrate on IPRs and related *sui generis* rights protecting commercially relevant data rather than on legislation protecting personal data integrity or regulating data transfer. This serves as the basis for the next section of this chapter, which briefly discusses selected areas where emerging tensions between IPRs and Big Data crystallize. Our concluding remarks argue that these tensions need to be discussed and addressed on a case-by case basis.

21.2 THE MOST RELEVANT IPRS AND *SUI GENERIS* RIGHTS IN BIG DATA SCIENCE: AN OVERVIEW

A number of IPRs and other protective rights may apply to various aspects and fields of application for Big Data, but essentially there are five types of IPRs and *sui generis* rights on which we concentrate. These encompass (1) patents, (2) copyrights, (3) the European database protection, and the important *sui generis* areas[2] of (4) trade secret protection and (5) regulatory exclusivities. The following section briefly explains the main features of these rights, and the analysis concentrates on the protection of data and data-related technologies, such as algorithms and bioinformatics tools.

21.2.1 *Patents on Software, Algorithms, and Diagnostics*

With companies working hard to innovatively collect, store, and retrieve data, the question of right to restrict access to information on the basis of granted IPRs is becoming a pressing consideration. As Nicholson Price[3] and Rachel Sachs[4] point out, the current US patent eligibility doctrines made it inherently difficult to patent Big Data sets, software algorithms, and validation methods used in Big Data. The question is whether the patent system for diagnostic methods, software, and algorithms is sufficiently robust in the United States and Europe so as not to allow patents to become routinely used legal avenues to protect access to data.[5]

United States
As a general rule, a patent claim must be directed to one of the four patent-eligible subject matter categories. Where a claim is not within one of these categories, the

---

[2] For the purpose of this short chapter, trade secret protection and regulatory exclusivities are considered as *sui generis* rights.
[3] Price, W. Nicholson, Big Data, Patents, and the Future of Medicine, 37 *Cardozo L. Rev.* 1401, 1420–25 (2016), available at https://papers.ssrn.com/sol3/papers.cfm?abstract_id=2659797 [https://perma.cc/R92S-CH2L].
[4] Cf. Sachs, Rachel E, Innovation Law and Policy: Preserving the Future of Personalized Medicine, 49 *U.C.D. L. Rev.* 1881–1987 (2016), available at http://ssrn.com/abstract=2596875 [https://perma.cc/NWQ5-5WGG].
[5] Michael Mattioli, Disclosing Big Data, 99 *Minn. L. Rev.* 535 (2014).

claim is not eligible for patent protection and should be rejected unless it falls within one of the judicial exceptions. A series of US judicial decisions has addressed these exceptions and the method of assessing patent applications based on one of these exceptions.[6] In its *Alice Corporation Pty. Ltd. v. CLS Bank International* decision, the US Supreme Court makes clear that a two-step test applies to determination of when an invention is patentable. First, the reviewer of the patent must determine if the patent covers an excluded area from patenting, such as an abstract idea or law of nature. If the patent covers an excluded area, the reviewer moves on to the second stage: whether there is an inventive concept that is an application of the abstract idea or law of nature.[7] This two-part test is a capstone to the Court's prior decisions in *Bilski v. Kappos*[8] and *Prometheus v. Mayo*.[9] This substantive approach has led to a situation where neither adding the words "apply it" to excluded subject matter nor the recitation of a computer can – without anything more – render the ineligible eligible. Although recent US Patent and Trademark Office (USPTO) guidance and US Circuit Court decisions give some hints on how to meet the heightened patent criteria, the judicial exceptions in the United States have made it much more difficult to broaden the protection of software and algorithms to restrict access to data under cover of patent protection.

European Union

In comparison, the European eligibility doctrine regarding software, data-related inventions, and diagnostic methods appears to be more flexible, despite the existence of an express provision on their excludability. Article 52 (2) of the European Patent Convention (EPC)[10] recites a list of "non-inventions," including abstract ideas, scientific theories, mathematical methods, and computer programs that are excluded "as such."

In the European Union, "technical character" is synonymous with invention; any demonstration and degree of technical character passes the patent eligibility threshold. The role of the technical feature is irrelevant, to the point that the mere use of technical means, such as a computer, may render a patent claim eligible. Accordingly, the question asked for computer-based methods is: does the

---

[6] See *Mayo Collaborative Servs. v. Prometheus Labs., Inc.*, 566 U.S. 66, (2012) (*Mayo*); *Association for Molecular Pathology v. Myriad Genetics, Inc.*, U.S., 133 S. Ct. 2107 (2013) (*Myriad*); *Alice Corp. Pty. Ltd. v. CLS Bank Int'l.*, 134 S.Ct. 2347 (2014) (*Alice*); *In re Roslin Inst.*, 750 F.3d 1333 (Fed. Cir. 2014) (*Roslin*); *Ariosa Diagnostics, Inc. v. Sequenom, Inc.*, 788 F.3d 1377 (Fed Cir. 2015) (*Sequenom*); *Ariosa Diagnostics, Inc. v. Sequenom, Inc.*, 802 F.3d 1282, 1286 (Fed Cir. 2015) ("December 12 Order") (*Per curiam* order denying petition for rehearing en banc); *Sequenom, Inc. v. Diagnostics, Inc.*, No. 15–1182, 2016 WL 1105544 (U.S. March 21, 2016).
[7] 134 S. Ct., at 7.
[8] 561 U.S. 593 (2010) (concerning business method patents).
[9] 566 U.S. 66 (concerning medical diagnostic and treatment patents).
[10] Convention on the grant of European Patents Done at Munich, October 5, 1973, 1065 U.N.T.S. 199 (hereinafter EPC).

method achieve a technical effect, or has it only nontechnical aspects, for example, aesthetic or economic?"[11]

In the European Union, mere games or business methods, for example, are not patentable,[12] but a method to analyze DNA *in silico* is patentable.[13] This also applies to simulations or modeling if the result is a teaching that can be used to achieve technical effects in the real world. For instance, a method of encoding audio information in a communication system may aim to reduce distortion induced by channel noise. Although the idea underlying such a method may be considered to reside in a mathematical method, the encoding method as a whole is not a mathematical method "as such" and hence is not excluded from patentability by Article 52(2)(a) and (3) of the EPC.[14] Similar reasoning applies to medical diagnostic methods and methods of treatment that are excepted from patentability under Article 53(c) of the EPC, but only if practiced on the human body. This requirement has been very narrowly interpreted to allow the patentability of specific genetic diagnostic methods.[15] Moreover, Article 53(c) explicitly states that these exceptions shall not apply to products, in particular, substances or compositions, for use in any of these methods.

In sum, in Europe, the patent eligibility standard has become a question of drafting, where many mixed claims and Big Data techniques could with clever drafting pass the patent eligibility threshold. It should not be forgotten that both in Europe and in the United States other patentability requirements, such as novelty, inventive step or nonobviousness, industrial application, sufficient disclosure, and clarity would still have to be satisfied.

21.2.2 Copyrights

In the United States and Europe, copyright protection may be relevant at different stages of Big Data research and development (R&D). Generally speaking, in order to obtain copyright protection, one has to demonstrate that the creation is original. The mere collections and sample sets of Big Data as such, without anything more, will not be protectable by copyright.[16]

If the originality criteria are met, however, copyrights could be held in relation to the manner in which data are selected and structured. It could also cover protocols or standard operating procedures organizing and describing such selection

---

[11] EPO – T 0208/84 (computer-related invention) of 15.7.1986.
[12] EPO – T-931/95 (pension benefit system partnership) of 8.9.2000.
[13] EPO – T-0146/07 (prenatal diagnosis/ISIS) of 13.12.2011.
[14] Cf. EPO Guidelines for Examination Part G, chap. II 3.3 (2016).
[15] EPO Opinion G-1/04 of December 16, 2005 (diagnostic methods). See also EPO – T-0146/07 (prenatal diagnosis/ISIS) of 13.12.2011, where patent eligibility was not even an issue.
[16] Cf. Michiel Verlinden et al., IPRs in Biobanking: Risks and Opportunities for Translational Research, 2 I.P.Q. 116, 116–29 (2011).

and structure. This may include the text and/or structure of questionnaires, coding systems, or software developed to (automatically) collect, store, process, search, and analyze samples and data. Copyright could also cover an original appearance or design of the database that will store (often standardized) data, biological material, or websites, where Big Data users and researchers can access biological material and/or data.[17] For example, the documents created to describe technical standards for the BioBrick RFC process are subject to copyright protection, as well as the software tools developed for synthetic biology applications and standards.[18]

Another issue that has recently gained traction is if it is possible to copyright biological sequence information, such as synthetically produced DNA sequences.[19] Here the advantage and drawback of traditional copyright features and concepts would have to be carefully considered and, if at all feasible, be reformed and adapted. This includes not only the preclusive effects of the very lengthy copyright terms and the availability of protection without registration but also established doctrines such as "fair use" that could permit more third-party uses of copyrighted DNA sequences than under patent laws. Ultimately, such copyright doctrines might provide the ground for the application of open-source principles to areas such as synthetic biology.[20]

In conclusion, any original, creative organization of data and the tools governing them will, under certain circumstances, be eligible for copyright protection, whereas an extension of copyright protection to synthetic biology is still a debatable issue.

21.2.3 EU Database Protection

In contrast to the United States, in the European Union, the investment in the content of a database can be protected by a "database right."[21] For example, a biobank including a collection of biological material with associated data that are

---

[17] Andrew W. Torrance & Linda J., Kahl, Bringing Standards to Life: Synthetic Biology Standards and Intellectual Property, 30 *Santa Clara High Tech. L. J.* 201, 226 (2014), available at http://ssrn.com/abstract=2426235 [https://perma.cc/H5B2-WNW8].

[18] Ibid., at 226.

[19] See. e.g., Duncan M. Davidson, Common Law, Uncommon Software, 47 *U. Pitt. L. Rev.* 1037, 1104–5 (1986); Irving Kayton, Copyright in Living Genetically Engineered Works, 50 *Geo. Wash. L. Rev.* 191 (1982); Donna Smith, Comment: Copyright Protection for the Intellectual Property Rights to Recombinant Deoxyribonucleic Acid: A Proposal, 19 *St. Mary's L.J.* 1083, 1096–108 (1988); Dan L. Burk, Copyrightability of Recombinant DNA Sequences, 29 *Jurimetrics J.* 469, 531–32 (1989); Andrew W. Torrance, DNA Copyright, 46 *Val. U. L. Rev.* 1 (2011); Christopher M. Holman, Copyright for Engineered DNA: An Idea Whose Time Has Come?, 113 *W. Va. L. Rev.* 699 (2011); Andrew W. Torrance, Synthesizing Law for Synthetic Biology, 11 *Minn. J. L. Sci. Tech.* 629 (2010); Christopher M. Holman, Developments in Synthetic Biology Are Altering the IP Imperatives of Biotechnology, 17 *Vanderbilt J. Ent. Tech. L.* 385 (2015), available at http://ssrn.com/abstract=2623153 [https://perma.cc/V36K-NCPQ].

[20] Holman, Copyright for Engineered DNA, at 385.

[21] See also Verlinden et. al., IPRs in Biobanking, at 111.

organized in a systematic or methodical way or a database in a "systems biology" (SysBio) project could be considered as a protected database.[22] The United States, however, has no equivalent database law, although databases can be protected by copyright if they qualify as a "compilation."[23]

In Europe, the different parties that invested or contributed to the establishment and development of the database could each claim *sui generis* rights on the whole or parts of the research project. In the case of biobanks or SysBio-related research, for example, such rights could become relevant at different stages of research and product developments.[24] Users can be prevented from extracting substantial parts of the data to create their own collection. Hence it is important to have clear arrangements on whether and under which conditions different parties could hold database rights and how stakeholders will be able to use the collection of data.[25]

The protection of database rights starts from the date when the database is completed or made publicly available. It does not require the fulfillment of any formalities or any registration. The protection covers a period of fifteen years.[26] Whenever the database is modified in a substantial way and this modification requires a substantial investment, a new term of fifteen years starts for the new construction of the database.[27]

21.2.4 Trade Secrets

Trade secrets offer protection for knowhow and business information that cannot be protected by conventional IPRs or that is otherwise elected not to be protected under conventional IPRs. This could, for instance, be an invention that does not fulfill the requirements to obtain patent protection, such as the eligibility, novelty,

---

[22] See Directive 96/9/EC of the European Parliament and of the Council of 11 March 1996 on the Legal Protection of Databases, chap. 3, 1996 O.J. (L077); see also Åsa Hellstadius, Sanna Wolk, & Richard Wessman, Intellectual Property and Biobanks, in *Biobanks as Resources for Health* 207–25 (Mats G. Hannson & Marianne Levin, eds. 2003). It is, however, highly controversial if EU database protection should be extended to cover collections of physical material.

[23] Cf. Mitchell Smith, *A Comparison of the Legal Protection of Databases in the United States and EU: Implications for Scientific Research* (2010), available at http://ssrn.com/abstract=1613451 [https://perma.cc/C6LF-5CBP]; Daniel J. Gervais, The Protection of Databases, 82 *Chi. Kent L. Rev.* 1109 (2007); Jane C. Ginsburg, Copyright, Common Law, and Sui Generis Protection of Databases in the United States and Abroad, 66 *U.Cin. L. Rev.* 151 (1997). Such a system has been proposed and rejected in the United States. Ibid., at 171.

[24] Verlinden et al., IPRs in Biobanking, at 111.

[25] Ibid. (referring to Global Alliance for Genomics & Health, *Framework for Responsible Sharing of Genomic and Health-Related Data* [2014], available at https://www.ncbi.nlm.nih.gov/pmc/articles/PMC4685158/ [https://perma.cc/XRP9-DRRG]); see also Timo Minssen & Jens Schovsbo, Legal Aspects of Biobanking as Key Issues for Personalized Medicine and Translational Exploitation, 11 *Person. Med.* 497, 497–508 (2014).

[26] Directive 96/9/EC of the European Parliament and of the Council of 11 March 1996 on the legal protection of databases, 1996, O.J. (L 77), 20–28.

[27] Ibid., at Article 10(III).

or nonobviousness criteria. An example highlighting this problem is Myriad Genetics (discussed more fully in Chapter 22), where an existing patent granting protection is invalidated, and the resulting database containing Big Data can remain protected under trade secret law. This is especially the situation in the United States, but the comparative situation across Europe is far more fragmented and reliant on national laws of the European Member States. In the United States, the application of an existing technology in a new sector could constitute a trade secret, even when such application seems obvious. Trade secrets also protect knowhow or information that is not described in a patent application but that remains secret and is crucial to optimize the use of an invention.

The trade secret holder cannot, however, object to the fact that a third party would develop independently identical production processes or algorithms, and the protection stops as soon as the information protected by the trade secret becomes (lawfully) publicly available or loses its commercial value. Hence certain information and data types are particularly difficult to protect by trade secrecy, such as products or services whose properties, structures, and setups are self-revealing. For example, the disclosure requirement in patent law and clinical trials data transparency legislation might make it impossible to protect some data that are not already covered by other IPRs. By contrast, valuable information that qualifies for commercially confidential information under the new European clinical trials data transparency legislation, such as manufacturing knowhow pertaining to the production of complex biologics or knowhow about sophisticated diagnostic methods and protein-folding patterns, could be more easily protected because the reverse engineering is so difficult.

The organization and ways of operating of a database could also be considered trade secrets because they would have an important impact on the quality of the health and life science–related data and the services provided. Trade secrets could, for instance, relate to the (systematic) approach chosen to collect, store, label, process, and track data or to the algorithm used to analyze the collected data. Researchers that, for example, access collections of biological data could be required to contractually commit themselves to respect the confidentiality of trade secrets. A third party not only would have to copy the database content or structure or software but also would need access to certain confidential knowhow or information to establish and operate the database or software in an optimal manner. In this respect, trade secrets could offer an additional protection of databases or software.

Until 2014, there has been no harmonized EU definition of a trade secret or a harmonized protection system for trade secrets. An EU Directive on the protection of undisclosed knowhow and business information against their unlawful acquisition, use, and disclosure is now in place.[28]

---

[28] Directive 2016/943, of the European Parliament and of the Council on the Protection of Undisclosed Know-How and Business Information (Trade Secrets) against Their Unlawful Acquisition, Use and Disclosure, O.J. (L 157) 1, 1–18.

By comparison, in the United States, at least as far as civil matters are concerned, the protection of trade secret misappropriation has so far been regulated entirely by state law. The Uniform Trade Secrets Act had already achieved substantial uniformity between the states, but there are also a number of differences and perceived procedural weaknesses. These perceived weaknesses in combination with technological and legal changes and an increased threat of cyber espionage motivated the adoption of a new federal civil private cause of action for trade secret theft that would provide businesses with a more uniform, reliable, and predictable way to protect their trade secrets anywhere in the United States.

The recently introduced Defend Trade Secrets Act (DTSA) amends the Economic Espionage Act to create a private civil cause of action for trade secret misappropriation. The DTSA does not eliminate or preempt the various state trade secret rights but rather would operate as an additional layer of potential protection.

21.2.5 Regulatory Exclusivities

Another form of protection that has become increasingly important to the commercial aspects of Big Data in the health and life sciences is regulatory market and data exclusivities, which are available for the protection of clinical trial data in both the United States and Europe. The European rules governing regulatory exclusivity[29] introduced the "8 + 2 + 1 year rule."[30] This rule, which applies to both small-molecule drugs and biologics, means that data exclusivity applies during the first eight years from the grant of the innovator company's marketing authorization. This implies that if a producer of a generic or biosimilar intends to apply for marketing authorization of a generic drug or biosimilar and wants to cross-reference to existing preclinical or clinical data, the authorities may during this period not accept such references due to data exclusivity restrictions. This means that the data exclusivity acts as a barrier preventing access to the data required for marketing authorization of a similar existing product, operating in much the same way as an IPR during the exclusivity period.

Following expiration of the first eight-year period, a generic company may start to cross-refer to the preclinical and clinical trial data of the originator in its regulatory applications. The data exclusivity period is, however, followed by a two-year market exclusivity period. Hence generic competitors cannot market their product for another two years, whereas they can now refer to the originator's data to prepare their application. Following the period of ten years (eight plus two) from the grant of

---

[29] Directive 2001/83, of the European Parliament and of the Council of 6 November 2001 on the Community Code Relating to Medicinal Products for Human Use, O.J. (L 311) 67, 67–128.
[30] Regulation 726/2004, of the European Parliament and of the Council of 31 March 2004 Laying Down Community Procedures for the Authorization and Supervision of Medicinal Products for Human and Veterinary Use and Establishing a European Medicines Agency (Text with EEA relevance), O.J. (L 136) 1, 1–33.

the innovator company's marketing authorization, the generic company may then market its product, provided that the innovator product does not qualify for yet another one-year market exclusivity.[31]

The European system recognizes specific *sui generis* forms of protection. These aim specifically at fostering the development of specific inventions and applications that are useful for the treatment of children ("pediatric extensions") or very rare diseases ("orphan drugs"). These may encompass dosage regimes useful for pediatric applications under Regulation (EC) No. 1901/2006 (for example, six months SPC extensions) and strong marketing exclusivities (ten to twelve years) for orphan drugs and pediatric orphan drugs under Regulation (EC) No. 141/2000.

In the United States, the Hatch-Waxman Act and related legislation provide for similar nonpatent marketing exclusivity. This is available to 505(b)(1) and 505(b)(2) NDA applicants, for example, either five-year "new chemical entity" (NCE) exclusivity, three-year new clinical investigation exclusivity, six months of pediatric exclusivities, or seven-year orphan drug exclusivity under the Orphan Drug Act.[32] In addition, specific market exclusivities are available under the so-called GAIN Act for the development and market approval of antibiotics.[33] Moreover, and in contrast to the more generally applicable European 8 + 2 + 1 system, the United States had introduced a much-debated special data and market exclusivities for the first approved innovator biologic drug. For biologics, the exclusivity term provided by the Biologics Price Competition and Innovation Act is twelve years from the date the reference product was first licensed.[34] The United States also has special market exclusivity provisions for the first approved interchangeable biologic product.[35]

While this brief overview could only draw a very rough picture, it is important to note that the specific design and new areas of application for regulatory exclusivities have become an increasingly important issue in general innovation policy debates.

21.3 EMERGING TENSIONS

This contribution has so far provided a brief overview on the most relevant IPRs for data-based life science research. Given the wide array Big Data applications and the great variety of IPRs, the choice of how to address, use, and interact with IPRs will

---

[31] See, e.g., Alexander Meier et al., An Assessment of Implications of Adaptive Licensing for Pharmaceutical Intellectual Property and Regulatory Exclusivity Rights in the European Union, 100 *Clin. Pharmacol. Ther.* 743, 743–753 (2016).

[32] 21 U.S.C. § 360bb(a)(2) (2008); see also 21 C.F.R. § 316.31 (2016).

[33] On July 9, 2012, the Generating Antibiotic Incentives Now, or GAIN, provisions were signed into law by President Barack Obama as part of the Food and Drug Administration Safety and Innovation Act; cf. Title VIII of the Food and Drug Administration Safety and Innovation Act (FDASIA), Pub. L. No. 112–144.

[34] See Public Health Service Act, § 351 (k)(7), as added by the BPCI Act.

[35] Depending on various factors, the length of market exclusivity varies between twelve and forty-two months; see Public Health Service Act, § 351(k)(6).

most likely differ among various areas of applications. This chapter concludes with a short, nonexhaustive discussion of selected emerging issues.

21.3.1 Antitrust and Big Data

While there are issues to be resolved between Big Data and IPRs, there is a growing awareness of the importance of data and specifically Big Data by market authorities. Antitrust agencies, those in the United States and competition agencies in Europe, are taking note of Big Data, and there is an increasing trend to examine closely the collection, use, and access of Big Data for anticompetitive effects.

Although much of the current focus on Big Data is directed toward Internet use and the collection and use of consumer data, there are strong indications that the scope of the law, especially in Europe, can be extended to Big Data in the life science sector.[36] Despite these indications, there remains no consensus on the application of antitrust law to Big Data. Disagreement aside, there is a growing number of decisions that highlight the use of antitrust rules to Big Data cases. Historically, the European and US agencies have been marked with different approaches to the assessments of anticompetitive behaviors. Although in the merger leading to Thomson Reuters, regulators in the European Union and the United States had concerns stemming from Big Data. Both took the position that the need for a company to collect vast amounts of financial data to effectively compete with the merged firm in the market for data terminals created a significant barrier to entry.[37] To address this concern, both authorities approved the merger on the condition that the merged firm would make copies of its database available for purchase by existing and new potential competitors. At the EU level, the European Court of Justice in *IMS Health*[38] set out clear rules stating that there are limitations to the extent IPRs can be used to protect access to data. Likewise, in the *Servier* case,[39] European competition rules were found to be applicable where companies acquire IPRs with the direct intent to reduce technological dissemination into the market, thus restricting the availability of data from product introduction.

---

[36] See D. G. Vestager, European Commission: Check against Delivery (2016), available at http://ec.europa.eu/commission/2014-2019/vestager/announcements/big-data-and-competition_en [https://perma.cc/6RR4-K7B8] (giving a recent speech on data as an asset and access to data for innovation). See also Edith Ramirez, et al., *Federal Trade Commission, Big Data: A Tool for Inclusion?* (2016), available at www.ftc.gov/system/files/documents/reports/big-data-tool-inclusion-or-exclusion-understanding-issues/160106big-data-rpt.pdf [https://perma.cc/3X3U-JYT2] (emphasizing the link between Big Data, medicine, and healthcare).

[37] Case COMP/M.4726, Thomson Corp./Reuters Group, of 19.2.2008, available at http://ec.europa.eu/competition/mergers/cases/decisions/m4726_20080219_20600_en.pdf [https://perma.cc/K2DF-5ZZA].

[38] Case C-418/01, *IMS Health GmbH & Co. OHG v. NDC Health GmbH & Co.*, 2002 E.C.R. I-3401.

[39] Decision COMP/AT.39612 "Perindopril (Servier)" of July 9, 2014.

The trend of the intervention of the competition rules into the rights of data owners is also occurring at the level of European Member States. For example, in the Cegedim[40] investigation, the French Competition Authority found that the refusal of access to data to those using rival software was unjustified. These are issues that remain unanswered in the antitrust narrative, but all indications are that the future holds more application of the antitrust rules.

21.3.2 Specific Areas of Science and Applications

The evolving use of standardized biological subject matter and data in "synthetic biology" and in "systems biology" (SysBio) raises science-specific tensions between IPRs and Big Data. Regarding the use of biological data standards, the most relevant field is probably SysBio.[41] SysBio involves the study of biological systems at a so-called systems level. One predominant reason and a critical prerequisite for the growth of SysBio is that the relevant scientific methodologies and research tools have become far more powerful and accurate. SysBio's interdisciplinary nature requires data, models, and other research assets to be formatted and described in standard ways to enable exchange and reuse of high-quality Big Data. Hence the SysBio community is heavily engaged in developing and agreeing on data standards. One issue concerns the potential of patents to function as data aggregators in biotechnology.[42]

"Large research infrastructures" represent another area of foreseeable challenges. For example, the enormous opportunities of Big Data and the gradual shift to more personalized, open, and transparent innovation models highlight the importance of effective governance and use of biological material and the associated data stored in "biobanks." Whereas much effort and money are being invested in the storing of biological material and increasingly sophisticated data sets in both private and public biobanks, there are often insufficient IPR strategies in place regarding the great variety of IPRs that can be obtained at the different construction and commercialization stages of biobanking.[43] While the choice of how to address and

---

[40] French Competition Authority, Decision no. 14-D-06 (August 7, 2014).
[41] Timo Minssen et al., Synthetic Biology and Intellectual Property Rights: Six Recommendations, 10 *Biotechnol. J.* 236, 236–41 (2015); Timo Minssen et al., Intellectual Property Rights, Standards and Data Exchange in Systems Biology, 11 *Biotechnol. J.* 1477, 1477–80 (2016).
[42] See also Burk, Dan, Patents as Data Aggregators in Personalized Medicine, 21 *BU J. Sci. Tech. L.* 233 (2015).
[43] See, e.g., Saminda Pathmasiri et al., Intellectual Property Rights in Publicly Funded Biobanks: Much Ado about Nothing?, 29 *Nat. Biotechnol.* 319, 323 (2011); Elise Smith, The Limits of Sharing: An Ethical Analysis of the Arguments for and against the Sharing of Databases and Material Banks, 18 *Accountability Res.* 357, 357–81 (2011); Michiel Verlinden et al., IPRs in Biobanking: Risks and Opportunities for Translational Research, 2 *Intell. Prop. Q.* 106, 106–29 (2015).

interact with IPRs might vary between different types of biobanks, it is clear that an appropriate balance in the user modalities of IPRs appears particularly important in open innovation scenarios and translational medicine.[44]

A further area with emerging issues is "personalized medicine," in particular "black-box medicine." This entails the use of combinations of large-scale, high-quality data sets with sophisticated and nontransparent predictive algorithms to identify and use implicit, complex connections between multiple patient characteristics."[45] In addition to pointing toward practical, ethical, regulatory, and privacy hurdles, Nicholson Price admonishes that the current IPR regime not only provides inadequate incentives for black-box medicine. He also points out that the incentives it does provide push the field in counterproductive directions.[46] Patents, the primary intellectual property driver of technological innovation, are a poor fit for black-box medicine. Patents are static, whereas black-box medicine is dynamic; patents are slow to issue, whereas black-box medicine evolves rapidly; and patents demand full and precise disclosure, whereas black-box medicine is inherently incapable of being fully disclosed.[47] In addition to basic and long-standing structural concerns, as discussed earlier, the recent US Supreme Court decisions[48] have – in contrast to European case law – severely restricted the general patent eligibility of diagnostic methods and algorithms.[49] Hence, as Nicholson Price argues, better-calibrated incentives are needed to properly enhance black-box medicine.[50]

Last but not least, as pointed out by Ruth L. Okediji, a numbery of tensions are emerging in the area of "private-sector uses of publicly available data."[51] The enormous innovation potential and economic value of Big Data will probably require a more considered and different set of intellectual property ownership rules.[52] One example relates to publicly available clinical trials data, where recent public and private initiatives, such as EU regulation No. 536/2014,[53] have resulted in more transparency and public availability of more complete sets of clinical trials data.[54] This will result in great opportunities but might also affect the availability

---

[44] Saminda et al., Intellectual Property Rights in Publicly Funded Biobanks, at 323.
[45] For a definition of "black-box medicine," see, W. Nicholson Price II, Black Box Medicine, 28 *Harv. J.L. Technol.* 419, 421 (2015).
[46] Ibid.
[47] Ibid.
[48] See notes 5–7.
[49] Price, Black Box Medicine, at 421.
[50] Ibid.
[51] Ruth L. Okediji, Government as Owner of Intellectual Property? Considerations for Public Welfare in the Era of Big Data, 18 *Vanderbilt J. Ent. Tech. L.* 331 (2016).
[52] Ibid.
[53] Regulation 536/2014, of the European Parliament and of the Council of 16 April 2014 on Clinical Trials on Medicinal Products for Human Use and Repealing Council Directive 2001/20/EC Text with EEA relevance, O.J. (L 158) 1, 1–76.
[54] W. Nicholson Price II & Timo Minssen, Will Clinical Trial Data Disclosure Reduce Incentives to Develop New Uses of Drugs?, 33 *Nat. Biotechnol.* 685, 686 (2015).

of IPRs and hence the dynamics of technology transfer and industrial involvement in translational medicine.[55]

21.4 CONCLUSION

A great variety of different IPRs and *sui generis* rights may apply to various aspects of Big Data applications. Clearly, some rights, such as European database rights and trade secrets, are becoming increasingly important for the commercial protection of Big Data, whereas other rights that have traditionally played a major role in innovation policy debates, such as patent rights, may not always be applicable and useful for the protection of specific data uses.

At the same time, the full effect and function of some of these IPRs – for example, as data aggregators – for the Big Data innovation framework are not entirely clear and demand further study. The (un-)availability of the aforementioned IPRs and *sui generis* rights might result in both a lack of well-calibrated incentives and under-investment in some areas but also in blocking effects for open innovation and anticommons scenarios in other areas. Also, their interplay with recent data transparency initiatives and their potential impact on open-innovation scenarios or public-private partnerships need to be elucidated. It can thus be assumed that nuanced approaches and IPR user modalities will have to be considered for different technological applications and that these need to be discussed and addressed on a case-by-case basis.

[55] Ibid.

22

The Pathologies of Data-Generating Patents

Ted Sichelman and Brenda M. Simon

22.1 INTRODUCTION

Should a patent confer exclusive control not only over an invention but also over the data generated by it, potentially indefinitely? Previously, we introduced the concept of "data-generating patents," which are patented inventions that by design produce valuable data through their operation or use.[1] In this chapter, we focus on concerns raised by biomedical data-generating patents, particularly in the context of the rise of Big Data. Many examples of biomedical data-generating patents have appeared throughout this volume, including patents covering genetic diagnostic tests, implantable and other medical devices, and consumer gadgets that track, store, and analyze information about patients and users.[2]

Consider the example of Myriad Genetics, which holds patents covering genes coding for an increased risk of breast and ovarian cancer. By selling its patented diagnostic tests, Myriad was able to develop an extensive database of genetic and phenotypic information about patients. Trade secret law provides protection for economically valuable information, such as Myriad's database, provided that it is not easily reproducible and reasonable efforts are made to maintain its secrecy.[3] Even after the US Supreme Court invalidated many of Myriad's patents, its database, which continues to be protected by trade secret law, has in many ways become more valuable than its patents. Allowing trade secrets to serve as economic complements to data-generating patents in this manner can result in substantial deadweight losses and barriers to downstream innovation that persist long after the patents can no longer be enforced.

---

[1] See Brenda M. Simon & Ted Sichelman, Data-Generating Patents, 111 *Northwest. U. L. Rev.* (2017). This chapter is adapted in part from this article, which contains relevant citations to all the assertions made herein.

[2] See Chapter 9 (discussing examples involved in the "medical Internet of Things").

[3] See Chapter 21 (describing trade secret protection).

We propose a framework for identifying those data-generating biomedical patents that are most likely to be socially problematic. Two factors are of key interest. The first factor, "preemptive potential," examines whether the data-generating patent strongly preempts others from generating the same types of data. The second factor, "foreseeability," concerns whether the patented invention generates data that can be used in secondary markets that are too distinct from that of the invention.

We propose and evaluate several remedies for problematic data-generating biomedical patents, including limiting patentability, mandating narrow disclosure or sharing of data, expanding defenses to infringement, and restricting available remedies. Although none of the options are without downsides, we tend to favor ex post remedies that can be tailored to the specific circumstances of a problematic data-generating patent.

In this chapter, we first describe the phenomenon of "data-generating patents" and its increasing significance in the era of Big Data. We then delve into legal and economic implications, particularly considering advances in technology that increase the value of generated data. We conclude by identifying the situations in which data-generating patents may reduce social welfare and proposing and analyzing various remedial measures.

22.2 THE EMERGENCE OF BIOMEDICAL DATA-GENERATING PATENTS

Patents and trade secrets are typically considered economic substitutes in the sense that if one decides to patent an invention, it is necessary to disclose the details of the invention and thus forgo trade secret protection. However, a minority of scholars has recognized that patents and trade secrets may additionally work as economic complements because the applicable legal doctrines do not require full disclosure of the invention. Data-generating patents differ from the traditional understanding of patents and trade secrets as complements in that these inventions – by definition – often generate information apart from the invention itself. In economic terms, data-generating inventions may yield information in distinct product markets. This information may be used to improve the invention itself or in an entirely different manner.

Data-generating patents have become of particular note in the current era of Big Data, in which technology now allows for low-cost data storage, retrieval, and analysis. In particular, the owner of a market power–conferring data-generating patent can use its legal rights to enjoy an advantage not only in the product market of the invention but also in the market for the information generated by the invention. Moreover, once the patent term ends, or even if the patent is invalidated, the holder continues to enjoy legal exclusivities afforded by trade secret law and its potentially indefinite term of protection. Beyond its legal rights, the data-generating patentee may also benefit from being the first (and only) provider able to gather and analyze data, by virtue of its twenty-year period of patent exclusivity. These potential economic consequences of data-generating patents were not contemplated in the delicate balance erected by the patent system and can – like Big Data more generally – potentially cause major social and economic harm.

22.2.1 The Rise of Data-Generating Patents

From Patents to Proprietary Databases of Genetic Disease Markers
The value of trade secrets obtained through data-generating patents is evident in the area of genetic testing, particularly the generation of proprietary databases of patients' genetic information derived from patented diagnostic tests.[4] Most notably, Myriad Genetics had been the sole provider in the United States of testing for the BRCA1 and BRCA2 genes, which are markers for breast cancer. Before the US Supreme Court's recent decision invalidating some of Myriad's patent claims, Myriad had the exclusive ability to collect clinical data from patients as a result of its patent protection for more than a decade, maintaining their information in a private database.

Myriad usually provides three types of test results when comparing a patient's genetic information with a naturally occurring genetic sequence: no variations, harmless variations, or mutations that are clearly harmful. For the first two types, no variations or harmless variations, the difference between the patient's sequence and the naturally occurring sequence does not indicate an increased susceptibility to breast or ovarian cancer. For the third type, where the mutations are clearly harmful, the patient is at increased risk for developing cancer.

Occasionally, however, the test results are more complicated to understand. For variants of unknown significance (VUS), the effects of the variations are difficult to interpret, so it is unclear whether the patient is at increased risk of cancer. Myriad states that the portion of patients with unknown variations is only 3 percent. For most BRCA testing carried out by other companies in Europe, where Myriad's patents have not been strongly enforced, the portion of cases resulting in unknown variations is as high as 20 percent. Myriad's lower unknown variation rate results from its ability to interpret its results in light of its very large, proprietary database. Trade secret protection of Myriad's massive database provides it with an advantage in

---

[4] Previous scholars have recognized that patents on medical diagnostic tests may allow for the control of information generated by the patented tests as a trade secret. See Dan L. Burk, Patents as Aggregators in Personalized Medicine, 21 B.U. J. Sci. Technol. 233, 233–49 (2015); John M. Conley et al., Myriad after Myriad: The Proprietary Data Dilemma, 15 N.C. J.L. Technol. 597, 616–18 (2014); Robert Cook-Deegan et al., The Next Controversy in Genetic Testing: Clinical Data as Trade Secrets?, 21 Eur. J. Hum. Genet. 585 (2013). However, unlike the treatment in this chapter, these scholars have limited their inquiry to the area of personalized medicine. Here we introduce the broad concept of data-generating patents, provide a general analytical framework to distinguish problematic from unproblematic data-generating patents, and offer and assess numerous prescriptive options to remedy any potentially detrimental effects.

the marketplace, enabling it to provide more thorough results than its competitors and market these benefits to prospective users.

In this manner, Myriad's patents – which generate data protected by trade secrecy – have provided a competitive advantage that is difficult and costly for competitors to replicate. Such barriers, coupled with the inability of the market to self-correct and lack of regulatory intervention, afford Myriad the ability to extend its market power well beyond the expiration or invalidation of its patents.

Data-Generating Patents across Technological Fields
Data-generating patents appear in numerous other biomedical applications. In the area of smart medical devices, such as heart monitors, smart contact lenses, and fitness trackers, patent holders can gather data about locations, times, and biometric data. Such devices can collect and store information about a user's actions at a given time, such as sleep habits, blood pressure, dietary intake, activity, stress levels, and productivity. While the collection of information by corporate and other entities is not new, advances in the means of aggregating and processing in the era of Big Data have dramatically altered the ability to use information.

22.2.2 Legal Consequences and Concerns of Patenting Data-Generating Inventions

Data-Generating Patents and Trade Secrets as Complements
Once a patent is filed, there is no duty to update its disclosure with newly found information relevant to the patent; indeed, there is an affirmative proscription against doing so. As such, inventors may choose to retain postfiling information about the invention as a trade secret. In this regard, the commercialized product, developed well after patenting, will often substantially differ from the invention previously described in the patent. Yet, because patent protection extends beyond what is disclosed in the patent itself, these commercialized products – and the information related to them – typically are protected by the original patent or by trade secret law.

To the extent that inventions are supposed to fall into the public domain once the patent term expires, this use of patents and trade secrets as complements arguably thwarts the goals of the patent system. Even in fields in which some disclosure of postpatenting data is required for regulatory purposes, such as medical devices or pharmaceuticals, this strategy can still be effective because such disclosed data are typically maintained as a secret by the applicable regulatory agency.

Data-generating patents present unique concerns that have not been sufficiently addressed. A data-generating patent will often yield information subject to trade secret law not merely about the invention itself but also about the invention's users and that may be advantageous in separate product markets. Such leveraging into secondary markets in the era of Big Data presents a use of patents and trade secrets as economic complements that is arguably well outside the "bargain" for exclusive rights contemplated by the patent system.

Traditional Trade Secret Safeguards Generally Do Not Apply to Data-Generating Patents

Ordinarily, trade secrets are subject to reasonable limitations to prevent against overreaching. Two oft-cited defenses in ensuring that trade secret law does not overreach are the ability to reverse engineer a product or process embodying a trade secret and simply independently discovering the trade secret. In contrast, neither reverse engineering nor independent discovery typically provides defenses to patent infringement.

In the case of data-generating patents, however, the ability to reverse engineer trade secrets is often illusory. When a data-generating invention is patented, would-be competitors are effectively foreclosed from reverse engineering for a substantial period because they are prohibited from making and using the patented invention during the twenty-year exclusivity period. In particular, a diagnostic test patent may entirely preclude substitute technologies, which, in turn, precludes competitors and others from generating similar data.

Indeed, Myriad effectively stopped contributing to public databases almost a decade ago, when it decided to maintain its users' data as trade secrets. Any company that wants to compete with Myriad can only interpret variations based on limited public data using incomplete analytical algorithms. By leveraging its patents, Myriad has managed to extend its exclusivity, even after its patents were effectively invalidated by the US Supreme Court. What began with patent protection over genetic information now includes trade secret protection for Myriad's databases of patients' full genetic sequences and phenotypic information, as well as the correlations and algorithms resulting from access to that wealth of data.

Although not quite as difficult as reverse engineering, independent discovery is also severely limited by the nature of data-generating patents. If the patent holder is dominant in the marketplace, it can preclude others, even those who independently invent, from practicing the patented invention. For the mutations at issue in the Myriad patent, there are no other genes that can be used to identify the mutations. When there are no equivalent alternatives to a patented data-generating invention, it may be effectively impossible to recreate the data generated by the data-generating patent holder, even fully independently.

Even after a data-generating patent expires or is invalidated, the patentee will tend to have a significant lead time that will handicap any competitor from entering the field postexpiration or postinvalidation, particularly where the patent provides its holder with market power. Such patents are not confined merely to genetic testing but can arise in any sector of the biomedical industries. The high costs of independently generating the data that the patentee obtained with the twenty-year lead time often ensures that there will be little risk of independent discovery and, ultimately, competition.

22.2.3 The Economic Effects of Data-Generating Patents

Data-Generating Patents and Innovation Incentives

One argument in favor of data-generating patents is that the additional protection they afford is necessary to provide optimal incentives to create data-generating inventions or the data generated by them. For instance, as we explained earlier, Myriad's medical diagnostic test for detecting the incidence of breast cancer is not particularly valuable absent a large database of information about genetic mutations. Perhaps such a database can only be amassed by a monopolist.

The main concern, however, is that innovation and improvements may be thwarted by providing too much protection for these types of data. Although patent holders will often be in the best position to make improvements or extend technology into new areas, they may choose not to do so, particularly where they have invested in a technology that has become the standard in a field and might be superseded by an improvement. The reluctance to improve a technology and the possibility of high transaction costs caution against merely expanding the scope of patent rights to enhance coordination, at least without some contrary empirical evidence. Absent further evidence, we believe that a cautious stance is called for, especially given the potential social costs of these inventions.

The Extension of Deadweight Losses by Data-Generating Patents

Typically, part of the quid pro quo for granting patent exclusivity is the assurance that information about the invention will become part of the public domain after patent expiration. By protecting information resulting from data-generating patents as trade secrets, however, it may be too costly for competitors to use the invention itself. Thus, while the data-generating invention technically falls into the public domain following expiration, the ability to retain key data generated by the invention may effectively preclude patent law's quid pro quo. Of course, the limitations of the patent disclosure requirements always result in some information being retained by the patent holder. What makes data-generating inventions different from other inventions is that the retained information does not just concern the use or operation of the invention itself but rather can affect disparate markets for the information and for a potentially indefinite duration.

Patents can impose substantial consumer deadweight losses during the patent term. For example, when a patent provides market power to its holder, prices for a patented product are often higher than the competitive price, precluding some consumers from purchasing who otherwise would have in a competitive market. Maintaining information contributed by consumers during the patent term as a trade secret thus could extend deadweight losses to the same class of consumers well past the expiration or invalidation of the patent. If patent term is optimally calibrated to induce innovation, then these additional deadweight losses are only worth the cost if the information protected by trade secret law provides social benefits greater than these costs.

22.3 IDENTIFYING AND ADDRESSING PROBLEMATIC DATA-GENERATING PATENTS

22.3.1 *Discerning Problematic from Unproblematic Data-Generating Patents*

As we explained earlier, not all data-generating patents necessarily result in net costs. Here we propose criteria that can be used to identify potentially problematic biomedical data-generating patents in the era of Big Data. In our evaluation, we focus on two main factors: the strength of preempting potential competition in data markets and expansion into unforeseeable markets. For the preemption factor, we propose assessing the magnitude of the effect on competition in the market regarding the data as opposed to the preemptive effect of the underlying invention itself. The greater the preemptive effect on marketplace competition related to the data, the more likely the invention is problematic. By "unforeseeable markets," we refer to whether the patent affords the ability to collect data in an area that is not directly related to the market covered by the patented invention. If the invention allows aggregation of data in unforeseeable markets, the likelihood that it is problematic increases.

Medical diagnostic inventions provide one example of how inventions may exhibit preemptive potential and allow for possible control over unforeseen markets.[5] For example, Myriad's patents foreclosed other methods of identifying mutations in the *BRCA1* and *BRCA2* genes. When broad preemptive scope is directly related to relevant data-generating patents, absent technological strides to design around the scope of the patents, the effect on competition in the market regarding the data is essentially preclusive during the twenty-year exclusivity period. Although aggregating data may lead to increased efficiencies, it may also result in more limited data analysis and improvements resulting from the data by the patentee or third parties. Additionally, when the ability to generate the data is exclusively in the hands of a

---

[5] Recent decisions from the Supreme Court have to some degree made it more difficult to obtain data-generating patents, particularly in the field of medical diagnostic testing. See *Mayo Collaborative Servs. v. Prometheus Labs., Inc.*, 132 S. Ct. 1289, 1305 (2012); *Alice Corp. Pty. Ltd. v. CLS Bank Int'l.*, 134 S. Ct. 2347, 2352 (2014). Yet many classes of biomedical data-generating inventions and some medical diagnostic tests still remain patentable.

single provider, the ability to assess the quality of results from the data aggregator is limited. As discussed earlier, after the patent expires or is invalidated, later entrants play a costly and extensive game of catch-up.

In terms of the unforeseeability factor, if Myriad used the gathered data to determine a propensity for developing another disease, such as muscular dystrophy, the data collected would reach unforeseeable markets. If the patent were of strong preemptive effect, this would afford the patent holder market power in independent markets during and even after the expiration or invalidation of the patent. This unforeseeable market power is, by definition, not contemplated in the scheme of patent rewards and corresponding social costs erected by the patent system and thus presents a large potential threat to social welfare.

Other factors may be useful in such an analysis, such as the general strength of the patent holder in the marketplace, commercial success, market size, the type of technology involved, and whether it makes the Big Data generated more valuable and whether the protected data implicate issues of major public concern, such as health, security, or privacy.

For example, the patent holder of a data-generating patent with a strong preemptive effect will often have unparalleled strength in the marketplace. In the case of genetic testing, the market will depend not only on the usefulness of the patent to consumers but also on the likelihood of insurance coverage. Thus the data generated by such a patent holder in the genetic testing space will very likely have an impact not only on private markets but also on consumer privacy and public health, which are concerns well worth considering in the overall calculus.

Although these additional factors can be helpful in the analysis, we believe that the likelihood that a given data-generating patent may be problematic will typically turn on the level of unforeseeability and preemption present in a given data-generating patent (or set of patents). For simplicity, we divide the landscape into four scenarios with an assessment of how problematic each scenario may be (see Figure 22.1). A full discussion of each scenario can be found in our earlier work.[6]

22.3.2 Proposals to Address Problematic Data-Generating Patents

Mitigating Innovation-Related Concerns
Identifying problematic data-generating patents ex ante will likely be a costly, difficult, and time-consuming task unless the rules used to do so are vastly over- or underinclusive. Thus we believe that ex post solutions – either through private or public actions in the courts or a regulatory arena – generally offer the most promise.

Substantially shortening the patent term or eliminating patent protection for data-generating inventions is unlikely to be optimal. A restricted exclusivity period would

---

[6] See Simon & Sichelman, *Data-Generating Patents*, at part III.A.

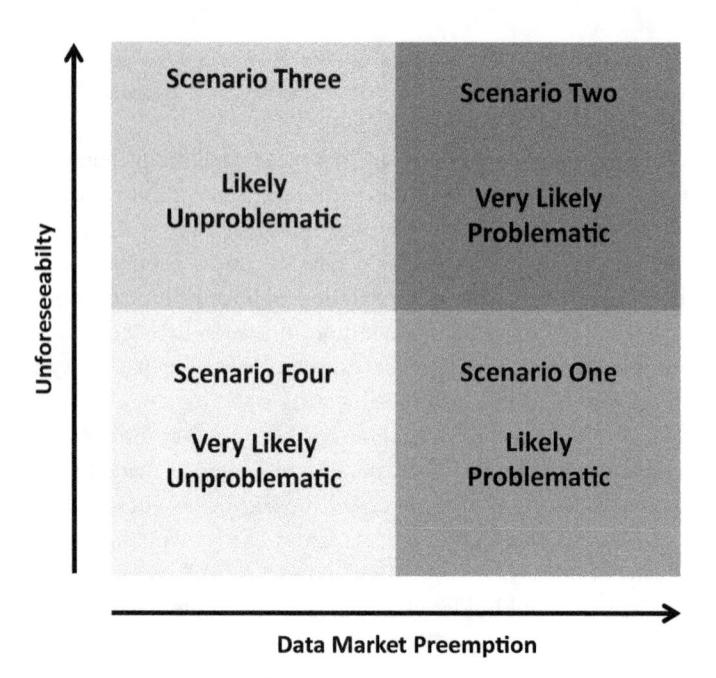

FIGURE 22.1 Data-generating patent scenarios.

cabin the patent holder's ability to gather data, but in addition to classification problems, it also might have the unintended consequence of nudging providers away from patent protection and toward secrecy. A benefit of trade secrecy is that it levels the playing field so that these inventors do not enjoy "superpatent" protection that allows them to use market power conferred by the patent to achieve dominance in the market for data protected by trade secret law. However, trade secrecy not only would reduce disclosure but also could cause providers to take extra precautions in preventing leakage of proprietary data-generating methods. These negative effects could potentially reduce innovation more than the social costs otherwise imposed by data-generating patents. Coupled with the difficulty of classifying harmful data-generating patents ex ante, shortening patent term does not appear to be a viable solution.

Eliminating patent eligibility for data-generating inventions, even harmful ones, would simply exacerbate the problems of shortening patent term. There may be other sound reasons for eliminating these classes of patentable subject matter, but with respect to reducing the costs of harmful data-generating patents – and there certainly are classes of these inventions that remain patentable – we do not believe such an approach is sensible.

A second solution would extend the patent misuse defense to bar enforcement of data-generating patents that improperly expand the scope of the underlying legal rights. Advances in Big Data techniques may increase the likelihood of pernicious expansion into secondary markets by enabling comprehensive linking and analysis of data across different industries and sectors. Extending the patent misuse defense, however, could present similar concerns to those discussed earlier. Specifically, to the extent that would-be patentees for problematic data-generating inventions could predict that their patents would be precluded from enforcement, they would opt for trade secrecy, making it far from ideal.[7]

A third option would be expansion of the independent invention exception to patent infringement for data-generating patents. A benefit of an independent invention defense is that it is applied ex post, so courts could tailor the remedy to target harmful data-generating patents. Indeed, courts could even allow reverse engineering of the patented invention as long as it was used to generate data that otherwise could not be collected without use of the invention. However, permitting even a limited exception could entail large monitoring costs.

Fourth, for data-generating patents that restrict basic research, such as Myriad's withholding of patient information from public databases, Congress or the courts could adopt an experimental use exception to infringement for data-generating patents. The exemption related to Food and Drug Administration (FDA) approval and the exception for medical and surgical procedures are potential models for a research-based exemption. Similar experimental use exceptions are also recognized internationally. While Congress might not adopt such an exception, the courts could plausibly adopt one, though they generally have been hesitant to do so. A research exemption could be tailored by the courts to apply only to harmful data-generating patents.

One downside of the independent invention and experimental use defenses is that they are complete bars to enforcement, at least in a particular lawsuit. If the data-generating patentee is effectively unable to enforce its patent against most infringers, such defenses effectively function as a denial of patentability altogether, increasing incentives for the inventor to retain its invention as a trade secret, with the attendant costs of doing so.

Another ex post solution is placing limits on patent remedies. Courts, for instance, could limit injunctive relief for infringing these types of patents, given the difficulty of reverse engineering and independently creating the data generated from them. Following the Supreme Court's decision in *eBay v. MercExchange*, courts have frequently denied injunctions in order to prevent "holdup" and other problems flowing from injunctive relief.[8] If courts can properly take into account the costs caused by data-generating patents yet still award monetary relief sufficient for inventors to seek patent protection, this solution could be ideal. However, systematic

---

[7] Similarly, expanding antitrust causes of action to allow for affirmative counterclaims to enforcement of problematic data-generating patents would not be an optimal solution in our view. See *USM Corp. v. SPS Techs., Inc.*, 694 F.2d 505, 512 (7th Cir. 1982) (Posner, J.).

[8] See *eBay, Inc. v. MercExchange, L.L.C.*, 547 U.S. 388 (2006).

errors in the award of monetary relief could result in de facto patent ineligibility for many data-generating inventions. This result would be especially concerning in an area where courts have already significantly contracted patent eligibility.

Addressing Disclosure-Related Concerns
Data-generating patents may capture information that will not fall into the public domain after the patent has expired or is invalidated. Some of the same potential solutions to the innovation-related concerns discussed previously would mitigate these disclosure problems. Here we examine solutions that more directly address disclosure issues.

One possibility is to force the holder of a harmful data-generating patent to publicly disclose the data otherwise protected by trade secret law. Such a mandate would be difficult to enforce because the patent holder could disclose a portion of its proprietary data, and it would be very costly for regulators to determine whether additional data were not disclosed. Moreover, without protecting that information as a trade secret, the patent holder would have less incentive to generate the information, potentially resulting in even less information for the public to use. Plus, the development of information that is available may come at a higher cost.

A less draconian way to encourage information sharing would be to mandate donation of data produced as a result of a data-generating patent to a regulatory agency, which would not disclose it for a certain period of time.[9] A limited period of data exclusivity might provide sufficient innovation incentives in this space, much as it has for biologics. Generally, confidential data submitted during the FDA approval process remain behind locked doors. Again, it may be too difficult to develop some mechanism to detect problematic data-generating patents ex ante. However, patents in some technological fields, such as genetic diagnostic tests, could include such a high percentage of data-generating patents that the costs of classification (and evasion of such by savvy patent applicants) may be dwarfed by the benefits of disclosure.

In the area of federally funded research, agencies could mandate such limited disclosure without intervention from Congress. For example, some have suggested amending the Bayh-Dole Act or increasing the authority of the National Institutes of Health (NIH) to ensure availability of information critical to public well-being. Recently, the NIH has instituted requirements for sharing human genomic data generated by NIH-funded research, although the data remain sequestered for a substantial period of time after submission, after which point it is made available through a tiered distribution system. Nonetheless, more stringent disclosure requirements would face strong industry opposition and monitoring and compliance

---

[9] See Chapter 20 (discussing a potential role for the FDA in clinical surveillance of algorithmic inventions).

challenges and may also greatly affect innovation incentives, although empirical evidence is lacking to draw a conclusion.[10]

Along these lines, public or public-private partnerships could incentivize the collection and analysis of data. Considering the use of data about consumers as part of the public infrastructure would encourage investment in their development. Congress could enact legislation or the courts could impose a remedy in trade secret law similar to the "essential facilities" doctrine in antitrust law to ensure that markets and the public would have access to critical information. In practice, it would seem too difficult to apply such an approach to all but a narrow class of inventions. Another option would be for the government to encourage the voluntary adoption of such sharing arrangements. These forms of data aggregation are rare in the United States, but they have enjoyed more success internationally; perhaps financial and other encouragement could increase their use domestically. Nonetheless, given the strong financial incentives to avoid such voluntary arrangements and difficulty in standardization, we do not view them as a likely solution.

A *sui generis* form of protection for data, such as that adopted by the European Union, would potentially encourage data-generating patent holders to disclose their information and charge for its use.[11] However, database protection in Europe is typically in the context of information that must be disclosed for its holder to monetize it. Given that the information produced by data-generating patents can be profitably maintained as a trade secret, it is unlikely that *sui generis* protection would affect behavior. Moreover, protecting databases in this way has been seriously considered in the past but not accepted in this country. Although this type of system would not require an explicit allocation of government resources, users still bear its costs in terms of both expenses and limitations on access. In addition, privatizing data in this way would limit the ability to build on and improve the data.

Similarly, prizes, tax breaks, or other rewards might provide sufficient incentives to innovate without many of the downsides of patents, but they also are not without costs. For instance, potential users of an invention will often bear its costs regardless of whether a patent or a prize provides the incentive for its creation. Additionally, data-generating patents seem particularly ill suited for nonpatent rewards. Data-generating patents, which may have preemptive effects and be leveraged to collect data in unforeseeable secondary markets, are likely to be quite difficult to value accurately ex ante.

Tailoring Solutions Based on Facts and Further Empirical Research

In sum, each potential solution to innovation and disclosure-related concerns has potentially significant limitations. Nonetheless, it seems clear that most of the

---

[10] Rarely used in the United States, compulsory licensing of the data could provide for broader information sharing but could unduly reduce incentives to patent.

[11] See Chapter 21 (describing *sui generis* protection of Big Data).

ex ante solutions, such as limiting patent term or narrowing patent eligibility, suffer from large error costs, as well as potentially substantial downstream costs in channeling these inventions into trade secrecy. As such, we disfavor them, particularly for innovation-related concerns. Mandatory disclosure of information produced by a narrow class of easily identifiable data-generating inventions might suffer less from these concerns, but without more information on the potentially negative effects on innovation incentives and the feasibility of monitoring compliance, we disfavor such solutions.

As for the ex post solutions, the options of enhanced independent invention, reverse engineering, and experimental use defenses, as well as limited denials of injunctive relief perhaps coupled with mandatory disclosure in extreme cases, could be promising if courts can properly tailor these remedies. Agencies can also implement ex post solutions, especially in the area of disclosure. For instance, one possibility would be to require contribution to a confidential government repository of data for certain classes of data-generating inventions, such as medical diagnostic tests, with release only after sufficient agency study of the information and its economic effects.

Ultimately, whether any of these solutions can be adequately implemented will depend on the competency of legislatures, courts, and agencies. Such competency can arguably be improved with more empirical study on the economic effects of data-generating patents. Here we have begun that process by recognizing the problem of data-generating patents, with an eye toward potential solutions and further study.

22.4 CONCLUSION

We have discussed biomedical data-generating patents as a unique illustration of patents and trade secrets acting as economic complements. Data-generating patents, which by design generate valuable data by their use, may provide the patentee market power not just over the invention but also over data generated by it. Trade secret law affords further protection for the generated data, even where the underlying patent allows its holder to preempt use or collection of the data in unforeseeable markets. Although the use of patents and trade secrets in this way may sometimes result in increased efficiency or provide additional innovation incentives in areas where they may be sorely lacking, in other circumstances they may produce detrimental effects. We have set forth factors for identifying potentially problematic biomedical data-generating patents and offered suggestions to mitigate the potential harm to innovation and disclosure that may result from their use. We hope our discussion serves as a useful starting point for future research into this complex intersection of intellectual property law and Big Data.

Epilogue

Professional Cooperation and Rivalry in the Future of Data-Driven Healthcare

Frank Pasquale

Authors in this volume have grappled with some of the most difficult issues in contemporary health law and policy. What is the proper balance between patient privacy rights and the public interest in research? How far should physicians trust machine learning as a tool for diagnosis or triage? How distinct are the research and clinical roles of modern healthcare institutions intent on quality improvement – and should law accelerate or slow down a blurring of boundaries here? Distinguished authors in this volume have answered each of these questions judiciously, carefully melding both legal analysis and state-of-the-art insights from computer science, philosophy, medicine, and social science.

The chapters also give us a glimpse of another critical set of conflicts on the horizon of law and medicine. Some experts in machine learning sincerely believe that, at bottom, all judgment (including medical or legal judgment) ultimately boils down to pattern recognition that will eventually be done better by machines than by humans. As attorneys and doctors contemplate a potential computationalist takeover of their professions, they might wonder whether machine learning is something to manage, question, or embrace. There will be fascinating opportunities for alliances to emerge among pairs of professions against an "odd man out." To see why, consider the logic of automation, which advances in data collection, analysis, and use have intensified.

According to one popular narrative of the future of work, it is not only routine jobs that robots will eliminate. Rather, the professions themselves stand on the brink of eradication. Record enough of what enough doctors and lawyers do, and machine-learning systems can catalog all potential scenarios, all potential responses to them, and the value of all possible outcomes of those responses. It is only a matter of time, according to this view, before a "master algorithm" replaces them all. Of course, once one actually tries to develop such an approach in either a hospital or a law firm, it immediately crashes into the harsh realities of data privacy laws, trade secrecy protections, attorney-client or doctor-patient confidentiality, and myriad other legal restrictions. Frustration at such impediments to surveillance may inspire technologists to pit lawyers against doctors or vice versa.

For example, those who lament the complex interactions among state and federal privacy laws and human subjects research rules (at the state, federal, and institutional levels) may welcome innovations such as smart contracts, automated compliance, and blockchains as a way to cut a Gordian knot of legal requirements. Mass adoption of such technologies could result from an alliance of providers and technologists against traditional attorneys and regulators. Law truly reduced to code promises infinite opportunities for personalization of data use restrictions and permissions. However, a translation of privacy compliance from statute and regulation to data propertization and contract would create obvious vulnerabilities for anyone duped or lured to accept one-sided terms. Law will always be necessary as a constraint on unconscionable data collection or uses.

Another divide may arise as managers at healthcare institutions and payers unite with technologists to record and evaluate more of the daily practice of physicians, nurses, and other caregivers. The managerial monitors in this scenario would probably need the help of lawyers to overcome opposition from caregivers to a pervasively monitored environment. They may aim to automate care, shifting expertise from fallible individuals to a network of computerized outcome measurements (touted as soon-to-be-omniscient in breathless media accounts of "deep learning"). But without caregivers' cooperation and buy-in, it is hard to imagine implementing sustainable quality-improvement initiatives, let alone the robot doctors that so many futurists thrill to.

Fortunately, regulatory authorities, professional associations, and large firms realize that for the foreseeable future, there are no shortcuts to app-driven diagnosis or perfected data governance. So, too, do serious academics. This collection is distinguished by the authors' willingness to do the hard work of proposing incremental improvement – both where such reforms advance the famed "triple aim" of healthcare (reducing cost, increasing quality, and improving access) and where some interests must be sacrificed in order to advance others.

Both attorneys and doctors have been adjusting to the demands of data scientists, machine-learning experts, and quantitative analysts for more and better data about the structures, processes, and outcomes of US healthcare. But as the power and prestige of technologists rise, a new set of questions emerges. What is the professional role of data scientists in the modern healthcare enterprise? Is HHS's recognition of the role of a "HIPAA deidentification expert" in some data-sharing scenarios a step toward formalizing the participation of computer scientists and technical experts in privacy compliance? Do data analysts have certain fiduciary duties to their direct clients and to the populations whose data they are analyzing?

This collection suggests several such duties. Data collectors should be very wary about exporting data collected in the health sector for other purposes, such as life insurance underwriting, employability scores, and other forms of profiling. Unless they are explicitly addressed, health disparities prevalent in the "real world" are prone to reemerge in its digital doppelgängers. Preserving trackability and traceability for drugs and devices is a task critically important to quality assurance. New modes of patient input need to be developed to supplement an ever-creakier framework of notice and consent.[1]

These ideas, and many more, have motivated a global movement for algorithmic accountability, led by journalists, attorneys, social scientists, and computer scientists. The idea here is not to make existing accountability structures algorithmic (by, for example, automating compliance or reducing ethical quandaries to a series of checkboxes). Rather, this movement has committed to establishing certain ethical and professional norms for data science – to make the users of algorithms more accountable for their effects. Many chapters in this volume promote algorithmic accountability and advancing existing practices of nondiscrimination, due process, and transparency into an increasingly technologized health sector.

To the extent that technologists in fields such as machine learning can develop their own distinct professional identity, steps toward the digitization of health monitoring and even diagnosis and treatment are likely to advance the triple aim. However, as historians and sociologists of the professions have shown, such an identity is hard to achieve. It will require mandatory education and ethical rules (with enforceable penalties for violations) designed to apply legal and medical principles of confidentiality, informed consent, and other norms to processes of medical data collection, analysis, and use. Standards to balance privacy and trade secrecy against scientific demands for open data and replicability will be critical. As technologists develop such standards (even if only out of fear of losing business or attracting law enforcers' attention in cases of troubling data use), this volume provides a wealth of insight into how to achieve such a balance. Its timely analyses and timeless methods should inform policymaking discussions, academic work, and corporate boardrooms.

---

[1] See, generally, Matt Zook et al., Ten Simple Rules for Responsible Big Data Research, 13 *PLoS Comput. Biol.* 1 (2017), available at https://doi.org/10.1371/journal.pcbi.1005399 [https://perma.cc/KC73-MKMT].

Index

AAMC. *See* American Association of Medical Colleges
accordance with existing laws
   in Healthcare Internet of Things design, 145–46
   in TPDA policy, 150
accountability
   as Healthcare Internet of Things design consideration, 144–45
   in TPDA mechanisms, 149–50
ACMG. *See* American College of Medical Genetics and Genomics
active breaches of identity, 185
ad hoc groups, 188
   in analytics, 182
   defined, 187
   identity management for, 185–86, 189–90
ADA. *See* Americans with Disabilities Act
advertisers and advertising, health-related Big Data for, 86
Affordable Care Act, U.S., 211
aggregated data
   in Big Data health care research, 254–55
   HIPAA and, limitations under, 258–59
   sources of, 269
   TPDAs and, 148–49
algorithm patents, 312–14
   in European Union, 313–14
   in U.S., 312–13
algorithmic analytics, 177–79, 182, 266
algorithmic classification, in analytics, 177–79, 182
all-payer claims databases (APCDs), 69, 112–13
   advantages of, 112
   Gobeille v. Liberty Mutual Insurance Co. and, 116–19
   growth of, 113

   pediatric care discrepancies in, 117
   prediction modeling through, 117
American Association of Medical Colleges (AAMC), 258
American College of Medical Genetics and Genomics (ACMG), 202–3
American Recovery and Reinvestment Act, U.S., 102–3
Americans with Disabilities Act (ADA), U.S., 69, 92–96
   data mining practices and, 96
   disability definitions under, 93–96
   discrimination protections under, 71–72
   eligibility criteria for, 93
   GINA and, 93–94
   privacy under, 260
   public accommodations under, 92–93
   "regarded as" provision in, expansion of, 94–96
   scope of, 85
analytics
   ad hoc groups in, 182
   algorithmic classification, 177–79, 182, 266
   behaviors and characteristics in, 175–76
   descriptive classification, 179
   development of, 175
   groups in, ethical significance of, 177–83
   identity in, ethical significance of, 177–83
   offline, 179
   personalization systems, 181–82
   profiling, 179–82
   shared ownership of, 180–81
   predictive classification, 182
   prescriptive classification, 179
   responses to, 175
Anderson, Chris, 50

anonymization, of Big Data, 249
  Expert Determination pathway, 281–82
anti-discrimination laws, for group privacy, 187
antimicrobial resistance, decrease of, 56–57
antitrust rules, 320–21
APCDs. *See* all-payer claims databases
Apopehnia, 51
ascriptive autonomy, 20
ascriptive groups, 187
assimilation model, defined, 69
autonomy, individual
  ascriptive, 20
  Big Data and, 109
  bioethics and, 20–22. *See also* Common Rule;
    Health Insurance Portability and
    Accountability Act Privacy Rule
    IRBs, 20–21
  civic solidarity and, 22
  commonwealths and, formation of, 22
  consumer-driven data commons and,
    23–26, 29
    advantages of, 25
    ethical standards of, 25–26
    rules of access for, 24
    value of, 24
  critiques of, 28
  evolution of, 20–22
  Hobbes on, 22
  Kantian notion of, 20
  norm of common purpose, 19–20
  voice as result of, 22–26
  weakness of, 21–22
Avastin, 81–82

Bacon, Francis, 31
best practices
  for Big Data health care research, 254
  Expert Determination pathways and, 280–82
Big Data. *See also* deidentification; health care
  research; health-related big data; health-
  related Big Data; intellectual property
  rights
  analytics of, 158
  anonymization of, 249
  autonomy issues for, 109
  biomedical, 190–91
    genetics research, 190
    implementation of, 191
  collection of, 100–1
    through consumer data, 101–2
    distrust of medical community as factor in,
      104
    through EHRs, 98–99, 102–4
    model for, 110–11

  as commodity, 262
  under Common Rule, 28–29, 246–47
    electronic communications and, informed
      consent in, 246–47
  defined, 1, 252
  ethical guidelines for, 4
  evolution of, 2, 311
  exclusions, 101–6
  FDA discretion over, 107–9
  genomic data flood, 2
  after *Gobeille v. Liberty Mutual Insurance Co.*,
    122–23
  health care fraud and, 75–79
    through postmarket analysis, 75
    regulatory requirements, 76–77
  health disparities and, 101–6
    among racial and ethnic minorities,
      104–5
  under HIPAA Privacy Rule, 28–29
  as homogeneous, 98–99
  informed consent and, 5
    through electronic communications,
      246–47
  integrated sets, 256
  linkage of, from multiple sources, 254
  longitudinal health records in, 252
  longitudinal population health data in, 252
  machine learning and, 31–32, 35–38, 40
  manufacturers' use of, 100–1
  with new technologies, 3–4
  organization of, 100–1
  in pharmacoepidemiology, 270–71
  pharmacovigilance and, 75–79
    through postmarket analysis, 75
    transformative role of, 75–76
  precision medicine and, 34–36, 101, 105
    traditional approaches to, 34–35
    machine learning and, 35–36
    epistemological shift and, 34–36
  privacy and, 36–40, 109
    losses of, 37–38
    violations of, 38–40
  regulation guidelines for, 4
  epistemology of, 30–34
    causation vs. correlation, 32–33
    theory vs. data, 30–32
    explanation vs. prediction, 34
  small data and, shift from, 15
  on social media, 3
  sorting of, 100–1
  in targeted populations, 99
  in twenty-first century, 26–28
  as valuable commodity, 205
  volume of data with, 252–53

Big Data to Knowledge Initiative, 15
bioethics
  autonomy and, 20–22. *See also* Common Rule; Health Insurance Portability and Accountability Act Privacy Rule
  top-down standards for, 23
biological sequence information, 315
biomarkers, 91
biomedical Big Data, 190–91
  genetics research, 190
  HIPAA and, 255–61
  implementation of, 191
biospecimens, 197–99
  duty to share, 215–16, 218, 220–21
  identifiable, 227
  non-identified, 227
black box medicine, 296–98
  benefits of, 297–98
  epistemology of, 35–36
  implementation of, 298
  informed consent and, 299
  intellectual property rights for, 322
  legality of, 295
  medical liability law and, 298
  Precision Medicine Initiative and, 295
  privacy and, 40
  risk-based approach to, 302–3
black box software, 294
body scores, 58
BRAIN Initiative, 15, 19
breaches, of group privacy, 185–86
Breyer, Stephen (Justice), 115

Cancer Moonshot, 15, 19
Caplan, Art, 157
causation, 32–33
  theories of, 32–33
  fairness and, 53–54
  health-related Big Data correlations and, 50–52
  law of, 52–54
CDIA. *See* Consumer Data Industry Association
CDL. *See* Common Data Layout
CDRH. *See* Center for Devices and Radiological Health
CDS products. *See* clinical decision support products
Center for Devices and Radiological Health (CDRH), 292
Centers for Medicare and Medicaid Services (CMS), 1
  under FCA, 73
  claims processing rates, 83
certification, of TPDAs, 147, 154–55

CFR. *See* Code of Federal Regulations
citizen education, 155
Civil Rights Act (1964), U.S., 95
clearinghouses, 138–41
  CDIA, 139
  CRAs and, 139
  under FCRA, 139
clients, for TPDAs, 148
clinical care, under Common Rule, 238–39
clinical decision support (CDS) products, 284, 287–93
  development of
    advances in, 289–90
    failures in, 288–89
  medical liability law and, 300
  new regulatory paradigms, 291–93
  next generation, 291, 294
CMS. *See* Centers for Medicare and Medicaid Services
Code of Federal Regulations (CFR), U.S., 196
collection, of data
  of Big Data, 100–1
  through consumer data, 101–2
  distrust of medical community as factor in, 104
  through EHRs, 98–99, 102–4
  model for, 110–11
  through clearinghouses, 139
  under HIPAA, 257
  by TPDAs, 152–53
  through data requests, 148
collective agency, 188–89
collective identity, 188–89
collectives, 187
Common Data Layout (CDL), 120–21
Common Rule, 20–21, 23–25
  Big Data under, 246–47
  electronic communications and, informed consent in, 246–47
  clinical care under, 238–39
  confidentiality and, 244–46
  control in research under, 244–46
  data access under, 28–29
  data exemptions under, 242–43
  development of, 238–41
    ethics in, 241
    National Commission for Protection of Human Subjects of Biomedical and Behavioral Research and, 238–40
    privacy issues, 239–41
    regulatory structure, 240–41
  duty to share under, 218
  ethical guidelines, 247–49
  during development process, 241

Common Rule (cont.)
  flexibility of, 247
  health research under, 207–8, 238–39
  HHS regulations for, 259–60
  HIPAA and, 247–48
  for identifiable private data, 243–44
    under public health law, 245
  individual privacy protections under, 223–25
    exemptions from, 224
  informed consent and, 26, 244–46
    Big Data and, through electronic communications, 246–47
    privacy and, under U.S. law, 196–97
  IRBs and, 244
  proactive approach to, 247
  problems with, 242–46
    distinction between research and non-research activities, 242–44
    with number of activities, 242–44
  professional standards, 247
  public trust elements in, 247–48
  regulatory structure of, 248–50
    during development process, 240–41
    standards, 247
  revised versions of, 241
commonwealths, 22
completion technique, 194–95
confidentiality
  with Big Data health care research, 255
  under Common Rule, 244–46
conscientious objection, to duty to share, 220–21
consent. *See* informed consent
consumer data. *See also* consumer-driven data commons
  Big Data through, 101–2
Consumer Data Industry Association (CDIA), 139
Consumer Privacy Bill of Rights (CPBR), U.S., 62, 143
consumer/credit reporting agencies (CRAs), 65–66
  clearinghouses and, 139
consumer-driven data commons, 23–26, 29
  advantages of, 25
  ethical standards of, 25–26
  rules of access for, 24
  value of, 24
control, in research, 244–46
copyrights, 314–15
  of biological sequence information, 315
  data selection, 314–15
correlations
  Big Data and, 32–33
  health-related Big Data and, 46–52
    background of, 46–49
    causation and, 50–52

failures within, 46–49
hypotheticals in, 46–49
mechanisms and, 47–48
costs, of Big Data health care research, 253
CPBR. *See* Consumer Privacy Bill of Rights
CRAs. *See* consumer/credit reporting agencies

data. *See* Big Data; small data
data access mandates, 154
data analysis. *See also* analytics
  in Precision Medicine Initiative, 163
  by TPDAs, 148
data brokers
  under FCRA, 60
  under FTC guidelines, 64
  for health-related Big Data, 60–62, 88–89
  HIPAA guidelines, 61–62
data collection. *See* collection
data determinism, 58
data manipulation, under FCA, 79–83
  as direct false claim, 81–82
  as reverse false claim, 82–83
data minimization, 62
data mining, 63
  ADA and, 96
  pharmacovigilance and, 78
data protection
  DPA, 194–95
  EU General Data Protection Regulation, 192
  for health-related Big Data, 58–60
    conservative approach to, 59
    FIPPs for, 59
    FTC guidelines for, 63–67
    reform proposals, 62–65
    technology challenges, 59–60
  reform proposals
    through data minimization, 62
    for health-related Big Data, 62–65
    through TPDAs, 147
data sharing schemes, 280
  under Expert Determination Pathway, 282
database protections, in EU, 315
data-generating patents, 324–36
  economic effects of, 329–30
    deadweight loss extensions, 329–30
    innovation incentives, 329
  evolution of, 326–27
    genetic disease marker proprietary databases, 326–27
    across technological fields, 327
  legal consequences of, 327–29
  problems with, 330–36
    under antitrust rules, 333
    disclosure-related issues, 334–35

identification of, 330–31
innovation-related issues, 331–34
sui generis protection of, 335
trade secrets and, 327–29
deadweight loss extensions, 329–30
DeCODE, 193–95
  DPA and, 194
  estimated data in, 193–94
  right to not know and, 202
Defend Trade Secrets Act (DTSA), U.S., 318
deidentification, of data
  through Expert Determination pathway, 273–74, 278–80
  anonymization of data, 281–82
  best practices for, 280–82
  data sharing under, 282
  HIPAA and, 273–75
  through Limited Data Set pathway, 274–76, 279–80
  through Safe Harbor pathways, 273, 276–80
Department of Health and Human Services (HHS), 259–60
descriptive analytics, 179
diagnostic patents, 312–14
  in European Union, 313–14
  in U.S., 312–13
difference-making causation, 32–33
dignitary harm, 230–31
direct false claim, 81–82
disabilities, definitions of, 93–96
discrimination
  ADA protections against, 71–72
  through health-related Big Data use, 58
  through redlining, 58
disease modeling, 56–58
disruption model, defined, 70
distrust of medical community, 104
DPA. *See* Icelandic Data Protection Authority
drug labeling, 76–77
  misbranding in, 76
DTSA. *See* Defend Trade Secrets Act
duty to share, health-related Big Data
  arguments for, 212–21
  informed consent in, 214
  for patients' property rights, 212–16
  reciprocity, 215–21
  for biospecimens, 215–16, 218, 220–21
  clarification of, 209–12
  under Common Rule, 218
  conditions for, 209–12
  conscientious objection to, 220–21
  through EHRs, 209
    opt-ins, 211
    opt-outs, 211

insurance type classification, 219
IRBs and, 221–22
re-identification in, 215

economic disenfranchisement, from TPDAs, 150–51
EHRs. *See* electronic health records
electronic communication, informed consent through, 246–47
electronic doctors, 266–67
electronic health records (EHRs), 73–74, 269–71
  Big Data through, 98–99, 102–4
  duty to share through, 209
  opt-ins, 211
  opt-outs, 211
  TPDAs and, 152
Emmanuel, Ezekiel, 74
employers, health-related data for, 86
Employment Retirement Income Security Act (ERISA) (1974), U.S., 69
  defined, 114
  Gobeille v. Liberty Mutual Insurance Co. and, 113–16
  preemption clauses in, 114–15
end of theory claims, 31, 50
epidemic prediction, 56–58
epistemic probabilities, 37
epistemology of big data, 30–34
Equal Credit Protection Opportunity Act, U.S., 66
Equal Pay Act, U.S., 95
ERISA. *See* Employment Retirement Income Security Act
Erlich, Yaniv, 194
ethics
  Big Data and, 4, 41
  in Common Rule
    during development process, 241
    guidelines for, 247–49
  Expert Determination pathway and, 279–80
  Limited Data Set pathway and, 279–80
  Safe Harbor pathway and, 279–80
  top-down standards, 23
ethnic minorities. *See* minorities
EU General Data Protection Regulation, 192
European Union, intellectual property rights in
  algorithm patents, 313–14
  database protections in, 315
  diagnostic patents, 313–14
  regulatory exclusivities, 319
  software patents, 313–14
  trade secrets, defined, 317
Evans, Barbara, 262
exceptionalism, health research for Big Data and, 206

Expert Determination pathway, 273–74, 278–79
  anonymization of data, 281–82
  best practices for, 280–82
  data sharing under, 282
  ethical considerations for, 279–80
  privacy protections in, 279–80

Faden, Ruth, 217
Fair Credit Reporting Act (FCRA), U.S., 60, 110
  clearinghouses under, 139
  CRA oversight under, 65–66
  FTC and, 66
  HIPAA and, 260
Fair Information Practice Principles (FIPPs), 59
  FTC and, 63–64
  Healthcare Internet of Things and, 143
fairness
  law of causation and, 53–54
  law of reason and, 53–54
Fallon, Richard, 20
false claims. *See* direct false claim; reverse false claim
False Claims Act (FCA), U.S., 6
  amendments to, 80
  CMS under, 73
    claims processing rates, 83
  data manipulation and, 79–83
    as direct false claim, 81–82
    as reverse false claim, 82–83
  historical development of, 80–81
  liability under, 81
  Medicaid and, 80
  Medicare and, 80
  pharmacovigilance under, 73
Family Educational Rights and Privacy Act (FERPA) (1974), U.S., 260–61
FCA. *See* False Claims Act
FCC. *See* Federal Communications Commission
FCRA. *See* Fair Credit Reporting Act
FDA. *See* Food and Drug Administration
FDCA. *See* Food, Drug & Cosmetic Act
Federal Communications Commission (FCC), 129, 136
Federal Policy for the Protection of Human Subjects (Common Rule). *See* Common Rule
Federal Trade Commission (FTC), 57
  data brokers and, 64
  Equal Credit Protection Opportunity Act and, 66
  extant powers of, 65–67
  FCRA and, 66
  FIPPs and, 63–64

  health-related Big Data and, protections for, 63–67
  Internet of Things device regulation, 129, 136
  regulation of privacy laws, 260
Federal Trade Commission Act, U.S., 110
FERPA. *See* Family Educational Rights and Privacy Act
financial institutions, health-related Big Data for, 86
FIPPs. *See* Fair Information Practice Principles
Floridi, Luciano, 159–60, 183–85. *See also* informational privacy
Food, Drug & Cosmetic Act (FDCA), U.S., 81
Food and Drug Administration (FDA)
  Big Data and, enforcement guidelines for, 107–9
  CDRH guidelines, 292
  CDS products regulated by, 284, 287–93
    development failures, 288–89
    development of, 288–90
    medical liability law and, 300
    new regulatory paradigms, 291–93
    next generation, 291, 294
  Internet of Things devices and, regulation of, 129
  medical software regulation, 284–88, 301
    for black box software, 294
    under Draft Software Policy, 285–86
    of IVDMIAs, 286–87
  mHealth applications and, 134–35
  pharmacoepidemiologic studies, 78–79
  pharmacovigilance by, 69
  SDAs and, 78–79
fraud
  health care, statutes against, 74
    for overbilling, 74
  in health-related Big Data, 56–57
free TPDAs, 151
FTC. *See* Federal Trade Commission

GAIN Act. *See* Generating Antibiotic Incentives Now Act
GDPR. *See* General Data Protection Regulation
Genera Morborum (Linnaeus), 34–35
General Data Protection Regulation (GDPR), 45
  TPDAs under, 152
Generating Antibiotic Incentives Now (GAIN) Act (2012), U.S., 319
genetic disease marker proprietary databases, 326–27
Genetic Information Nondiscrimination Act (GINA), U.S., 93–94, 190
genetic testing, 101
genetics research, 190

genome sequencing, 101
genomic data flood, 2
GINA. *See* Genetic Information Nondiscrimination Act
Ginsburg, Ruth Bader (Justice), 115
Gobeille v. Liberty Mutual Insurance Co., 113–24
  APCDs and, 116–19
  Department of Labor regulations influenced by, 119–21
  ERISA and, 113–16
  incentives for data sharing after, 122–23
  long-term legal impact of, 115–19
    on health services research, 117–19
    on Medicaid, 118
    on Medicare, 118
    on states' programs and initiatives, 116
  voluntary data contributions by payers after, 121–22
government subsidies, for TPDAs, 150–51
Gramm-Leach-Bliley Act, U.S., 260
group privacy, 176–77, 183. *See also* collectives
  for ad hoc groups, 188
    defined, 187
    identity management for, 185–86, 189–90
  anti-discrimination laws for, 187
  for ascriptive groups, 187
  in biomedical Big Data, 190–91
    genetics research, 190
    implementation of, 191
  breaches of, 185–86
  for collectives, 187
  moderate interpretation of, 186
  right to inviolate personality and, 185–90
  strong interpretation of, 186
  weak interpretation of, 186

Hatch-Waxman Act, U.S., 319
HCUP. *See* Healthcare Cost and Utilization Project
Health Care Cost Institute, 121–22
health care data. *See* health care research; health-related Big Data
health care fraud. *See also* False Claims Act
  Big Data and, 75–79
    through postmarket analysis, 75
    regulatory requirements, 76–77
    transformative role of, 75–76
  through overbilling, 74
  pay and chase model, 79–80
  statutes against, 74
health care research, for Big Data. *See also* deidentification; genetics research
  challenges for, 253–55
    with aggregated data, 254–55
    best practices standards, 254
    confidentiality issues, 255
    linkage of data from multiple sources, 254
  under Common Rule, 207–8, 238–39
  compared to other research uses, 225–35
  cost savings from, 253
  data facilitation in, 205
  data protection for, 206–7
  exceptionalism and, 206
  in *Gobeille v. Liberty Mutual Insurance Co.*, 117–19
  HIPAA and, 206–7
    aggregated data limitations, 258–59
    collaborative research under, 258
    deidentification of data, 273–75
    enhancement strategies for, 261–63
    limited data sets in, 272–73
    sharing observational research, 271–75
  human subjects in, 226–28
    Common Rule standards for, 226–28
    individually identifiable, 226–28
  IRBs and, 228–30
    privacy protections and, societal lapses in, 230
    sensitivity of health information, 229–30
    social media and, 230
  overview of, 252–53
  policy options for, 235–36
  of private information, 228
  professional cooperation in, 337–39
  public trust in, 263
  risk assessment of, 230–35
    administrative burdens of, 232
    application of uniform daily life risks standard, 232–34
    dignitary harm and, 230–31
    mediation of risk in, 234–35
    minimal risk determination, 231–33
    recognition of risk in, 230–31
  volume of data, 252–53
health disparities, 101–6
  among racial and ethnic minorities, 104–5
Health Information Technology for Economic and Clinical Health (HITECH) Act (2009), U.S., 102–3, 269
  HIPAA and, 272
Health Insurance Portability and Accountability Act (HIPAA), U.S.
  Big Data health care research and, 206–7
    aggregated data limitations, 258–59
    collaborations in, 258
    deidentification of data, 273–75
    enhancement strategies for, 261–63
    limited data sets in, 272–73
    sharing observational research, 271–75

Health Insurance Portability and Accountability Act (HIPAA), U.S. (cont.)
  biomedical data and, 255–61
  Common Rule and, 247–48
  data brokers under, 61–62
  data collection under, 257
  data disclosure exceptions, 123
  data sharing schemes, 280
  draft development of, 255–56
  FCRA and, 260
  FERPA and, 260–61
  HITECH Act and, 272
  individual privacy protections under, 224
  overview of, 251–52
  PHI and, 257–59
    reclassification of, 259–60
  privacy laws and, 260–61, 269, 279–80
  purpose and function of, 261
  regulations under, 126, 257–58
    reforms of, 259–60
  risk assessment and, 257
  wearable technology under, 257
Health Insurance Portability and Accountability Act (HIPAA) Privacy Rule, 20–21, 23–25
  data access under, 28–29
  data brokers under, 61–62
  data disclosure exceptions, 123
  health-related data and, 90
  informed consent in, 26
health records. *See* electronic health records; longitudinal health records
health services research, 117–19
Healthcare Cost and Utilization Project (HCUP), 90
Healthcare Internet of Things (IoT). *See also* Third-Party Data Auditors
  CPBR and, 143
  design considerations for, 143–46
    accordance with existing laws and norms, 145–46
    accountability in, 144–45
    individual awareness in, 143–44
    innovation protections, 146
    transparency in, 144–45
  FIPPs and, 143
health-related Big Data, 44–46. *See also* deidentification; duty to share; *Gobeille v. Liberty Mutual Insurance Co.*; health care research
  APCDs, 112–13
  body scores in, 58
  commercial use of, 57–58
  as commodity, 262
  correlations and, 46–52
    background of, 46–49
    causation and, 50–52
    failures within, 46–49
    hypotheticals in, 46–49
  data brokers for, 60–62, 88–89
    HIPAA guidelines, 61–62
  data protection policies for, 58–60
    conservative approach to, 59
    FIPPs for, 59
    FTC guidelines for, 63–67
    reform proposals, 62–65
    technology challenges, 59–60
  debate over, 56–58
  decrease in antimicrobial resistance, 56–57
  defined, 44–45, 98
    by GDPR, 45
  deprecation of, 59–60
  discriminatory uses of, 58
  disease modeling, 56–58
  disease prediction and, 91–92
  for employers, 86
  epidemic prediction, 56–58
  expansion of, 2–3
  for financial institutions, 86
  fraud in, 56–57
  FTC guidelines for, 63–67
  after *Gobeille v. Liberty Mutual Insurance Co.*, 122–23
  high-risk patients and, identification of, 56–57
  under HIPAA Privacy Rule, 90
  for interested parties, 86–87
  Internet of Things and, 45–46
  law of causation and, 52–54
    fairness and, 53–54
  law of reason and, 52–54
    fairness and, 53–54
  legal implications of, 45
  for marketing and advertising, 86
  misuse of, 56
  from non-biomedical sources, 2–3
  through open data sources, 89–90
  patients' property rights for, 212–16
  pharmacovigilance and, 56–57
  studies of, 3
  privacy protections for, 90
  professional cooperation strategies with, 337–39
  as public good, 262
  public health surveillance and, 56–58
  regulatory arbitrage and, 60–62
  through social media, 87–88
  subsumption approach, 5–6
  through wellness programs, 88

HHS. *See* Department of Health and Human Services
high-risk patients, identification of, 56–57
HIPAA. *See* Health Insurance Portability and Accountability Act
HIPAA Privacy Rule. *See* Health Insurance Portability and Accountability Act Privacy Rule
HITECH Act. *See* Health Information Technology for Economic and Clinical Health Act
Hobbes, Thomas, 22
hospital referral regions (HRRs), 121–22
human subjects
  in Big Data health care research, 226–28
  Common Rule standards for, 226–28
  individually identifiable, 226–28
  National Commission for Protection of Human Subjects of Biomedical and Behavioral Research, 238–40
hypothetico-deductive method, 30–31

Icelandic Data Protection Authority (DPA), 194–95
identifiable biospecimen, 227
identifiable private data, under Common Rule, 243–44
  public health law and, 245
identifiable private information, 227
identity
  active breaches of, 185
  of ad hoc groups, 185–86, 189–90
  in analytics, ethical significance of, 177–83
    offline, 179
    personalization systems, 181–82
    profiling, 179–82
    shared ownership of, 180–81
  collective, 188–89
  informational, 183
  passive breaches of, 185–86
identity-constitutive privacy, 183
in vitro diagnostic multivariate index assays (IVDMIAs), 286–87
individual autonomy. *See* autonomy
individual awareness
  in Healthcare Internet of Things design, 143–44
  TPDAs and, 149
individual privacy, protections for
  additional structures for, 223–24
  for biospecimens, 224
  under Common Rule, 223–25
    exemptions from, 224
  under HIPAA, 224

historical development of, 223
IRBs and, 223–25
in U.S., 225
informational identity, 183
informational privacy, 176, 183–85
informed consent
  in analytics, 185
  Big Data and, 5
  through electronic communications, 246–47
  black box medicine and, 299
  under Common Rule, 26, 244–46
    Big Data and, through electronic communications, 246–47
  in duty to share, 214
  in HIPAA Privacy Rule, 26
  privacy and, under U.S. law, 196–202
    of biospecimens, 197–99
    in CFR, 196
    under Common Rule, 196–97
    denial of consent, 201
    individual perspectives on, 199–202
    under NPRM, 197–200
innovation protections
  in Healthcare Internet of Things design, 146
  in TPDAs, 150
Institutional Review Boards (IRBs), 20–21
  Big Data health research for, 228–30
    privacy protections, societal lapses in, 230
    sensitivity of health information, 229–30
    on social media, 230
  Common Rule and, 244
  duty to share and, 221–22
  individual privacy protections, 223–24
  right not to know and, 203–4
integrated Big Data sets, 256
intellectual property rights (IPRs), Big Data and
  algorithm patents, 312–14
    in European Union, 313–14
    in U.S., 312–13
  antitrust rules, 320–21
  for black box medicine, 322
  challenges with, 311
  copyrights, 314–15
    of biological sequence information, 315
    data selection, 314–15
  database protections, in EU, 315
  diagnostic patents, 312–14
    in European Union, 313–14
    in U.S., 312–13
  for large research infrastructures, 321–22
  overview of, 312–19
  for private sector use of public data, 322–23

intellectual property rights (IPRs), Big Data and (cont.)
  regulatory exclusivities, 318–19
    in European Union, 319
    in U.S., 319
  software patents, 312–14
    in European Union, 313–14
    in U.S., 312–13
  for specific applications, 321–23
  for specific areas of science, 321–23
  sui generis rights, 312–19
    for data-generating patents, 335
  for SysBio, 321
  trade secrets, 316–18
    EU definition of, 317
    in U.S., 318
international law, privacy in, 176
Internet of Things (IoT) devices. *See also* Healthcare Internet of Things; mobile Health applications
  ethical frameworks for, 125
  FCC regulation of, 129, 136
  FDA regulation of, 129
  FTC regulation of, 129, 136
  health-related Big Data and, 125
  legal frameworks for, 125
  regulatory frameworks for, 125
IPRs. *See* intellectual property rights
IRBs. *See* Institutional Review Boards
IVDMIAs. *See* in vitro diagnostic multivariate index assays

Kant, Immanuel, 20
Kennedy, Anthony (Justice), 114–15
Kyllo v. United States, 39–40

labeling. *See* drug labeling
laboratory developed tests (LDTs), 286–87
Lacks, Henrietta, 215
large research infrastructures, 321–22
LDTs. *See* laboratory developed tests
legal rights, 176
legislation, for health-related data. *See specific legislation and acts*
LHRs. *See* longitudinal health records
liability law. *See* medical liability law
Lifeline program, 110–11
Limited Data Set pathway, 274–76
  ethics and, 279–80
  privacy protections in, 279–80
Linnaeus, Carolus, 34–35
longitudinal health records (LHRs), 252
longitudinal population health data (LPHD), 252

machine learning, 31–32, 35–38, 40
marketing, health-related Big Data for, 86
mechanisms, 47–48
  accountability, 149–50
  transparency, 149–50
Medicaid. *See also* Centers for Medicare and Medicaid Services
  FCA and, 80
  after *Gobeille v. Liberty Mutual Insurance Co.*, 118
medical devices. *See* Internet of Things devices; mobile Health applications
Medical Electronic Data Technology Enhancement for Consumers Health (MEDTECH) Act, U.S., 134
medical liability law, 298–304
  for black box medicine, 298
  CDS products, 300
  future recommendations for, 304–5
  for health care enterprises, 303–4
  medical malpractice by providers, 299–303
  patient recovery under, 298–99
  purpose of, 298
medical software, FDA regulation of, 284–88, 301. *See also* clinical decision support products; Internet of Things devices; mobile Health applications
  for black box software, 294
  under Draft Software Policy, 285–86
  of IVDMIAs, 286–87
Medicare. *See also* Centers for Medicare and Medicaid Services
  FCA and, 80
  after *Gobeille v. Liberty Mutual Insurance Co.*, 118
medicine. *See* black box medicine
MEDTECH Act. *See* Medical Electronic Data Technology Enhancement for Consumers Health Act
minorities, racial and ethnic
  distrust of medical community by, 104
  health disparities among, 104–5
MMAs. *See* mobile medical applications
mobile Health (mHealth) applications
  through apps, 132
  clearinghouses and, 138–41
    CDIA, 139
    data collection in, 139
    regulation of, 139
  practical concerns with, 135–38
  quantified-self, 131
  regulation of, 129
    concerns over, 134–35
    by FDA, 134–35

smartphones, 130–34
software platforms for, 133
wearables, 131–32
under HIPAA, 257
mobile medical applications (MMAs), 133
moderate interpretation, of group privacy, 186
moral informational privacy, 176
moral rights, 176

NAHDO. *See* National Association of Health Data Organizations
naïve inductivism, 31
Narayanan, Arvind, 194
NASHP. *See* National Academy for State Health Policy
natalizumab, 118, 270
National Academy for State Health Policy (NASHP), 120
National Association of Health Data Organizations (NAHDO), 120
National Commission for Protection of Human Subjects of Biomedical and Behavioral Research, 238–40
National Institutes of Health (NIH), 107, 198–99
National Research Act, U.S., 242
National Research Council, 235
next generation CDS products, 291, 294
NIH. *See* National Institutes of Health
Nissenbaum, Helen, 39
non-identified biospecimens, 227
non-identified information, 227
norm of common purpose, 19–20
Notice of Proposed Rulemaking (NPRM), 197–200

Obama, Barack, 319
Obermeyer, Ziad, 74
objective probabilities, 37–38
Office for Civil Rights (OCR), of Department of Health and Human Services, 129
Office for Human Research Protections (OHRP), 244
Office of the National Coordinator for Health Information Technology (ONC), 129
offline identity, 179
OHCAs. *See* organized health care arrangements
OHRP. *See* Office of Human Research Protections
Okediji, Ruth L., 322–23
ONC. *See* Office of the National Coordinator for Health Information Technology
open data sources, 89–90
opt-ins, duty to share, 211
opt-outs, duty to share, 211
organized health care arrangements (OHCAs), 258
Orphan Drug Act, U.S., 319

Parasidis, Efthimios, 100
passive breaches of identity, 185–86
patents. *See* algorithm patents; data-generating patents; diagnostic patents; software patents
patienthood, 189
patients' property rights, for health-related Big Data, 212–16
pay and chase model, 79–80
PCAST. *See* President's Council of Advisors on Science and Technology
pediatric care, discrepancies in, 117
Personal Genome Project, 229
personalization systems, 181–82
pharmacoepidemiology
  Big Data in, 270–71
  studies in, 78–79
pharmacovigilance. *See also* False Claims Act
  Big Data and, 75–79
  through postmarket analysis, 75
  transformative role of, 75–76
  data mining and, 78
  defined, 77–78
  under False Claims Act, 73
  by FDA, 69
  health-related Big Data and, 56–57
  studies of, 3
  SDAs and, 78–79
  studies of, 3
  World Health Organization on, 79
PHI. *See* protected health information
Pietsch, Wolfgang, 31
post-approval research pathways, 274–79
  Expert Determination, 273–74, 278–79
  anonymization of data, 281–82
  best practices for, 280–82
  data sharing under, 282
  ethical considerations for, 279–80
  privacy protections in, 279–80
  Limited Data Set, 274–76
  ethics and, 279–80
  privacy protections in, 279–80
  Safe Harbor, 273, 276–78
  ethical considerations for, 279–80
  privacy protections in, 279–80
precision medicine
  Big Data and, 34–36, 101, 105
  traditional approaches to, 34–35
  machine learning and, 35–36
  epistemological shift and, 34–36
  genetic testing and, 101
  genome sequencing and, 101
  NIH and, 107

Precision Medicine Initiative, 15, 19, 106–7
  black box medicine and, 295
  defined, 271
  methods of, 161–63
    data analysis, 163
    data collection, 162–63
    for participants, 161–62
  results, 163–72
    participant characteristics, 163–64
  risk assessment in, 163–72
    for longitudinal study design, 171–72
    of nature of genetic information, 170–71
    overview of, 172–74
    for permitted but unwanted use of information, 167–70
    for unintended access to identity, 163–67
prediction modeling, 117
predictive analytics, 182
prescriptive analytics, 179
President's Council of Advisors on Science and Technology (PCAST), 63
Price, Nicholson, 291, 312, 322. *See also* black box medicine
privacy. *See also* group privacy; Health Insurance Portability and Accountability Act Privacy Rule; individual privacy
  under ADA, 260
  Big Data and, 36–40, 109
    losses of privacy, 37–38
    violations of privacy, 38–40
  for Big Data health research, IRBs and, 230
  under Common Rule, 239–41
  contextual integrity theory, 39
  in Expert Determination pathway, 279–80
  family resemblance theory, 39
  identity-constitutive, 183
  informational, 176, 183–85
  informed consent and, under U.S. law, 196–202
    of biospecimens, 197–99
    in CFR, 196
    under Common Rule, 196–97
    denial of, 201
    individual perspectives on, 199–202
    under NPRM, 197–200
  in international law, 176
  in *Kyllo v. United States*, 39–40
  in Limited Data Set pathway, 279–80
  right to inviolate personality and, 183–85
    group privacy and, 185–90
  technological challenges to, 256
  top-down standards for, 23

Privacy Act (1974), U.S., 59, 240
privacy laws
  ADA, 260
  FCRA, 60, 110
    clearinghouses under, 139
    CRA oversight under, 65–66
    FTC and, 66
    HIPAA and, 260
  FERPA, 260–61
  FTC regulation of, 260
  Gramm-Leach-Bliley Act, 260
  HIPAA and, 260–61, 269, 279–80
  HITECH Act, 102–3, 269
  PHI under, 257–59
    reclassification of, 259–60
private information, health research for, 228
profiling, of identity, 179–82
protected health information (PHI), 257–59
  reclassification of, 259–60
protection. *See* data protection
public accommodations, under ADA, 92–93
public good, health-related Big Data as, 262
public health law, 245
public health surveillance, 56–58
public trust. *See also* distrust of medical community
  in Big Data health care research, 263
  in Common Rule, 247–48

racial minorities. *See* minorities
Racketeer Influenced and Corrupt Organizations Act (RICO), U.S., 81
Ramirez, Edith, 138
reason, law of, 52–54
  fairness and, 53–54
reasonable expectation of privacy, 39
reciprocity argument, 215–21
redlining, through health-related Big Data, 58
regulations, on data
  adjustment of, 6
  Big Data and, 4
  for health care fraud, 76–77
  under Common Rule, 248–50
    during development process, 240–41
    standards for, 247
  under GDPR, 45
    TPDAs under, 152
  after *Gobeille v. Liberty Mutual Insurance Co.*, 119–21
  health-related Big Data, 60–62
  under HIPAA, 126, 257–58
    reforms of, 259–60
  Internet of Things devices, 129, 136

through mHealth applications, 129
  clearinghouses, 139
  concerns over, 134–35
  by FDA, 134–35
  under SOFTWARE Act, 134
regulatory arbitrage, 60–62
regulatory exclusivities, 318–19
  in European Union, 319
  in U.S., 319
Rehabilitation Act (1973), U.S., 94
reidentification, in duty to share, 215
relationality, defined, 159
reports, by TPDAs, 148–49
  aggregate, 148–49
research. *See also* genetics research; health care research
  defined, 243
reverse false claim, 82–83
RICO. *See* Racketeer Influenced and Corrupt Organizations Act
right not to know, 202–4
  ACMG recommendations, 202–3
  DeCODE and, 202
  IRB members and, 203–4
  limitations of, 204
right to inviolate personality, 183–85
  group privacy and, 185–90
Riley, Margaret Foster, 205
risk assessment. *See also* high-risk patients
  of Big Data health research, 230–35
    administrative burdens of, 232
    application of uniform daily life risks standard, 232–34
    dignitary harm and, 230–31
    mediation of risk, 234–35
    minimal risk determination, 231–33
    recognition of risks, 230–31
  HIPAA and, 257
  in Precision Medicine Initiative, 163–72
    for longitudinal study design, 171–72
    of nature of genetic information, 170–71
    overview of, 172–74
    for permitted but unwanted use of information, 167–70
    for unintended access to identity, 163–67
Rorty, Richard, 22

Sachs, Rachel, 312
Safe Harbor pathway, 273, 276–78
  ethical considerations for, 279–80
  privacy protections in, 279–80
Schauer, Fred, 256

scientific inquiry and knowledge, Big Data as influence on, 30–34
  causation vs. correlation, 32–33
  theory vs. data, 31
  explanation vs. prediction, 34
SDAs. *See* signal detection algorithms
security, TPDA limitations, 152–53
self-service TPDAs, 151
self-subsidized TPDAs, 151
Sensible Oversight for Technology which Advances Regulatory Efficiency (SOFTWARE) Act, U.S., 134
sensitivity of health information, 229–30
Sentinel Initiative, 100
Sentinel System, 6
shared ownership of identity, 180–81
The Signal and the Noise (Silver), 51
signal detection algorithms (SDAs), 78–79
Silver, Nate, 51
Skopek, Jeffrey, 202, 210
small data, Big Data and, 15
social media
  Big Data health research on, 230
  Big Data on, 3
  health-related Big Data through, 87–88
software. *See* medical software
SOFTWARE Act. *See* Sensible Oversight for Technology which Advances Regulatory Efficiency Act
software patents, 312–14
  in European Union, 313–14
  in U.S., 312–13
solidarity, civic
  autonomy and, 22
  development of, 26–28
Solove, Dan, 39
Steffanson, Kari, 202
strong interpretation, of group privacy, 186
subsumption approach, 5–6
sui generis rights, 312–19
  for data-generating patents, 335
Sweeney, Latanya, 229
systems biology (SysBio), 321

technology. *See also* Internet of Things devices; medical software; mobile Health applications
  Big Data and, 3–4
  data protection challenges, for health-related Big Data, 59–60
  under HITECH Act, 102–3
  under MEDTECH Act, 134
  ONC and, 129
  PCAST and, 63

technology (cont.)
  under SOFTWARE Act, 134
  TPDAs and, 147
Third-Party Data Auditors (TPDAs), 142–43, 146–55
  benefits of, 147
  certification of, 147, 154–55
  client hiring of, 148
  considerations of, 150–54
  data analysis by, 148
  data collection by, 152–53
    through data requests, 148
  data policy considerations, 149–50
    accordance with existing laws, 150
    accountability mechanisms, 149–50
    for individual awareness, 149
    for innovation protections, 150
    transparency mechanisms, 149–50
  data protection through, 147
  defined, 146–47
  EHR systems and, 152
  free, 151
  under GDPR, 152
  government subsidies for, 150–51
  limitations of, 150–54
    economic disenfranchisement as, 150–51
    with expanding amounts of data, processing issues, 151–52
    security issues, 152–53
    technical, 152
    in user education, 153–54
  policy goals of, 147
  policy recommendations for, 154–55
    for certification process, 154–55
    for citizen education, 155
    data access mandates, 154
    for regulations process, 154–55
  report formulation by, 148–49
    through aggregate reports, 148–49
  self-service, 151
  as self-subsidized, 151
  setup completion by, 147
  technological advances and, 147
TPDAs. *See* Third-Party Data Auditors
trade secrets, 316–18
  data-generating patents and, 327–29
  EU definition of, 317
  in U.S., 318

transparency
  as Healthcare Internet of Things design consideration, 144–45
  in TPDA mechanism, 149–50
21st Century Cures Act, U.S., 271
Tysabri. *See* natalizumab

uniform daily life risks standard, 232–34
Uniform Trade Secrets Act, U.S., 318
United States (U.S.). *See also* Americans with Disabilities Act; False Claims Act; Federal Trade Commission; Food and Drug Administration
  algorithm patents in, 312–13
  CFR in, 196
  Consumer Privacy Bill of Rights, 62
  CPBR, 62, 143
  diagnostic patents, 312–13
  GINA, 93–94
  health-related Big Data and FTC protections and, 63–67
    under HIPAA Privacy Rule, 90
  HHS, 259–60
  HIPAA Privacy Rule, 20–21, 23–25
    data access under, 28–29
    data brokers under, 61–62
    health-related Big Data under, 90
    informed consent in, 26
  informed consent in, privacy and, 196–202
    of biospecimens, 197–99
    in CFR, 196
    under Common Rule, 196–97
    denial of, 201
    individual perspectives on, 199–202
    under NPRM, 197–200
  regulatory exclusivities in, 319
  RICO, 81
  software patents in, 312–13
  trade secrets in, 318
user education, TPDAs and, 153–54

Venter, Craif, 195–96
voluntary data contributions by payers, 121–22

weak interpretation, of group privacy, 186
wellness programs, health-related Big Data through, 88
Wertheimer, Alan, 216–17
World Health Organization, 79